Best Wishes
in the gifts and grace
of God's love -
Leonard A. DeCfue

Publisher
Imprint and Trademark

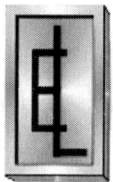

Eccles Living

Printed in the U.S.A.
ISBN 978-0-9903544-0-6

This prophetic text provides a serious perspective from the Holy Bible regarding our world society, politics and religions. Predictions about the past, present and future are linked to reality. My creative thesis offers new insight about coming global conflicts and the divine plan for humanity. It is not written as a novel, but rather a non-fiction truth about startling stages now unfolding in the last days.

Gratitude is foremost offered to God for his guidance in these mysteries which include bodily redemption into heaven, but my thanks also goes to Oakie for his help with graphics, to Karen for work on PDF format and to a friend who found scarce spelling errors in the first few copies that were corrected.

Dedication

To My Father and Mother
Who Led by Example
With a Life of Love, Hope, and Devout Faith

Leonard and Alice DeClue

LET MY PEOPLE GO

When I say, The God of your fathers has sent me to you: what should I say is his name? And God said to Moses, "I AM THAT I AM. So shall you say unto them, I AM has sent me to you." Exodus 3,1-15

Moses And The Burning Bush

Blessed are they who read, hear and keep the words of this prophecy. Seal not the sayings of this book: for the time is at hand. He who overcomes will not be hurt by the second death. To him I will give to eat of the tree of life in the paradise of God. Revelation 1,3; 2,7&11; 22,10

Table of Contents

PREFACE

"I saw in the right hand of him that sat on the throne a book written within and on the backside sealed with seven seals. The Lion of the tribe of Judah has prevailed to open the book and loose its seven seals." Revelation 5,1-5

Understanding biblical prophecy relating to the end of the world is a popular subject and the general public has a great desire to know how the time in which we live fits into the scheme of things. Many literary works and motion pictures have centered around the spectacular or cataclysmic aspects of prophetic writings without consideration of this limited and partial context. These productions are often thrilling or partly informative but we are left with more questions than answers about details of the end times, especially in matters of peace and security that now concern many people in our global society.

Mainstream theology tends to interpret the Apocalypse as a major catastrophic event comprised of extreme natural disorders and annihilation of nuclear war. This perception inaccurately combines independent components of Scripture into one fast track approach and often nullifies most relevant passages of the last days as history. The simplistic idea that events are all going to happen at once overlooks important succession of autonomous prophetic landmarks and ignores the inclusive political climate of the end time.

Failure to acknowledge the true nature of Armageddon and to separate it from other prior wars predicted in the bible that lead to an evil world government distorts the entire meaning of the day of the Lord. It is a fallacy to believe the person of the Antichrist will come to power by peaceful means or that his rule will be threatened by an earthly war. The final battle of God Almighty is not one of man against man but rather of an evil humanity against Christ's heavenly army in a display of real conflict that can only be symbolically expressed by imaginative art forms such as science fiction movies.

Reason is the most basic motive in prompting the vision and writing of this book. There is a logical progression of thought about fundamental issues and events foretold before the glorious Second Coming of Christ. Given the individual sovereignty and vastly different ideologies of the peoples on earth, the concept of an evil world dictator will not happen without war. What is biblically defined as the final wrath of God in the end should not be confused with great military struggles before that time is reached.

Old Testament prophets hold the keys to many of the specifics of the last days, but without the New Testament and particularly the book of Revelation it would be nearly impossible to comprehend the details. While studying contents of the seven seals, stark indication of three different swords became obvious to me in connection with what Jesus outlined in the gospel as precursory and ultimate signs of the end. My feeling was that prophecy separated battles before the end and it intrigued me to take a closer look.

After several years of persistent research of grouping Scripture verses according to the clues associated with the three swords, it became evident to me that opening of the book of seven seals in Revelation was a sequence of profound messages parted in a set time clock. The great sword of the second seal is distinct in time and purpose from the sword in the forth seal and these swords are similarly divided from the sword of Christ which is the wrath of the Lamb in the sixth seal. Each seal begins a new period of time where the pieces of the total prophetic puzzle come together in a believable reality.

Swords contained in the seals correspond to predictions by Jesus of nation rising against nation as being apart from kingdom rising against kingdom and that being apart from his return in judgment.[1] In short, there are two world wars given here in advance of the final battle. What many scholars do, however, is focus on the last omens stated in the gospel that involve God's end wrath and the Second Advent. They mistakenly teach that battles other than their idea of Armageddon have already happened either in the last century or in the first century when the Romans destroyed the second Jewish temple.

We are led to believe by the prevailing theory of eschatology that the development of World War III will be the end of the world. This pervasive viewpoint has been common since the nuclear arms buildup among superpower nations reached the capacity to destroy our modern society. It is certainly possible for mankind to annihilate itself, but we must ask ourselves if complete destruction is a practical military objective or if limited nuclear strikes at strategic targets between hostile nations could stop any further damage?

Central questions posed in this book are whether or not humanity can survive World War III and if so what follows for the rest of mankind? The assertion that our world will be greatly crippled yet retain its viability may not be hard to accept, but the claim of surviving another nuclear world war before the end is no doubt startling. We simply are not accustomed to think that far in advance, nor is it appealing to concede to the historical lesson of an unending bloody struggle for power that continues to the end time and only then culminates in catastrophic natural disorders and Christ's judgment.

Any proposal of a World War IV is unfamiliar to our theological lexicon. Nonetheless we need to realize the Apocalypse is set forth in stages that fulfill all prophetic things, not just a portion of them. Evangelists emphasize the gospel must be preached in all the world before the end comes, but how many teach that Jesus spoke these words in relation to great world wars as just the beginning of sorrows? These facts are often distorted or omitted and any description of divine vengeance is diluted with misleading pacifism.

Much inquiry was made in preparing this study toward isolating the names of ancient peoples who are mentioned in the prophets with respect to the end times. Well-organized ideas provide new insight of which countries these ancient names refer to in today's society and what role they are given in current and future events. The resulting scope of research identifies virtually all major nations and many smaller ones. It further reveals a scenario of changing world order reflected in the seals and ensuing fate of humanity.

Revelation of biblical prophecy given in a historical sense or in the present and future exhibits the infinite knowledge and power of the higher living being of God. No other deity has accurately communicated to us beforehand the affairs of ancient history, the plan of salvation accomplished in Christ or a detailed description of events in the last days clearly forming in our time. God wants us to know that our faith in him and moral behavior have everything to do with the quality of our existence in this mortal life as well as the right to enter his eternal kingdom in heaven or face everlasting damnation.

Jesus explained in his discourse of end things that the love of many shall grow cold because iniquity will abound.[2] This link is the critical underlying root cause of all our cultural problems. Whatever form sin takes it is self-serving as opposed to true charity and also detracts from the natural order of human dignity. The fundamental principle of Christianity teaches God is love.[3] It is impossible to love without God since we create the absence of genuine goodwill by denying his benevolence in all good gifts and shift gratitude for giving and affection to ourselves as existing independent of his care.

End times prophecy like that concerning the ancient Hebrew nation is inextricably interwoven with people's obedience or rejection of divine law. If our priorities are in line with the ways of God set forth in Scripture and in our conscience, he gladly gives us the necessities and reasonable desires of earthly life *"that you may live and prosper, and may have long life in the land."*[4] In other words *"seek ye first the kingdom of God, and all these things will be added unto you."* [5] The acting out of faith in the right manner invites God into our lives so we can secure his omnipotent protection and his blessings.

Any ideal concept of brotherhood can only be achieved through values of virtue that characterize the holiness of God. This excellence is not abstract in that we don't know or can't attain, but application of the golden rule of loving our neighbor as our self requires love of God for he is the power whereby we love and receive favors of happiness. Hence we are taught *"He who abides in love, abides in God, and God in him."*[6] Selfless love reaches beyond physical things into the spirit realm as *"I seek not yours, but you."*[7]

Ethics is fractured in the practice of sin by causing deception and confusion about what is right and wrong eventually leading to some sort of reason without conscience that justifies sin. This vacuum of morality gives many living in sin a false idea that their ways are hid from God or that he doesn't mind or that he doesn't exist. Of sin *"the sensual man does not perceive the things that are of the Spirit of God, because it is examined spiritually."*[8] And of judgment *"all things are naked and opened unto the eyes of him whom we have to do."* [9] Our denial of spirituality in God does not change reality.

The physical and spiritual aspects of prophecy cannot be separated. Opposing forces of God's spirit versus those of the world and demonic spirits distinguish children of light and darkness. There is only one way to please God and that is through his forgiveness of sin and keeping the commandments of divine law. It is deception to believe that God is the Father of everyone and all people have their own ways of finding him without guilt or accountability. Mercy has its limits and God has no fellowship with evil.[10]

Iniquity is a form of slavery especially as it becomes habitual and takes on forms of addiction as *"everyone who commits sin is a slave of sin."*[11] Jesus said to the hypocrites *"You are of your father the devil, and the lusts of your father you will do, for he is a liar, and the father of it."*[12] All who refuse to admit their sin are not necessarily possessed by demonic spirits, but by their own vanity they are victims of their flesh and choose to be part of an evil family that opposes righteousness and thereby rejects truth and love.

Teaching the kingdom of God is within us and we must keep our eyes on the narrow path of a heavenly calling to eternal life may seem strange, but plagues of judgment revealed in Scripture are certainly not a fantasy. We should know *"preaching the cross is to them that perish foolishness"* because they *"receive honor one of another, and seek not the honor that comes from God only."*[13] We have to resist temptations that saturate our culture for *"If any man love the world, the love of the Father is not in him."*[14]

It is prudent in the preface to provide some historical evidence of both the human and divine person of Jesus since the substance of my book is about his salvation, his Lordship and his return to earth as our Messiah and judge. External issues of divine justice in these last days center on mankind's acceptance or refusal of the mission of Jesus to reconcile our sins to God by the sacrifice of himself since *"This is the work of God that you believe on him whom he sent."*[15] What is told and fulfilled in the Holy Bible about the divine birth, the life, the death and the resurrection of Jesus is not rumor or myth.

Accounts of the gospel recorded in the New Testament speak not only of a few people who saw and were with Jesus on a daily basis, but they inform of multitudes that watched the great miracles no other person had ever done and heard the irrefutable wisdom of someone who knew his infinite purpose in completing Scripture. For anyone who looks at history as a science or verifiable fact, there are no lies or error in the eyewitness reports of Jesus. To this realism *"we know that his testimony is true"* as *"we beheld his glory, the glory as of the only begotten of the Father, full of grace and truth."*[16]

In the record of Luke, he explains a stir among the first Christian disciples to aptly document who Jesus is, what he did and his eminent return *"Forasmuch as many have taken in hand to set forth in order a declaration, even as they from the beginning were eyewitnesses, it seemed good to me also, having had perfect understanding of all things from the very first, to write the certainty of those things."*[17] Sacred writings have been preserved with care so we may know for sure who is manifest in the person of Jesus.

Specific reference to the risen Christ states *"he showed himself alive after the passion by many infallible proofs, being seen of them forty days"* and of them who saw, spoke and ate with him *"that same Jesus, whom ye crucified, God raised up, whereof we all are witnesses."*[18] These people knew Jesus, saw him die on a cross, buried him and were baffled to see him rise from the dead. But he told them about Scripture of those things and even they did not understand until he appeared, talked and ate with them after he rose. It is a mistake to rationalize Jesus in human terms or deny his resurrection.

No other can lay claim to what Jesus did by offering himself to die for sin or stand in his place as an eternal being who shares the Godhead with the Father and the Holy Spirit. The very Hebrew word for God used in the bible is a plural form of deity. In the creation story of Adam and Eve at the very start of the human race *"God said, Let us make man in our image, after our likeness."*[19] God was not talking to himself, but Jesus took part in all of creation as in the beginning *"the Word was with God, and the Word was God"* and of his earthly ministry *"the Word was made flesh, and dwelt among us."*[20]

About his divinity Jesus declared *"I came down from heaven, for I proceeded forth and came from God."*[21] He clearly proclaimed *"All things the Father has are mine"* and he spoke of *"the glory which I had before the foundation of the world."*[22] Further he exclaimed *"I am the bread of life, which comes down from heaven, and gives life to the world."*[23] When asked if he was the Christ, he answered *"I am: and you shall see the Son of Man sitting at the right hand of power and coming in the clouds of heaven."*[24] He said of his glory and majesty *"All power is given to me in heaven and in earth."*[25]

Doctrine of the Most Holy Trinity holds that there are three distinct persons of God who share a union that cannot be explained in our physical terms, but that heavenly reality can be known in part by the exercise of faith.[26] This teaching is expressed in various ways in the bible and Jesus summarized it in the commission of baptism *"in the name of the Father, and of the Son, and of the Holy Spirit."*[27] The authority is singular yet in three persons of God and in such consciousness *"There are three that bear record in heaven, the Father, the Word, and the Holy Spirit; and these three are one."*[28]

Both Scripture and church tradition leave no doubt that Jesus was conceived and born of a virgin thru the Holy Spirit. Although divine in nature he took on human flesh and revealed himself by word and by great miracles.[29] Before his death, he professed to his disciples that *"the Son of man shall be betrayed, and they will condemn him to death, and will deliver him to be mocked and scourged and crucified, and on the third day he will rise again."[30]* He laid down his life willingly out of love for those who believe in him as *"No one takes it from me, but I lay it down of myself, that I may take it up again."[31]*

Some may think of God as being vindictive and legalistic but the truth is Jesus came to reveal the spirit of love to humanity as a commendable way of life *"that they all may be one, even as you Father in me and I in you; that they also may be one in us, perfected in unity."[32]* Of this he said *"I am in the Father, and the Father in me"* and likewise if anyone chooses to believe and receive his spirit *"we will come unto him, and make our abode with him."[33]* Are not those who spurn love the ones who are really spiteful and practice a vain legalism of their own? Unwittingly or not, they reap what they sow.

This writing is submitted to all readers in order that true knowledge might be gained which is victory of resurrection life over the inordinate lusts of the flesh and endless life after death. Setting aside grave predictions made in the bible, its intent for all is to know the Lord and be an epistle of Christ *"written not with ink, but with the Spirit of the living God"* who speaks through the tables of our hearts.[34] Thus, *"if anyone is in Christ, he is a new creature."[35]* Understanding doctrine and prophecy profits nothing if we don't have an inward sense of God in our spirit who gives freedom in following divine law.

The parable of the vine illustrates our connection to Christ in the grace of forgiveness and communion of love in his spirit. Jesus exhorted *"I am the true vine, you are the branches. He who abides in me, and I in him, he bears much fruit. Abide in my love."[36]* This is the crux of the gospel for *"Whoever is born of God does not commit sin, because his seed abides in him and he cannot sin."[37]* As we accept that grace and keep love in our spirits *"the truth shall make you free"* from the bondage of iniquity. Jesus greeted his disciples with *"Peace be to you"* and said to them *"Receive the Holy Spirit."[38]*

Every man or woman has a measure of faith.[39] We can either build on that gift doing what we know is right or deny it becoming deceived in our minds and hearts to truth. Foreign doctrines are being accepted even in some churches as part of a peculiar and insincere Christianity that perverts the life we are expected to live. The real war is within us to overcome the spiritual powers of darkness that defy divine ordinances meant to preserve life and replace them with a selfish myriad of idolatries which breed death. Our destiny is a matter of our free will to either serve God or be a slave of his creation.

All kinds of false dogma are being devised and advocated in these last days as *"evil men and seducers shall wax worse and worse, deceiving, and being deceived."[40]* Many people are inclined to believe these erroneous teachings or take a passing interest in what is thought of as vogue. Warnings are made to *"be no more children tossed to and fro and carried about with every wind of doctrine, by the sleight of men."[41]* Likewise, *"Beware lest any man spoil you through philosophy and vain deceit, after the tradition of men, after the rudiments of the world."[42]* Truth in Christ cannot be compromised.

As in many instances of ancient Jewish history, the prevailing aim of prophecy is for men to know God's judgments ahead of time so they have the opportunity to repent and thereby avoid punishment. In his great mercy and willingness to turn the tide of his justice, God desires that none should perish.[43] Similar to the laws of physics, man is given the choice to set a mode of action or inaction. The message often heard in times past to repent and believe in the kingdom of God urgently applies to our world today.

There is an enormous "if" in various places of the bible concerning the collective will of a nation or the combined volition in the community of believers to reverse the plagues of impending divine justice. Much strength is stored in numbers and this conditional relationship is dependent on the people's decision to recognize the danger, change their ways and walk in the statutes of divine law. Following are examples of verses from Scripture that demonstrate our only hope against catastrophic disasters of the end times:

> "If my people, which are called by my name, shall humble themselves, and pray, and seek my face, and turn from their wicked ways; then will I hear from heaven, and will forgive their sin, and will heal their land." II Chronicles 7,14

> "At what instant I shall speak concerning a nation, and concerning a kingdom, to pluck up, and to pull down, and to destroy it; If that nation against whom I have pronounced turn from their evil, I will repent of the evil I thought to do unto them." Jeremiah 18,7-8

> "For the day of the Lord is great and very terrible, and who can stand it? Now therefore says the Lord: Be converted to me with all your hearts, in fasting, and in weeping and in mourning. And rend your hearts, and not your garments, and turn to the Lord your God, for he is gracious and merciful, patient and rich in mercy, and ready to repent of the evil." Joel 2,11-13

Question arises in light of these verses if we will respond fully enough as a nation or as a Christian community in the appropriate manner to appease the anger of God? No easy answer can be given to this query since nobody can presume when God will close the window of opportunity for a nation or for the Christian church as a whole to reconcile with his authority. At this point there remains a strong illusion of better things to come based on our own ability to grapple with distresses around us. Solidarity in prayer is sorely needed in asking God to extend his mercy and shorten the extent of his justice.

We should reflect on the ancient judgments passed upon the Jewish people due to their rejection of repeated urgings for contrition by the prophets and also consider the direction our society is taking in worsening transgressions against God's commandments. This growing backward trend is not encouraging. An epidemic of errors and heresies has led to a form of neo-paganism and atheism that is inducing the ruin of innumerable souls. At the heart of this is Jesus who is the sign of contradiction between good and evil because he is the power of grace over sin and our only insurance against self-destruction.[44]

Unless a dramatic shift is made in our public conscience from the false hope of its secularism and idolatry, what needs to be addressed is who if anyone can benefit from the potent force and wide ranging affects of prophecy? Is God wasting his time? In response we need to distinguish between humanity as a whole including its public institutions and that segment of society who demonstrates true faith. Those totally converted to Christian principles provide an underlying optimism in an otherwise disturbing outlook.

Judgment is meant not only to punish for obstinate misdeeds and disbelief but also to persuade conversion and purify the body of believers from their own iniquity. This kind of negative reinforcement is intended to clean the house of God from hypocrisy and a half-hearted commitment to the faith. The purification periods of world wars will bring many detached church members and nonbelievers to their knees in godly repentance. Only then can they live in united holiness and complete the mission of discipleship.

Before the end is reached, Christians have the promise of being saved from that time of extreme wrath against a world duped in an evil apostasy.[45] Jesus taught the faithful to look up for their redemption *"even at the doors"* as they see the signs of the end come to pass.[46]   He instructed to watch and pray so they *"may be accounted worthy to escape"* the snare for all who dwell on the face of the earth.[47]   Further he said that blessed are those servants when he comes and described phases of a second and third watch.[48]

The thought that Christians will be physically removed from the world to escape death has a verifiable basis in many passages of both the Old and New Testaments. This concept of gathering of Christ's servants from earth to heaven has a common terminology of rapture in some Protestant circles and also called the parousia by Roman Catholics. What has caused theological debate about the subject of this happening is not if it will occur, but rather when it will occur either at the Second Advent or at some point before. This topic is essential to our times and we must consider its implications.

Seeing that Jesus spoke in the gospel of Luke about three watches in reference to when *"one will be taken and the other left"*, my well documented research diverges from the belief of rapture or parousia being a single event and instead presents a three part theory separated in time and grouping of who will be taken.[49]   The suggestion offers a rational alternative to those who would put most if not all matters of prophecy at the end or to those who think rapture will take place prior to any tribulation. These issues are discussed at length from Scripture in the introduction and in respective chapters.

My book is written to make it as simple as possible to comprehend the realities of our time and obtain the hope it offers. There is nothing in print to my knowledge that breaks down prophecy in such order and detail. Free from any theoretical bias about things of the end, the work was done with an open mind and heart to truth in the bible. The Catholic Confraternity-Douay and King James versions are used as a basis of biblical study and comparison because of their validity. These older translations are considered authentic transcripts and exhibit a strong overall language consistency.

Intricacies of prophecy are scattered throughout the bible and in many places hidden in allegory, but the text is designed so that even those who are unfamiliar with the subject can read with interest its meaning. Writing of the book was much like a pianist who must cross hands while playing. Although most do not play, many enjoy listening and want to hear the sounds of compositions repeatedly. Similarly, meditation and study may be required to grasp some of the ideas so if certain passages are not clear at first glance then continue and come back when needed. Complex issues call for an extended analysis.

Overlapping is necessary in that concepts may not be fully understood until they are explained in subsequent chapters. With this in mind readers might consider finishing the book from start to finish rather than skipping around. References are often made to the section of the bible from which quotes are taken. Italics are used to highlight the gist of bible verses and footnotes are provided to the industrious to find Scripture citations for the purpose of further individual or group instruction. It may be helpful to make notes of questions and then read the biblical setting of quotes to clarify interpretation.

Varied wording of most verses between two sources chosen for reflection express the same meaning, but not all of them are categorized in the same manner. This problem in locating matching quotes is apparent in the indexing format of the Catholic version for the Psalter. Since any minor discrepancies exist, footnotes are solely printed according to chapters and linguistic lines numbered in the King James Version of the bible. These guidelines conform to other translations that contain a similar order to look at particular points of interest. Verifying statements can add to a learning experience.

The seven seals are much like a secret code that stretches into virtually all prophetic matters of the last days. Key words and phrases in each of the seals are clues to broader messages contained in various places of the bible. Thorough examination of this course leads to a great number of passages that further explain its extensive and abstruse scope. In essence my text breaks the secrecy of the seals and untangles the linked verses to each seal from the other ones to complete the perception of their individual significance.

Every effort has been made to limit any repetition and avoid excessive discussion. Although a multitude of quotes are made from the bible more so than any publication of its kind, these concise instructions are given in an intelligible manner. Few people bother to read the book of Revelation due to the difficulty of deciphering its symbols and how these mysterious visions correlate to each other, but even fewer still have attempted an in depth analysis of its meaning. The implications of end times prophecy are meant to be known and the timing for a serious look at this aspect of Scripture is upon us.

Nearly everyone either owns or in our age of communication has access to a copy of the Holy Bible and it is strongly recommended that they take time to read at least some of the corresponding citations provided herein. My assertions are not made up from some extraordinary visions of my own, but rather are written from a commonplace source. To the extent that these quotes may be unsettling for some, they are not of myself but taken from the word of God. We must grasp the teaching of these prophecies in their occurring at distinct seasons of the future. Only time will prove the order of these things.

To those who wish to inspect or check the quotes used, it should be mentioned that some passages are condensed to focus on the meaning of a topic and are often comprised of more than one citation. The cohesiveness of the same messages written by different prophets in separate periods reinforces their divine authority. Correspondingly, multiple references are added in the footnotes to further support my conclusions. These citations are by no means inclusive but are more than sufficient to guide more scrutiny.

Discussion is made in appropriate chapters of any of the more prominent errors that exist in prophetic theology. Comparisons are made between these diverging opinions to express their disunity and show how they relate to the actual wording of Scripture. Some of the pitfalls that cause inconsistent and misleading views are reviewed to expose their inappropriateness. Certain verses require the isolation of particular words or phrases to examine their root intent. This research of the original Hebrew and Greek language is extremely helpful in interpreting the English translations chosen for study.

Hard medicine is offered in the ensuing pages for a sick and dying world. As to the theological import of my treatise, a practical adjustment needs to be made in the limited and partial perceptions that most people have of the end. We need to examine theology and start thinking about prophetic events that are happening now and other affairs that are forecast in the bible before the final period. Our slumber must stop and dialogue has to be directed at basic aspects of the last days and how these things progress in stages.

There is a broad based lack of satisfaction among Christians in finding a coherent interpretation of the last days. Even non-Christians want to know what Christianity holds for the world and expect more than a muddled understanding exhibited in a sort of big bang theory of the end. Scholars too by means of their own profession need be open to rational discussion and at least privately must have reservations about simplistic ideas that have little relevance to current events or diverse issues concerning the end.

People may wonder why a lion is pictured on the front cover, but this symbol has deep roots in mystery for Christ who descended from the tribe of Judah as heir to the throne of David. His connection to an evolving crucible in the seven seals is also depicted as the Lamb of God who is the paschal sacrifice in salvation and marvelous exodus into heaven. Marble background on the cover reflects Job's wish for his words to be graven with an iron chisel and with lead in the rock forever.[50] These ardent lessons require us to admit if it looks like a duck, swims like a duck and quacks like a duck, it is a duck.

My purpose in writing is not one of cynicism, but rather to inform and fill the wide understanding gap that exists about biblical prophecy. The Book of Remembrance: A Story That Is Told is an enhanced revision of The Book Of Seven Seals that I wrote and published in 1996. My general perception of coming things remains the same and events following the 9/11 tragedy support my initial thoughts about the second seal, but insight of Scripture is shown more clearly in greater detail and accuracy than before through study and by observing changes that have taken place in global political affairs.

Since significant changes are made in the use of certain quotes to support my concepts of the divine word and multiple other verses are included with additional definition, the new publication is not intended as some sort of second edition of my first attempt. That read was only a vague shadow of what needed to be finished at a suitable moment. Fresh updates which apply to signs of our times provide compelling reasons to see pending judgments and reconcile with our Creator. Complete coverage of horrors and hopes for modern humanity waits to be lived out in expectation we need to consider and teach.

This work is presented as non-fiction. Given the threats of terrorism and the violent political situation in the greater Middle East region and elsewhere, world changing events are rapidly taking place. Due to heightened tensions and the fluid nature of military actions, there is no way of telling what events will transpire leading to and prompting the engaging of WWIII as it is described in the second seal before the time of readership. Incidents may have transpired that were speculative when writing. Yet the implications and outlook of bible prophecy are long term and extend beyond the end of this age.

---

[1] Mathew 24,7; Mark 13,8; Luke 21,10
[2] Mathew 24,12
[3] 1John 4,16
[4] Deuteronomy 5,33
[5] Mathew 6,33; Luke 12,31
[6] I John 4,16
[7] II Corinthians 12,14
[8] I Corinthians 2,14

[9] Hebrews 4,13
[10] I Corinthians 10,20-21; II Corinthians 6,14
[11] John 8,34; Romans 6,19-20; II Peter 2,19
[12] John 8,44
[13] John 5,44; Corinthians 1,18
[14] I John 2,15
[15] John 6,29
[16] John 1,14; 21,24
[17] Luke 1,1-4
[18] Acts 1,3; 2,32&36
[19] Genesis 1,1&26
[20] John 1,1&14
[21] John 6,38; 8,42
[22] John 16,15; 17,5&24
[23] John 6,33-35
[24] Mathew 26,64; Mark 14,62; John 9,37
[25] Mathew 28,18
[26] I Corinthians 13,12-13
[27] Mathew 28,19
[28] I John 5,7
[29] Isaiah 7,14; Luke 1,26-35
[30] Mathew 20,18-19; Luke 24,7
[31] John 10,17-18
[32] John 17,21-23
[33] John 14,11&23
[34] II Corinthians 3,3
[35] II Corinthians 5,17
[36] John 15,1-9
[37] I John 3,9
[38] John 8,31-32; 20,21-22
[39] Romans 12,3
[40] II Timothy 3,13
[41] Ephesians 4,14
[42] Colossians 2,8
[43] John 3,16
[44] Luke 2,34
[45] Mathew 24,13
[46] Mathew 24,33; Luke 21,28
[47] Luke 21,35-36
[48] Luke 12,37-38
[49] Mathew 24,40-42; Luke 17,34-36
[50] Job 19,23-24

Chapter One
INTRODUCTION

"Before it came to pass I told it to you. I showed you new things from this time, even hidden things, and you did not know them. They are created now, and not from the beginning." Isaiah 48,3-7

Thought that the book of Revelation is not meant to be literally understood may have had merit in times past, but the world has developed into a time where the final things of prophecy can be discerned and will be perceived by the happening of actual events on earth. The common belief that the last days are strictly a matter of divine providence prohibits us from recognizing the preliminary signs of the end by stifling study and leaves the unwarranted impression that it will come suddenly with no means of escape.

God does not have to sit down and write himself a book to know what is going on nor are the warnings of his word to be only construed in terms of recorded history. Many bible quotes appear in each of the chapters of my book that form a solid foundation for building the arguments of each stage in its thesis on the seven seals. These are offered in an orderly fashion most often intermixed with discussion. What may seem interesting to readers is the matter of fact style of narration used in context of controversial issues.

One of the most misinterpreted verses of the prophets states *"Howl you: for the day of the Lord is at hand; it shall come as a destruction from the Almighty."*[1] The implication of this reading had many Christians shook up in the church around two thousand years ago and the same sentiment remains a puzzling reality today. This idea of uncertainty about impending doom is upheld by the isolation of these types of Scripture with the teaching by Jesus *"But of that day and hour no one knows, not even the angels in heaven, but the Father only."*[2] Question arises then if omens are any of our business?

The faulty logic that Jesus taught nobody knows what is going to happen blinds our eyes from seeing he only informed we don't know exactly when things will occur. He foretold of a specific sequence of events that are portents to be grasped and examined in the whole of Scripture to more fully comprehend his gospel. What good are signs if they are not seen as such? God wants to impart the knowledge of his word within the limits of his providence as those who ask will receive and he who seeks will find.[3]

Sensing a pressing anxiety in the early church, the apostle Paul wrote *"that you be not shaken in mind, that the day of Christ is at hand."*[4] He knew that other things spoken by the prophets had to take place before that time and they had no cause for concern about some unusual danger. St. Paul spoke about *"the times and the seasons"* of the end saying there was no need for him to further explain those separate periods of prophecy leading to the coming of Jesus in judgment. He did, however, reveal a key factor about the end: *"But you, brethren, are not in darkness that that day should overtake you as a thief."*[5]

In plain words, the apostle was telling the faithful that those who trust in Christ the Lord being spiritually ready will simply not be there in the time of punishment against a global apostasy. They will be taken alive to heaven ahead of that time.[6] There is no way to account for that absolute miracle of miracles in our human terms, but rapture has an integral place in theology and thus cannot be dismissed as superstition. This concept is actually tri-form and its three settings are fully explained in phases or watches.

Saint Paul did not want believers to be ignorant of mysteries as they relate to the hope of rapture or to the ministry of the gospel in the salvation of Jews.[7] A central ground of confusion for some scholars has been the failure to distinguish between the wrath of God as it is defined by the final plagues on earth from the eternal damnation of evil souls. To do so evades the very important lesson St. Paul made that *"God has not appointed us to wrath"* which is physical ruin and death he pointed to as a *"sudden destruction"* in this world upon the wicked immediately before and during the end period vengeance.[8]

General references to the end times described as *"the last days"* and *"the latter times"* contain a plurality in the very terms themselves.[9] They imply there is more than one stage in fulfilling future predictions. Jesus said not *"one jot or one tittle shall in no wise pass from the law, till all is fulfilled."*[10] These things are written in much detail and it is up to us to examine Scripture in order to identify their meaning in both spiritual and physical application. Let us accept this task and proceed with determined faith for *"there is nothing covered, that shall not be revealed, neither hid, that shall not be known."*[11]

Any approach to learning the Holy Bible requires prayerful reflection and an open heart to God's spirit as *"he will guide you into all truth, and he will show you things to come."*[12] We need to see and accept the divine word's face value since *"there is none else,* declaring *the end from the beginning and from ancient times the things that are not yet done."*[13] The prophets said of the Lord's anger *"in the latter days you shall consider it perfectly"* and likewise *"none of the wicked shall understand, but the wise shall understand."*[14] Of this Jesus asked *"how is it that you do not discern this time?"*[15]

Complex issues of prophecy about the church in times of wars remain unsolved or in dispute. No single voice is put forth in these matters that relate to the very life of this institution or its role in the last days. As private or isolated the church may be, it still lives in the world and has to formulate its opinion. Whatever excuses like apathy, fear of reprisal, stubborn intellect or personal gain, some scholars would rather stay away from the difficult and embarrassing task of reviewing outdated or inaccurate positions.

Most of prophetic Scripture is oriented to the present or future, not times of the past. The church should be the keeper of these things that have great inherent potential for discipleship. St. Paul wrote *"if the trumpet gives an uncertain sound, who shall prepare himself to the battle?"*[16] He said not to be children in understanding but in understanding be men *"For God is not the author of confusion."*[17] We are admonished to be *"perfectly joined together"* in the same mind and in the same judgment.[18] In relation to prophecy it has the power to convict and convert both unbelievers and the unlearned.[19]

Jesus ordered his apostles at the great commission to teach *"all things whatsoever I have commanded you."*[20] For evangelization to be fully effective it has to embody a thorough inspection of Christ's teachings for instruction including his extensive warnings about his Second Coming. The apostle John said of this expectation that *"The testimony of Jesus is the spirit of prophecy."*[21] This testimony of atonement and redemption by the risen Christ is clearly manifest in the revelation of end times prophecy. Dialogue of its particulars can no longer be passed off as broad symbolism or historical allegory.

The focus of my work is realism and to the extent that predictions are being fulfilled in our world, we must face those events in the measure of their context. In the overall gloomy or even ugly picture of man's tendency toward evil and ultimate judgment, we should remember Christ informed us to pray to the Father that *"Thy kingdom come"* and *"Thy will be done in earth, as it is in heaven."*[22] No time in history even comes close to the consummation of a spiritual awakening like this in earth. Yet why do we pray in this manner if we don't believe? Many do, but wonder how it will take place.

Considerable evidence is found in Scripture to support the tenet of a new age being born at Christ's judgment for future generations in a *"world without end."*[23] Relevant chapters examine biblical references to the dawning of this time and what it holds for a humanity that still must accept Christ's salvation to overcome the weakness of sin and death. Mortality of our flesh will never change regardless of how long or well we live, but God's holy plan is disclosed in the defeat of evil for those who inherit the earth.

Great prophetic wisdom is hidden in the prayer of the Our Father by asking God to *"lead us not into temptation, but deliver us from evil."* This represents an anxiety among Christians during times of wars at the close of separate dispensations of grace that will include many Jews before the end. Two distinct periods of temptation and evil relate to when the Antichrist first appears in the world and later takes over it. The prayer involves timings of rapture for those not led into temptation and for those delivered from evil.

Gentile and Jew are the same in accepting Christian faith, but there remains a period when many Jews and Gentiles will yet come to that belief.[24] Isaiah wrote of God that *"Behold, you shall call a nation that you know not, and nations that knew not you shall run to you because of the Lord your God, and for the Holy One of Israel."*[25] This verse recognizes the Lord our God and Jesus as the Holy One of Israel. It reveals the calling of a nation of Gentile believers to him not relating to the ancient Jews, but also speaks of another time to follow when those of Gentile nations will turn to the Lord.

Christ will come back to deliver in times of wars and judge at the Second Advent. The gospel will be spread so *"O Lord, my strength, and my fortress, and my refuge in the day of affliction, the Gentiles shall come unto you from the ends of the earth. Behold, I will this once cause them to know, I will cause them to know my hand and my might, and they shall know that my name is The Lord."* His hand is in the watches and his might in glory, but this day of affliction is in WWIV when many more Gentiles repent saying *"Surely our fathers have inherited lies, vanity, and things wherein there is no profit."*[26]

When Jesus went to the synagogue as his custom was on the Sabbath day, he pointed to himself as he read from the writings of Isaiah about the anointed one who would bring the promise of healing and restoration to Israel. This passage relates to his ministry *"To proclaim the acceptable year of the Lord, and the day of vengeance of our God."*[27] The extensive period of grace in salvation has not been completed nor has the time of final wrath begun but when these things are fulfilled *"as the earth brings forth her bud, so the Lord will cause righteousness and praise to spring forth before all nations."*[28]

There will be no questions about the risen Christ in that new world, but until his wrath comes upon the earth God will continue to draw people into the Christian faith *"For from the rising of the sun to the going down, my name shall be great among the Gentiles."*[29] The gospel was rejected by many Jews even though they saw miracles of Jesus, heard his teachings and he rose from the dead according to Scripture yet since *"It was necessary that the word of God should first have been spoken to you, but seeing you put it from you and judge yourselves unworthy of everlasting life, we turn to the Gentiles."*[30]

Ministry of the gospel to Jews has mainly been a closed door from the beginning of Christianity. Yet St. Paul asked us if God has cast away the Jewish people on account of their stubbornness to believe in the new covenant of faith in Christ as opposed to holding on to the self-righteous works of Mosaic Law. His answer was no and he spoke of a time

3

of *"the receiving of them."* In his metaphor of the olive tree whose root is Christ with its branches being the church, he said *"God is able to graft them in again."* And blindness in part is happened to the Jews *"until the fullness of the Gentiles be come in."*[31]

There will be a turning point in belief toward Christianity for Jews whom St. Paul called *"the election."* We need to learn about the salvation that will be manifest in this special anointing of Jews and how it will affect discipleship. It is ordained of God and has to be accepted in a spirit of love. This truth is central to understanding the timeframe of the first watch and a subsequent change in the reign of church hierarchy within the Catholic faith. The transformation is a unique sign of other matters prior to the end.

Christians for the most part realize that Jews will come to salvation, but generally don't know that will happen only as a part of their race in the last days and as a whole nation after the Messiah returns in glory. Jesus revealed to us *"Many that are first shall be last, and the last shall be first."*[32] The meaning of this saying applies to the ministry of the gospel to *"Jew first and then to Greek."*[33] Although Christ was at first rejected by the Jews, a Jewish segment is predestined to minister and evangelize the faith.[34]

To comprehend the prophetic order of succession in administration of the gospel as being primarily directed at Gentiles versus Jews, it is necessary to distinguish the kinds of Scriptural terminology used to describe these groups. When the patriarch Jacob was at the place named Peniel, an angel told him that his name would be called Israel, not Jacob.[35] Even though Jacob was renamed Israel in this very early ancient time, the following record of the prophets often refers to the term Jacob as well as to Israel.

These terms of Jacob and Israel are used in Scripture as speaking of a people not an individual. Generally the two groupings refer to the Jews either in blessing or curse, but the term Israel is applied in certain verses to the Gentiles as the children of God. St. Paul warned the Gentile church not to be *"wise in your own conceits"* since *"all Israel shall be saved"* when God *"shall turn away ungodliness from Jacob."* He thus referred to the Jews as Jacob and said about the olive tree metaphor to their conversion *"how much more shall these, which be natural branches, be grafted into their own olive tree?"*[36]

Similar to the great day of Pentecost when the disciples of Jesus received a special anointing of power when God's spirit came upon them, the Apocalypse reveals that a group of 144,000 from the twelve tribes of Israel will be sealed by angels for the service of God.[37] This large number seems literal and reflects living human beings who become celibate priests that appear to all be from bloodlines of Jewish decent.[38] Their place is prominent in Scripture and this group is even given a name: *"Now hear, O Jacob my servant, and Israel whom I have chosen, and you Jeshurun whom I have chosen."*[39]

Manifold wisdom of God is timeless with respect to whom his whole family in heaven and earth is named.[40] Scripture reveals many things about his decision to anoint certain Jews, but the intent is by *"the Lord of harvest to send forth laborers into his harvest."*[41] This mystery is clearly seen in the sealing of these chosen servants called Jeshurun, a term that means darling or to be upright. The marking of these God fearing men in their foreheads by angels is suitably called what the Catholic translation describes as the alphabet letter Thau in ancient Hebrew which has form of the sign of the cross.[42]

Jewish people have an integral place in nearly all matters of prophecy. They were given divine law and their holy men of God including the prophets and the apostles wrote and handed down the books of the Old Testament and most of the New Testament. The mere fact that they have survived persecutions since they lost their ancient homeland is a

4

great testimony to their experience in history of the power and authority of God. Christ came from the royal bloodline of King David by virgin birth of the Jewish woman named Mary who being *"full of grace"* was chosen as the vessel of Incarnation.[43]

The current Jewish kingdom in the Promised Land fulfills a prophetic reality that has a primary focus for biblical events of the end times. It is not by chance that Jews have been migrating back to their state in the land of Canaan from all over the world. This is being accomplished according to Scripture and we need to know the role they have as a nation. We cannot ignore the political or spiritual impact that Jews will have on the church or the world. They have much to do with the ongoing battle of good and evil.

Of the expanding apostasy and its persecution of the church, *"the gates of hell shall not prevail against it"* since Jesus will save the faithful and bring his kingdom to earth.[44] God has not forgotten his promises, neither his everlasting covenant made in the blood of Christ.[45] The divine purpose in the Jewish people is establishing the new covenant with all nations on earth for his glory, not theirs. To this truth it is written *"For my name sake will I defer mine anger, and for my praise will I refrain for you, that I not cut you off, for how should my name be polluted? And I will not give my glory to another."*[46]

It is so purposed that the disturbing problem for the world is the peace of Jerusalem, a complexity existing in the present which will become more pressing as the final stages of prophecy unfold. Government officials are bewildered due to failure of peace proposals. Conflict between religious beliefs and political ideologies together with major economic concerns have formed a great powder flask that threatens the stability of world peace. Terrorism and wars are becoming more bloody while military expansion is on the horizon as open support and an arms quest for the destruction of Israel and its allies grows.

We must understand the political ramifications of Scripture in the struggle for control over Jerusalem that worsened with the assault of 9/11 against the World Trade Center and the U.S. government. The very act of 9/11 and ensuing battles are a factual reflection of prophecy that is explained in the second seal as a prelude to WWIII. Great changes since the fall of Soviet communism are foreseen in the bible. This new separation of political ideologies and influence of radical Islamic sects to form or expand their own rule raises perplexing questions for Russia and other nations that are answered in Scripture.

As the watchmen plea day and night *"you who make mention of the Lord, keep not silence, and give him no rest, till he establish, and till he make Jerusalem a praise in the earth."*[47] Shedding of light upon God's plan for this holy city is needed to save souls and lives. Ignorance and silence on these matters of prophecy can only foster deception and promote evil designs to destroy life and govern without God. We must employ the element of prognostic truth to speak to any sanity that exists to limit the dangers imposed by those who are mistaken about the outcome of their actions or their beliefs.

Without the grace of God to reveal his word, how can anyone change the beliefs of countless Moslems, Hindus, Buddhists, atheists and other practices including Judaism which refuse to accept Jesus as Savior whom Moses taught *"The Lord thy God will raise up unto thee a Prophet from the midst of thee, of thy brethren, like unto me, unto him ye shall hearken, whosoever will not, I will require it of him."*[48] There is no real harmony in the conflicting theologies of religions since truth does not contradict itself. Jesus plainly said *"He who does not honor the Son, does not honor the Father who sent him."*[49]

Many non-Christians consider Jesus as a great teacher or even a prophet, yet at the same time deny his divinity or atonement for sin. How can anyone who thinks of Jesus as a holy man accept only some of what he taught and still reject the rest of what he said or did? He either spoke the truth about himself and the world or he didn't. Our study of the gospel should consider the whole of his mission. Common ground exists for dialogue among diverse religions and the subject of the prophets is one that has a basis in Judaism, Christianity and Islam. Bible clarification can only benefit everyone involved.

Faulty religious convictions or the lack of any faith in atheistic communism often serve as an ideology for war, but God's kingdom cannot be taken by force. When we put ourselves in place of God or misuse his word, our motives are by definition a selfish mode of authority and out of line with the divine will. Instead of prospering, nations become locked into an abusive and destructive political platform for raw power under the guise of freedom that results in corruption, oppression and loss of human rights.

A conspicuous irony of the end period is that all religions and governments will fall prey to domination of the Antichrist *"who opposes and is exalted above all that is called God, or that is worshiped, so that he gives himself out as if he were God, and his coming is according to the working of Satan."*[50] Selfish and deceptive works of idolatry will lead to glorification of the human person in the Antichrist whose power is in the prince of darkness. The certainty is all people on earth will succumb to this epitome of blasphemy and pride in our flesh with little choice except execution of those who resist.

Knowledge of God is not just a mental concession, but a communion with him in our hearts that comes through his word as *"faith comes by hearing, and hearing by the word of God."*[51] His judgments are given to cleanse us from our faults and receive his life as *"Come now and let us reason together says the Lord; though your sins be as scarlet, they shall be white as snow."*[52] Learning details of prophecy without gaining divine wisdom is useless because *"the devils also believe, and tremble."* They no longer have a choice to serve God but are reserved in *"chains of darkness unto the judgment."*[53]

Unless someone is reprobate in mind and heart much like the devils themselves, each of us has the choice to accept the grace and mercy of God even for serious sins. Those who are estranged from God *"profess that they know God; but in works they deny him"* and such exhibit the hypocrisy of *"having a form of godliness, but denying the power thereof."*[54] Herein lies the distinction of knowledge as one of human reason alone whose glory in itself is egoism and that true wisdom of knowing God for *"My people are destroyed for the lack of knowledge, seeing you have forgotten the law of God."*[55]

Grace is given to the humble, not to the proud as *"Everyone who is proud in heart is an abomination to the Lord."*[56] Isaiah wrote of the day of the Lord that it *"shall be upon everyone that is proud and lofty, and he shall be brought low."*[57] We are taught to be *"doers of the word, and not hearers only."*[58] Jesus wants to help those who feel they have done too much wrong and no longer are worthy of forgiveness. It is their pride that stops them from healing, but *"draw nigh to God, and he will draw nigh to you."*[59]

We stand in times of great perils, yet through the misfortune of wars an extraordinary revival will take place within the Christian faith. This change will be reflected in more unity, holiness, new conversions and a drawing back of some who have fallen away from faith in its obligation to worship. As wickedness becomes more and more pronounced, Jesus will succeed by reaching many souls in repentance *"to open their eyes, and to turn them from the power of Satan unto God, so they may receive forgiveness of sins, and inheritance among them which are sanctified by faith that is in me."*[60]

Divine mission is given to the church to preach Christ's gospel to the ends of the earth *"that those who believe in him may not perish, but may have life everlasting."*[61] For all practical purposes that ministry will end since Jesus explained *"the night is coming, when no one can work."*[62] The kingdom of God on earth can only come by Christ himself to *"destroy them which destroy the earth."*[63] Iniquity shall end in our world and phases of its demise by swords in the seven seals are summed up in contention as *"I will overturn, overturn, overturn it, until he comes whose right it is: and I will give it to him."*[64]

Some of the signs of the end are already evident in our world. Jesus informed there would be great earthquakes, famines, pestilences and fearful sights from the sky.[65] These kinds of recent disasters have taken countless lives and resulted in extreme costs for many nations. Those who survive are often left injured, sick, homeless and broken with radically reduced lifestyles. The alarming external conditions of our environment are direct warnings of divine justice against abounding iniquity in our world and its growing widespread acceptance as something to be sought after as a normal way of life.

Distortions of nature will become more prevalent and severe reaching catastrophic proportions in the end. The full effects of entities like global warming are just starting and we are reaping what we sow in poor stewardship of our environment. Man himself will be responsible for much of the atmospheric and geological abnormalities that give rise to severe calamities of the bible. We will experience awesome repercussions of our actions as things like nuclear wars disturb the physical elements of our universe.

Besides our bad influence, God is in control and earthquakes have devastated entire countries either directly or by producing tsunamis so big as to shock scientists. Changing weather patterns have caused untold damage by massive hurricanes, great floods, tornados and dreadful mudslides. Famines spread in large parts of the world due to intensive droughts. Wildfires consume enormous areas of land. Aids is still epidemic and viruses like Ebola pose new threats to human life while other deadly strains pop up in staples of livestock. Biological and chemical weapons add to our worries.

The issue of iniquity was raised by Jesus as a veridical sign of the last days and *"For which things' sake the wrath of God comes on the children of disobedience."*[66] There is an absolute link between the plagues we see and our behavior as individuals, a church and a nation. In the battle between virtue and vice that goes on in every human life, it is apparent that spiritual forces of evil have seduced mankind in general into a stupor of hedonism, materialism and egoism. To this St. John wrote *"the lusts of the flesh, and the lusts of the eyes, and the pride of life are not of the Father, but are of the world."*[67]

Awful and inclusive judgments will happen as long as the condition and direction of man's choice is to follow after the world and powers of darkness. Transgressions against morality have taken many forms in our own society and everywhere. All divine laws are being violated while an unknowing public is trapped in apathy and indifference by the lack of conscience and hardness of heart. Our reality is dominated by pride, greed, discord, hatred and violence. Yet God pleads *"I have no pleasure in the death of the wicked, but that the wicked turn from his way and live, for why will you die?"*[68]

In a time when intercession and penance are most needed from the church for a world on the brink of terrible destruction, there has been an increased loss of faith in no small part of members so *"that in the latter times some shall depart from the faith, giving heed to seducing spirits and doctrines of devils."*[69] While many members have been drawn away in varying measures by their own infidelity, divisions in the clergy over doctrine to make the gospel more tolerant of sin have further eroded discipleship as Jesus warned of those who *"come to you in sheep's clothing, but inwardly are ravening wolves."*[70]

Seeds of doubt and distrust are being sown from within and without. A prime example is the sex scandals and law suits involving the Catholic Church which have added to its financial strain and severely damaged its image of sanctity. Every diabolical method possible is being used by evil powers to drain strength from the church and take away our only hope of obtaining divine mercy to somehow change the downward spiral of human existence. Evangelization has stagnated while many stay away from church without feeling any need for confession or compassion to pray for the tragedies around us.

For the joy of the church to be full, its mission of intercession and evangelization must embrace Jesus' teaching to *"abide in me and my words abide in you."*[71] These efforts for conversion require us to keep the Sabbath and recognize prophetic truth in fortitude and *"so much more as you see the day approaching."*[72] The world is sinking into an abyss of despairing iniquity from which appears little hope for reparation. Rebellion against God and *"falling away"* from active faith are shaping great apostasy of the end and preparing humanity for the institution of a singular false Christ and satanic worship.[73]

Concerning the length of timeframe for the three swords in the seven seals, the most frequent question asked is how long will it take to accomplish these things and when will Jesus return in final judgment? What behooves us most to address this mystery according to Scriptural clues is that there are preceding watches to the glorious return of Christ and this inquiry must be determined in the present tense of the succession of those times. The Second Advent of Christ to judge the wicked needs to be distinguished from his prior and unseen proximate return, the parousia, to rapture the faithful in three stages.

After Jesus rose from the dead, his apostles asked him if he would then restore the kingdom to Israel. His response was *"It is not for you to know the times and seasons, which the Father hath put in his own power."*[74] The application here is that the apostles were not living in those periods and hence could not see all those things connected to the end that he had taught them. It simply was not time to fully understand or experience all the matters of prophecy in their proper perspective of world events. Jesus nevertheless instructed *"It is given unto you to know the mysteries of the kingdom of heaven."*[75]

In due time those mysteries would be revealed since *"I have many things to say unto you, but you cannot bear them now."*[76] He likewise noted *"every Scribe instructed in the kingdom of heaven, brings forth from his storeroom things new and old."*[77] The seasons and times of the end are given to us to know and bear in the inspiration and fulfilling of Scripture. In allegory as Christ's mystical body, the church must take up its burden of his redemptive passion. Prophetic symbolism of this road to Calvary involves her agony, scourging, condemnation, crucifixion, entombment and resurrection.[78]

The most telling indication Jesus made in timeframe of end signs is *"This generation shall not pass away, till all these things be fulfilled."*[79] His encompassing statement was made in reference to our ability to recognize these things as *"when you see these things come to pass, know you that the kingdom of God is nigh at hand."*[80] Independent signs separated by time and circumstances need to be understood before we can realize what to look for. That is why Jesus was specific about these things and our purpose is to prepare now for him since nobody has a guarantee to live to see a new world on earth.

With respect to rapture, his advice is to watch and pray always for *"when these things begin to come to pass, then look up, and lift up your heads, because your redemption is at hand."[81]* Things are plural in relation to his warnings and as they pertain to rapture this clue is when they begin to happen, but *"he who shall endure to the end shall be saved."[82]* Jesus definitively outlined the separate timings of rapture as *"if he comes in the second watch, and if in the third watch, blessed are those servants."[83]* These watches occur within the beginning of sorrows in world wars he described before the end time.[84]

No clear verse indicates exactly when the generation of the last days starts or its years of life. The parable of the fig tree and *"when its branch is now tender, and the leaves break forth"* was given by Jesus as a sign to happen during the development of the State of Israel.[85] Issues of the end times could not happen until this statehood was formed and Jesus made this point with specific references to the doors of rapture that first open in a watch that is in events leading to WWIII which now appear to be upon us.

Whatever the case may be as to the timeframe between now and the end, any foresight contains framework that has to be considered as events develop and transpire within the stages set forth in the seven seals. Suffice it to say we are living in the times of the end and we should be concerned with those things that are happening now in the context of those times. It is imperative that we understand the place of Jewish government in the sequence of global wars and the next chapters discuss the clear Scriptural comparison between their ancient history and their progression in prophecy of the last days.

St. James wrote *"If any man lack wisdom, let him ask God, and it shall be given him"* and *"receive with meekness the engrafted word."[86]* The theme of my book that became evident to me parallels the ministry of John the Baptist who was sent to *"Prepare the way of the Lord, make straight in the wilderness the paths of our God."[87]* My message speaks to conversion in reference to Christ's return to save and judge rather than his first coming to atone for sin. The sacrament of baptism reflects the spiritual water of God's word that leads to our rebirth in his spirit to live a new way as *"you must be born again."[88]*

Despite the unnerving aspects of anguish resulting from divine justice that will affect many of the righteous along with the wicked, the Lord's counsel is to *"Fear not: for I am with you."[89]* In all the horror and panic that will take place around us until Christ's return in judgment, the one motivating force we can count on is his love since *"There is no fear in love; but perfect love casts out fear."[90]* To this St. Paul exhorted *"For God has not given us the spirit of fear, but of power, and of love, and of a sound mind."[91]*

Among the fruits of the Holy Spirit are virtues of fortitude and prudence that instill in us the courage of longsuffering and provident conduct. If we cannot have peace in our external world, we can strive to have it in our spirits and be an example of stability to others. The intent of my work is to secure and build upon the foundations of faith, hope and charity toward the unity of all Christians in a spirit of renewal and evangelization. That supernatural life allows us to rise above fear and sorrow in comfort and joy.

My text presents some candid answers to tough questions about contemporary society and world affairs in terms of biblical truth. Many diverse compliments were made to me from prominent people in response to the limited distribution in publication of my first exegesis on this topic. One reply stands out in my mind from a Catholic priest who being a theologian said I had done something no man has yet been able to do. In all humility, I can find no other interpretation of the Apocalypse that is written in such an open, timely and comprehensive fashion or I would acquire and study it myself.

Lessons of my work may cause many to begin their serious contemplation of the bible or reconsider their beliefs and views about the end of the world. These pioneering ideas have potential to produce a fresh interest in current issues of prophecy as they are now taking place and what events we can expect in the future. Debate about this subject has gone on from the beginning of Christianity and no doubt these discussions will continue until all things are accomplished, especially when they affect our daily lives.

Attention to the creative nature of this work needs to be drawn to Scripture itself as in answer to questions of the faithful about our times, *"The Lord hearkened, and a book of remembrance was written before him for them that feared the Lord, and thought upon his name."*[92] This verse implies that the book is one of uncovering the knowledge of God in recalling his prophetic purpose so that our search for truth can be understood and we can prepare for promises that await us. It is about the Lord as the Alpha and Omega.[93]

In the difficult task of writing I have often had to remind myself of Jesus teaching that *"my yoke is easy, and my burden is light."*[94] Only toward completing initial thoughts did any realization come to me that my work might actually be part of God's plan in these perplexing times. If this is true, then so be it for I have nothing to add or subtract from Scripture since it has all been said but not yet done. My hope is the new eschatology will have widespread distribution, generate dialogue and bear fruit of discipleship.

Sound doctrine of godly wisdom learned in secret places of study and prayer is meant to be broadcast everywhere as *"what you have whispered in the inner chambers will be preached on the housetops."*[95] I have tried as much as possible to give balance to this writing with respect to aspects of divine mercy and divine justice since siding with either is not fair to anyone. There is no stopping of the gospel *"for if this counsel or this work be of men, it will come to naught: But if it be of God, you cannot overthrow it."*[96]

At least some readers may find it surprising that I am Roman Catholic by baptism and also by the living out of that faith in active participation in the Liturgy of the Mass and other church ministries. The Catholic faith is expressed in various ways in my book in light of the divine word to better understand certain doctrines and devotions. My intent in this is to foster greater unity and a more effective practice of Christian faith. I am an American born citizen and although exceptions are made in my study about U.S. policy and laws, my gratitude for the freedoms of citizenship and patriotism remain.

In ancient history Job wished his words were *"printed in a book, graven with an iron pen and lead in the rock forever, for I know that my redeemer lives, and he shall stand at the latter day upon the earth."*[97] I have often felt an identity with the desire in this verse to share my reflections about a subject that has eternal pertinence for humanity. There is a sense of urgency in my being about these things, but I have faith in God's timing and trust for his glory that *"my words shall not return unto me void, but shall accomplish that which I please, and it shall prosper in the thing whereto I send it."*[98]

The prophet Daniel mused to himself *"I understand not"* about prophecies he wrote since *"the words are closed up and sealed till the time of the end."*[99] I do not have all the answers, but my study of Scripture points to major issues of the end times that now need to be addressed. Isaiah wrote of apathy, negligence and deception that exist in facing facts of our times that *"the vision of all is become unto you as the words of a book that is sealed. Therefore the Lord said their fear toward me is taught by the precept of men."*[100] Who then do we fear or are we responsible for teaching his divine word?

St. Peter admonished *"I stir up your pure minds by way of remembrance: That you may be mindful of the words of the prophets, knowing this first, that there shall come in the last days scoffers, and saying, Where is the promise of his coming?"*[101] Given the present state of our affairs, the reality of that promise is not slack but *"the days are at hand, and the effect of every vision."*[102] So many people are unprepared since they don't understand the bible or take the Holy Spirit to heart. They are too busy with cares of this life to be concerned with the things of God and they are blinded by their own lusts.[103]

My book will hopefully change some of that as it is written in love to inspire and convert, not to condemn. Even in the obscurity and darkness of these days, people have a deep hunger to fill inner emptiness only God can satisfy. Readers may find my work enlightening, but with a flavor that is bitter as well as sweet. Jesus told believers *"you are the salt of the earth; but if the salt loses its strength, it is no longer of any use."*[104] So it is and not only with sweat but with tears did I write the sad parts of this story.

Like gold embedded in a rock, features of the last days are fixed in the sequence of opening the seven seals. Issues raised in my study fit the parable Jesus gave that *"No one puts a patch from a new garment on an old garment, and no one pours new wine into old wineskins."*[105] While the church needs to keep established doctrines and traditions that are sacred and serve to build faith of its members, it must open itself to the revelation of divine prophecy and the inherent sorrows to be endured, yet the hopes to be obtained. Can we afford to ignore *"the shadow of death"* that hangs over the world?[106]

---

[1] Isaiah 13,6; Joel 1,15
[2] Mathew 24,36&42; 25,13; Luke 12,39-40
[3] Mathew 7,7-8; Luke 11,9-10
[4] II Thessalonians 2,2
[5] I Thessalonians 5,1&4
[6] I Thessalonians 4,16-17
[7] Romans 11,24-25
[8] I Thessalonians 5,3&9
[9] I Timothy 4,1; II Timothy 3,1
[10] Mathew 5,18
[11] Mathew 10,26; Luke 8,17; 12,12
[12] John 16,13
[13] Isaiah 46, 9-10
[14] Jeremiah 23,20; Daniel 12,10
[15] Luke 12,56
[16] I Corinthians 14,8
[17] I Corinthians 14,20&33
[18] I Corinthians 1,10
[19] I Corinthians 14,24-25
[20] Mathew 28,20
[21] Revelation 19,10
[22] Mathew 6,10-13; Luke 11,2-4
[23] Ephesians 3,21

[24] Romans 9,24; Galatians 3,27-29
[25] Isaiah 55, 5
[26] Jeremiah 16,19-21
[27] Luke 4,16-21
[28] Isaiah 61,1-11
[29] Malachi 1,11
[30] Acts 13,46
[31] Romans 11,1-28
[32] Mathew 19,30;20,16; Luke 13,24-25& 30
[33] Romans 1,16
[34] Zechariah 12,10-14
[35] Genesis 32,28-30; 35,10
[36] Romans 11,24-26
[37] Acts 2,1-4; Revelation 7,2-4
[38] Revelation 14,3-4
[39] Isaiah 44,1-2
[40] Ephesians 3,10-21
[41] Mathew 9,38; Luke 10,2-3
[42] Ezekiel 9,3-4
[43] Isaiah 7,14; Luke 1,27-28
[44] Mathew 16,18
[45] Deuteronomy 7,8-9; Romans 9,4-5
[46] Isaiah 48,9-11
[47] Isaiah 62,6-7
[48] Deuteronomy 18,15&18-19
[49] John 5,23
[50] II Thessalonians 2,4&9
[51] Romans 10,17
[52] Isaiah 1,18
[53] James 2,18-20; II Peter 2.4; Jude 6
[54] II Timothy 3,2-8; Titus 1,16
[55] Hosea 4,6- 7
[56] Proverbs 16,5 & 18
[57] Isaiah 2,12
[58] James 1,22
[59] James 4,8
[60] Acts 26,18
[61] John 3,16
[62] John 9,4
[63] Revelation 11,18
[64] Ezekiel 21,27
[65] Mathew 24,7; Mark 13,8; Luke 21,11
[66] Colossians 3,5-6
[67] I John 2,16-18
[68] Ezekiel 33,11
[69] I Timothy 4,1-2
[70] Mathew 7,15; Acts 20, 29
[71] John 15,7
[72] Hebrews 10,25
[73] II Thessalonians 2,3
[74] Acts 1,7
[75] Mathew 13,11; Mark 4,11; Luke 8,10
[76] John 16,12
[77] Mathew 13,52
[78] Mathew 16,24; 20,23; I Corinthians 11,26

[79] Mathew 24,34; Mark 13,30; Luke 21,32
[80] Luke 21,31
[81] Mathew 24,33; Mark 13,29; Luke 21,28 & 36
[82] Mathew 24,13; Mark 13,13
[83] Luke 12,35-38
[84] Mark 13,8
[85] Mathew 24,32-34; Mark 13,28; Luke 21,29-32
[86] James 1,5&21
[87] Isaiah 40,3; Mathew 3,1-3; Mark 1,3; Luke 3,4
[88] John 3,5-8
[89] Isaiah 43,5
[90] I John 4,18
[91] II Timothy 1,7
[92] Malachi 3,16
[93] Revelation 1,8-18; 22,12-13
[94] Mathew 11,30
[95] Mathew 10,27; Luke 12,3
[96] Acts 5,38-39
[97] Job 19,23-25
[98] Isaiah 55,11
[99] Daniel 12,8-9
[100] Isaiah 29,11-14
[101] II Peter 3,1-4
[102] Ezekiel 12,23
[103] Mathew 13,18; Luke, 8,5-8
[104] Mathew 5,13; Mark 9,50; Luke 14,34
[105] Mathew 9,16-17; Luke 5,36-38
[106] Psalm 23,4-5

Chapter Two
CAPTIVITY OF ISRAEL
"I spoke unto you in your prosperity, but you said, I will not hear. This has been your manner from your youth, that you obeyed not my voice."
Jeremiah 22,21

In order to gain a proper perspective of the State of Israel's present day affairs and its prospects of remaining in the ruling power of government, some background information is provided in this chapter of how God revealed himself to the Jews and their response to him as a chosen people. Prophetic mysteries in the bible and many specific aspects of the divine plan for the last days are found in the record of Jewish history and prophets before Christ became man. Their experience of the majesty and power of God is a testament to all nations of his supreme authority and foreknowledge of world events.

The ancient Hebrews were slaves in the land of Egypt for several generations before they were delivered and only after many trials over forty years in the desert did they eventually reach the Promised Land. Their bondage as strangers in a foreign land for some four hundred years as well as their emancipation and going out of that land were fulfillments of prophecy to a nation which had not even been born.[1] God told these things to the patriarch Abraham when as yet he had no children to inherit the Land of Promise.[2] Divine law was given to Jews in that early time as a binding covenant.

Israel was still in its infancy as a people when they migrated to and settled in Egypt from the land of Canaan. They came there because of severe famine that *"covered the face of the earth."*[3] One of Jacob's sons had found favor with the Pharaoh and was appointed magistrate over all Egyptian affairs. When his brothers came to buy food they were surprised to see Joseph in a lofty position since out of envy they sold him as a slave during his youth. In meekness he invited his whole family to dwell there as *"God did send me before you to preserve you a posterity in the earth and save your lives."*[4]

Being a prophet himself Joseph knew that the hardest years of the famine were yet to come and since he had persuaded the Pharaoh to prepare by storing up corn, he also knew there was plenty of food for his father and brethren. Jacob recognized the opportunity and God spoke to him as he journeyed to Egypt with his family and their possessions for *"I am God, the God of your father: fear not to go down to Egypt, for I will there make of you a great nation."*[5] In that time the whole twelve tribes of Jacob numbered only about seventy souls and Joseph gave his family the best land and provisions in Egypt.

Considering the special care of divine providence allowed to the Israelites who were already quite wealthy when they began their sojourn, they were fruitful and multiplied prolifically since *"They became so numerous and strong that the land was filled with them."*[6] After Joseph and his brothers died, reports of the large Hebrew population and their great influence were received with displeasure by a wicked king who feared they would rise up against Egypt and leave. The king decided to organize cruel taskmasters over these foreigners to oppress them into forced hard labor and servitude.

Devious and vile methods were used to make the lives of the Jews miserable through slavery and attempts failed to murder their newborn males *"But the more they afflicted them, the more they multiplied and grew."*[7] Brutal bondage continued very long over the passage of time and their groaning for rescue went up to God who called Moses from a burning bush to answer their plea as he said *"Come, now! I well send you to Pharaoh to lead my people, the Israelites, out of Egypt."*[8] Moses then went to his people and informed them the God of their fathers spoke to him that he would deliver them.

Although the Pharaoh responded to Moses by increasing the burden on the Jews and by beating them, God fulfilled his word that *"I will redeem you with a stretched out arm, and with great judgments."*[9] Many terrible plagues came upon the Egyptians at the word of Moses so even the magicians of Pharaoh declared *"This is the finger of God."*[10] But the Pharaoh remained obstinate to let the Jews go out of Egypt to worship their God. So Moses told him and his nation that the Lord warned *"For by now I would wipe you from the earth. But I have spared you to make my name resound throughout the earth."*[11]

Never before had such calamities struck Egypt as waters became blood and swarms of frogs, flies, lice and locusts swept the land while boils, pestilence, great hail and sand storms destroyed men, livestock and crops. No doubt the Egyptians learned the Hebrew God was far more powerful than any deity known since the Jews were saved from these plagues.[12] In the final judgment *"the Lord slew every first born in the land of Egypt, for there was not a house without its dead."*[13] It was only then that the Pharaoh let the Jews go out of Egypt as he said to Moses *"be gone, and you will be doing me a favor."*

During the night that every first born of the Egyptian families and their livestock were killed, all the Hebrew families prepared the Passover according to instructions by Moses.[14] In this rite each household sacrificed a lamb whose blood was put *"on the two side posts and on the upper door post of the houses."* They were taught to roast the lamb and eat it with bitter herbs and unleavened bread in a manner *"with your loins girt, sandals on your feet and your staff in hand, like those who are in flight."* And the Lord said *"when I see the blood, I will pass over you, when I smite the land of Egypt."*

Shroud of mystery covers the perpetual Passover ritual that Jews still celebrate each year. They know it is meant to remember how their ancient freedom was won, but much deeper symbolism lies in the unblemished lamb's blood as the liberty found in Christ who is *"the Lamb of God."*[15] The unleavened bread is a figure of purity and the sign of the cross was made by placing blood on the upper and opposite doorway posts. Bitter herbs reflect persecution and war, while their expectancy of going into the Promised Land is one that signifies their redemption in rapture from the final end time apostasy.

After the Jews fled from Egypt with gifts of anything they needed from Egyptians, the Pharaoh pursued them with his army to make revenge and bring them back as slaves. But his defeat was sure at the Red Sea as Moses stretched his hand out and *"the Lord caused the sea to go back, and made the sea dry land, and the waters were divided."* Then the Israelites amazingly crossed *"into the midst of the sea on dry land, with water like a wall to their right and to their left."* When the enemy army followed, the sea suddenly closed around them and *"the Lord overthrew the Egyptians in the midst of the sea."*[16]

According to the Hebrew census of pilgrims to the Promised Land, there were over six hundred thousand men of war not counting all the women, children and others.[17] They endured harsh penalties for unbelief and wandered extensively in the wilderness yet God miraculously provided bread from heaven that appeared on the ground, gave them pure water to drink and sent wild fowl for their meat. By divine acts they won famous battles against their enemies. Their only problem was keeping the law God gave to Moses.

Ample warnings were given to the Israelites not to forget their God who brought them out of Egypt *"lest when you have eaten your fill, and built fine houses, and increased your silver and gold, you then become haughty of heart.*"[18] This counsel was given due to their pride in thinking that riches would be derived from their own doings. Moses told them of the promise *"It is not because of your merits or the integrity of your heart that you are going to take possession of their land. Remember then, it is the Lord, your God, who gives you the power to acquire wealth, for you are a stiff necked people."*[19]

Besides the covenant God made with the ancient patriarchs, the main reason the Jews were chosen is to make an example to all nations that *"the Lord is God and there is no other."*[20] They were selected to be a people set apart from the diverse sinful ways of the heathen and *"be holy, for I the Lord your God am holy."*[21] Their glory was not meant for themselves, but the message Moses tried to instill in them was that *"not by bread alone does man live, but by every word that comes from the mouth of the Lord."* The purpose to love and serve him is life itself as *"he is your life, and the length of your days."*[22]

Judgments were passed against the nations that Israelites overthrew *"Because their land is become defiled, I am punishing it for its wickedness by making it vomit out its inhabitants."*[23] These peoples were stronger than the Jews and they had large fortified cities so the chance to victory without God was little to none. But they did conquer and Moses instructed them as they went to cross the Jordan River into the Land of Promise to *"Understand, it is the Lord your God who will cross over before you as a consuming fire; he it is who will reduce them to nothing and subdue them before you."*[24]

No apology is necessary from God for his justice since *"the invisible things of him from the beginning of the world are clearly seen, being understood by the things that are made, even his eternal power and Godhead."* Everyone from their childhood has the ability to know God and do what he expects. Whether his law is written before us or not, all people are innately endowed with a conscience to discern good from evil. There is no excuse for a foolish heart whose secrets will be revealed in eternal judgment since those whose works are vanity and sin simply have *"changed the truth of God into a lie."*[25]

Stark reality of this tendency in human nature to obscure and deny truth is obvious in one of the greatest divine interventions in human history. The Hebrews gathered at Mt. Sinai having cleansed their garments in expectation as they were informed *"on the third day the Lord will come down on Mount Sinai before the eyes of all people."* Moses was told by the Lord *"I come to you in a thick cloud so the people may hear when I speak with you and believe forever."* They then heard a trumpet blast and saw the glory of the Lord in fire and smoke like from a furnace as the mount trembled before them.[26]

Scripture plainly indicates the Israelites heard the actual voice of God as he uttered the Ten Commandments *"which the Lord spoke unto you, in the day of the assembly."*[27] They vowed *"We will do everything that the Lord has told us."* Moses took Aaron the high priest, his sons and seventy elders up the mount *"and they beheld the God of Israel."* They must have seen or heard a sort of vision for he *"used to speak to Moses face to face."* But even Moses only got a glimpse of God for *"I will make all my beauty pass before you, but my face you cannot see for no man sees me and lives."*[28]

An awesome display of power was witnessed by the Hebrew nation to reveal God's law and purpose. Moses went up the mount again to receive the Ten Commandments engraved on tablets of stone by God's hand and also to learn the details of making the tabernacle and service of the priests. As he stayed there forty days and nights, the Israelites committed a grave sacrilege by forming a molten calf of gold to worship it with sacrifice saying *"This is your God, O Israel, who brought you out of Egypt."* In anger Moses broke the tablets and many were slaughtered for their rebellion.[29]

If it were not for the wise and prayerful intercession of Moses, God would have killed all the Israelites and fulfilled his covenant of the Promised Land through Moses' seed. He again wrote the Ten Commandments on new tablets of stone to replace the broken ones. These were put in the Ark of the Covenant to be the center of Jewish tradition and homage.[30] Moses said to his congregation *"I have set before you life and death. Choose life then, that you and your descendants may live by loving the Lord, heeding his voice."*[31] But he knew they would not listen then or in the distant future.

Following are biblical quotes that summarize the warnings God gave to the Jews and to foreigners who live among them. The prophetic application of these passages is for both ancient history and for the last days. Since the Ten Commandments are so basic and important to Jewish law or to any civilized society, these are recorded here to remind us of the standards of morality needed to establish true brotherhood in any community as well as obtaining the loving protection and many blessings of divine providence.

Clarification of the sixth commandment is needed since the word adultery appears in most if not all bible translations as its sole forbidden act. The proper sense of the word adultery is impure acts because this law forbids all sexual sins, not just those that violate marital fidelity. Behaviors like homosexuality and fornication are defined in the bible as sins that prohibit anyone from entering the kingdom of God.[32] It is a grave deception to believe otherwise since chastity is required outside the sanctity of marriage. Jesus said whoever even lusts after a women *"has committed adultery with her in his heart."*[33]

"I am the Lord your God. You shall not do as they do in the land of Egypt, where you once lived, nor shall you do as they do in the land of Canaan where I am bringing you. Do not defile yourselves by any of these things by which the nations whom I am driving out of your way have defiled themselves. You however, whether natives or resident aliens, must keep my statutes and decrees forbidding all such abominations by which the previous inhabitants defiled the land; otherwise the land will vomit you out also for having defiled it, just as it vomited out the nations before you. Heed my charge not to defile yourselves by doing the customs done before you." Leviticus 18,1-5&24-32

"But if you do not heed me, refusing to obey my commandments and breaking my covenant, then I in turn will give you your deserts. You will be lost among the Gentiles, swallowed up in your enemies' captivity. Those of you who survive in the lands of their enemies will waste away for their own and their father's guilt. Thus they will have to confess that they and their fathers were guilty of having rebelled against me, so that I too had to defy them and bring them into their enemies' land." Leviticus 26,14-42

"But it is not with you alone that I am making this covenant under the sanction of a curse; it is just as much with those who are not here among us today as it is with those of us who are now here present before the Lord our God. In keeping with the curses of the covenant inscribed in this Book of the Law, future generations, your own descendants who will rise up after you, as well as the foreigners who will come here from far-off lands, when they see the calamities of this land, all its soil being nothing but sulfur and salt, a burnt out waste, they and all the nations will ask 'Why has the Lord dealt thus with this land?' And the answer will be 'Because they forsook the covenant which the Lord, the God of their fathers, had made with them. The Lord was angry and uprooted them from their soil and cast them into a strange land, as it is this day.' Both what is still hidden and what has already been revealed concern us and our descendants forever, that we may carry out all the words of this Law." Deuteronomy 29,13-15&21-29

The Ten Commandments

1) I am the Lord your God. You shall not have other gods before me.
2) You shall not take the name of the Lord your God in vain.
3) Remember to keep holy the Sabbath day.
4) Honor your father and mother.
5) You shall not kill.
6) You shall not commit impure acts.
7) You shall not steal.
8) You shall not bear false witness against your neighbor.
9) You shall not covet your neighbor's wife.
10) You shall not covet you neighbor's goods.

Exodus 20,1-17; Deuteronomy 5,2-22

These commandments seem simple enough and anyone in their right mind can discern that they are guidelines meant for our own good and that of our society. The dignity of any man or woman lies in being a creature of God who reflects his holy image in us free from our own ruinous passions. This liberty is the path of love that can only be obtained by observing divine law grounded in truth and justice. Harmony between God and man procures the necessary result of peace among men. Any other choice leads to discord and dishonor in selfish wickedness that ultimately results in bloodshed and destruction.

Once the twelve tribes of Israelites first settled in the land God had provided for them, *"the Lord gave them peace on every side, just as he promised their fathers."*[34] Without explaining the details of which nations were conquered or how the sections of the biblical land of Canaan were apportioned, it was Joshua who with many miracles led the Jews after Moses died.[35] He proclaimed *"Every promise has been fulfilled for you with not one single exception."*[36] What took place long ago was exactly according to prophecies from the time of Abraham, but the initial peace for Jews was short lived.

When Joshua and other elders who outlived him died, the next generation arose who *"did not know the Lord, or what he had done for Israel."* They forgot the law taught to their fathers and abandoned the Lord who brought them there as *"they followed the other gods of the various nations around them."*[37] Temptation to do evil existed because the command God gave to totally doom the cities they took for inheritance was not followed. They were to *"save alive nothing that breathes"* of any person or their livestock and utterly destroy their false gods with fire not taking anything for spoil.[38]

What happened in the early stages of Jewish dominion with respect to a loss of power and affliction by their enemies was a direct outcome of their greed and lust for things they were not to have in the first place. The remnant of peoples left who were not Jews resulted in mixing of marriage and worship of their false gods. As Joshua warned to his brethren, these people became *"a snare and a trap for you, a scourge for your sides and thorns for your eyes."[39]* In anger of their recurring sins, the Lord said *"I will not henceforth drive out before them of the nations which Joshua left when he died."[40]*

As a consequence of violating their covenant with God, he allowed these prior peoples to remain in the land as punishment to the Jews for their continued disobedience of divine law.[41] Those nations persecuted and made war with the Israelites throughout the extensive period in which judges ruled over Israel. These judges who more or less had partial jurisdiction were mainly military leaders who the Lord chose to deliver the Jews from their despoilers. When they repeatedly repented of their iniquity in hard times *"the Lord took pity on their distressful cries of affliction under their oppressors."*

Rebellion was met with retribution and repentance led to restoration of order among the Jews. This cycle of peace and adversity went on for hundreds of years as Israelites would not listen to their judges who clearly brought divine mercy to their cause. They kept refusing to abide in the safety of the covenant and persisted in testing God's patience to fulfill his word that they would perish from the land. The positive reinforcement of his goodness should bring us to lasting repentance and loyal gratitude, but instead in their pride *"when the judge died, they would relapse and do worse than their fathers."[42]*

Succeeding the period of judges, a monarchy was formed in Israel that for a brief time rivaled the power and glory of any kingdom on earth. A prophet named Samuel who was highly respected everywhere in the land was the last of the judges who *"judged Israel all the days of his life."[43]* There was peace in his rule as his enemies were beaten by great miracles of God and many Jewish cities were returned to their control.[44] When Samuel grew old, the Israelites sought him to *"Make us a king to judge us like all the nations and our king shall judge us, and go out before us, and fight our battles."[45]*

Samuel was displeased with the idea of kingship since the Hebrews were governed by theocracy from the start. God was their supreme ruler and ministry of his laws was given to the priests or prophets who had a divine commission. Trust was to be placed in him by living out the civil matters and sacred rituals of his precepts. These traditions were not accepted since their hearts were blinded to the lessons of their history and they wanted to be like others who governed themselves. They sought a scapegoat to cover their iniquity other than the one prescribed in the law regarding their rite of atonement.[46]

Thus God told Samuel *"they have not rejected you, but they have rejected me, that I should reign over them."[47]* He later anointed Saul with oil saying *"the Lord has anointed you to be prince over his inheritance, and you shall deliver his people out of the hands of their enemies, that are round about them."[48]* Upon presenting Saul to the people, they rejoiced saying *"God save the king"* and he was made their king. Saul conquered nations who threatened Israel, but as his pride and greed grew he took spoils from his enemies that were to be doomed and even sacrificed them to God in sacrilege.[49]

Saul was rebuked by Samuel as *"The Lord has rent the kingdom of Israel from you this day, and has given it to your neighbor who is better than you."* He boldly told him *"it is like the sin of witchcraft to rebel, and like the crime of idolatry to refuse to obey."[50]* Then Samuel anointed David as king and *"Saul feared David because the Lord was with him, and was departed from himself."[51]* David's fame was great since he saved Israel from their enemy when he killed the giant Goliath.[52] Saul persisted many times to kill David out of envy and even slaughtered scores of priests who helped him.[53]

It came to pass that Samuel died and Saul apparently committed suicide at the finish of a losing battle.[54] Subsequently David had a struggle with the house of Saul, but took his place as king over all the tribes of Israel.[55] His early years of reign were in Hebron, but he moved his throne to Jerusalem where he ruled for over thirty more years. He won many battles in far territories not previously governed by Israel and in this way he not only secured his borders, but extended the colonial boundaries of servitude toward Israel. In his ambitious plans *"the Lord preserved David in all enterprises he went about."*[56]

Early on as king in Jerusalem, David brought the Ark of the Covenant there to place it in a tabernacle he had pitched.[57] The Lord appeared to him at that spot to fulfill a critical prophecy given to Moses about where the Jews would go to worship after they settled in the land of heritage.[58] With respect to this sanctuary, it was *"the place which the Lord chooses and designates as his dwelling."* Moses warned *"Take care not to offer up your holocausts in any place you fancy, but offer them up in the place the Lord chooses from among your tribes, there you shall make whatever offerings I enjoin upon you."*[59]

The sanctuary site was definitely a matter of divine decision that would be pointed out in the proper time of circumstance. Enclosed in the Ark were the Ten Commandments and its resting place was to be the single focus of gathering for prayer and ritual. It was determined to be the absolute seat of mercy and blessing of God as *"the dwelling place for his name."* David desired to make a permanent structure for housing the ark of God, but the prophet Nathan revealed to him that the Lord said after he died one of his sons *"shall build a house to my name, and I will establish his throne forever."*[60]

This prophetic promise applies to Jesus the Messiah of Israel who would build God's house not in a temple made by human hands, but in hearts of his people. That covenant is based on divine promise where Christ would fulfill the law, yet the location of his Lordship on earth is certain as *"I have chosen this place, that my name may be there forever, and my eyes and my heart may remain there perpetually."*[61] And further *"I have given a place to my people Israel, they shall be planted and dwell therein and moved no more."*[62] Question of these lasting things is not if, but when it will happen.

Solomon took his father David's place as king and built the first physical temple in the pattern given to him that God showed to his father, but his throne and the temple were conditional as the Lord said to him *"If you do according to all that I have commanded you, there shall not fail you a man of your stock to be ruler in Israel."* On the contrary *"if you turn away and serve strange gods, I will pluck you up by the root out of my land and this house I will cast away, and make it a byword and an example among the nations."*[63] Thus the right of his lineage to succeed the throne was restricted.

David was not only king but also a prophet as *"the spirit of the Lord has spoken by me and his word by my tongue."* To him *"it was appointed concerning the Christ of the God of Jacob"* that *"Although my house be not so with God, yet he has made me an eternal covenant, ordered in all things."*[64] Here he distinguished the divine nature of Christ from his own house since the promise holds *"I will be his father and he shall be my son, I will settle him in my house and in my kingdom forever, and his throne shall be established for evermore."*[65] This kingdom is of the Almighty through Jesus his only Son.

Many issues of prophecy are presented by David in his lineage and in his psalms. He knew that the covenant of an everlasting kingdom was *"for a great while to come."* Of the Messiah who would take the throne of Israel, he called him his Lord who sits at the right hand of God.[66] David was an important link in explaining the divine being of Christ next to that of God as *"The Lord is among the chariots of God, as in Sinai, in the holy place."[67]* Jesus was with God at Mt. Sinai and in the tabernacle tent. In his connection to Christ, David said God *"has made me remarkable above all men."[68]*

Although there is prophetic significance in the place chosen in Jerusalem for building the temple, it is not synonymous with the house that the Lord will secure to the name of God in the promise to David or is it the same as God's home in heaven. The house of Christ is one built by the Holy Spirit in souls of people who obey his law. Even though he may have an earthly throne, his throne is in heaven with God and his kingdom is eternal in both respects. Those of his house who being mortal have promise of that which is immortal already revealed to us by the resurrection of Christ from the dead.

Seeing that Christ's kingdom is of God's home and eternal kingdom in heaven, they who are of his house have a greater inheritance than what is temporal on earth. The hope of the Messiah combines or unites that kingdom which is above with anyone in humanity who loves and serves him in divine will. This kingdom is and has been only partially reflected on earth by those who rest in the grace of God's love. Yet in the time of fulfillment of all things albeit in the course of harsh judgment, a new spiritual awakening will occur at the Second Advent for the Jews and for mankind as a whole.

Mystery of the human and divine nature of Christ as the Son of David is a prominent theme of Scripture. The prophets attest *"that a King shall reign and prosper, and shall execute judgment and justice in the earth. They shall dwell in the land I gave to Jacob, and my servant David shall be their prince forever."[69]* Of his house and reign, *"As the host of heaven so will I multiply the seed of David, and his seed shall endure forever and his throne as the sun before me."[70]* Jesus holds the key of David and he alone *"shall open and none shall shut, and he shall shut and none shall open."[71]*

Regarding the lineage of Christ as *"the root and offspring of David"*, Jesus satisfied the bloodline promise of the Son of God *"who was born to him according to the flesh of the offspring of David."[72]* When the angel Gabriel came to the Virgin Mary announcing that she would conceive the Son of God in her womb by the power of the Holy Spirit, he told her to name him Jesus and declared *"the Lord God shall give unto him the throne of his father David, and of his kingdom there shall be no end."[73]* So it is the Savior became man, but of his reign *"Jesus Christ of the seed of David was raised from the dead."[74]*

To all who love and obey God *"Know you not that you are the temple of God, and that the Spirit of God dwells in you?"[75]* Isaiah wrote *"Hearken unto me, my people, and give ear unto me, my salvation is gone forth, look upon the earth, those that dwell therein shall die, but my salvation shall be forever."[76]* Jesus is the mediator of a covenant that concerns not only blessings in this brief human life but of *"an incorruptible inheritance, undefiled and unfading, reserved in heaven."* Whoever receives his life is reborn of an everlasting seed sustained *"by the word of God, which lives and abides forever."[77]*

In the days of King Solomon, his people dwelt without any fear and none of the kings on earth had such riches and wisdom.[78] He exercised authority from the borders of Egypt to the Euphrates River and faithfully constructed the Jewish temple consistent with the detailed pattern that had been shown to his father by the Lord.[79] Despite his great wealth and savvy, his downfall was due to his incessant lust of foreign women who seduced him to make and worship false gods. With this stubborn grave sin, he broke his covenant with God and then in anger the Lord told him *"I will divide and rend your kingdom."[80]*

About five hundred years had passed from the Hebrew exodus out of Egypt at the time Solomon ruled in Jerusalem.[81] An incomplete census taken by his father recorded well over one and a half million military men and after David died these Israelites became a great people who could not be counted for multitude.[82] The expansive dominions of David and especially Solomon were renown among all nations because of the amazing power and works of their God. At this pinnacle of fame and fortune, the kingdom was split when Solomon died and then began its fall as they turned to evil ways.

All the Israelites were ready to crown Roboam king over Israel in his father's stead, but he showed himself as a very harsh ruler that would stiffen their labor. In response, ten of the twelve tribes revolted and they decided to govern themselves. It had already been shown to Jeroboam by a prophet that ten tribes would break off and follow him as king.[83] Only the tribe of Benjamin remained loyal to Roboam who was from David's tribe of Judah. The northern kingdom of Samaria was called the house of Israel and the other kingdom located in and around Jerusalem was termed the house of Judah.

Since the Jewish temple of worship was in Jerusalem, Jeroboam feared that his people would go over to the kingdom of Judah. He devised a wicked plan to keep them under his control by making altars to false gods.[84] Ordained priests of the Levite tribe were cast off and he placed base men to minister at the feasts of idols. To some extent his scheme backfired since the priests and other God fearing Jews went to Jerusalem, but overall the kings and people who succeeded Jeroboam in Samaria followed his rebellious lead in doing abominations until their destruction and captivity by the king of Assyria.[85]

Unlike the house of Israel who consistently disobeyed divine law, the kings of Judah exhibited a mixed and sometimes stark contrast in their faithfulness to God. When they or those in Samaria were humbled by plagues to cry out for the Lord's help, his wrath turned away and they repeatedly saw his miraculous mercy in saving them. They lived in a long period where all nations were at war as predicted *"There shall be no peace to him that goes out and comes in, but terrors on every side."*[86] God wanted peace for Israel, but sorrows came because as he explained *"You have left me and I have left you."*[87]

Little by little, the beautiful cities of the Jews were wasted and they lost dominion of all their former tributaries. The surrounding nations who once honored and served them rose up to be their enemies and then plundered them, stripped them of wealth and took away the spoils of war. To add to their distress, civil wars and famines were common plagues of daily life. Even though the Lord grew weary of their sins, his final justice for either kingdom did not happen overnight. He was patient and measured in dealing with his people's sins providing many occasions for them to see his truth and repent.

Looking back on history in the waning hours of the two kingdoms of Israel, it was much like the period of judges where a cycle of rebellion and amends took place. In spite of a few good kings that ruled in the house of Judah to spur the Jews to faith, they most often forgot God and paid the sore price of their iniquity. The house of Israel lasted over two hundred years and came into captivity after a three-year siege as *"the king of the Assyrians took Samaria, and carried Israel away to Assyria."* The Lord ended this house and *"removed them from his sight, and there remained only the tribe of Judah."*[88]

Several years after the Assyrians conquered Samaria, their new king sought to take the rest of Jewish land captive. The kingdom of Judah existed for over a hundred years past its counterpart and despite the pillage of cities in Judah, the Assyrians failed to conquer Jerusalem. The prophet Isaiah foretold to the attacking king that *"the virgin the daughter of Zion has despised you and laughed you to scorn."* Then at night an angel of God *"slew in the camp of the Assyrians a hundred and eighty five thousand."* When the king awoke, he was shocked to find his soldiers were dead and he returned to Assyria.[89]

Iniquity in the house of Judah grew grievously to the point that they were worse than the heathen nations who had been there before them. Even the holy temple in Jerusalem was defiled with idols to false gods and the city was full of innocent blood.[90] The Lord's verdict was known that *"I will remove Judah also out of my sight, as I have removed Israel."* His judgment was clear that *"I will give all Judah into the hand of the king of Babylon, and he shall carry them captive into Babylon."*[91] But they spurned the truth of his word and believed the false prophets who *"made this people trust in a lie."*[92]

In the ending period of Jewish rule, the king of Babylon came against Jerusalem after sending many bands of men from his vast dominion to destroy the cities of Judah. At that time he took thousands of prisoners and much booty including the *"vessels of the house of the Lord."*[93] He then set up a governor in Jerusalem who later revolted from him. Consequently the king came back, besieged the city, broke down the walls and burnt everything including the temple with fire. Except for a few, the Jews who surrendered or were not killed by the sword or by hunger were all taken prisoner to Babylon.[94]

There was no longer any remedy for the ancient Hebrews to hold onto any semblance of the great kingdom they once had. The displacement and dispersion of the Jews was foreseen in a prophetic parable of good figs and rotten figs. To the good figs of those who were lucky enough to go captive to Babylon by divine providence, the Lord said *"I will set my eyes upon them for good, and I will bring them again to this land."* But to the bad figs of those left in the land or who escaped to Egypt *"I will deliver them into all the kingdoms of the earth for their hurt to be a reproach and proverb."*[95]

Issues relating to the return of Israel from captivity are studied in the next chapter, but a profound irony is professed in Scripture for the Jewish nation regarding their captivity. The adage that history repeats itself holds true in reference to the eventual fate of present day Israel. Biblical predictions about the State of Israel parallel the ancient deliverance of Jews from their enemies to establish their kingdom but also their ensuing experience of destruction, captivity and dispersion due to wickedness. These matters are an integral part of the swords of second and fourth seals as well as what events intervene.

This succinct paradigm of divine justice is *"the days come says the Lord that I will bring again the captivity of my people Israel and Judah, in the latter days you shall consider it."* Like many other similar prophecies, the context of this passage is in the end times and it clearly indicates an inclusive period of vengeance not only for the combined houses of Israel but also *"a full end of all nations whether I have scattered you."* God will yet remember his covenant with Jews for *"I will not utterly consume you, but I will chastise you in judgment, that you may not seem to yourself innocent."*[96]

It is necessary to distinguish from Scripture what role the Jews occupy as an entity of government as opposed to their place in the Christian church. There is a great dichotomy explained in my book as pertinent chapters reveal the dualism of Jews who either believe in or reject the holy gospel of Christ as *"he shall be for a sanctuary; but for a stone of stumbling and a rock of offense to both houses of Israel, and many of them shall stumble, fall, and be taken."*[97] For Jews and Gentiles in the end period of the Antichrist's rule, the Lord said *"I will bring the captivity of your captives in the midst of them."*[98]

23

Obligation to keep the Ten Commandments is a law for all mankind in the sense of our human conscience *"For the eyes of the Lord behold all the earth, and give strength to those who with a perfect heart trust in him."*[99] From the beginning *"It is he who sits on the circle of the earth and brings the princes to nothing, he makes the judges of the earth as vanity."*[100] Conditional blessings or curses that God gave to Moses affect every nation. Divine justice is the same throughout time *"For I am the Lord, I change not."* Nobody can alter the statutes of his law to instruct us in either life or death.[101]

God is not prejudice against any race with respect to his desire to plentifully bestow many good gifts that anyone needs to be whole in spirit, soul and body. His axiom for happiness and eternal salvation applies to everyone and in light of Scripture we see that every nation, kindred, people and tongue are represented in heaven to stand forever in the presence of God and Christ.[102] These are they who choose the way of life in the journey on earth and receive the promised gift of blissful resurrection. But in the here and now of our mortal being God also promises to satisfy the desires of our heart as follows:

> "If you live in accordance with my precepts and are careful to observe my
> commandments, I will give you rain in due season, so that the land will bear
> its crops, and the trees their fruit, you will have food to eat in abundance so
> that you may dwell securely in your land. I will establish peace in the land
> so you may lie down to rest without anxiety. I will rid the ravenous beasts
> out of your country, and keep the sword of war from sweeping across your
> land. And five of you shall chase a hundred and a hundred of you shall put
> ten thousand to flight. You will rout your enemies and lay them low with
> your sword. I will look with favor upon you, and make you fruitful and
> numerous. Ever present in your midst, I will be your God, and you will be
> my people."   Leviticus 26,3-12

What more could we want? These are the wishes and longings for all people to inherit their land in peace and prosperity. Who doesn't want plenty of sustenance, tranquility of mind, good health, safety from harm and a happy family? Even more, God promises to feed the hunger of our spirit to know our Creator in a personal relationship in which he can minister to our special intentions. There is a very positive connection in Christ with each aspect of our well being not only in our external environment, but in spiritual, mental and physical needs since he *"shall quicken your mortal bodies by his Spirit that dwells in you."*[103] The promise is complete to suit our separate individuality.

On the other hand, divine chastisement is much like our own laws as repeat offenders receive more severe punishment. In handing out his penalties, God is considerate of the degree of our perverseness as Jesus said *"For with what judgment you judge, you shall be judged, and with what measure you measure, it shall be measured unto you."*[104] His rulings in agreement with God the Father are based on the principle that the worse we are in our moral actions and the more stubborn we are to repent from sin, the more intense we derive retribution. These alarming statutes are summarized in the next passage:

> "But if you do not heed me and do not keep all these my commandments, then
> in turn I will appoint over you terror, consumption, and the burning ague,
> and I will cause sorrow of heart, and you shall flee when none pursues you,

and your land will bear no crops, and its trees no fruit, your strength shall be spent in vain, and I will unleash the wild beasts against you, rob you of your children, and destroy your cattle, and send pestilence among you, and cut off your supply of bread, and make your cities waste, and bring your sanctuaries unto desolation, so devastated will I leave the land that your enemies will stand aghast at the sight of it."   Leviticus 26,14-32

Cultural anomaly and tragedy throughout history can be traced to the single causality of ingrained forms of iniquity. Sin is not without cost in itself or by the punitive orders of divine providence. Some of the judgments stated above are evident in varying depths everywhere in the world. These are not all inclusive of the chastisements given in the bible, but they provide a general idea of God's displeasure and methods of disposing his anger. There is no maybe in respect to any of the blessings or curses God gave to Moses for mankind. The determining pivotal factor rests in the choice to be faithful.

Zionism in a true prophetic and philosophical sense is inclusive for humanity in that it refers to our place as children of God with the promise of blessing here on earth and also eternal life in heaven as he *"is God of gods, and Lord of lords, who regards not persons, and loves the stranger in giving him food and raiment."* Thus Jews were taught to *"Love you therefore the stranger."*[105] They who are foreigners should be welcomed as equals since only *"One law shall be to him that is home born and to the stranger that sojourns among you"* and also *"as you are, so shall the stranger be before the Lord."*[106]

Foreigners from other nations who submitted themselves to divine law and desired to live among the Jews had the same privileges as the Hebrews themselves, except for the priesthood reserved only for the Levite tribe.[107] They were allowed to take part in sacred rituals such as the Passover, rite of atonement and offerings of sacrifice. The meaning of being Jewish is spiritual as *"he is a Jew who is so inwardly."* This imprint is of God and symbolized in the oblation of animals by the priest who sprinkled blood on the altar and burnt the inward fat and kidneys.[108] Our inward parts belong to Christ.

Commands to the Jews to destroy the lives of their enemies and their belongings as they came into the Promised Land may seem like a contradiction to permit foreigners to live among the Jews and take part in traditions. The reason God ordered an apparent genocide of the nations conquered by Israelites was because of their iniquity and its evil influence. Once the land was cleansed of these heathen ways, anyone who desired to seek and serve the Lord was to be considered no different from Jews.

Equality of human rights provided under the law of God was expressed by Solomon after he completed building the first Jewish temple. His prayers were made not only for his nation, but for all other nations as he petitioned the Lord *"concerning the stranger, which is not of your people, but is come from a far country for your great name's sake, if they come and pray in this house, then hear you from the heavens, and do according to all that the stranger calls to you for: that all people of the earth may know your name, and fear you, and may know that this house is called by your name."*[109]

What is meant for Jews in relation to common brotherhood and prosperity according to divine commandments never materialized in ancient history. Jesus informed that the whole law is based on the principle of loving God and our neighbor.[110] Any society will fragment and crumble under the weight of its apostasy without that love which comes from our submission to the Holy Spirit. If we don't honor and abide in the salvation of

Christ, he won't recognize us before God the Father and the consequences of our refusal go far beyond any adversities of this life into the realm of eternal damnation.[111]

America is a present day example of how iniquity can weaken and corrupt a nation that is still the most powerful and Christian society on earth. These noble attributes are increasingly becoming more relative as internal and external influences detract from the strength of our government, military, economy, educational system, social order, health, values and family unit. What may have been a legitimate claim of boasting and worthy model to others has in many ways turned into a matter of shame. Our motivating and sustaining force of divine love has largely been replaced by selfishness and pride.

Atheism and idolatry are being promoted by a more subtle use of secularism founded on the principle that every issue of state should be devoid of God because his name is an inherent affront against personal freedom and civil rights. Separation of state and church was never intended to create an atheistic counterculture that establishes laws contrary to divine will and teaches doctrines which infringe on religious freedom. It clearly was not formed to abrogate God from the public arena, but instead to safeguard faith in him and his way as a criterion to be weighed in our political conscience for profit.

Attempts to remove God or any symbolism of Christianity from the public sector have become more ardent, pervasive and visible. Misuse in the interpretation of law such as those regarding abortion, pornography and homosexual rights blatantly annuls our human dignity. The slaughter of millions of innocent unborn babies and the widespread sins of gross sexual impurity are matters that cry out daily for divine vengeance. These profane acts of the baby boom generation and their siblings were not accepted by their ancestors. Why now do we think our laws are exempt from morality and scrutiny of God?

We have built empires in our culture for criminal incarceration and rehabilitation of mental problems, alcoholism and drug abuse. Besides our physical institutions, doctors and counselors treat countless people who suffer from depression, paranoia and a host of other emotional disorders. Major programs have developed to deal with the abuse and neglect of children due to the breakdown of the family system and high rate of divorce. Do we really need more jails, more counseling and more prescription drugs? The lasting solution to these social insecurities and violence is in divine grace and forgiveness.

Our national economy is in a precarious position. Long gone are days when anyone could find employment that paid high wages along with medical and pension benefits. Major corporations have had to restructure, outsource labor to foreign workers and file for bankruptcy. Extreme overhead costs have reduced productivity, business investment and available full-time jobs. Natural disasters, terrorism and energy prices have jolted our economy while the trade deficit soars and military funding piles up debt. Inflation hits hardest in primary sectors of subsistence requiring many to find extra work.

Housing, health care, food, utility and insurance costs have skyrocketed resulting in tighter budgets that curtail consumer spending and reduce economic growth. These and other big prices together with unemployment and more taxes shatter living standards in severe hardship for many households. Our aging population due to birth control and abortion poses a funding crisis for Social Security, Medicare, Disability, Medicaid and other programs like Education. As more people live to reach retirement age, less workers are available to pay for basic needs, wasteful projects and reckless borrowing.

With all technological resources at our disposal, our nation is still perplexed as how to deal with economic ailments, social problems, grave threats of terrorism, chronic disease and disruptions in nature. The concept of secular education excludes teaching biblical truths and contradictory theories like evolution put in its place. Schools of psychology are geared to self-actualization rather than faith and philosophy taught as human reason, not divine inspiration. Why have we made God a subject of vanity? Or are we unable to discern his being or see that urgent ills of our society result from his anger?

Financial plagues deeply struck the American banking system with a threat of collapse resulting in huge monetary bailouts by the federal government. Lending abuses fostered by greed and lax regulation created pervasive losses in mortgage-backed securities due to falling home prices and rising foreclosures. This staggering drop of capital prompted a credit crisis that further crippled the housing industry and highly impaired business in general. Efforts to revive the economy and avoid a deeper recession or depression have reached unseen levels causing an extreme drawback in massive taxpayer liability.

Nearly all economic indicators give little hope of quick solution to setbacks relating to business and personal bankruptcies. Many reasons, including a flooded housing market and tighter credit, can be given to expect a continued drain on pocketbooks and loss of income. The plummet in housing values has left millions of people with negative or reduced equity in their homes. This upside-down effect in the bedrock of most people's savings increases the risk of default and inhibits home equity loans forcing many into a mode of survival. Construction companies have cut back or just stopped building.

Vast sums of money have been lost in stock market shares reducing the solvency of pension funds, slashing capital in retirement accounts and harshly affecting a broad spectrum of industry. Like housing value decreases and the federal rescue plan for banks and other institutions, these incredible amounts are in the trillions of dollars. Financial upheaval then forced the U.S. to set aside core principles of capitalism. State and local government budget deficits have multiplied tax burdens on our citizens in a deteriorating economy. Most gains in stocks go to the wealthy yet another crash could come.

How has the richest nation on earth fallen into a state of financial peril? The great tumult and drastic fluctuations in world markets indicate the fragile nature of our means of livelihood and how quickly things can turn for the worse. U.S. fiscal credibility has suddenly come into question with a lack of confidence among investors and the obvious vulnerability seen by its rivals and enemies. Signs of our times provide ample grounds for a distressing outlook in national defense and domestic welfare that is laden with serious dangers to the fundamental rights of our lives, liberty and felicity.

Nothing is wrong with the way our founding fathers wrote the articles of our freedom, but the error is in the constitution of our hearts to invent unjust laws and live a gospel of our own making. Jews were instructed by God to *"lay up my words in your heart and in your soul, and you shall teach them to your children."[112]* This practical guide to true knowledge is shunned by those *"Ever learning and never able to come to the knowledge of the truth."[113]* To this base egoism *"Woe unto them that are wise in their own eyes and prudent in their own sight, for the wisdom of their wise men shall perish."[114]*

What is known as the American dream has been lost for many in privation while they who have enough property don't enjoy security of a happy family or faith in God. Any sense of real harmony whether in our homes or in our community must come by uniting the divine will with that of our own. The melting pot associated with our country is much more than the influx of mixed races, but it is a sordid blending of incompatible values of good and evil within our soul. Our only politically correct remedy for misfortune and ruin rests in response to the words In God We Trust printed on our currency.

The United States of America is facing a serious judgment of war like none other yet recorded in its history. Terrorism is a plague that has already reached the boundaries of our homeland and the full extent of its damage is still to be realized. Events which have transpired since 9/11 present a scenario of a broader and violent world war described in the second seal. This country's place in that particular period of Scripture is soundly defined and so are those who seek to destroy the State of Israel and its allies. Jews have returned to the Holy Land and control over Jerusalem is the primary matter at hand.

---

[1] Genesis 15,13-14; Exodus 12, 40-41
[2] Genesis 12,6-7; 13,14-15
[3] Genesis 41,56-57
[4] Genesis 45,3-21
[5] Genesis 46,2-4&26-27
[6] Exodus 1,6-7
[7] Exodus 1,8-17
[8] Exodus 3,2-10
[9] Exodus 6,6-8
[10] Exodus 8,19
[11] Exodus 9,15-16
[12] Exodus 9,4&11&26
[13] Exodus 12,29-33
[14] Exodus 12,3-13
[15] John 1,29&36; Revelation 5,12
[16] Exodus 14,15-31
[17] Numbers 1,45-49
[18] Deuteronomy 8,11-14
[19] Deuteronomy 8,17-18; 9,5-6
[20] Deuteronomy 4,32-39
[21] Leviticus 19,2
[22] Deuteronomy 8,3; 30,20
[23] Leviticus 18,25
[24] Exodus 23,27-30; Deuteronomy 9,3
[25] Romans 1,20-32
[26] Exodus 19,9-20
[27] Exodus 20,22; Deuteronomy 10,4
[28] Exodus 24,3&9-10; 33,11-23; Psalm 68,17
[29] Exodus 32,4-28
[30] Deuteronomy 10,1-5
[31] Deuteronomy 30,19-20

[32] Leviticus 18,22-25; 20,13-16; Romans 1,24-32
[33] Mathew 5,28
[34] Joshua 12,7-24; 21,43-45
[35] Exodus 3,8; 6,2-4; Joshua 24,8-13
[36] Numbers 34,1-12; Joshua 23,14-15
[37] Judges 2,10-14
[38] Deuteronomy 7,2-5; 12,2-3; 13,15-17; 20,10-18
[39] Joshua 23,11-13
[40] Judges 2,15-23
[41] Judges 3,1-5
[42] Judges 2,18-19; Romans 2,4
[43] I Samuel 3,19-20; 7,15
[44] I Samuel 5,6-12; 7,10-14
[45] I Samuel 8,4-8&20
[46] Leviticus 16,10&20-22&29-31
[47] I Samuel 8,7
[48] I Samuel 10,1&24; 11,15
[49] I Samuel 14,47-48; 15,16-21
[50] I Samuel 15,22-28
[51] I Samuel 16,13; 18,12
[52] I Samuel 17,4-9&50-51
[53] I Samuel 22,17-19
[54] I Samuel 25,1; 31,1-6
[55] II Samuel 3,1; 5,1-5
[56] II Samuel 8,11-14; I Chronicles 18,1-13
[57] II Samuel 6,12; I Chronicles 16,1
[58] II Chronicles 3,1
[59] Deuteronomy 12,4-14
[60] II Samuel 7,7-17; I Chronicles 17,9-15
[61] II Chronicles 7,16
[62] I Chronicles 17,9
[63] I Chronicles 28,2-20; II Chronicles 7,1-22
[64] II Samuel 23,1-6
[65] I Chronicles 17,11-17
[66] Psalm 110; Mathew 22,41-45
[67] Psalm 68,17
[68] I Chronicles 17,16-27
[69] Jeremiah 23,5; Ezekiel 37,25
[70] Psalm 89,35-36; Jeremiah 33,22
[71] Isaiah 22,22; Revelation 3,7
[72] Romans 1,2-4; Revelation 5,5
[73] Luke 1,26-38
[74] II Timothy 2,8
[75] I Corinthians 3,16
[76] Isaiah 51,4-6
[77] I Peter 1,4&23
[78] I Kings 4,20-25; 10,14-27
[79] I Chronicles 28,11-19
[80] I Kings 11,1-11; II Chronicles 9,22-28
[81] I Kings 6,1
[82] I Kings 3,8; I Chronicles 21,5-6
[83] I Kings 11,29-31
[84] I Kings 12,26-33
[85] II Kings 17,5-13&22-23; II Chronicles 11,13-17
[86] II Chronicles 15,5-6

[87] II Chronicles 12,5
[88] II Kings 17,6-18
[89] II Kings 19,20-21&32-37
[90] II Kings 21,2-16; II Chronicles 33,2-9
[91] II Kings 23,27; Isaiah 39,6; Jeremiah 20,4-5
[92] Jeremiah 28,15; 36,22-31; 37,1-2
[93] II Kings 24,1-16; II Chronicles 36,5-10
[94] II Kings 25,1-12; II Chronicles 36,11-20
[95] Jeremiah 24,4-10; 38,2-3; 43,4-13
[96] Jeremiah 30,3-14&23-24
[97] Isaiah 8,14-15; Romans 9,30-33
[98] Ezekiel 16,53
[99] II Chronicles 16,9
[100] Isaiah 40,21-26
[101] Malachi 3,6
[102] Revelation 7,9-10
[103] Romans 8,11
[104] Mathew 7, 2; Mark 4,24; Luke 6,38
[105] Deuteronomy 10,17-19
[106] Exodus 12,48-49; Numbers 9,14; 15,14-15
[107] Deuteronomy 10,8
[108] Leviticus 3,1-17; 4,8-9; Romans 2,29
[109] I Kings 8,41-43; II Chronicles 6,32-33
[110] Mathew 22,37-40; Mark 12,29-31
[111] Mathew 10,32-33; 25,41-46
[112] Deuteronomy 11,18-19
[113] II Timothy 3,7
[114] Isaiah 5,20-24; 29,14

Chapter Three
RETURN OF ISRAEL
"For they are a nation void of counsel, neither is there any understanding in them. Oh that they were wise, that they understood this, that they would consider their latter end." Deuteronomy 32,28-29

According to biblical chronology, more than a millennium had passed from the time of ancient Hebrews entering Egypt to when they went out to establish and then surrender their own kingdom. In that extensive period of history the Jews became a great nation and inherited the Land of Promise only to lose it because of their sins. Final judgments of captivity were a matter of their choice, not God's intent since it was and still is his desire *"that it might be well with them and with their children forever."[1]* The microcosm of their iniquity and responding divine justice is pertinent to the fate of all nations.

Jews have been an object of ridicule since they first experienced repercussions of their persistent rebellion against divine law. It was irrational to reject such close contact with divine power and care in favor of idolatry. Many who have a cynical attitude toward them, however, reflect their own vanity and fail to learn the lesson of serving God for his sake and their own. The truth is he did not spare his chosen people and won't spare any other *"For his eyes are upon the ways of man, and he sees all his doings."[2]*

With respect to historical prophecy, the Lord's infallible word was in front of the Jews for nearly every step they made. So many miracles were done on their behalf they came to expect these great works as an immutable privilege. When various dangers were eminent, they were repeatedly warned as *"the Lord sent unto them all his servants the prophets, rising early, but they mocked the messengers of God, and despised his words, and misused his prophets."[3]* Hence, they fell by the sword and the two houses of Israel went separately into captivity of Assyria and of the inclusive empire of Babylon.

Captives of the kingdom of Judah taken to the land of Babylon were instructed by the prophet Jeremiah not to try an escape but rather stay to build houses, plant orchards, raise families and settle there. False prophets had told them they would be delivered to go back home, but this was not the Lord's plan since *"after seventy years be accomplished at Babylon, I will visit you, and perform my good toward you, in causing you to return to this place."[4]* These captives would surely have been killed if they left before then.

There was a partial return for the Jewish people to the area in and around Jerusalem after the Lord fulfilled his word to *"punish the king of Babylon, and that nation for their iniquity."[5]* At the appointed time, the Persian empire conquered Babylon and due to divine intervention King Cyrus wrote a decree that *"the Lord God of heaven has charged me to build him a house at Jerusalem, which is in Judah."[6]* Even though the fallen kingdom of Judah was originally comprised of only two tribes, Jews of other tribes were among their captives since many of them moved to Judah prior to their captivity.

Genealogies of some fifty thousand Hebrews who migrated back to Jerusalem are recorded in the first and last periods of their return.[7] As the Persian King Cyrus allowed, they took many provisions and much wealth with them to rebuild the temple including the vessels of the Lord's house that were found. Despite attempts made by adversaries to stop the temple from being built, the work was completed over the span of two Persian kings. Decades later the Jewish scribe Ezra was sent by another king with a company of Jews and treasures to set up magistrates to govern all of Judah under divine law.[8]

Upon arriving at the rebuilt temple in Jerusalem, Ezra learned from the elders that *"the people of Israel and the priests have not separated themselves from the people of the lands, doing according to their abominations."*[9] After all the hard work and brief time in which they kept the law, the Jews again turned to heathen ways and began to marry the foreigners who lived in neighboring lands. Contrary to Ezra's efforts to purge his people from abuses of the law, iniquity continued until their enemies persecuted them with great affliction so that the wall and gates of the city were broken down and burnt.[10]

While Ezra as priest yet had provincial authority over the Israelites in Judah, the third Persian king of that time granted permission to a Jew named Nehemiah to go and rebuild the wall and gates of Jerusalem.[11] He was given letters by the king to govern in his land and obtain all the timber needed for construction. Being a God fearing man he not only led many workers to finish the project, but he restored proper order of the priesthood and of keeping the Sabbath day.[12] Only then was the Lord's house kept from profanity.

In the ancient period of the bible that describes the return of Jews to Judah, they were provided many favors by the kings of Persia but their rule was not one of sovereignty and their land was a small portion of what they had before captivity. Although they rebuilt the temple and had limited jurisdiction, they still grieved to the Lord as *"for the land that you gave unto our fathers, behold, we are servants in it."*[13] Their congregation was just a fraction of their great prior numbers and even in this time of blessing and restoration they persisted in being a rebellious people who as a result were torn by their enemies.[14]

Records of what happened to Jews in the Holy Land after this period are written in the apocrypha books called the Machabees that are part of Catholic cannon in sacred texts. These writings show that a relatively strong community of Jews existed in Judah during the Grecian empire that followed Persian reign. Continued chastisement of the Jewish people progressed severely by the armies of Greece, but they were often turned back by the devout faith of a few.[15] These brave men were heroes in defense of divine law and sanctity of the temple thereby helping to reconcile their brethren to God.[16]

The prophets had much to say about the rise and fall of the great kingdoms on earth from the Jewish captivity to the birth and ministry of Christ. With general reference to Babylon and subsequent control over the Holy Land, the Lord said *"many nations and great kings shall serve themselves of them also, and I will recompense them according to their deeds."*[17] More specifically, visions of the prophet Daniel who was among captives to Babylon foretell detailed information regarding the bloody succession of power by the ancient world dominions of Babylon, Persia, Greece and the Romans.[18]

Scholars have meticulously traced the wide range of prophecies made in the book of Daniel regarding these regime changes. Fulfillment of those global events in an ancient early age adds credence to the divinely inspired nature of the bible since no human reasoning could have possibly predicted the exact outcome of so much history. The king of Babylon after he was humbled professed this truth, *"I blessed the Most High that lives forever, he does according to his will in the army of heaven, and among the inhabitants of the earth, and none can resist his hand and say: Why have you done it?"*[19]

Biblical prophecies concerning the return of present day Israel should not be confused with isolated prophecy of the ancient return of Jews under the servitude of Persia. Basic clues are provided in the Old Testament to identify predictions that pertain to the end times. Besides terms like the last or latter days and the word end, these passages usually make reference to promises of the Messiah and often are discussed in the context of a second captivity and subsequent return. Other key phrases compare as it was then to a future tense and sometimes indicate a generation that is a daughter of the past.

Prevalent verses of the prophets about how the Israelites evolved from captivity stem largely from the euphemism stating *"the remnant that is escaped of the house of Judah shall again take root downward, and bear fruit upward."*[20] This prophecy refers to those who went captive to Babylon and were nourished so that they grew in number. Only a portion of these returned to Jerusalem so the rest eventually migrated to various nations over time with those from the house of Israel who survived the captivity of Assyria. Very few Israelites escaped captivity and even fewer of these lived to tell about it.

In tracing the Jewish remnant of prophetic Scripture who are gathered out of foreign countries in return to their homeland, it is critical to recognize that there is also a final remnant who will return from the captivity of the Antichrist. Thus, another return will yet occur in a time apart from what has occurred in our world. This great irony resulting from a repeated desolation of Israeli society staggers our intellect since how can these things happen again in the face of warnings and history? Why would Jews or humanity be so senseless to close their hearts to God and his word to their ultimate doom?

Any thought of kingdom come for mankind is based on obedience to divine law in accordance with the atonement and power of Christ to overcome sin through his love. Moses spoke more than once of the Israelites' certain destiny of old and of their children in the latter days since *"it shall come to pass, when all these things are come upon you, the blessing and the curse, then provided that you and your children return to the Lord, and heed his voice with all your heart and soul, the Lord will turn away your captivity, and he will again gather you from all the nations wherein he has scattered you."*[21]

Even before the Jews reached the Land of Promise, Moses admonished them *"For I know that evil will befall you in the latter days, because you will do evil in the sight of the Lord to provoke him to anger through the work of your hands."*[22] The principle for their future is dependent on the choice to serve God and obtain his grace as *"Oh that you had hearkened to my commandments! Then had your peace been as river, their time should have endured forever."*[23] Only God can secure their inheritance since *"In returning and rest shall you be saved, in hope shall your strength be, but you would not."*[24]

Matters relating to the long term forecast for Jews to inherit the Promised Land are not conjecture. Yet the fulfillment of this expectation hinges on acceptance of the salvation of Christ in compliance with divine will. Many might ask why God chose the Hebrews if he can't control them or is their obstinate conduct merely an object of disdain? On the contrary *"For I know the thoughts that I think toward you says the Lord, thoughts of peace and not evil to give you an expected end, then you shall call upon me, and I will hear you, and you shall seek me and find me, and I will turn away your captivity."*[25]

Neither the claim of land inheritance nor the eventual reconciliation of Jews with God are negotiable. Due to ignorance or fear of reprisal, some theologians choose to ignore the divine purpose in calling the Israelites, but the Lord emphatically proclaimed *"I have not spoken in secret, in a dark place of the earth: I said not unto the seed of Jacob, Seek you me in vain."*[26] This passage is found in the context of salvation for all humanity as *"Look unto me, and be saved all the ends of the earth: for I am God and there is no other, for every knee shall be bowed to me, and every tongue shall swear."*[27]

We need to understand that the end of the world is not an end of mankind since *"God himself that formed the earth and made it, he has established it, he created it not in vain, he formed it to be inhabited."*[28] Despite wickedness and perdition of the world, there has been a divine intent for all to reflect a godly image *"since the day God created man upon the earth."*[29] For Jews, *"As I live says the Lord God, I will reign over you with a strong hand, and I will make you subject to my scepter."*[30] And to others *"I will return and will bring them again, every man to his heritage, and every man to his land."*[31]

After the age prior to the great flood, civilization began in Noah's time so *"the Most High divided to the nations their inheritance."*[32] Only God calls *"the generations from the beginning"* and determines the boundaries and length of their existence.[33] With respect to the Jews, the Lord appeared to Abraham saying *"I will give unto you, and your seed after you, the land wherein you are a stranger, all the land of Canaan for an everlasting possession, and I will be their God."* This unchangeable oath was made to Abraham through his son Isaac as *"I will establish my covenant with Isaac."*[34]

Abraham was first given the promise of land before he had any children as *"he that shall come forth out of your own bowels shall be your heir, unto your seed I have given this land from the river of Egypt unto the great river, the river Euphrates."*[35] His wife Sarah was already old at that time and due to unbelief she persuaded Abraham to *"go in to my maid, perhaps I shall get children through her."*[36] He did so and a son named Ishmael was born by her maid called Hagar.[37] Although this offspring was firstborn and became the father of all the vast Arabic tribes, he was not the heir of promise.

Regardless of the hard feelings between Arabs and Jews stemming from the question of a firstborn son's birthright to a double portion of a family's inheritance, the fact remains that nobody can change exceptions to this tradition when God so chooses.[38] After being barren for over ninety years Sarah did conceive and bear the chosen son whom God said *"call his name Isaac, and I will establish my covenant with him for an everlasting covenant and with his seed after him."*[39] The Lord confirmed this particular promise to both Isaac and to his son Jacob by appearing to them in their lifetimes.[40]

Borders of the Promised Land extend far beyond the area where ancient Canaanites lived. This territory is in numerous citations of Scripture that includes the boundaries of several adjacent nations beside the land of Canaanites.[41] The considerable expanse of property from the river of Egypt to the Euphrates River was never fully instituted as a single Jewish government even in the kingdoms of David and Solomon. It remains to be seen in our present world exactly how much of this land will be annexed through the spoils of war before the Jews are again taken away captive and scattered.

God was not joking when he promised a specific location of inheritance under his law for the Israelites. In a broader sense, there is a present gap in Christian theology to grasp and integrate the earthly promise of the kingdom of God with that of eternal life in heaven. The remnant of Jews who will be brought into their land to serve God are only a part of the overall divine plan for humanity as Abraham was told *"you shall be a father of many nations."*[42] That oath to him is to all who believe, *"I will make you exceedingly fruitful, and I will make nations of you, and kings shall come out of you."*

Although Abraham had other children after Sarah died, the promise of him as father of many nations was not in them, but rather in Christ who was born a Jew. In Jesus we have the hope of eternal life and also his word that *"Blessed are the meek, for they shall inherit the earth."*[43] To this David wrote *"the righteous shall inherit the land and dwell therein forever.*"[44] The heart of claims to Abraham is more than material for *"Fear not Abram: I am your shield and exceeding great reward."* He was justified in his faith in God *"who gives life to the dead and calls things that are not as though they were."*[45]

Circumcision of all Jewish males and the male servants was commanded by God to Abraham as *"a token of the covenant between you and me."*[46] This outward sign was given as an ordinance to symbolize a spiritual commitment of the faithful to obey divine law. Moses prophesied to the Jews that *"the Lord your God will bring you into the land which your fathers possessed, and you shall possess it, and he will do you good and will circumcise your heart and the heart of your seed to love the Lord that you may live."*[47] The significance is in purity of spirit in Christ who circumcises our sin.[48]

What has puzzled some scholars about the promises to Abraham is if and how the unending aspect for future generations will take place. The Lord declared *"Abraham shall become a great and mighty nation and all the nations of the earth shall be blessed in him."*[49] These oaths are made to Jews and Gentiles, but there is only one seed of Christ for *"if you are Christ's, then you are the seed of Abraham."*[50] God's design for Jews is *"as you were a curse among the heathen, so will I save you and you shall be a blessing."*[51] They will become a leading example to all nations of faith and love.

Many view the end of the world with only a cursory study of the meaning of the word end. It does not mean that the world is going to blow up in pieces or that all life on earth will be extinguished as Jesus noted *"for the elect's sake those days shall be shortened."*[52] Scriptural usage of the end has two different meanings as it applies separately to the end of any free society under the period of the Antichrist's rule and also to the end of mans' iniquity on earth as a result of judgment at the Second Advent. Human wickedness and demonic powers will pass away in damnation leaving an elect faithful remnant.

Have we as Christians forgotten what the apostles of Christ were looking for even after he rose from the dead?[53] Of course they had their eyes fixed on heaven since they saw firsthand that Jesus is risen, but they wanted the peace on earth that would come from their Redeemer *"To perform the mercy promised to our fathers and to remember his holy covenant"* so they *"might serve him without fear in holiness and righteousness, all the days of our life."*[54] After wars this hope will come by the wrath and judgment of Christ *"whom heaven must receive until the times of restitution of all things."*[55]

Those who have believed in Christ and now do are still the first fruits of his Messianic kingdom.[56] It shall come to pass that *"Jerusalem shall be called a city of truth, and the mountain of the Lord of hosts, the sanctified mountain."* In that time *"Thus says the Lord: I am returned unto Zion and will dwell in the midst of Jerusalem."*[57] In healing from all devastation of the last days, *"Behold, I will reveal unto them the abundance of peace and truth."*[58] God will not forget his new covenant in Christ to dwell with us and in us *"for I will forgive their iniquity, and I will remember their sin no more."*[59]

The dilemma of Scripture for a final return of Israel to statehood in their homeland is explained in very simple language as *"the Lord shall set his hand again the second time to recover the remnant of his people."*[60] Passages of prophecy relating to this yet second return of the Jews are logically mingled with the judgment and captivity of the present day State of Israel. For them to return again, they obviously must come from outside that land having been expelled by reason of divine justice despite the fact that it has taken over two and a half millennia of exile to come back and rule in the first place.

Since their permanent return is described with many blessings, there is a deceptive tendency among some scholars to apply that prosperity to the present and associate the latter end destruction with what happened in ancient history. This view denies another return by negating the pending punishment of the existing Jewish state. It further distorts contemporary affairs by misconstruing certain biblical verses that relate to a temporary defense of Israel for a lasting salvation by the Messiah. But as explained in following chapters, God will defend Israel in a war before they surrender in the next one.

Jesus is not coming back to a nation that is already established in its land but to one that is shattered at home and scattered abroad to bring back and restore them. This great irony is well documented as *"Except the Lord had left unto us a very small remnant, we had been as Sodom, and we should have been like Gomorrah."*[61] The people of these ancient cities were annihilated by God with fire and brimstone that came out of heaven for their gross sins of impurity and idolatry. In allegory to that destruction, *"It is of the Lord's mercies that we are not consumed, for the Lord will not cast off forever."*[62]

Notwithstanding the harsh retribution to come, the Lord *"remembered his covenant forever, the word which he commanded to a thousand generations for an everlasting covenant."*[63] He said to Moses of this promise that *"when they are in the land of their enemies, I will not cast them away to destroy them utterly, and break my covenant."*[64] Likewise, *"yet I will leave a remnant, that you may have some that shall escape the sword among the nations, when you shall be scattered through the countries."*[65] Iniquity will not be found when they return again *"for I will pardon whom I reserve."*[66]

Parallelism is an integral component of Scripture as prophecies about the future are reflected in the events of the past and connotations used for explaining things to come are somewhat hidden in various passages since the same terminology is repeated. Strict attention needs to be given to the context of particular verses as well as hints in wording because God explained *"I have multiplied visions, and used similitudes, by the ministry of the prophets."*[67] In the course of study, these applications of metaphor and analogy are closely examined to interpret how they pertain to the future in relevant chapters.

Given these complications, many specific predictions are otherwise relatively direct and simple in meaning. The structure of all elements in end times prophecy is based in the gospel of Jesus that corresponds to the event sequence in opening of the seven seals of Revelation. Consistent with this, stages of ancient history involving migration of Jews into the Promised Land to secure their borders followed by their rebellion and judgment parallel their current plight reflected by major world wars prior to the Second Advent. Only after those things will they return in peace and abide in God's love.

Concerning the second gathering of the Israelites, the Lord specified that *"I will turn their mourning into joy, and they shall come again from the land of the enemy, and there is hope in your end that your children shall come again to their own border."*[68] The context of this verse to come again is led by the Messiah in freedom *"For the Lord has redeemed Jacob and delivered him out of the hand of one that was mightier than he."* Their salvation in the latter days is from captivity since *"The Lord will not turn away the wrath of his indignation till he has executed the thoughts of his heart."*[69]

Redemption in Christ is comprehensive since he has all power in heaven and earth, but all things of the prophets and the law are still to be revealed. His enemies in our world are yet to be made his footstool. Jesus said *"I am not come to destroy, but to fulfill"* for in him is the summation of promise in the new and everlasting covenant.[70] It is written that Jews will receive Christ since *"I will put my law in their inward parts and write it in their hearts, and I will be their God, and they shall be my people for I will forgive their iniquity and remember their sin no more."[71]* This reference is to their life on earth.

Either we accept the divine word for what it is or we don't, but the answers about real life are there for those who want to know. It is our business to understand God's will and intercede on behalf of mankind accordingly. Too often we concentrate solely on our own salvation and gratification without having any comprehension of how the bible affects our society and what Christ did for the whole of humanity. The immense consequence of the forgiveness of sins has a strong bearing for an elect seed of Christ from many nations who by divine providence will endure and survive even past the end.[72]

Examples of the revelation in God's spirit for his kingdom on earth are quite clear in Scripture and mostly found in the Old Testament. These passages are not some fantasy of a near perfect global society but *"the remnant of Israel and such as are escaped of the house of Jacob will stay upon the Lord, the Holy One of Israel in truth. The consumption abridged shall overflow with justice, an abridgement in the midst of the land."[73]* This remnant of Gentile and Jew is the elect of any races for whom wars and natural disasters will be curtailed and cease so that they may inherit a new world in peace.

In the fury of his wrath God will remember mercy in order to accomplish his purpose *"Like as I have brought all this great evil upon this people, so will I bring upon them all the good that I promised them."* When the Jews are gathered again, they will at last enter the binding covenant of God in Christ as he said *"I will give them one heart and one way, that they may fear me forever for the good of them and of their children after them. I will plant them in this land assuredly with my whole heart and whole soul. And it shall be an honor before all the nations of the earth, and they shall fear and tremble."[74]*

The Messianic promise is just what the nomenclature indicates both in a spiritual and physical sense. Jesus is not only coming back in glory of judgment to condemn, he is coming as a deliverer of those who are left that would not submit themselves to the Antichrist. He once asked the rhetorical question of *"shall not God avenge his own elect, who cry to him day and night? Yet when the Son of Man comes, shall he find faith on the earth?"[75]* Yes is the answer to divine loyalty in defending the faithful and his vengeance will destroy a global apostasy of the end wherein Christians are martyred.

It is important to recognize that Jesus predicted that *"Jerusalem shall be trodden down by the Gentiles, for there will be great distress in the land, and wrath upon this people. And they shall fall by the edge of the sword, and shall be led away captive into all nations."[76]* This prophecy has nothing to do with demolition of the second Jewish temple almost two thousand years ago by the Romans, but its context is in end time events of Christ's gospel. He was clearly warning present day Jews of a future time when the Antichrist will obtain world control by military conquest for a short period.

Divine justice is not pronounced without cause since we are creatures of conscience and spirit whereby sound reason dictates good values and faith obtains a communion with our Creator in gratitude and dependence for our well being. Yet many have lost a sense of guilt for their sins as they impose themselves above God's law and substitute heresy for the true life given by his grace. Isaiah wrote about those who mulishly justify their sins, *"Woe to you apostate children, says the Lord, that take counsel but not of me, and that cover with a covering but not of my spirit so they may add sin to sin."[77]*

Hypocrisy is a cunning malady we choose to bring upon ourselves as *"that which comes out of a man is what defiles the man. All these evil things come from within."[78]* Jesus asked *"Why do you call me, 'Lord, Lord', and do not practice the things I say?"[79]* Christians are not made by the lip service from their mouths, but those who don't walk the walk of holiness that comes not from their ego but of God's spirit he said *"in vain do they worship me."[80]* They set their own rules of conduct apart from divine law and their actions show *"where your treasure is, there will your heart be also."[81]*

People who refuse to confess serious sins that are repeatedly specified in Scripture as shameful and worthy of anathema are accountable to God since *"the pride of your heart has deceived you."[82]* Although some do, no one needs to make a kind of image out of wood or stone to commit idolatry as *"these men have set up their idols in their heart, and put the stumbling block of their iniquity before their face."[83]* Sin clouds the mind so that some think their immoral actions are a new freedom and claim to be in right standing in the Lord's house when their homage and offerings to him are a sacrilege.

Covenants to Abraham, Moses and David of the kingdom of God in heaven and earth are in Christ as they speak of his seed, his people and his house with reference to being of the Almighty God. All Messianic prophecies discussed in my book point to him who will complete the promises, but has already shown himself to be the only begotten Son of God, paid the price of atonement in his blood and revealed the eternal incorruption of resurrection to heaven. Jesus is light some choose to hide from as *"everyone who does evil hates the light, neither comes to the light, lest his deeds be reproved."[84]*

Judgment against Jews who have returned to their land is written, *"The end is now come upon you, and I will judge you according to your ways."[85]* Likewise the psalmist wrote *"the stone which the builders refused is become the head stone of the corner."[86]* The chief stone of God's living temple is Jesus who after quoting this verse prophesied of Jews returning in salvation since *"Whosoever shall fall upon that stone shall be broken, and on whomsoever it shall fall it will grind him to powder. Therefore the kingdom of God shall be taken from you and will be given to a people who yield its fruits."[87]*

Scripture verses involving the stumbling block for Jews reveal a distinction between the spiritual and physical nature of promise *"For they are not all Israelites who sprung from Israel, nor because they are descendants of Abraham are they all his children."[88]* Jesus accused certain Jews who would kill him *"If you were Abraham's children, you would do the works of Abraham."* The promise of their kingdom relies on following the path of faith in his endless salvation as he frankly told them *"if you believe not that I am he, you shall die in your sins. You neither know me, nor my Father."[89]*

Failure to accept the atonement and way of Christ as a prerequisite to inherit the Land of Promise will lead to the ruin of Jews who now reside there. Much detail is found in the prophets about the evil practices and wicked political decisions to be lived out by the present day Israelites. These issues are examined more closely in relevant chapters, but their sinfulness will be like the past as *"Verily you are defiled in the way of your fathers, and you commit fornication with their abominations."[90]* Still further in metaphor, *"My people have been lost sheep, they have forgotten their resting place."[91]*

The paramount question for Jews in the Holy Land is whether or not they will incur the curses set forth in the law for disobedience. Scripture plainly reiterates they will again invite the plagues of judgment since many verses point to the sorrow that *"My eyes do fail with tears, for the destruction of the daughter of my people."[92]* Prophecy shows in the context of the last days *"when the house of Israel dwelt in their own land, they defiled it by their own way and by their doings."[93]* Of this God said *"I know that you would deal very treacherously, and was called a transgressor from the womb."[94]*

By the time of the Second Advent our world will be broken in pieces and Jews will have already been scattered abroad. This is the unfortunate setting in which the Messiah will come as *"He that scattered Israel will gather him, and keep him, as a shepherd does his flock."[95]* God's mercy is out of love and respect for his covenant, but above all else *"It is not for your sake that I will do this, O house of Israel, but for my holy name's sake, which you have profaned. And I will sanctify my great name that the Gentiles may know that I am the Lord, when I shall be sanctified in you before their eyes."[96]*

Creation of the present State of Israel is a fulfillment of prophecy that sets the center stage for the development and completion of other major events of the end times. While most passages about the return of Israel apply to the final Messianic promise, other connected verses refer to current statehood by forecasting issues of morality, wars and captivity. Of today's Jews *"the children of Israel shall return, and shall seek the Lord their God, and David their king, and they shall fear the Lord and his goodness in the last days."[97]* Their zeal will be short lived since the bulk of prophecy shows infidelity.

Writings of the prophet Hosea reveal that many Jews will abandon divine law, but also point to those who keep their faith in Christ. Of their fleeting obedience he explained *"for your goodness is as a morning cloud, and as the early dew it goes away."* Material things will replace their faith *"as they were increased so they sinned against me."* The security of God's providence is temporary since *"though I have redeemed them, yet they have spoken lies against me, for the spirit of whoredom has caused them to err."* Due to their fall from his grace *"Woe unto them, for they have fled from me."[98]*

Much like ancient history, the Jewish nation will again forget who helped them and warned them about the dangers of iniquity as *"Israel has cast off the thing that is good."* Similarly, false prophets will arise who deny judgment and teach prosperity but *"the pride of Israel shall be humbled before his face."* Yet it is vital to grasp that God will bless and protect Israel from their enemies before the captivity of their kingdom as *"I will be to them as one that takes off the yoke on their jaws, and I put his meat to him that he might eat. I carried them in my arms, and they knew not that I healed them."[99]*

Hosea prophesied that because of their backsliding *"the days of visitation are come, the days of recompense are come. Israel is swallowed up: now is he become among the nations like an unclean vessel."[100]* Even as they turn to evil ways and bring destruction upon themselves, a portion of them will remain faithful since *"though you, Israel, play the harlot, yet let not Judah offend."[101]* This analogy of different roles in morality relates to ancient history when their kingdom was split in two parts and the house of Judah was obedient to God despite the persistent iniquity of the neighboring house of Israel.

Christian Jews will separate themselves from the abominations committed by their brethren and try to lead them to repentance, but *"though they called them to the Most High, none at all would exalt him."* Many will refuse conversion as *"the people that do not understand shall fall."[102]* But believers will know the truth about judgment for *"it is time to seek the Lord, till he come."* They will realize the hope of their rapture just prior to the end period. Deliverance is in the midst of turmoil and war since *"Also, O Judah, he has set a harvest for you, when I returned the captivity of my people."[103]*

Division in spirituality among Jews is expressed by contrasting descriptions of their values as on one hand *"They return, but not to the most High."* On the other, some will retain their love for God and his law since *"Judah yet rules with God, and is faithful with the saints."*[104] These will serve Christ with the remainder of the church in that time. Not all Jewish Christians will live in their homeland because many Jews have refrained from migrating there to begin with and some will flee before their kingdom's fall. Wherever they reside in the world *"the Lord will feed them as a lamb in a large place."*[105]

Other prophets attest to a period of blessing upon Israel and their subsequent rebellion as the Lord said *"I have brought up children, and exalted them, but they have despised me. Your silver is turned into dross, your wine is mingled with water."* Of the holy city in Jerusalem *"How is the faithful city that was full of judgment become a harlot? Justice dwelt in it, but now murderers."*[106] It is evident that the State of Israel will thrive under God's care prior to its collapse for rejecting his new covenant since *"when I had fed them to the full, then they committed adultery and assembled in the harlot's houses."*[107]

Religious leaders will be a major contributing factor in causing the Jews to sin and be dispersed by the cruel sword of the Antichrist. Of this fallacious debauchery *"they were scattered because there is no shepherd, but the shepherds fed themselves and fed not my sheep."*[108] There will be a great cleansing from God for *"I will purge out from among you the rebels, and them that transgress against me."*[109] The bible is very clear about what will finally happen to their government as *"Zion shall be redeemed with judgment and the destruction of the transgressors and of the sinners shall be together."*[110]

An interesting analogy is presented by the prophet Ezekiel about the sure progress in development and then latter ruin of the modern Jewish establishment.[111] It alludes to the creation of their statehood after World War II by saying *"when you were born, your navel was not cut, neither were you washed in water, nor swaddled, but you were cast out in the open field in the abjection of your soul."* In these early years, no nation had pity on the Jews when they were persecuted by wars, but God had mercy as *"I said unto you when you were in your blood: Live; yea, I said unto you in your blood, Live."*

These references apply to the unexpected military success of Jews in their 1967 and 1973 battles for survival. God is still watching over Israel for their good and as explained in the second seal he will defend them in World War III so that they will expand for *"I have caused you to multiply as the bud of the field, and you increased, and grew great, and you did prosper into a kingdom."* To the surprise and dismay of many who now seek to destroy Israel, *"your renown went forth among the nations for your beauty: for it was perfect through my comeliness, which I had put upon you says the Lord God."*

Israel is portrayed in Ezekiel's prophecy as a woman who grew from the troubles of her infancy into an exceedingly beautiful lady with riches and glory. This metaphor has certainly not yet taken place nor has the time come when *"you did trust in your own beauty, and played the harlot because of your renown."* As the sins of Israel become apparent, she is characterized *"as a wife that commits adultery, which takes strangers instead of her husband."* Therefore the Lord foretold that he will bring her lovers against her and *"I will judge you as adulteresses and as they that shed blood are judged."*

One of the most vivid analogies of present day Israel's course of behavior is made in comparison to what happened to the Jews in ancient history as *"Behold, every one that uses a common proverb, shall say this against you: As the mother was, so also is her daughter."* The spiritual symbolism of a marriage with God indicates *"your time was the time of love, yea, I swore to you, and entered into a covenant with you, and you became mine.*" But as past defiance, "*you are your mother's daughter who cast off her husband and her children, as you have despised the oath in breaking the covenant.*"[112]

Similarities between the present and past for Jewish rule in the Holy Land are found in many instances of biblical prophecy. To understand the parallelism of various passages that have profound implications for Jews and the world, it is necessary to discern this intent in those messages. For instance, Ezekiel chastised the people of his day, but in the same tone referred to the future as "*Go you, serve you everyone his idols, and hereafter also.*"[113] Likewise, Jeremiah wrote "*I will plead with you says the Lord, and with your children's children will I plead.*"[114] Each of these verses points to different times.

Pervasive deception will cover the minds of Israelites once they are free from threats of their enemies. They will again fall into a stupor of pride thinking no nation will defeat them. Jesus warned about the last days that "*many false prophets shall arise, and shall deceive many.*"[115] The word of the Lord will be far removed from the people "*for from the prophets of Jerusalem is profaneness gone forth into all the land, they say to everyone that walks in the imagination of his own heart, No evil shall come upon you.*"[116] These false prophets "*have seduced my people, saying Peace, and there is no peace.*"[117]

Corruption will become incurably malignant in Jewish society since "*Her princes have judged for bribes, and her priests have taught for hire, and her prophets divined for money.*"[118] Contrary to predictions of Scripture about pending captivity "*they prophesy unto you a false vision and divination, and a thing of nothing, and the deceit of their heart.*" After so long a time, it is a pity that their nation will again witness the favor of God only to deny him and pervert his holy word by saying "*you shall not see the sword, neither shall you have famine, but I will give you assured peace in this place.*"[119]

Curses against the Jews in the end times are obvious to anyone who chooses to see the truth "*for the virgin daughter of my people is broken with a great breach, with a very grievous blow.*"[120] Yet given all these clear warnings, "*the word of the Lord is become unto them as a reproach, and they will not receive it.*"[121] Their obstinate refusal mirrors the perverse common attitude that will prevail in the world as they say "*Prophesy not to us right things, speak to us smooth things, cause the Holy One of Israel to cease before us.*"[122] Of these malicious desires and lies "*my people loved such things.*"[123]

Urgings by God for repentance from his people are repeatedly made to remind them of his love and desire to bless instead of punish for "*If you will return, O Israel, says the Lord, return unto me, and if you will put away the abominations out of my sight, then you shall not be moved.*"[124] The tragedies of divine justice could have been avoided "*If they had stood in my counsel, and caused my people to hear my words, then they should have turned them from their way.*" But due to their lusts and blind deception "*every man's word shall be his burden: for you have perverted the words of the living God.*"[125]

When the Israelites revel in newly found wealth and power, they will not listen to the pleadings of God that "*if you thoroughly amend your ways and your doings, then I will cause you to dwell in the land I gave to your fathers, forever and ever.*"[126] Of this calling to repentance "*I have spread out my hands all the day unto a rebellious people, which walk in a way that was not good, after their own thoughts.*"[127] The reality of that time is they will not hearken as "*Hear, O foolish people, and without understanding, who have eyes and see not, and ears, and hear not. Shall I not visit for these things?*"[128]

Prophecies written in Lamentations specifically reiterate that the timeframe of these judgments are upon the daughter of the Israelites. These predictions about the returned generation of Jews reveal *"the joy of our heart has ceased, the crown is fallen from our head: woe unto us."*[129] Of their loss of power over the Holy Land, *"she that was great among the nations, how is she become tributary!"* They will not expect this retribution because of the lies of their prophets and the blindness of their iniquity for *"Jerusalem has grievously sinned, therefore she is removed; she remembered not her last end."*[130]

Current Jewish statehood has great significance for end time events, but their present reign in the Holy Land is no guarantee of securing its promise. We need to distinguish between their physical return and their spiritual return since these two subjects are interdependent for any permanency of residence to take place. The fact is that as the world falls into deep apostasy and incurs the wrath of God, they will also be judged since he said *"I will punish all them which are circumcised with the uncircumcised."*[131] Even more expressly, it is written *"I will judge you in the land of your nativity."*[132]

The sad outlook for Israel is the consistency of Scripture passages showing that God will repeat their dispersion as *"I will scatter them among the nations, which they and their fathers have not known, and I will draw the sword after them."*[133] Our world has changed from ancient history and Jews will go captive in places they have never been before *"so shall you serve strangers in a land that is not yours."*[134] Despite false claims of liberty *"We looked for peace, and no good came, for a time of healing, and behold fear! My sorrow is above sorrow, astonishment has taken hold of me."*[135]

Regarding those of the Jewish population who survive through great world wars and end time disasters to come upon the world, *"the remnant shall return, even the remnant of Jacob unto the mighty God."*[136] After all these afflictions are accomplished *"At that time will I bring you again for I will make you a name and a praise among all people of the earth, when I turn back your captivity before your eyes, says the Lord."*[137] It is Christ who at the Second Advent *"will gather you out of the countries you are scattered with a mighty hand, and with a stretched out arm, and with fury poured out."*[138]

Application of bible prophecies of the return and defense of Jews in WWIII is often misinterpreted as an exclusive indication of their inheriting the Holy Land and an end of global wars. This irrational view distorts the entire context of the day of the Lord and Jesus' teaching about the end time affairs of Jewish statehood. Israel will be judged and if they are to be scattered again, the covenant that they will inherit their land under the reign of the Messiah must still be fulfilled. The restoration of their kingdom is in a future time after they realize the divinity of Christ and live in harmony with God.

While there is a sense of hope among Christians that God will repair the damage that humanity brings on itself by creating a global society founded in the Holy Spirit of love and truth, others either ignore or dispute the passages of Scripture that clearly point to a happy ending for mankind. It is an error to misplace all these inspiring and pleasant promises of our earthly existence by saying they only refer to the spiritual Zion in heaven. The promise of eternal life in God's dwelling above by resurrection in Christ is different from the assurance of his kingdom for mortal humans on earth.

Predictions that pertain to a new hope for mankind should be accepted as such and not confused with matters that relate to heaven. Both worlds have the unending design of our Creator for the benefit of his creatures to share in his glory and be united in divine grace. By means of great judgments and the purging of evil works, the remnant of nations will learn from its mistakes and come into the bond of Christ. Scripture passages about this subject discussed in closing chapters distinctly describe a world of continued peace, prosperity and goodwill. Man will no longer seek bloodshed for selfish gain.

In the meantime, refusal to discern and appropriately respond to the seasons and times of the word of God will needlessly inflict great disasters upon our world. Since major events of prophecy involve Israel, what needs to be addressed is when and how it will be judged. This perplexing issue is now very pressing upon the enemies of Israel who for greed, power or thought that they are fulfilling God's word want to destroy the Jewish nation. Why would anyone want to fight a losing war in this time or in another be allied with an evil Antichrist who despite brief victory will be condemned by Christ?

No peace can ever be achieved without inviting Jesus in our hearts, nor can society have lasting progress if forms of idolatry are held against his atonement for iniquity. There is no other salvation given to us in this life or the next. As in any era of the past, every nation has paid the price for their sins by the plagues of divine justice. God has not changed, but unfortunately neither has man's desire to follow after his own devices that foster discord in our world by selfish pursuits. The bottom line is that all of man's wisdom, might and riches will never sustain anyone from God's scrutiny and wrath.

Following chapters present a scenario of global events written in biblical prophecy that corresponds to the gospel of Jesus as it relates to opening of the seven seals in the book of Revelation. These guidelines provide an outline of the last days where many intricacies of the prophets and apostles can be put in proper order and understood in the context of developing stages. What is happening in the present with respect to political and military conflicts conforms to predictions of the end times. Only by study and discerning this connection can anyone have an accurate perception of our reality.

---

[1] Deuteronomy 5,29; Psalms 81,13-14
[2] Job 34,21-22; Romans 11,21-22
[3] II Chronicles 36,15-16; Jeremiah 25, 4-7
[4] Jeremiah 29,4-10
[5] Jeremiah 25,11-13
[6] II Chronicles 36, 20-23; Ezra 1,1-3
[7] Ezra 2,1-65; Nehemiah 7,4-67
[8] Ezra 6,15; 7,12-25; 8,1-20
[9] Ezra 9,1-2
[10] Ezra 10,3-5; Nehemiah 1,3
[11] Nehemiah 2,7-10; 5,14; 8,5
[12] Nehemiah 13,10-11&30

[13] Ezra 9,8-9; Nehemiah 9,34-37
[14] Deuteronomy 4,27; 28,62; Jeremiah 42,2
[15] I Machabees 1,26-52
[16] I Machabees 4,41-60; 5,63; 13,3&33; 14,4-6
[17] Jeremiah 25,14
[18] Daniel 2,39-40; 5,25-28; 7,3-6; 8,20-21; 11,2-20
[19] Daniel 4,34-35
[20] II Kings 19,30-31; Isaiah 37,31-32
[21] Deuteronomy 4,30-31; 29,14-15; 30,1-4; 31,29
[22] Deuteronomy 31,29
[23] Psalm 81,11-15; Isaiah 48,18-19
[24] Isaiah 30,15
[25] Jeremiah 29,11-14
[26] Isaiah 45,19
[27] Psalm 37,9; Isaiah 45,22-23
[28] Isaiah 45,17-18
[29] Deuteronomy 4,30-35
[30] Ezekiel 20,33-38
[31] Jeremiah 12,15-17
[32] Genesis 10,32; Deuteronomy 32,8
[33] Isaiah 41,4
[34] Genesis 17,8&21; 21,12
[35] Genesis 15,4&18
[36] Genesis 16,1-4&16
[37] Genesis 16,10-12; 21,9-12; 25,12-16
[38] Genesis 27,32-40; 48,8-20; Numbers 8,13-16
[39] Genesis 17,17-21
[40] Genesis 26,1-5; 28,10-14; 48,3-4
[41] Exodus 3,8; 6,2-8; 23,23-31; Numbers 34,1-14
[42] Genesis 17,4-7&15-17
[43] Genesis 25,1-10; Mathew 5,5
[44] Psalm 37,29
[45] Genesis 15,1; Romans 4,17
[46] Genesis 17,10-14
[47] Deuteronomy 30,5-6
[48] Colossians 2,10-12
[49] Genesis 18,18
[50] Galatians 3,16&29
[51] Zechariah 8,13
[52] Mathew 24,22; Mark 13,20
[53] Acts 1,6: Romans 10,1
[54] Luke 1,67-75
[55] Acts 3,21
[56] Romans 8,22-29; James 1,18; Revelation 14,4
[57] Zechariah 8,3
[58] Jeremiah 33,6-9
[59] Jeremiah 31,34
[60] Isaiah 11,11
[61] Genesis 19,24-28: Isaiah 1,9; Jude 7
[62] Lamentations 3,22-31
[63] Psalms 105,8-11
[64] Leviticus 26,42-45
[65] Ezekiel 6,8
[66] Jeremiah 50,19-20
[67] Hosea 12,10

[68] Jeremiah 31,11-17
[69] Jeremiah 30,23-24
[70] Mathew 5,17-18; Hebrews 10,13-17; 13,20
[71] Jeremiah 31,33-34
[72] Romans 4,13
[73] Isaiah 10,20-23
[74] Jeremiah 32,37-42; 33,9
[75] Luke 18,7-8
[76] Luke 21,20-24
[77] Isaiah 30,1
[78] Mark 7,20-23
[79] Luke 6,46
[80] Mathew 15,8-9; Luke 6,43-45
[81] Luke 12,34
[82] Obadiah 3
[83] Ezekiel 14,3
[84] John 3,19-20; 8,12
[85] Ezekiel 7,2-4
[86] Psalm 118,22; Isaiah 28,16
[87] Mathew 21,42-44; Luke 20,17-18; I Peter 2,5
[88] Romans 9,6-7
[89] John 8,19-24&39-47
[90] Jeremiah 11,10; Ezekiel 20,30-31
[91] Jeremiah 50,6
[92] Lamentations 2,11
[93] Ezekiel 36,17
[94] Isaiah 48,8
[95] Jeremiah 31,10; Ezekiel 34,12-13
[96] Ezekiel 36,22-23
[97] Hosea 3,4-5
[98] Hosea 4,7&12; 6,4; 7,13
[99] Hosea 7,10; 8,3; 11,3-4
[100] Hosea 8,8; 9,7
[101] Hosea 4,15
[102] Hosea 4,14; 11,7
[103] Hosea 6,11; 10,12
[104] Hosea 7,16; 11,12;
[105] Hosea 4,15-17
[106] Isaiah 1,2-22
[107] Jeremiah 5,7
[108] Ezekiel 34,5-8
[109] Ezekiel 20,38
[110] Isaiah 1,27-28
[111] Ezekiel 16,3-42
[112] Ezekiel 16,8&44-45&59-60
[113] Ezekiel 20,39
[114] Jeremiah 2,9
[115] Mathew 24,11&24; Mark 13,22
[116] Jeremiah 23,15-17
[117] Ezekiel 13,9-19
[118] Micah 3,11
[119] Jeremiah 14,13-15
[120] Jeremiah 14,17
[121] Jeremiah 6,10
[122] Isaiah 30,9-13

[123] Jeremiah 5,31
[124] Jeremiah 4,1; 7,23-24
[125] Jeremiah 23,21-27&36
[126] Jeremiah 7,5-7
[127] Isaiah 65,2
[128] Jeremiah 5,21-29
[129] Lamentations 5,15-16
[130] Lamentations 1,1-9
[131] Jeremiah 9,25
[132] Ezekiel 21,30-32
[133] Jeremiah 9,16
[134] Jeremiah 5,19
[135] Jeremiah 8,15-21
[136] Isaiah 10,21
[137] Zephaniah 3,20
[138] Ezekiel 20,34

Chapter Four
OPENING OF THE FIRST SEAL
THE WHITE HORSE

"When the Lamb had opened the first of the seven seals, I saw a white horse and he who sat on it had a bow, and a crown was given to him, and he went forth conquering and to conquer." Revelation 6,2

Most theologians perceive the four different colored horses that appear separately in each of the first four seals of the Apocalypse as a panorama of disasters in the world without any real order of occurrence. Since the seven seals are located before numerous other distinctive judgments and vividly descriptive visions, the mistaken tendency of this view has been to downplay or trivialize their overall importance. Prevalent opinion of the symbolism reflected by the four horses is that all of them are simultaneously out of the barn on earth in the respective forms of falsehood, war, famine and pestilence.

Overly simple views of the four horses as an ongoing group of present day plagues fail to discern that each seal has grave significance for the world as a period of time in which other bible prophecies are instrumented. Detailed analysis of the wording of each seal reveals that they have individual components relating to a sequence of end times events. Virtually all biblical predictions concerning eschatology, including things like the seven trumpet and seven vial judgments of Revelation, can be properly understood in stages reflected in the opening of the seven seals as they relate to the gospel of Jesus.

Scholars who correctly see Jesus as the rider of the white horse in the first seal, whose kingly crown is eternal in the divine plan rather than a temporary form of a false Christ, generally consider his triumph over evil and death as applying to the salvation of souls in heaven without recognizing how the gospel applies to earth, especially in regard to the seasons and times of the last days. Physical aspects of prophecy are not only given to us to be construed in retrospect, but also provided as visible signs of our times. The Lord's conquering applies to wars as well as to souls until he fully conquers in the end.

Despite the bogus prophets who have come as the Messiah leading countless people to follow their falsehoods, the symbolism in the first seal does not apply to some limited or global evil force. Jesus predicted *"many shall come in my name, saying I am the Christ, and shall deceive many."*[1] This spirit of antichrist now pervasive in the world will reach its peak in the person of the Antichrist, but he will not appear or take control until the events of the third and fourth seals. Although Christ's enemies are not yet his footstool, his crown and his bow display his power to defeat them through his atonement.

The overall inadequacy of current Christian theology with respect to identifying what things precede the Second Advent has been the inability to separate passages of the bible in terms of chronological timing and therefore inappropriately lump these prophecies into an end times catchall of anarchy. At the start of the Apocalypse it is written that these messages were given to the church by God *"to show unto his servants things which must shortly come to pass."* Study is essential for *"Blessed is he that reads, and they that hear the words of this prophecy, and keep those things therein: for the time is at hand."*[2]

Saint John the apostle wrote the book of Revelation on the island of Patmos where he was sentenced to exile for speaking the word of God and for his testimony of Jesus Christ. He saw an awesome vision of Jesus in great power and *"out of his mouth went a sharp two-edged sword.* " Jesus introduced himself saying *"I am the first and the last: I am he that lives, and was dead, and behold, I am alive for evermore."* As supreme judge who will render to every person according to their works, including damnation of fallen angels along with unrepentant sinners, he said *"I have the keys of hell and death."*[3]

Scripture testifies to the fact that from the beginning of the world God determined the outcome of our earthly reality for individuals and nations in accordance with his law and justice. There is sound reason for the prophetic messages of the bible and that is to communicate the sole glory of God and his salvation, but in so doing warn of pending dangers in the hope of extending his mercy through the conversion of sinners. Why would we neglect that opportunity to prolong his grace by proclaiming his word? As a church we are instructed to *"Quench not the Spirit"* and *"Despise not prophecies."*[4]

Of ancient time Isaiah wrote of the prophetic word of God as *"I have declared the former things from the beginning, and they went forth out of my mouth, and I showed them, and they came to pass."*[5] This verse clearly indicates that these mysteries were revealed and made known before they came to pass. We must share that wisdom as the Lord and Redeemer of Israel ordained: *"Who, as I, shall call and shall declare it, and set it in order for me, the things that are coming, and shall come? Fear you not, neither be afraid: have I not told you from that time, and declared it? You are my witnesses."*[6]

Preaching of the gospel seldom touches on the divine justice that is solely entrusted to Christ, but this aspect of his teachings is an important means of leading people to truth in discipleship as he said *"The works which the Father has given me to finish bear witness of me, that the Father has sent me."*[7] Many don't bother to study how prophecy applies to our world because of its complexity and dire threats. They still say *"The vision is for many days to come."*[8] What may have been uncertain in the past will become evident as the intent of these writings is *"Seal not the sayings of the prophecy of this book."*[9]

During his public ministry Jesus spoke of eternal life for all who believe in him and he declared *"Before Abraham was, I am."*[10] Despite his many works of divine power and schooling of people about the prophets, the Jewish religious leaders betrayed Christ by bringing him to crucifixion for this claim to his eternal being. They would not believe he was the Promised One of whom it is written *"To whom then will you liken me, or shall I be equal? Lift up your eyes on high, and behold who has created these things."*[11] They tried to cover up his resurrection with bribery and lies after he rose from the dead.[12]

When Moses was called from a burning bush to deliver the Israelites from slavery, the Lord referred to himself as *"I AM THAT I AM"* and added *"Thus shall you say to the children of Israel, I AM has sent you."*[13] Connection between this description of God's name and how Jesus spoke of himself is no coincidence. Although separate, he shares in one being with the Godhead of the Father and the Holy Spirit so *"that you may know and believe me, and understand that I am he: before me there was no God formed, neither shall there be after me. I, even I, am the Lord, and besides me is no savior."*[14]

Even the apostles of Jesus did not fully comprehend his divinity or atonement until after he rose from the dead. Only then did they realize his divine mission in becoming human flesh. Of Jesus being God *"All things were made by him, and without him was not anything made that was made. He was in the world, and the world was made by him, and the world knew him not."*[15] Other religious beliefs and secular atheism still inhibit or prohibit the divine purpose for everyone to know the love of Christ *"who is the image of the invisible God. And he is before all things, and by him all things consist."*[16]

No person has ever done the wonderful miracles Jesus performed on earth and for this reason he said *"Though you believe not me believe the works so that you may know and believe the Father is in me, and I in him."*[17] Similarly, the evidence of prophetic events happening in our world is proof of his divine instruction about the last days. His unity with God is verified by this reality and by his doctrine that *"I and my Father are one."* He said of his union *"I can of my own self do nothing"* and because of this binding force of the Holy Spirit from God *"he that has seen me has seen the Father."*[18]

The two edged sword that came out of the mouth of Christ in St. John's vision has the same symbolism as the bow he saw in the hand of Christ as he goes forth as a conqueror on the white horse of the first seal. These emblems in all simplicity refer to the word of God as given to us in Scripture and as such apply to both physical and spiritual matters. With respect to the manifest nature of truth in his sword *"the word of God is quick, and powerful, and sharper than any two edged sword, piercing even to the dividing asunder of soul and spirit, a discerner of the thoughts and intentions of the heart."*[19]

Some might feel uncomfortable with the thought that Jesus is portrayed with weapons of warfare, but he asserted *"the Father has committed all judgment unto the Son."*[20] There are limits to the patience and mercy of God as well as to the extent that his servants must suffer the wrongs of their enemies. We do not have laws against crime without reason, nor can all wars be considered unjust.[21] The judgment of Christ is in harmony with God as *"Vengeance is mine, it is I who bring forth life and death, I who inflict wounds and heal them, I will repay my foes and requite those who hate me."*[22]

Above all else, the real mystery of Revelation is Jesus Christ who shares the throne of God. There is only one seat of power in heaven that rules over all creation and this singular authority is in *"the throne of God and of the Lamb."*[23] Christ is pictured as a lamb because he is the unblemished paschal sacrifice whereby we receive reconciliation and the promise of eternal life. He is the beginning and the end of all things seen and unseen. He is the very power of creation in whom there is no sense of time or space and by whom the *"things which are seen were not made of things which do appear."*[24]

Jesus declared *"I am the resurrection and the life: he that believes in me, though he was dead, yet he shall live."* Of this life giving power he said *"as the Father has life in himself, so has he given to the Son to have life in himself."*[25] His glory is in the Father *"as you have given him power over all flesh, that he should give eternal life to as many as you have given me."*[26] He assured us that *"my words shall never pass away."* As this applies to fulfilling end times prophecy he is *"Far above all principality, and power, and might, and dominion, not only in this world, but also in that which is to come."*[27]

Opening of the seven seals in the Apocalypse is literally centered at the throne of God as the seals appoint seasons and times of a book whose chapters remain to be recorded in reality. St John saw a great vision of God the Father on his seat of glory as *"I saw in the right hand of him that sat on the throne a book written within and on the backside, sealed with seven seals."*[28] This book was so important that except for Christ the Lamb *"no one in heaven, or on earth, or under the earth, was able to open the scroll or to look thereon."*[29] Only he can unlock the divine plan to establish God's kingdom.

Symbolic visions and corresponding prophecies concerning the horses of the first four seals relate primarily to a series of intermittent wars and an intervening famine that lead to the ultimate wrath and judgment of the Lamb in the last three seals. Jesus is able to complete his salvation as *"You are worthy to take the book, and to open the seals thereof:*

for you were slain, and have redeemed us to God by your blood." He is at the right hand of God so *"That in the dispensation of the fullness of times, he might gather together in one all things in Christ, both which are in heaven, and which are in earth."*[30]

There is no other Christ and as rider of the white horse in the first seal, he went forth to triumph with a bow. Scripture plainly shows the meaning of the bow as *"Your bow was made quite naked, according to the oaths of the tribes, even your word."*[31] This verse directly connects his bow to the entire bible in light of conversion and performing the prophecies that will establish the new covenant in Christ. Use of the word naked denotes both the perception and action of God's word in that the covering will be removed. We will understand these ancient mysteries as well as experience them.

Harsh passages about the Lord's bow and the sword of his mouth are frequently expressed in the bible. God raised up Christ in righteousness and *"called him to his foot, gave the nations before him, and made him rule over kings. He gave them as dust to his sword, and as driving stubble to his bow."*[32] From the beginning of his revenge on his enemies, God firmly declared *"I will make my arrows drunk with blood and my sword shall devour flesh, and shall consume the earth with her increase, and set on fire the foundations of the mountains, for he will avenge the blood of his servants."*[33]

Salvation in a spiritual sense was accomplished when Jesus died on the cross as he then said *"It is finished."*[34] Nevertheless this act of atonement is not the end of his work in terms of his word. Illustration in the bow of Christ as a means of conquering embraces the whole of his gospel with respect to forms of judgment in the end times against the wicked since *"Unless they be converted, God will sharpen his sword, he will bend and aim his bow, he ordained his arrows against the persecutors."*[35] Likewise in anger, *"out of his mouth goes a sharp sword, that with it he should smite the nations."*[36]

Earthly events have always been under the control of Jesus, but the sequence of these things for the last days begins with the opening of the first seal. For all practical purposes in distinguishing what predictions correlate to this seal, it should be noted that although Christ's divinity and word are timeless, there is a limited but extensive scope in this particular stage of prophecy. In order to determine the opening and closing point in time for this period, it is necessary to examine certain statements in the gospel of Jesus about the end of the world that have not been previously discussed in prior chapters.

When asked what signs will precede the end, Jesus disclosed beside the occurrence of false prophets that *"When you shall hear of wars and commotions, be not terrified: for these things must first come to pass: but the end is not by and by."*[37] The idea here in his initial prophecies is that the end will not happen all at once and in the very early starting stages there will be wars and insurrections. It is critical to perceive that these affairs are separate and plural. Further, they should not to be confused with other signs of wars he said would yet follow because those periods are described in terms of the by and by.

Pertinent questions for the first seal are how the Lord's bow as his conquering word applies to our world and whether or not these prophecies have been fulfilled. In other words, what wars and commotions was Jesus talking about and are they to be understood historically or in a future tense? These early wars are associated with the first seal and they happened in the last century with the great events of WWI and WWII. In regard to the ensuing conflicts of lesser insurrections, there have also been many isolated battles in various parts of the world that took place since the conclusion of those times.

Unlike the other seals of Revelation that express their respective swords, there are few biblical citations relating to the first seal. Other seals have much detailed information that applies to separate wars and what happens in the intervening periods of those battles. Of the first seal, Jesus predicted in just a few words some major and lessor events that have already happened. Scholars tend to ignore the separation of these wars from the times of other great global wars he predicted or else mistakenly combine these other wars with Armageddon. In either case, they fail to see all the prophetic wars before the end.

Historians have recorded the vast changes in the world's political structure due to the turmoil since WWI. All these military struggles whether on a large or small scale were largely a result of hatred and a lust for power by oppressive regimes.[38] The cruelty that mankind is capable of was reflected in these wars. They show insufficiency in ideologies that are opposed to divine law and exhibit the inability to govern without God. The hand of divine justice has always been in all our earthly affairs due to selfish lusts but we simply would not have all this destruction if the nations knew the love of Christ.

Other than a descriptive reference to the Jewish holocaust of WWII as a prelude to the birth of present day Israel, the only correlation in the bible to the start of the last days in Jesus' gospel is an extraordinary vision that St. John saw and wrote in chapter twelve of Revelation.[39] In this sign *"there appeared a great wonder in heaven: a woman clothed with the sun and the moon under her feet, and upon her head a crown of twelve stars."*[40] Who this woman represents and the spiritual battle she leads against evil have enormous significance for the church and the world. This vision is pertinent to the first seal.

Much can be said about the real spiritual conflict that pits the influence of holy angels of God against demonic forces led by the fallen angel called the Devil, Satan or Lucifer. This unseen underlying war of good and evil has everything to do with the reality we live in for *"we wrestle not against flesh and blood, but against principalities, against powers, against the rulers of darkness of this world."*[41] We need to understand this ongoing battle and cooperate with God's line of authority in the spiritual realm to obtain his sovereign help in dealing with iniquity in society and its ensuing bloodshed.

From the beginning of humanity when Adam and Eve were persuaded by Satan to eat the forbidden fruit of knowing good and evil, therefore making us all subject to death yet having the choice of life by grace, God then told the Devil *"I will put enmity between you and the woman, between your seed and her seed."* He was not talking about Eve as the mother of a holy seed, but this prophecy pertains to the mother of Jesus and his salvation over death. Though somewhat obscure in translation God also said to Satan *"she will crush your head, as you attempt to bite at her heel."*[42] Her power is in Christ.

One of the most basic tenets of Christianity is that Jesus was born of a virgin who conceived him by the Holy Spirit of God. This chosen one called Mary is special among the children of God and was set apart in holiness free from sin in order to bear the Son of God as it is written *"Behold, a virgin shall conceive, and bear a son, and shall call his name Immanuel."*[43] Her virginity is complete in every way in body, soul and spirit just as the Angel Gabriel greeted her *"Hail, full of grace, the Lord is with you. Blessed are you among women."*[44] Her sanctity is unique in Scripture as the new spiritual Eve.

No one can comprehend the experience of being the Mother of God, nor can they fully grasp her position to him as daughter or the virtues of her motherhood. If anyone would stop and contemplate the intimate connection that Mary has to Jesus even from her virgin womb, they would realize her purity in the flesh and her high place in heaven. She is the woman in Revelation who leads the battle against Satan and his angels of darkness for the salvation of souls from damnation. As commander of God's forces and mother of his seed, it is her sole mission to glorify Christ and bring forth his reign in our hearts.

Prophecies written about the struggle of her who was clothed with the sun against the Devil have important meaning for the last days. St. John wrote *"behold, a great red dragon, having seven heads and ten horns, and seven crowns upon his heads."*[45] This vision of evil forces speaks to the heart of darkness as the color red denotes a banner of bloodshed and its huge size indicates the great extent of its power. The dragon itself is Marxist atheism with its ten horns of communication that directly oppose divine law. Its seven heads are the nations it rules with ideological, political and military power.

Biblical references to Jesus' mother are decisive for us to embrace in our hearts since Satan, knowing in his wrath that he has a short time *"cast out of his mouth water as a flood after the woman, that he might cause her to be carried away by the flood."*[46] This flood is a myriad of heresies that are being forwarded against the purity of Mary's soul, her perpetual virginity and her place as Queen of Heaven. But as the true handmaiden of the Lord who said to the Angel Gabriel *"be it done unto me according to your word"*, her very nature is obedience to the grace of faith and revelation of divine love in Christ.

Reason and faith work hand in hand as we study to determine the various doctrines of truth in Scripture. With respect to the person of Jesus' mother Mary she said of herself in a prophetic sense *"Behold the handmaid of the Lord."* This description of her applies to chief ambassador of the Lord and mother of his children as it is written, *"O Lord, I am your servant, and the son of your handmaid."* Spiritual rebirth is in and through her for *"save the son of your handmaid."*[47] Jesus doesn't need salvation, so why then do some *"sit and speak against your brother, you slander your own mother's son?"*[48]

Eternal life can only reach us in the form of Jesus who shapes us in his image through his spirit who reveals to us the Most Holy Trinity. Christ is the only mediator between God and all humanity, but those of his mother's seed *"keep the commandments of God, and have the testimony of Jesus Christ."*[49] The seed of Mary is that of Christ not only in his flesh, but also in his spiritual mission to his mystical body in the church. Thus Isaiah wrote that God's children *"are borne by me from the belly, who are carried from the womb."*[50] Mary is that holy womb from which Christ's life comes to sustain us.

Believers are sent to bear witness of salvation since Jesus prayed to the Father *"as you have sent me into the world, even so have I also sent them into the world."* But in this response of our submission to intercede for souls, *"unto whomever much is given, of him shall much be required."*[51] It is no surprise God has chosen distinct ministries of the church based on our humility to serve him.[52] We are all called to be instruments of his grace and this life giving power is his, not our own. For our own good and that of the church, we must be sensitive to leadership he appoints in both heaven and earth.

Divine motherhood can only be attributed to Mary who is often simply referred to as Our Lady. She is mother of the church and spoken of as the one *"that looks forth as the morning, fair as the moon, clear as the sun, and terrible as an army with banners."*[53] This verse corresponds to the woman clothed in the sun who fights against the red dragon and shows the amazing power of Our Lady to instill her guiding light in us and lead us in battle. She is the one of prophecy who is the Queen of Heaven whose royal place is next to Christ as *"upon your right hand did stand the queen in gold of Ophir."*[54]

On the cross before he died, Jesus said to his mother who stood by his beloved apostle St. John *"Woman, behold your son!"* and then he told St. John *"Behold your mother!"*[55] The relationship he indicated is spiritual and consistent with other biblical verses that point to her place in the work of salvation. Scripture clearly teaches to the backsliding church that *"the Lord has created a new thing in the earth: A woman shall compass a man."* This passage exhibits the permeating grace that emanates from Our Lady and plainly refers to her majesty as a *"habitation of justice, and mountain of holiness."*[56]

Accepting the maternal work of Our Lady in salvation by her universal mediation of graces may be an adjustment for some who have not understood her power and protection in leading us to Christ. In the battle against the dragon, the story says *"to her were given two wings of a great eagle."*[57] The eagle is the word of God and its two wings are the faith and charity revealed therein that she lived out. This prophecy to us about teaching Scripture allows her to find refuge in the desert of our souls as *"the earth helped the woman, and swallowed up the flood which the dragon cast out of his mouth."*[58]

Issues concerning Our Lady have caused much controversy for the Christian faith. It is a serious error to put her aside as an obstacle in reaching Jesus or to reduce her place to an ordinary woman who fortuitously became his mother. She is spouse of the Holy Spirit in the most true way and what *"God has joined together, let no man put asunder."*[59] The only child born to her was Jesus and this divine son miraculously passed through the veil of her virginal womb without disturbing her virginity. Jesus had relatives called brethren by custom, but Mary's legal husband Joseph only knew her spiritually.[60]

Devotions to Our Lady are seen by many as a misguided Catholic phenomenon due in part to the instruction of Jesus for us to pray in his name to the Father.[61] We certainly have access to God through Christ *"if we ask anything according to his will"*, but this axiom does not restrict other forms of prayer as we are to *"Let no man beguile you of your reward in voluntary humility and worshiping of angels."*[62] Ancient Israelites were warned by God of the angel who led them *"Beware of him, and obey his voice, provoke him not; for he will not pardon your transgressions: for my name is in him."*[63]

Although we normally do not see angels, the Lord chose to *"give his angels charge over you, to keep you in all your ways."*[64] Like Christ, we are not of this world and he has blessed us *"with all spiritual blessings in heavenly places."* We must *"seek those things which are above."*[65] St. Paul admonished those who object to the veneration of heavenly beings since such are *"vainly puffed up by his fleshly mind, and not holding the Head, from which all the body increases with the increase of God."*[66] Images such as the cross and other artistic expressions of faith are designed as symbols, not idols.

There is a difference between worship that belongs to the Godhead and humility we must have for those over us in the spiritual realm, but these forms of prayer are mutually dependent.[67] The bible states of Our Lady that *"You are fairer than the children of men. Your arrows are sharp in the heart of the king's enemies. He is your Lord. The king's daughter is all glorious within, therefore shall the people praise you forever and ever."* [68] She joyfully echoed this psalm saying *"My soul does magnify the Lord, my spirit rejoices in God my Savior, for from henceforth all generations shall call me blessed."*[69]

In these sinful and tumultuous times we need all the help we can get and God wants us to honor whomever he has placed in charge of us for our own good. As this concerns Our Lady, her connection to the Most Holy Trinity is one of royalty. The woman clothed with the sun and the moon under her feet reflects divine light in queenly sovereignty as she has *"upon her head a crown of twelve stars."*[70] These stars signify the twelve tribes of Israel who remain children of promise, the twelve Apostles upon whom Christ founded his church and also the apostolate of those consecrated to her Immaculate Heart.

The battle over minds and hearts of humanity that exists in our spiritual reality must be recognized today. Our Lady has been appointed captain over God's troops and her powerful intercession before him has become very limited by our neglect and failure to see her place in Scripture. Jesus is the only door into the kingdom of God, but his mother Mary is the gate of that kingdom. These terms are not a contradiction, nor are they the same thing as the Lord is *"strength to them that turn the battle to the gate."*[71] Jesus is not himself the gate, but *"this gate of the Lord, into which the righteous shall enter."*[72]

Prophetic implications of the dragon's assault on the church are severe and have direct application to what has been occurring in recent time as *"his tail drew the third part of the stars of heaven, and did cast them to the earth."*[73] These stars are not demons who fell from grace long ago, but they are the pastors, priests and religious who have become deceived about the truth. Those of the clergy in any of the Christian confessions who teach false doctrines and moral errors have brought many souls of their flocks down with them from the true light of heaven thus becoming in great danger of damnation.

Why the sign of the woman clothed with the sun is so central in importance to the first seal hinges on the fact that it coincides with the first things Jesus said would happen in the last days. This vision is a physical sign that was given in the fully documented event of Fatima that took place in Portugal during WWI. That famous visible announcement of the last days by Our Lady's appearance included many warnings of the consequences of deeply seeded iniquity. The common belief that this supernatural apparition was a myth or hoax prohibits us from grasping spiritual war and obstructs the plan of God.

Fatima was a profound event that has a direct correlation to Scripture and unless we respond to this divine intent we hasten God's justice and hinder his grace in our lives. This revelation of the Queen of Heaven and Mother of the Church first of all provides us with safe refuge in her as a messenger of Christ, but also one who made predictions and gave certain visions that substantiate prophecies made in the bible. The messages of Our Lady, contained in six visitations in 1917 to three children ages 7 to 10 years, are grouped into three parts called secrets and all of these have been released to the public.

Examination of the Fatima messages told by the eldest child named Lucia are relevant to the timeframe of the first seal and also to the future as these things stand the test of time and we understand their relation to God's word.[74] Only a few years before Pope John Paul II revealed the final secret in the year of 2000, he noted that Our Lady seems to read the signs of our times with special insight. Vatican officials were perplexed with the symbolic language of the third secret saying it is not easy to decipher, but they accept the teachings of Fatima as a truth having partial application to the present time.

For many who have little or no knowledge of Fatima, Our Lady first visited the three children while they were tending their sheep. They saw her dressed in white, shining as it were brighter than the sun whose rays of light from God engulfed their hearts and souls. In her hand she held a rosary with beads and a crucifix all shining like stars. She told them she came from heaven and set an appointed time for them to come back each month to meet her. During her visits she repeatedly asked them to pray the rosary daily to make intercession for the sins of the world and thereby bring God's grace to end WWI.

All godly prayer is powerful since *"The effectual fervent prayer of a righteous man avails much."* Jesus said we would be heard *"If you abide in me, and my words abide in you."*[75] The rosary is based in Scripture and made up of the Our Father, Hail Mary and Glory Be. These prayers are taken from the words of Jesus, greetings to his mother and the truth of eternal Trinity in the Godhead. We profess our Eucharistic unity in saying the rosary for *"bind the sacrifice with cords, even to the horns of the altar."*[76] That daily sacrifice is timeless and *"neither will any of the cords thereof be broken."*[77]

No doubt the primary theme of Fatima is an urgent call to conversion and penance in keeping with the gospel. Our Lady told the children that Jesus wanted them to establish worldwide devotions to her Immaculate Heart as a means of obtaining the salvation of souls and of preventing war. She explained that WWI would end, but a more terrible war would follow if people did not stop offending God. Without a concerted effort within the church to clean its house and intercede, God has judged godless nations and he has and will continue to use them to chastise Christian peoples who leave the path of Christ.

Warnings of Fatima emphasize the obligation of the church for holiness, prayer and evangelization. We should realize the main problem in our world is internal as it relates to our spiritual state so as more and more Christians fall away from truth, the closer we come to judgment. How can we please God and be his example of charity if we don't obey his commandments? This is the crux of Our Lady's prophecy about WWII and the additional threat that Russia would spread its errors of atheism throughout the world, bringing new wars, persecutions of the church and annihilation of certain nations.

In regard to this second secret, a special request was made by Our Lady to consecrate Russia to her Immaculate Heart for its conversion and for peace. She predicted a Pope would do that resulting in Russia's conversion and a period of peace. No Pope heeded her call until the pontificate of John Paul II in 1984 when he entrusted all nations to her care. Shortly after his official act, the world witnessed the fall of Soviet communism and a frail end to the cold war with relative peace. The issue of WWII and any of the isolated wars since then is history, but the predicted time of any sense of peace is temporary.

Marxist atheism either expressed openly or in covert ways under a guise of religion or secularism has indeed spread throughout the world as foretold in the second secret. This growing apostasy in Our Lady's warnings has a direct influence on ending peace and the result of new wars that will cause the complete genocide of certain nations. The bearing of these divine punishments against iniquity in these predictions therefore has an implicit meaning for the future. We must see that Our Lady's prophecy of peace is not indefinite and its termination has a looming perspective of coming nuclear world wars.

Should anyone who recognizes the gross sins in our world be surprised at the evident prospect of extreme divine justice? Or is the present threat of global terrorism related to the age old conditions of our obedience to divine law that underlines the clear warnings set forth in Fatima? On the day Our Lady gave these three secrets, the children saw a great angel with a flaming sword that looked like it would set the world on fire. His profound cry to all of mankind for "Penance, Penance, Penance" is a threefold summons that corresponds to the apocalyptic wars and final wrath of the end times.[78]

Signs of the last days explained in Christ's gospel have application to Fatima because it marked the starting events of wars, but Our Lady's prophecies include still new wars that come after WWII. We need to separate the wars and commotions of the last century from the great wars Jesus spoke of as yet the beginning of sorrows. The angel with the flaming sword spoke to a sequence of circumstances or separate periods when he called three times for penance. Catholic officials see his flaming sword as being formed by humanity itself now lost in sin and they recognize its potential for self-destruction.

In vision of the angel who stood at the left hand of Our Lady, the children said flames of his sword died out when they were extinguished by the splendor of light from her right hand. This strong power of hers over evil forces that would destroy our world is largely dependent on those who believe in and pray to her. Vitality of the church in living out our faith and its devotions to her plays a pivotal role in the balance of divine justice. Yet the vision that the children saw of her heart encircled with thorns shows how often we offend her instead of pleasing her. We must be realistic about this principle.

Vatican officials have confirmed that the bible is not simply a matter of intellectual communication, but our study of it is a life giving process where God reveals himself and his plan to his children. They hold that the prophetic word of God is revealed to us by his spirit and that this revelation came to an end with the fulfillment in Christ, but it has not yet been made fully explicit. Comprehending prophecy then remains a vital task for the apostolic church to gradually grasp its full significance and not only see the God of the past, but be open to this charisma concerning his kingdom with scrutiny, not scorn.

Events of Fatima need to be interpreted in the broader light of Scripture, especially as they relate to the woman clothed with sun and how these things apply to matters of the end. Our Lady's battle extends to the Second Advent when she will triumph with Christ, but her progeny in Revelation reflects persecution and also deliverance of rapture as *"her child was caught up unto God, and to his throne."* This act to a mysterious man child is a measure of fullness in the Gentile church, yet the dragon then *"went to make war with the remnant of her seed"* who likewise in sorrow will await their redemption.[79]

Communication of the third secret was held back until long after WWII by the child Lucia who alone survived as a nun to disclose the prophecies of Our Lady. Sister Lucia did not think anyone would understand this vision if it was given too prematurely. In a letter to Pope John Paul II dated 12May1982 she wrote that the third secret is a symbolic revelation referring to the spread of atheism due to the failure to heed Our Lady's call to repentance and reparation. She emphatically said that if we have not seen the final part of this inclusive prophecy, we are going toward it little by little with great strides.

Expectation about the third secret primarily among Catholics had been very high from the time when other messages of Fatima were known. The third vision is of a Pope who leads the church ministers up a steep mountain to its apex where stood a big wooden cross with two angels underneath gathering the blood of martyrs to sprinkle it on those who made their way to God. During their ascent, they saw the destruction of a great war as they passed through a large city that lay half in ruins. Then as they reached the cross at the top, each of them suffered martyrdom by soldiers who shot bullets and arrows.

This striking portrayal of WWIII and Golgotha of the church is disturbing to say the least. Vatican officials have interpreted the third secret to represent an interminable Way of the Cross for the church, but they restrict its context to the twentieth century largely due to the fact that Pope John Paul II was the Pope of suffering who brought the fall of Soviet Communism. The assassination attempt on his life in 1981 was seen as an end to a tragic and bloody period of history and his decision to release the final secret in 2000 was viewed as one of hope by saying the vision is not an irrevocably fixed future.

Predictions of Fatima are presently interpreted by church officials in terms of adjacent events of history that occurred around the time of Fatima and in the specific prophecies already fulfilled such as WWII and that of Pope John Paul II. It was disappointing for the faithful to hear the announcement that there is no great mystery in the third secret, nor does it unveil the future. The decision by Catholic authorities to look mainly at the past to explain warnings of Our Lady has left the impression on many that Fatima is passé and no longer of any interest. This question has yet to be fully explained and resolved.

Analysis of the commentaries made by Vatican officials clearly indicates that they see the third secret as an assault by atheistic systems against the church and all Christians. They did not dismiss this threat as something of the past, but on the contrary said the call to conversion and penance remains timely and urgent today. In essence, they assured that the Way of the Cross still applies to the church without giving any details except that it is no fantasy of mankind's capacity of reducing himself to ashes. Specifics about new wars, however, can be found in the bible and any idea of total doom is not its impetus.

In discerning the pertinence of Fatima for the future we need to keep in mind that Sister Lucia knew the interpretation of the final vision was long range and thought at an old age we still are moving toward the end little by little. She said that the understanding of the final secret belonged to the Pope himself but Pope John Paul II instead deferred that authority to another time. The true relevance of the Way of the Cross for the present and future is not forgotten since an infallible papal definition may yet be made to connect the reality of terrorism, a broad arms build-up and wars to the messages of Fatima.

The principle that the future is not unchangeable rests on our willingness to obey the will of God and to intercede for the world, especially through the sign he gave us in Our Lady at Fatima. Devotions to her have steadily diminished and few people realize the critical need for penance. Our ability to appease God's anger is relative, not absolute. He looks at the overall practice of faith in the church, not just qualities of a few.[80] Some things like the Second Advent and harsh biblical end signs are fixed in the future since repentance is virtually in hindsight of divine justice, not from the foresight of it.

Great mystery exists in the Calvary of the church as by sufferings, even in metaphor of its agony, condemnation, crucifixion and sepulcher, she will arise in eminent rebirth at the return of Christ in glory. The thought that humanity will utterly obliterate itself is not the divine plan, but the new covenant in Christ will be established for a remnant left of mankind. We must look to Scripture to grasp the sorrowful passions of the church in the remaining times of the end. Our Lady foretold at Fatima that entire nations would be literally annihilated by wars, but she did not imply the same fate for all of them.

Our comprehension of the bible involves our reason and it grows with meditation and study. Of necessity this process includes the correlation of our reality to prophetic signs that are being fulfilled and those affairs that logically follow. The Apocalypse refers to the mystery of God happening in context of the Old Testament *as he has declared to his servants the prophets.*[81] These writings provide a sound basis for determining many details of Christ's gospel yet to be preached. We must not let fear and ignorance get in the way of our quest to learn the word of God and the instruction of Our Lady.

Wars and persecution of the church are obvious events associated with the Way of the Cross. As these things relate to the second secret, the prophecy is open ended in regard to the savage aims of atheist systems, but as they apply to the third secret there is a sense of finality in the cross that is given to the church as a whole. This symbolic Calvary of the mystical body of Christ leads to the epitome of apostasy when the Antichrist takes control over the church through war and afterward rules the world thereby perverting all religious worship to him alone.[82] We simply cannot ignore this fact of Scripture.

Freedom of religion still exists in the vast majority of societies on earth although that right is either severely restricted or denied in some nations. True faith has been damaged by the spread of many errors, but it certainly has not been lost. Despite the false finger pointing of the past, the Antichrist has not even been made known let alone advance his power to the summit of the church. It is grave sin for whoever has accused any Pope of this evil. Many have failed to see the context of when the Antichrist will appear, how he will gain his influence in the church and the bloodshed preceding his ruthless reign.

When the third secret was made public, the tragedy of 9/11 or the increasing impact of world terrorism had not been contemplated. World peace is vanishing and global war is becoming a serious reality, but this connection to the end period is only in passing and has no direct bearing on the final battle of Armageddon. WWIII conforms to Jesus' prediction that nation shall rise against nation and only starts the beginning of sorrows in the gospel to be endured by the church. The conclusion for a viable church is still in another world war in which Jesus foretold that kingdom shall rise against kingdom.

What should be recognized in matters of the church is that Jesus said *"the servant is not greater than his lord. If they persecuted me, they will persecute you."*[83] In regard to the analogy of his passion for the church he exclaimed *"you shall indeed drink of the cup that I drink of"* and further prophesied *"the night is coming, when no man can work."*[84] The remnant of the church will go through great darkness in a symbolic form of its own tomb when *"you shall be hated of all nations for my names' sake."* This mission in the Way of the Cross is to *"fill up that which is behind of the afflictions of Christ."*[85]

We should not loose sight of Fatima where the miracle of the sun took place before some seventy thousand people. This awesome sign is biblical and such a big crowd was not under some kind of mass hallucination. The multitude of spectators at one moment all turned to see the sun making movements outside of cosmic laws. For several minutes they saw the sun spinning like a wheel, dancing in the sky and come out of its place as thought to fall upon the earth. Terror came upon everyone, but it did not hurt their eyes to look into the sun for so long and colors of the rainbow shined on everything.[86]

Details about future wars are not provided in the messages of Fatima but rather a set of general consequences of our failure to meet the conditions for peace. The elements of divine justice are present and we must be practical in our outlook. False hopes will not bring correction in lax morals, nor will idle pursuits turn the tide of apostasy. We must realize from the first secret that the somber vision of human souls plunged together with demons amid groans of pain and despair in a sea of fire reflects these times of ours when a civilization without God is being constructed on a path to its eternal perdition.

Assessing the perils of the last days requires us to consider that *"judgment must begin at the house of God: and if it first begin at us, what shall the end of them be that obey not the gospel of God?"*[87] The only recourse we have to alter this suffering is by sincere prayer, humble penance and charitable outreach. We need revival but frequent calls for a new evangelization are stagnated while wounds of division become deeper. The reality of hardness in human hearts is that even after future judgments *"the rest of the men which were not killed by these plagues yet repented not of the works of their hands."*[88]

In the year before the events of Fatima in 1916, an angel appeared to the three children to prepare them for the visits of Our Lady. During these three apparitions, the Angel of Portugal taught the children to pray for conversion of sinners and offer their sufferings and sacrifice to God for the pardon of sin and for peace in their country. They saw the angel in the form of a young man, transparent and brilliant as crystal in the rays of the sun. A great vision was shown to them as the angel held a chalice in his left hand and over it in the air was a Eucharist from which drops of blood fell into the chalice.

Lessons given by the angel have critical significance for the Christian faith and for the ability of it members to intercede for a dying world. The angel exhorted the children to adore the Most Holy Trinity, Father, Son and Holy Spirit. Then he instructed them to offer the Body, Soul and Divinity of Jesus Christ present in all the tabernacles of the world for the outrages, sacrileges and indifference with which Jesus Himself is offended. He urged them to begin zealous prayer through the infinite merits of His most Sacred Heart and of the Immaculate Heart of Mary for the conversion of poor sinners.

The matter of the true nature of the Eucharist, which was established by Jesus at the Last Supper on the evening of his betrayal, has caused a major division in doctrine for the meaning of participating in this Christian rite. Catholics believe that the celebration of the Last Supper involves the transformation of ordinary bread and wine into the actual body and blood of Christ, while other confessions deny his presence professing that the bread and wine are merely symbolic as a type of memorial. Either we receive the very person of Jesus in the communion of eating and drinking this food or we don't.

Belief in the divine species of the Eucharist is central to the proper Christian order of worship and we must examine Scripture to understand this holy tradition. Jesus indicated his great desire to eat the Passover with his disciples and as they were eating he took bread, and gave it to them saying *"Take, eat; This is my body which is given for you."* Likewise, he took the cup saying *"This is my blood of the new testament, which is shed for many for the remission of sins."* He commanded them to *"do this in remembrance of me"* thereby establishing the priesthood in the practice of this communion rite.[89]

Breaking of the bread was a common ritual among the early Christians, but even then as is now there was doubt about its true significance. St. Paul needed to admonish them by asking *"The cup of blessing which we bless, is it not the communion of the blood of Christ? The bread which we break, is it not the communion of the body of Christ?"*[90] He spoke to them as wise men who were taught the truth, yet heresies and irreverence took place in their gatherings to celebrate the Lord's Supper *"For he that eats and drinks unworthily, eats and drinks damnation to himself, not discerning the Lord's body."*[91]

Much like the veil of Christ's human flesh that hid his divinity, his body and blood are hidden in the elements of bread and wine. We need to go beyond appearances and see with the eyes of our heart to experience the sacred presence of Jesus in the Eucharist. It is an issue of faith to believe the word of God as *"we are made partakers of Christ"* and we must accept his sacrificial offering as *"we have an altar."*[92] It is written *"For there are three that bear witness in earth: the spirit, and the water, and the blood; and these three are one."*[93] This presence of Christ in his spirit, word and blood is present tense.

Why would we accept, as some Christian confessions do, only the divine nature of the bible and of the Holy Spirit, but deny the holy presence of Christ in the Eucharist that comes through his word and spirit by means of the priesthood? Many of Jesus' followers were offended and went away because he claimed *"the bread that I will give is my flesh."*

And he further clarified, *"He that eats my flesh, and drinks my blood, dwells in me, and I in him."* His instruction aptly applies to the Last Supper where he instituted the Eucharist by his power as *"the words that I speak unto you are spirit, and they are life."*[94]

After Jesus rose from the dead, he appeared to his apostles at an appointed place in Galilee saying *"I am with you always, even unto the end of the world."*[95] He spoke of the Eucharist where his presence in the Consecrated Bread is lasting in all the tabernacles of the earth. The word end does not signify a ceasing, but despite the persecution in the end period, this testimony will continue and Jesus will establish it anew as: *"I will not anymore eat thereof, until it be fulfilled in the kingdom of God."* Of this consummation for our world he explicitly revealed *"until the kingdom of God shall come."*[96]

Residence of Jesus in the Eucharist in the sense of time is permanent for humanity. His glorious return will coincide with his Eucharistic reign for all people since *"You, O Lord, shall endure forever, and your remembrance unto all generations."* This psalm speaks of the Second Advent and its result when *"the heathen shall fear the name of the Lord, and all the kings of the earth your glory."*[97] Another psalm likewise describes the destruction of the wicked and makes a Eucharistic connection to that time as *"The Lord reigns: let the earth rejoice, and give thanks at the remembrance of his holiness."*[98]

It is not by chance that Jesus used the term remembrance to refer to himself in the Eucharist because that sublime gift was prophesied long before he made it a sacrament. Thus Isaiah wrote, *"Yea, in the way of your judgments, O Lord, have we waited for you, the desire of our soul is to your name, and to the remembrance of you."* This passage equates his name with his remembrance and also describes end times sorrows in the hope of rapture. That hope is closely attuned to adoring and receiving the Eucharist for *"they visited you in trouble, they poured out a prayer when you chastened them."*[99]

Throughout many psalms, an urgent prayer is made for deliverance from bloodshed. Jesus urged us to watch and pray that we might be accounted worthy to escape death and the Antichrist's snare.[100] That bond with him lies in the Eucharist for *"salvation is in the tabernacles of the righteous."* Thus here *"shall the congregation of the people compass you about: for their sakes therefore return you on high."* To this Hidden Jesus in his consecration of bread and wine *"his secret is with the righteous."*[101] In their times of redemption, *"The meek shall eat and be satisfied: your heart shall live forever."*[102]

True worship of God in Christ cannot be separated from the secret of his tabernacles, nor should this new covenant be put apart from the hope of rapture *"For in the time of trouble he shall hide me in his pavilion, in the secret of his tabernacle shall he hide me."*[103] Surely it is written *"My times are in your hand, you shall hide them in the secret of your presence."*[104] Jesus spoke of his Father who *"is in secret, and sees in secret"* for God is in him and also present in the Eucharist with him. So then *"He that dwells in the secret place of the most High shall abide under the shadow of the Almighty."*[105]

Writings of the Psalter have direct relevance to the Lord's house and the manner of our Sabbath homage as *"bring me unto your holy hill, and to your tabernacles, unto the altar of God."*[106] It is in his tabernacles that *"God is in the midst of her, the holy place of the tabernacles of the most High."*[107] We must understand our part in this profound truth of his altar for *"We will worship at his footstool. Arise, O Lord, into your rest; you and the ark of your strength."*[108] Moreover, *"From the end of the earth will I cry unto you, I will abide in your tabernacle forever: I will trust in the covert of your wings."*[109]

In the Liturgy of the Mass we *"proclaim the death of the Lord, until he comes."*[110] By proclaiming Christ's death and eternal victory over it in the Eucharist, the church shares in a prophetic union with him in his Calvary and resurrection. After his Second Advent, there will be no need to suffer his passion or defend faith *"for when your judgments are in the earth, the inhabitants of the world will learn righteousness."*[111] Jesus said *"And I, if I be lifted up from the earth, will draw all men unto me."*[112] Like him, the church will live out the Way of the Cross before humanity will be drawn to the Eucharist.

Until then we must face the surge of evil that Jesus predicted would plague us even as the time of Noah when they *"Knew not, until the flood came, and took them all away."*[113] This apostasy has reached the interior of the church since *"there shall be false teachers among you, who subtly shall bring in damnable heresies, even denying the Lord that bought them."*[114] So it is today we find moral and doctrinal heresies that are based in diverse forms of secular humanism and materialism. These vain pursuits of lusts and of human means to govern our way of life subvert the very salvation of the gospel.

Sharp schisms have occurred openly in Protestant denominations over moral issues like homosexuality that are clearly defined in the bible as worthy of damnation.[115] What is holy has been replaced with the profane even to the point of elevating gay people to high positions of their clergy. They have lost any reason of divine justice and hence destroy the basis of atonement in repentance. These types of rebellion that subject Christ to human volition are being widely propagated, while ecumenical efforts at interfaith unity often become muddled in accepting contradictory dogmas as part of the truth.

Struggles to keep the pure faith in the church so it can reflect the real image of Christ have grown into a severe identity crisis, but *"when the flood arose, the stream beat vehemently upon that house, and could not shake it: for it was founded upon a rock."*[116] That rock is Christ as he is expressed in his word, his spirit and his blood for *"He is the Rock, a God of truth and without iniquity."*[117] We are told to *"Enter into the rock, and hide yourself in the dust"* since our egoism must die to let Jesus live in us. Through faith *"we look at the things which are not seen"* to receive him in the Eucharist.[118]

Similar to the Ark of the Covenant that was the center of ancient Jewish worship, the Eucharist is purposed as the primary focus of Christian life. Much more than the Ark that held divine law, the Eucharist is the source of life itself to obedience of that law *"For the bread of God is that which comes down from heaven and gives life to the world."*[119] No exception can be made to this rule, nor to the sacred priesthood of whom Jesus ordered that ceremony to be done in his name. We are totally separated from sin in this practice as *"you cannot be partakers of the Lord's table and of the table of devils."*[120]

Contentions against the divine nature of the Eucharist contradict the word of God and thus have spawned a multiplication of divisions that hinder his spirit in union of Christ. Jesus is our *"high priest over the house of God"* wherein he serves *"a greater and more perfect tabernacle, not made with hands."* He established the new covenant whereby *"We are sanctified through the offering of the body of Jesus Christ once and for all."* It is in this offering accomplished for all time that we commune with him *"By a new and living way, which he has consecrated for us, through the veil that is his flesh."*[121]

Profession of faith in Christ is meant to be a voice of unity, not continuing discord that has fractured the church and also has led many to believe they can just do as they please or simply don't need the church in their lives. Jesus founded his church upon the apostle Simon whom he surnamed Peter to create order as *"You are Peter, and upon this rock, I will build my church."* He ordained an enduring office in him since *"I will give you the keys of the kingdom of heaven, and whatsoever you shall bind on earth shall be bound in heaven, and whatsoever you shall loose on earth shall be loosed in heaven."*[122]

For centuries many have maligned the papacy, which is a direct commission from the Lord designed as a guardian of truth to keep it intact. The very name Peter that Jesus gave to Simon means rock and indicates strong identity he intended in this leadership role with himself. This is not to say that anyone can replace Christ, but this unique Vicar of Christ remains through the succession of office in the same way that bishops, pastors and priests are ordained in the sacrament of holy orders.[123] There is a divine mandate for the priesthood to minister to God and give prescribed sacraments to his people.

Organizational structure is mandatory for any kind of large business since it could not function without a line of authority complete with delegated duties. The church isn't any different in method of administration as *"God has set the members as it pleased him."*[124] We simply don't appoint ourselves to ministry *"For not he that commends himself is approved, but whom the Lord commends."*[125] As this applies to the keys of the kingdom of heaven in making decisions on earth that are bound or loosed in heaven itself, the power was not given to many but to one. The Pope has advisors, but he decides.

Protestant churches that have become increasingly divided and strife between Catholic priests are largely the result of shepherds and theologians who have little or no regard for authentic magistracy in the Pope and bishops united to him. Under the guise of liberty and a false claim to a deeper understanding of Scripture, they have betrayed the truth in various ways in an attempt to adapt to the mentality of the world. These errors are impelled by the illusion of being more easily agreed with and followed, but morality and doctrine are unchangeable as they reflect the real presence and gospel of Christ.

More than ever before, we must heed the divine instruction to *"Obey them that have the rule over you, and submit yourselves: for they watch for your souls, as they must give an account."*[126] So too must all give an account who contradict infallible issues of faith that concern the sacraments and teachings of the church. Instead of trying to bring Jesus down to our level of thinking, we have to believe in the word of God as it is and allow the Holy Spirit to enlighten our hearts to do what is right since *"Let the wicked forsake his way. For my thoughts are not your thoughts, neither are your ways my ways."*[127]

Spiritual warfare is at the core of our quest for peace, but evil forces are successfully working to undermine the structure of the church, separate people from it and attack its sacraments and devotions. This mischief is foremost directed at the Eucharist which *"from the rising of the sun unto the going down of the same, in every place there is sacrifice, and there is offered to my name a clean oblation."* It is this perfect offering of Christ's blood in the Liturgy of the Mass that is mocked by those who say that *"the table of the Lord is polluted, and the fruit thereof, even his meat, is contemptible."*[128]

Signs of the last days include the lack of fidelity in the sacrament of marriage as Jesus said it would be as in the days of Noah when *"they were eating and drinking, marrying and giving in marriage."*[129] His implication is a mad search for pleasure and a disregard for the sanctity of marriage since much sin and great violence existed in the earth before the flood. Mankind's greatest fear is its own destruction and many people are hiding that fear in a careless attitude of *"Let us eat and drink, for tomorrow we shall die."* The irony in this futility is *"Surely this iniquity shall not be purged from you until you die."*[130]

High divorce rates and domestic violence have caused a breakdown of the family unit in many societies. This phenomenon has alienated countless church members, especially Catholics, and brought about the acceptance of careless remarriage, sexual promiscuity, cohabitation and homosexuality as normal Christian lifestyles. Many divorced Catholics do not bother to seek annulment of an invalid marriage or ask a priest's advice about their status with the church. Great numbers stay away from Sunday Mass because they see no means of reconciliation, but these people are either mistaken or unwilling to repent.

Other sacraments are being violated in unprecedented ways by errant opinions that affect all Christian faiths. The sacrament of confession was instituted when Jesus told his apostles *"whose sins you shall forgive, they are forgiven them, and whose sins you shall retain, they are retained."*[131] This power is given to the priesthood through Jesus himself, yet it is seldom advocated or practiced reflecting a general reluctance to address and turn from sin. Many people deny any need for confession and this deceptive refusal of grace leads to infringement of the sacraments of baptism and confirmation.

Renewal of the whole of gospel truth is sorely needed in the church today. In order to restore unity we have to go beyond superficial efforts that are based on parts of divine teaching *"as you have not kept my ways, but have been partial in the law."*[132] Souls are not edified by compromise or neglect of God's word as *"Not by might, nor by power, but by my spirit says the Lord."*[133] His spirit is not divided, nor can we deviate from the path he has chosen for us to lead a holy life. We are seriously warned to *"make straight paths for your feet, looking diligently lest any man fail the grace of God."*[134]

Ministry and practice of the sacraments as well as insistent calls to devotions are the lifeblood of the church. These lessons taught by Our Lady at Fatima and by the Angel of Portugal apply not only to the Catholic faith, but to all Christians. This work of prayer and penance is only on the fringe of our ministry, while the Eucharist is being denied, ignored or disgraced by sacrilegious communions. The Sabbath Day is no longer holy to those who neglect it and its fullness is lost to those who diminish the fact that *"we being many are one bread, and one body: for we are all partakers of that one bread."*[135]

Faith is essential to please God since he has chosen unseen things to bring to nothing the things that are seen so that no flesh can glory in his presence.[136] It is *"by one offering he has perfected forever them that are sanctified."* This offering of the Eucharist is the very image of Christ who *"has given himself for us as an offering and a sacrifice to God for a sweet smelling savor."*[137] Doubting or denying his presence in the Eucharist is a decisive and pressing matter in the manner of worship, *"Wherefore lift up the hands which hang down, and the feeble knees, lest that which is lame be turned away."*[138]

How is it that some churches have a pulpit in which they preach, but have not an altar or tabernacle that are clearly defined in the bible for use in the Christian rite which began at the Last Supper ? It is true that believers in Christ are themselves the tabernacles of his spirit, but shall we thereby negate the source of his grace in the Eucharist? Do these then put themselves above the blood of Christ or simply lack enough faith to *"go on unto perfection"* in his word? The truth in this is *"our God is a consuming fire"* against the works of our flesh so *"that those things which cannot be shaken may remain."*[139]

Ordinances for the service of the priests under ancient Hebrew law were of a worldly sanctuary, but through the new covenant *"the priesthood being changed, there is made a necessity a change also of the law."* As our eternal high priest in heaven Jesus is now *"a minister of the sanctuary, and of the tabernacle, which the Lord pitched, and not man."*

The Lord's house is established around his altar and his tabernacle where he becomes and remains our Consecrated Bread through the Holy Spirit. This daily work of the ministry was appointed to holy men of God from the very beginning of Christianity.[140]

Opposition to the Pope and to devotions of Our Lady present a great challenge for the church to heal the fractured elements of the Protestant Reformation and correct internal discord among Catholic priests and teachers. There are no easy answers to the problems of agreement except those offered in Scripture as *"God is Spirit, and they that worship him must worship in spirit and truth."* In this union with Christ of marriage to his church *"they two shall be one flesh."* It is in his Eucharistic covenant that Jesus will *"present to himself a glorious church, not having spot, or wrinkle, holy and without blemish."*[141]

For those who accept the prophets as a source of truth and those willing to learn, Jesus urged us to *"Search the Scriptures for they speak of me."*[142] He prayed to God the Father for the faithful at Gethsemane to *"Sanctify them through your truth: your word is truth so they may be made perfect in one, that they may believe that you have sent me."*[143] Harmony in doctrines of faith and morals is intrinsic to our salvation and the conversion of others. We need to be honest about the teachings of God's word for *"Whereas there is among you envying, strife, and divisions, are you not carnal, and walk as men?"*[144]

There are many prophecies about Christ before he became man and beside his divine birth, the most important concerns his atonement for sin. Isaiah wrote *"by his knowledge shall my righteous servant justify many, for he shall bear their iniquities."* This passage is very explicit about the passion and death of him who is called the Savior and Redeemer as *"he was wounded for our transgressions, and with his stripes we are healed, because he poured out his soul unto death."* He was made *"an offering for sin"* since he was *"brought as a lamb to slaughter"* and hence *"cut off out of the land of the living."*[145]

It is a mistake to see the Messiah as only a victor who would bring external peace and not see his prophetic mission to end the root cause of all adversity that results from sin. No one is justified by his own works, nor is anyone capable of acting out of true love without grace. That spiritual mercy to commune with God was revealed in the blood of Christ to free us from sin as *"he has sent me to bind up the brokenhearted, to proclaim liberty to the captives, and open the prison to them that are bound."* Thus heed *"How beautiful are the feet of him that brings good tidings and publishes salvation."*[146]

Jesus was foreordained before the foundation of the world by God to make amends for our iniquity and he was clearly manifest on earth according to the prophets for *"they pierced my hands and my feet, they part my garments among them, and cast lots upon my vesture."*[147] Not only his death, but also his resurrection was foretold since *"you will not suffer your Holy One to see corruption."* Although he died, his body did not decay but he rose in glory for *"You are my Son, this day have I begotten you."* So it is God said of him *"I will make him my firstborn, his seed also will I make to endure forever."*[148]

Resurrection from death into eternal life with God in heaven and world peace on earth are basic prophecies of Christ since *"He will swallow up death in victory, and the rebuke of his people shall he take away from all the earth."* Persecution of Christians will cease and the remnant left of humanity will know the Lord as *"he will destroy the web that is spread over all nations, and it shall be said in that day, Lo, this is our God, we have waited for him, and we will rejoice in his salvation."*[149] Apostasy and secularism will end so that mankind will then follow the way of love in the tabernacle of Jesus.

Scripture is very consistent with respect to the triune nature of the Godhead as the apostle Peter said to him *"You are the Christ, the Son of the living God."* His apostle Thomas exclaimed *"My Lord and my God."*[150] Jesus was born in Bethlehem since from there *"shall he come forth unto me that is to be ruler in Israel"* and *"Of the increase of his government and peace, there shall be no end."* Of his sovereign and divine place, *"For unto us a child is born, a son is given, and his name shall be called Wonderful, Counselor, The mighty God, The everlasting Father, The Prince of Peace."*[151]

Titles given to the Messiah indicate someone who is more than an ordinary prophet or corporeal king, but rather a person who is one in being with the Almighty. The apostle John wrote *"We know that the Son of God is come, that we may know him that is true, and we are in him that is true, even his Son Jesus Christ. This is the true God, and eternal life."* Likewise, *"God has spoken to us by his Son, being the brightness of his glory, and the express image of his person."* No man has seen God the Father, but *"the only begotten Son, which is in the bosom of the Father, he has declared him."*[152]

Rational explanations cannot be made for the countless miracles Jesus performed on earth. Who else has shown the power to instantly cure the blind, the deaf, the dumb, the crippled, the lepers and other diseases or to cast out demons, raise the dead, walk on water, calm a raging storm or feed thousands with a few morsels of food? These are only some of his works as *"there are also many other things which Jesus did."* Throughout church history even more great signs were manifest by those with faith in his name as *"God also bearing them witness, with divers miracles, and gifts of the Holy Ghost."*[153]

Supernatural charismata of God's spirit are given to the faithful for the edification of the church. These unusual talents induce conversion and express the nature of the Trinity as *"there are varieties of gifts, but the same Spirit, and there are varieties of ministries, but the same Lord, and there are varieties of workings, but the same God."*[154] Our purpose in Christ is to be conformed into his image as he is the source of life in spiritual rebirth and in resurrection.[155] Jesus was *"the first begotten of the dead"* so that *"being made perfect, he became the author of eternal salvation to them who obey him."*[156]

Circumstances about the prophetic word of the Savior point to the birth, death and resurrection of a divine person to redeem mankind from sin in eternal life of resurrection by destroying the very power of death in sin *"For since by man came death, by man came also the resurrection of the dead."*[157] Jesus is the new Adam from whom we obtain the promise of being with God. He became man so *"that through death he might destroy him who had the empire of death, that is, the devil."*[158] That final time of judgment will not come until the return of Christ in glory when the elect of God inherit the earth.

The conquering king in the first seal acts in both spiritual and physical ways to bring the world to conversion. Plagues or curses of divine justice have the effect of purifying the people of God to repentance and purging the wicked from our world. Everyone has the choice of embracing Jesus as the true means of life and adoption by God in which we become his children as *"Thus says the Lord, ask me of things to come concerning my sons, and concerning the work of my hands."*[159] Of this high calling Jesus said *"He who hears my word, and believes on him who sent me is passed from death into life."*[160]

Human beings as such can never see the face of God the Father, but by faith in his Son they are delivered from the power of death in hope of resurrection. We have assurance of that promise since *"because you are sons, God has sent forth the Spirit of his Son into your hearts, crying Abba, Father, and if a son, then an heir of God through Christ."*[161]

This eternal reward is God the Father himself whom we cannot behold in our flesh, but *"Blessed are the pure in heart, for they shall see God."* To these saints in heaven we should pray for *"we also are compassed about with so great a cloud of witnesses."*[162]

Spirituality in separating ourselves from the vices of our flesh is attained by inner grace for God is *"the Father of spirits."*[163] As water is a basic element of physical life and used in baptism to signify our cleansing from sin, Jesus spoke about the living water of his spirit to nourish our hearts similar to *"a well of water springing up into everlasting life."* To the thirsty he is *"the fountain of living waters"* wherein *"as many as received him, to them gave he power to become sons of God."*[164] From this one fountain springs *"the wells of salvation"* in which we draw joy from his Eucharistic presence.[165]

In this time of uncertainty and adversity that we now live, the only real solace we can depend on is the word of God and the safety that exists in his spirit within the community of the church. Despite its internal difficulties, we need to defend not abandon the church. Our focus should be on the truth and holiness of the faithful as we labor together to bring healing to the only institution created by Christ to glorify God. Christianity is not just a private matter for we are members of the Lord's body and commanded to observe the Sabbath in the testament of our faith.[166] It is right to give him thanks and praise.

Anyone who desires to know God and be at peace with him needs to simply open their heart and soul to him since *"we all like sheep have gone astray."*[167] Salvation is free for *"all you that thirst, come to the waters, and you that have no money, make haste, buy, and eat."*[168] It is in coming to the waters of his Eucharistic Table that our submission and faith in Christ becomes complete. Go *"taste and see that the Lord is good."*[169] Herein is satisfaction money can't buy and heavenly rewards we won't lose as *"Do not labor for the food that perishes, but for that which endures unto life everlasting."*[170]

Our testimony of Jesus stems not only from what he already fulfilled in Scripture, but also from his witness to things that have not yet happened. The biblical message of God's kingdom in Christ on earth has not been revealed, nor has humanity experienced great sufferings foretold before that time due its iniquity. We are told *"all scripture is given by inspiration of God and is profitable for doctrine. Preach the word: be instant in season, out of season."*[171] Thus, *"we have the word of prophecy, as to a lamp shining in a dark place, until the day dawns and the morning star rises in your hearts."*[172]

Essential issues of prophecy concerning the divinity of Christ and his ministry on earth show *"that Christ should suffer, and that he should be the first to rise from the dead."*[173] Jesus said if he had not come in the word of truth and power of God, there would be no sin for disbelief *"But now they have no cloak for their sin."* We cannot conceal the entire dimensions of truth that are revealed in God's word without being held accountable. Those doctrines have been, are now and will be manifest in our world. In continuum, *"light shines in the darkness, and the darkness overcame it not."*[174]

The knowledge of good or evil is much more than an intellectual process, but it is our service to either one or the other as *"no man can serve two masters."*[175] Jesus explained that *"none is good, save one that is God."* Our virtue comes not of ourselves but by the grace from his Son since *"The steps of a good man are ordered by the Lord."*[176] This means to guide and also to form us is in receiving him as he said *"I am the way."* He is the potter and we are the clay, yet so many are self-righteous. Even before Jesus became man, he *"was the true light that enlightens every man who comes into the world."*[177]

Although the Lord's bow in the first seal represents the whole of God's word, his victory is not conclusive within this seal's timeframe as he has not already triumphed, but *"he went forth conquering, and to conquer."*[178] Wars and commotions of the last century are the first things he said would come to pass. The foremost question now is if terrorist actions, ongoing battles and new military threats indicate the start of the second seal's sword where *"nation shall rise against nation."* This dreadful world war and that in the fourth seal when *"kingdom shall rise against kingdom"* have many biblical details.[179]

Fear of total nuclear annihilation and confusion in identifying the true significance of WWIII has caused the common perception that this war is the end of the world. That thought is not the focal point of Scripture and many future aspects of prophecy still lie beyond this widespread conflict regardless of its potential for complete destruction. The scope of WWIII has enigmatic yet profound implications for the church and undoubtedly will affect some nations more than others. Its end will set the stage for revealing who the Antichrist is and his subsequent prevailing military struggle to rule the world.

Anxiety and remorse have overcome many in our global culture because of military incursions, natural disorders, economic conditions and social maladies. The uncertainty and adversity in which we live has caused the public in general to think about their very existence to find reasons that explain these plagues and offer solutions to reverse this flood of dismay. Irrespective of status or creed and attempts to hide from or deny our reality, most people are aware of our situation and are seeking a way toward reform. Our obedience to divine law will determine what degree we alleviate these curses.

None of us can alter the course of prophetic truth, but its revelation in our minds and hearts can change our lifestyle and attitude for the better. Only God knows in advance how broad, how deep and how long his word will take hold in our civilization to create a repentant change in our paths to appease his anger. His warnings are made so we can ask for mercy with clean hearts and avoid our sorrow by being ready in the watches before it is too late for him to respond for help. Salvation is in Christ and we must turn from the bankruptcy of faith that has caused so many to justify sin and follow falsehoods.

Instruction in the kingdom of God is a fundamental prerequisite for conversion and matters of prophecy are central to that knowledge, especially as it applies to signs of the last days now in progress. Countless people are searching for meaning in our troubled world and earnestly are turning to the bible to make sense out of great dangers we face. Many ask whether or not current events are predicted and where these things will lead, yet they are left with ambiguous answers that do not account for major developments that biblically take place before the final wrath and judgment of Christ.

It would seem out of reach to effectively deal with various pitfalls of opinion about the end times and clarify issues of truth that have been distorted concerning Christian faith, but *"it is God who works in you both the will and the performance."* He draws us in spirit to choose his good pleasure as *"not I, but Christ lives in me."*[180] With respect to his word *"Give ear, O you heavens, and hear, O earth: My doctrine shall drop as the rain, my speech shall distil as the dew, and as showers upon the grass: Because I will publish the name of the Lord."*[181] We have not seen the fullness of this prophecy.

Honest discourse in Christian theology is not an abstract process since it involves God himself who is interested and able to communicate his message, particularly in this day of literacy and technology. He is not idle, nor is his work without fruit as *"you are God's husbandry."*[182] We labor together with him while one plants and another waters the seed of his word. When even two or three gather in his name, he said *"There am I in the midst of them."* The sure stakes vested in the bible are far greater than ever before and hence worthy of our attention since *"it is not a vain thing for you: because it is your life."*[183]

---

[1] Mathew 24,5; Mark 13,6; I John 4,1
[2] Revelation 1,1-3
[3] Revelation 1,9-18; 2,23
[4] I Thessalonians 5,19-20
[5] Isaiah 48,3
[6] Isaiah 44,7-8
[7] John 5,36-47
[8] Ezekiel 12,27-28
[9] Revelation 22,10
[10] John 8,58
[11] Isaiah 40,25-26
[12] Mathew 27,62-66; 28,1-15
[13] Exodus 3,14-15
[14] Isaiah 43,10-11
[15] John 1,1-10; Ephesians 3,9
[16] Colossians 1,15-17
[17] John 10,36-38
[18] John 5,30; 10,30; 14,9
[19] Hebrews 4,12
[20] John 5,22
[21] Romans 12,18
[22] Deuteronomy 32,35&39-41
[23] Revelation 3,21; 22,3
[24] Hebrews 11,3
[25] John 5,26; 11,25
[26] John 17,2
[27] Mathew 24,35; Mark 13,31; Ephesians 1,21
[28] Revelation 5,1
[29] Revelation 5,2-10
[30] Ephesians 1,10
[31] Habakkuk 3,9
[32] Isaiah 41,2
[33] Deuteronomy 32,22&42-43
[34] John 19,30
[35] Psalms 7,12-13
[36] Revelation 19,15

[37] Mathew 24,4-6; Mark 13,5-7; Luke 21,8-9
[38] James 4,1-3
[39] Ezekiel 16,4-6
[40] Revelation 12,1
[41] Ephesians 6,12
[42] Genesis 3,14-15
[43] Isaiah 7,14
[44] Luke 1,28
[45] Revelation 12,3
[46] Revelation 12,15
[47] Psalm 86,16; 116,16; Luke 1,38
[48] Psalm 50,20
[49] Revelation 12,17
[50] Isaiah 46,3
[51] Luke 12,48; John 17,18
[52] Mathew 18,3-5; 23,11-12; Luke 22,25-26
[53] Song of Solomon 6,10
[54] Psalm 45,9
[55] John 19,26-27
[56] Jeremiah 31,21-23
[57] Revelation 12,14
[58] Revelation 12,16
[59] Mathew 19,6; Mark 10,8-9
[60] Mathew 1,18-25; 12,46-47; Luke 8,19-21
[61] Mathew 6,6; 7,11; John 14,13-16; 15,7
[62] Colossians 2,18; James 4,3; I John 5,14
[63] Exodus 23,20-21
[64] Psalm 34,7; 91,11
[65] Ephesians 1,3; Colossians 3,1-2
[66] Colossians 2,18-19
[67] Revelation 19,10; 22,8-9
[68] Psalm 45
[69] Luke 1,46-55
[70] Revelation 12,1
[71] Isaiah 28,6
[72] Psalm 118,20
[73] Revelation 12,4
[74] Fatima in Lucis's Own Words, Vol. I & II; ewtn.com/ fatima/index. html
[75] John 15,7; James 5,16
[76] Psalm 118,27; Mathew 6,9-13; Luke 1,28&42
[77] Isaiah 33,20; 54,2
[78] Ezekiel 21,27
[79] Luke 12,35-38; Revelation 12,4-5&17
[80] Jeremiah 15,1-2; Ezekiel 14,14-20
[81] Revelation 10,7
[82] II Thessalonians 2,3-4; Revelation 13,2&7-8
[83] Mathew 10,24-25; John 15,20
[84] Mark 10,39; John 9,4
[85] Mathew 24,9; Colossians 1,24
[86] Genesis 9,12-16; Isaiah 54,7-10
[87] I Peter 4,17
[88] Revelation 9,20; 16,11
[89] Mathew 26,26-28; Luke 22,19-20
[90] Acts 2,42-46; 20,7; I Corinthians 10,15-16
[91] I Corinthians 11,27-29

[92] I Corinthians 10,17; Hebrews 3,14-15; 13,10
[93] I John 5,8
[94] John 6,51-63
[95] Mathew 28,20
[96] Mathew 26,29; Mark 14,25; Luke 22,16-18
[97] Psalm 102,12-22
[98] Psalm 97,1&12
[99] Psalm 30,1-6; 50,5; Isaiah 26,8-20
[100] Luke 21,34-36
[101] Psalm 7,6-8; 118,15-18; Proverbs 3,32
[102] Psalm 22,23-26
[103] Psalm 27,4-5; 77,12-13
[104] Psalm 31,15&20
[105] Psalm 91,1; Mathew 6,6&18
[106] Psalm 43,3-4; 84,1-3; Hebrews 12,22-24
[107] Psalm 46,4-5
[108] Psalm 132,7-8; Isaiah 66,1-2
[109] Psalm 61,2-4
[110] I Corinthians 11,26
[111] Isaiah 26,9; Jeremiah 31,33-34; 32,40
[112] John 12,32
[113] Mathew 24,38-39; Luke 17,26-27
[114] II Peter 2,1-3
[115] Leviticus 18,22-25; Romans 1,25-32
[116] Luke 6,48-49
[117] Deuteronomy 32,4; Psalm 18,1-2
[118] Isaiah 2,10; II Corinthians 4,5-18
[119] John 6,33&50&58
[120] I Corinthians 10,21
[121] Hebrews 9,11; 10,10-23
[122] Mathew 16,17-19
[123] Ephesians 2,19-22; 4,11-12; I Timothy 3,1&8
[124] I Corinthians 12,18
[125] II Corinthians 10,18
[126] Romans 12,4-5; Hebrews 13,17
[127] Isaiah 55,7-9; Romans 10,6-8
[128] Malachi 1,11-13
[129] Genesis 6,11-13; 7,23; Mathew 24,37-42
[130] Isaiah 22,13-14; Luke 12,16-21
[131] John 20,21-23; James 5,16; I John 1,9
[132] Malachi 2,6-9
[133] Zechariah 4,6; I Corinthians 2,12-13
[134] Hebrews 12,13-15
[135] I Corinthians 10,17
[136] I Corinthians 1,21-29
[137] Ephesians 5,2; Hebrews 10,1&14
[138] Malachi 1,13-14; 2,12-13; Hebrews 12,12-13
[139] Hebrews 6,1-2; 12,25-29
[140] II Corinthians 3,6-11; Hebrews 7,12; 8,2; 9,1
[141] John 4,23-24; Ephesians 5,26-32; II Peter 3,14
[142] John 5,39
[143] John 17,17-23
[144] I Corinthians 3,3; I Timothy 6,3-5; Titus 3,3
[145] Isaiah 53,3-12
[146] Isaiah 52,6-7; 61,1-2

[147] Psalm 22,16-18; Ephesians 1,3-9; I Peter 1,20

[148] Psalm 16,10; 89,18-29; Colossians 1,18

[149] Isaiah 25,7-9

[150] Mathew 16,16-17; John 20,26-29

[151] Isaiah 9,6-7; Micah 5,2

[152] John 1,18; Hebrews 1,1-4; I John 5,20

[153] John 21,24-25; Hebrews 2,3-8

[154] I Corinthians 12,4-11; Ephesians 4,11-12

[155] Romans 8, 29; Colossians 1, 15&18

[156] Hebrews 5,9; Revelation 1,5

[157] I Corinthians 15,20-26

[158] Hebrews 2,9-16

[159] Isaiah 45,11

[160] John 5,24

[161] Romans 8,13-16; Galatians 4,6-7

[162] Mathew 5,8; Hebrews 12,1& 22-24

[163] Hebrews 12,9

[164] Jeremiah 17,13; John 1,12; 4,14; 7,37-38

[165] Psalm 46,4; Isaiah 12,3; 49,10

[166] Exodus 31,13-17; Hebrews 10,25

[167] Isaiah 53,6

[168] Isaiah 44,3-4; 55,1-4

[169] Psalm 34,8

[170] Mathew 6,19-20; John 6,26-27

[171] II Timothy 3,16-17; 4,1-2

[172] II Peter 1,19-21

[173] Mark 9,31; 10,33-34; Acts 26,22-23

[174] John 1,5; 15,22-25

[175] Mathew 6,24; Luke 16,13

[176] Psalm 37,23; Luke 18,19; John 14,6

[177] Isaiah 30,21; 64,8; John 1,9

[178] Revelation 6,2

[179] Mathew 24,7; Mark 13,8; Luke 21,10

[180] Philippians 2,13; Galatians 2,20

[181] Deuteronomy 32,1-3; Psalm 68,11

[182] I Corinthians 3,7-9

[183] Deuteronomy 32,47; Mathew 18,20

Chapter Five
OPENING OF THE SECOND SEAL
THE RED HORSE

"When he opened the second seal, there went out another horse that was red: power was given to him who sat thereon to take peace from earth that they should kill one another, and he was given a great sword." Revelation 6,3-4

Civilization stands at the most dangerous period in its history and as of the 9/11 tragedy that took place on American soil in September of 2001, we may have entered an apocalyptic world war clearly defined in Scripture. This battle relates to the great sword of the second seal that takes peace from the earth and must be considered with a global rather than regional perspective. It is still the first stage in the beginning of sorrows described in Jesus' gospel, but this sword starts perilous times of the last days predicted by St. Paul resulting from men of corrupt minds whose folly shall be manifest.[1]

Although what can appropriately be called WWIII is only one of two great biblical wars remaining before the end time, we should realize its unmatched capacity for much destruction and have no delusions about our ability to stop it. Since so many people think of a third world war with a morbid concept of total doom in which we are all going to die, it is important to set the record straight with respect to its true relevance. This chapter does not minimize the impact of nuclear war nor suppress an urgent need for prayer and penance, but we must know the proper alignment of prophetic affairs.

For those of Christian faith and anyone disposed to truth, this time of bloodshed can be likened to a crash course in spirituality and in justice. The surprise of 9/11 prompted a reality check for a lot of people who woke up to the fact it reflected an act of war by an ingenious enemy whose overall identity we could not readily see. From its inception, the 9/11 attack on the World Trade Center and the U. S. government had a military strategy to disrupt economic stability, divide the nations and enlist a worldwide army to conquer the earth. Effects of this mischievous and organized plan increase day by day.

In this critical moment we have to take our faith seriously and recognize the signs of Jesus' gospel that are being revealed in present events. We are being tested with a severe trial to educate us toward sincere practice of our faith and spiritual humility to realize that our jeopardy is due to a regression of morality and denial of God. The real battlefield is in our hearts and unless we look inward to the cause of our misery, no amount of wealth, technology or military superiority will save us. We cannot put our destiny in our own hands and continue to profane the divine word and sacred covenant in Christ.

Strangely enough many Americans cried out in prayer to God after the 9/11 disaster, but this enthusiasm soon faded and reverted to a state of denial regarding our national security. Countries around the world incurred loss of life and economy from 9/11 and have since been victims of violent acts. The strength of terrorist cells has grown as like minded factions of this abhorrent ideology increase in number, draw together, harden resolve, acquire financing and build their arsenal. A major question for many societies is if they should seek isolation, join the revolt or engage this enemy in war.

Politicians and news media commentators have been grappling to analyze what kind of war we are involved in and how to define its bounds. Some have suggested that it is a clash of civilizations and others label it as a religious war of Moslems against Christians, while still others call it a battle against civilization itself. Disparity between cultures and religions as reasons for this war is misleading because these entities are inherently diverse. The thought of nihilism as a basis for terrorism is applicable since there are no social or political limits to this radical brand of ideology for society.

Attempts to diagnose the ongoing terrorist war require a determination of who is the enemy behind this battle and how to treat this disturbing problem. Are those responsible for violence really who they say they are and is there any room to negotiate a peaceful settlement? Some have used the terms radicals or extremists to describe various groups assembled as an Islamic jihad because other Moslems do not agree with their plans. A definite split exists in Islam that crosses all sectarian and national lines with respect to Islamic principles, methods of governing and interaction with other cultures.

Making the distinction between extremist and moderate Islamic camps is crucial since most Moslems want to live in peace, yet are often subjected to forms of injustice as well as bitter sectarian conflicts and civil wars in their own countries that have nothing to do with the outside influence of other nations. Many Moslems enjoy freedoms, economic opportunity and acceptance in western societies they cannot find elsewhere. Islamic forums have repeatedly denounced terrorism, affirmed the rights of life and religious freedom and advocated cultural harmony in the absence of prejudice.

Moslem peoples like those of other faiths cannot be stereotyped into a philosophical class. All human beings have a conscience to interpret the meaning of social values, morality and ideology. We have the innate ability to determine vain hypocrisy where it applies to falsehood. Moslems as a whole do not accept the indiscriminate slaughter by terrorists that is often directed at their own people and religious mosques. They can see what is done in the name of holy war is a pretense for power and greed. This battle is not against Islam, but it is against a tyranny void of good will and justice.

As some observers point out, the terrorist agenda of today parallels the fascism of Nazi Germany. Many similarities can be drawn from the conditions that led to WWII, but its basis is in the pride and corruption of men who proclaim a liberty they cannot find. Instead they are captive to their own lusts that have no limits or equity and can never be satisfied. We cannot play God, nor can we obtain peace and security by oppression for *"if you have bitter envying and strife in your hearts, lie not against the truth. This wisdom descends not from above, but it is earthly, sensual, devilish."[2]*

Deception runs deep for those who think they are part of an army of the Messiah to liberate humanity. If they have any inkling to Scripture, they would realize no human army will bring God's kingdom, but the Messiah will come from heaven itself with his angelic forces to destroy evil powers and wicked works of mankind. He does not need our frail help to conquer since his power and glory far exceeds anything we can imagine. We will know the timing of his judgment since *"the heavens shall be rolled together as a scroll, and all their host shall fall down, as the leaf falls from the vine."[3]*

With respect to the last days, we should not try to put the cart before the horse or look only to the very end of things before their beginning. Signs that immediately precede the Second Advent such as asteroids falling all over the earth have no direct relation to conventional or nuclear wars. These man made conflicts will be done with by the time of God's full wrath in the form of unsurpassed natural disorders and final judgment. In the meantime, we ask *"Why do wars and quarrels come among you? You lust, and have not, because you ask amiss, that you may consume it upon your passions."[4]*

Extremists who proceed in the name of Islamic jihad fail to admit the Messiah's place against an evil world ruled by the Antichrist and ignore the spiritual meaning of jihad in relation to the inner struggle of all mankind against our own iniquity. There are both practical and celestial aspects in the fallacy of their intentions in interpreting the oracles of God since *"solid food is for the mature, for those who by practice have their faculties trained to discern good and evil."[5]* Darkness cannot overcome the light of divine truth, but that light shines in contrast to the sphere of iniquity and deception.

Decisions about what is right and wrong for anyone who is mentally capable would seem to be an easy and obvious process, but the function of our inner spirit whereby we can know the goodwill of God has everything to do with our perception. When we allow our own intellect and passions to govern our lives, we become conscious of only what we want to see and our hearts follow after deception. We can never grasp the word of God if we pick and choose only those things that spuriously support our contrived claims. Without honesty and humility how can we expect to know his will?

Eminent dangers threatening the world result from the perplexing breakdown in ethics that is so pervasive in all our societies. Far more innocent blood is now being shed daily by the legalized atrocity of abortion than what is being lost by terrorism. This grave sin is only one of many that plaques us in the balance of divine justice. Some of our highest political, judicial and religious minds are perverting our laws, yet are aloof to the adverse nature and repercussions of their policies as *"they speak vanity, with flattering lips and with a double heart do they speak."[6]* Civil liberty does not abrogate divine law.

Our real deficiency is not in a better army or more military hardware, but it is in our hearts to see and follow after truth. The paradox of our souls is captivity in the lusts of our flesh and the need to be free by forgiveness from God for *"there is one lawgiver, who is able to save and to destroy."* We have put many strange gods before him and often taken his name in vain yet *"Humble yourselves in the sight of the Lord, and he shall lift you up."[7]* We do not have any other logical choice so *"Woe unto them that call evil good and good evil, who put darkness for light, and light for darkness."[8]*

How many blame their ill fortunes on someone else and don't accept responsibility for our afflictions in ourselves? The guilt that leads to wars has to be shared by opposing enemies, but we must be objective with respect to terrorism. Should the U.S. have taken the damage of 9/11 as a slap on the face and then turned the other cheek to invite another slap? Jesus taught *"if the Goodman of the house had known in what watch the thief would come, he would have watched, and would not have suffered his house to be broken into."[9]* This ordinary principle concerns practical and spiritual defense.

Difference of right and wrong applies to morality, but it involves social justice and the reproach of war to safeguard our public welfare. We cannot avoid bloodshed by passive detachment as *"are you unworthy to judge the things that pertain to this life?"[10]* Scripture instructs to *"Open your mouth for the rights of the destitute, decree what is just, defend the needy and the poor."[11]* Jesus likewise observed *"Why even of yourselves judge you not what is right?"[12]* They knew not God for he said *"as I hear, I judge, and my judgment is just, because I seek the will of the Father who sent me."[13]*

There comes a point when the unseen spiritual war between good and evil angelic forces breaks through the veil of our physical reality. We must deal with it on the surface of that reality and most often we only then realize the urgency to pray in humility for divine assistance. St. John saw this vision of an angelic war *"and Satan, who deceives the whole world, was cast into the earth, and his angels cast out with him."*[14] What is happening on earth is demonic and we should know *"if we would judge ourselves, we should not be judged. But when we are judged, we are chastened of the Lord."*[15]

This is not a season to be complacent about everything as if we are mere spectators in a game. The war we are in is not subject to our fancy but of God who *"confirms the word of his servant, and performs the counsel of his messengers."*[16] We must heed these warnings as *"Hear, and give ear: be not proud: Give glory to the Lord your God, before he cause darkness, and before your feet stumble upon the dark mountains, and while you look for light, he turns it into the shadow of death and makes it gross darkness."*[17] Of his counsel, *"Be you not as the horse, or as the mule, that has no understanding."*[18]

People in general don't want to change their ways, nor do they want to think about things that will disrupt their comfort zone. They usually take a position of extremes by either denying the reality around them thinking injury will never reach them or claim that nothing can be done to change it so they go on with their apathy. Yet in daily facing the absence of peace and lack of sound discourse, most of us are forced to ask why so much grief is being felt and to look for solutions. We must be sober to analyze our conditions and not lose heart in our ability to secure some measure of divine mercy.

One of the most puzzling aspects of Scripture is *"Who will hearken and hear for the time to come?"*[19] It is not as though God has no effect like he was talking to the wind for *"I will instruct you and teach you in the way which you shall go. I will guide you with my eye."* In this wise, *"The eyes of the Lord are upon the righteous, and his ears open to their cry."*[20] There is a positive side of the bible as *"Your word is a lamp unto my feet, and a light unto my path. Teach me, O Lord, the way of your statutes, and I will keep it unto the end: many shall see it, and fear, and shall trust in the Lord."*[21]

After divine law was written in stone, Moses said *"it is not hidden from you, neither is it far off. But the word is very nigh unto you, in your mouth, and in your hearts, that you may do it."*[22] Of prophecy Jesus also taught *"I have told you before it comes to pass, that when it is come to pass, you may believe."*[23] God will reveal the events that are and are to come in the last days since *"I will bring the blind by a way that they knew not, I will lead them in paths that they have not known: I will make darkness light before them, and crooked things straight. These things will I do, and not forsake them."*[24]

Who are the blind that God will teach or how can the blind be led to see which way to walk? Jesus rebuked *"For judgment I am come into this world, that they which see might not see; and they which see might be made blind."* This saying pertains to egoism and its deception, but he told of a different blindness to that self so we have faith and receive grace from above since *"If you were blind, you would have no sin. But now you say, 'we see', your sin remains."*[25] We must be blind to our human ability because *"Who is blind, but my servant? I am the Lord, and my glory will I not give to another."*[26]

Great hope is given for the last days albeit in times of judgment for *"Behold, the former things are come to pass, and new things do I declare: before they spring forth I tell you of them."* The gist here is that the end times will be revealed before these things fully transpire since *"The Lord shall go forth as a mighty man, as a man of war shall he stir up zeal: he shall cry, yea, roar; he shall prevail against his enemies."* It is in this context of prophecy spread to the ends of the earth we are given a new song and praise to the rock of our salvation: *"let them shout from the top of the mountains."*[27]

Many of us tremble when we envision the end of the world, but we need to trust in God through the present sorrow and dispel confusion that his final wrath is now upon us. The only thing we have to fear is sin for if our hearts are pure before him, then all suffering and even death become pale in light of divine love and assurance of eternal life. It is written *"The great day of the Lord is near, it is near, and hastens greatly, even the voice of the day of the Lord."*[28] This verse denotes a separation in times of nearness and our focus in these seasons of watches is directed at the Lord's voice.

Do we need to see the heavens opened in a vision of the throne of God, behold a bodily form of the Holy Spirit and literally hear our Creator's voice or that of a prophet appearing from the dead? Does Jesus have to physically prove to each of us he rose from the dead? These kinds of visible signs have been witnessed in the past, yet many refused to believe who have deceived a myriad of souls to reject the atonement of Christ.[29] No one can restrict the intervention of God or the miraculous gifts he bestows on his children, but his voice remains clearly manifest to us in Scripture.

It may be hard to grasp but there is an appointed time for the revelation of end times prophecy as *"The Lord gave the word: great was the company of those who published it. You, O God, did send a plentiful rain, whereby you did confirm your inheritance, when it was weary. To him that rides upon the heavens of heavens, he does send out his voice, and that a mighty voice."*[30] This horn of the divine plan is global for *"The voice of the Lord is upon the waters, the God of glory thunders. The voice of the Lord divides the flames of fire, and in his temple does everyone speak of his glory."*[31]

Let us have no doubt about God's desire to unveil the Apocalypse to us as a means of conversion with the hope of redemption since *"the glory of the Lord shall be revealed, and all flesh together shall see that the mouth of the Lord has spoken."* He gives power to those who confess their iniquity, amend their ways and submit to his providence for *"He shall feed his flock like a shepherd, he shall gather the lambs with his arm, and carry them in his bosom."* We must know *"the Lord will come with a strong hand, and his arm shall rule, his reward is with him, and his work before him."*[32]

An awesome response awaits the message of biblical prophecy as Job's heart trembled and leaped when he taught *"Hear attentively to the noise of his voice, and the sound that goes out of his mouth. He directs it under the whole heaven, and his lightning unto the ends of the earth. After it a voice roars: he thunders with the voice of his excellency, and he will not stay them when his voice is heard. He seals up the hand of every man; that all men may know his work."*[33] This vision speaks of the noise and the sound of his voice to resound through the ends of the earth so we might understand the divine plan.

We have sought, but not found the true meaning of end things as these matters were hidden until they have now become pressing in our reality. The world stands open to the bible and in many respects is desperate for the voice of God, whether it is for mercy, for correction or for a greater design than we can offer to achieve peace and justice. Of our corrupt morality or ability to govern without God *"All nations are counted to him as nothing and vanity. Who has directed the Spirit of the Lord or has been his counselor? To whom have you likened God or what image will you compare to him?"*[34]

Are we so foolish to think that God does not see or judge our evil ways for *"when will you be wise? He who formed the eye, shall he not see? Shall he who instructs nations not correct?"*[35] Many look for a sign to believe and even the faithful seek a miracle to overcome severe obstacles to evangelization. There are a variety of gifts from the Holy

Spirit, but the ones most needed today are in the wisdom, knowledge and sovereignty of God. We must open ourselves to these graces in relation to his prognostic word to find our roots and what manner of fruit we bear for we are judged by those doings.

In all simplicity, the fear of the Lord is to hate evil and embrace his truth for *"the Lord gives wisdom: she is a tree of life to those who grasp her, then you will understand rectitude and justice, and equity; yea, every good path, saving you from the way of evil men, who rejoice in perversity."* Wisdom was given to holy people in all ages, but now points to reform from an ominous waking as *"Wisdom cries aloud in the street, down the crowded ways she calls out, at the city gates she utters her words: Turn you at my reproof, behold I will pour out my spirit upon you, I will make known my words."*[36]

Before the full force of WWIII, what appears as a great act of God's love in our affairs relates to the principle that *"where sin abounded, grace did much more abound."*[37] He wants to dispel confusion and trepidation about the end times so we can face these things with courage whereby our trust in him gives peace that passes human intellect and endures all things. That kind of understanding is of our heart to lead us in a union with him that has no end. By discerning and keeping his saving grace in the midst of all this treachery *"we are more than conquerors through him that loved us."*[38]

Miracles of healings that Jesus performed were intended to induce the divine power of conversion that brings life and peace to all who accept it. He had compassion for our physical infirmities, but was more concerned about the sickness of our spirit. When he healed a severely crippled man, he said *"you are made whole: sin no more, lest a worse thing come unto you."*[39] No fate is worse than damnation and for that reason he taught *"he who believes in me, the works that I do he will do also, and greater works than these shall he do."*[40] Our highest calling is to reveal all truth in his salvation.

Going forth of the Lord's voice is itself a prophecy to open our minds and hearts to the realities of his word as *"I will open rivers in high places, and fountains in the midst of valleys: I will make the wilderness a pool of water and the dry land springs of water."*[41] This great outreach of revival is directed by the Lord in his spirit for *"Fear not, for I am with you: I will bring your seed from the east, and gather them from the west, I will say to the north, Give up, and to the south, Keep not back, bring my sons from far, and my daughters from the ends of the earth, even every one that is called by my name."*[42]

That which began about two thousand years ago on Pentecost, when God's spirit came upon Jesus' disciples in tongues of fire, has come to a stage of maturity among Gentiles. The fullness of grace has yet to be imparted in a segment of Jews and will not reach its completion until after the Second Advent as *"I will pour out my spirit upon all flesh."*[43] In the interim times, there will be severe trials of world wars and then great tribulation in the order of nature. Everyone who is called to Christ must live in the path of faith by keeping his word and to that noble testimony we must all bear witness.

Given billions of people who now live on earth and the instant technology of media sources, prediction of a worldwide move to restore human hearts to God by his prophetic word would seem unprecedented in scope for he said *"Bring forth the blind that have eyes, and the deaf that have ears. Let all nations be gathered together and let the people be assembled: who among them can declare this, and show us former things? Let them bring forth their witnesses, that they may be justified; let them hear and say, It is truth."*[44] This work will cross language barriers and challenge global journalism.

77

Usage of the word former in Scripture needs to be considered in its context since this reference to matters of prophecy describes the future as if it were written in history. God is all knowing and in his mind *"As I have thought, so shall it come to pass. I have spoken it, I will also bring it to pass; I have purposed it, I also will do it."*[45] He wants us to inquire of these things and moreover for us to *"Produce your cause, bring forth your strong reasons: Let them show the former things, what they be, that we may consider them, and know the latter end of them, and declare us things for to come."*[46]

Of the time when God would reveal his prophetic word Jesus said *"If he called them gods, unto whom the word of God came, why say you of him whom the Father sanctified, and sent into this world, you blaspheme?"*[47] The idea of being a god is in our ability to judge for *"the Lord God said, Behold the man is become as one of us, to know good and evil."* We are created in God's image with an inner spirit, but by sin that spirit dies an enduring death beyond the grave. Only he can give life as *"he deals with you as sons, but if you are without discipline, then you are bastards and not sons."*[48]

Flesh is created out of dust and to dust it shall return for *"God judges among the gods. How long will you judge unjustly? I have said you are gods, but you shall die like men, and fall like one of the princes."* The wicked will die like all do, but their evil spirit will perish in damnation as the memory of kings is not forgotten in history. We should consider recompense of evil in this life as even now *"all the foundations of the earth are out of course"*, but we must also give an account of our soul that passes on into eternal life or death for *"Shall we not much more obey the Father of spirits and live?"*[49]

Mankind was given dominion over the earth and it is God's desire that we replenish it, but we have caused problems like pollution, global warming and much bloodshed. We let creation become the object of idolatry whereby it rules us in the consumption of our lusts. Law and order are quickly being lost because we reject the divine life offered to us whereby we might succeed in sovereignty over our world. It is in this context we are told to *"Blow you the trumpet in Zion: the land is as the Garden of Eden before them, and behind them a desolate wilderness, yea, and nothing shall escape them."*[50]

Modern technology has improved the lives for a vast majority of the human race either directly or indirectly. Some kind of comparison could be drawn to the biblical Garden of Eden as much progress has been made in diverse industries such as medicine, housing, agriculture, transportation, energy and communication. These advances have provided comforts and luxuries in material things unknown to prior generations. Many societies have come to expect this affluence as a normal pattern of daily life and trust in science alone rather than the grace from above that imparts knowledge and sustains life.

Blessings of God on earth and in heaven are not determined by our mere creation, nor are we all his children. It is bane to deny conscience, try to redefine sin and treat him as an object of our whim. God is absolute and so is his word for it will *"Show the things that are to come hereafter, that we many know that you are gods; yea, do good, or do evil, and let us speak, and behold it together."*[51] Of these prophecies we are told *"O Zion, get you up into the high mountain; O Jerusalem, lift up your voice with strength, lift it up, be not afraid: Say to the cities of Judah, Behold your God!"*[52]

Prophets were sent in times past rising early to warn people of judgment so they might repent and receive mercy from God. Though we may not have a clear record of all who brought a voice of wisdom to our troubled world, *"Surely the Lord God will do nothing, but he reveals his secret unto his prophets."*[53] Jesus predicted *"you shall be brought *before rulers and kings for my sake, for a testimony against them."*[54] His teachings will reach their ears for *"Kings shall shut their mouths at him: for that which they had not been told shall they see, and that which they had not heard shall they consider."*[55]

God gave us the reason of conscience so he could communicate with us and he gave us his law to establish that reason for our own good, but many see this higher reason of our spirit as a source of human pride where we disavow his law and his very existence by putting ourselves above him. Reason then becomes a matter of mind drawn by lusts and blind to truth by displacing virtue with vice. From the start, death came by human desire to govern life itself in effect replacing him who gives life with self *"For covetousness is the root of all evils."*[56] This root of egoism is in deception and in death.

Would that we all be like the psalmist who wrote *"Oh how I love your law! It is my meditation all the day. My soul is continually in my hand, yet do I not forget your law. I have inclined my heart to perform your statutes always, even unto the end."*[57] Jesus said *"My sheep hear my voice"* but we are not all his sheep for *"The heart is deceitful above all things, and desperately wicked: who can know it? I the Lord search the heart, I try the reins, even to give every man according to his ways."*[58] This inner darkness blocks our ability to know our own selves unless we submit to the light of his grace.

Spiritual reason is the power to discern between good and evil since either we choose the source of life from God or follow death in the lusts of our flesh. Jesus rebuked the scribes, *"Woe unto you, hypocrites! For you shut up the kingdom of heaven, and have left undone right judgment, mercy and faith. You have taken away the key of knowledge. You serpents, brood of vipers, how can you escape the damnation of hell?"*[59] The key to truth is divine grace and it is in this faith we *"yield ourselves as those that are alive from the dead, and our members as instruments of righteous unto God."*[60]

Hypocrisy results from deceptive lusts of the flesh that offer no freedom as *"These are wells without water, they speak great swelling words of vanity. While they promise liberty, they are servants of corruption."*[61] Jesus made an analogy of wickedness to an evil tree that could not bring forth good fruit because its seed was evil. Those who bring forth bad fruit become conceited slaves of themselves for *"Cursed be the man that trusts in man, whose heart departs from the Lord."*[62] Of this seed, *"they shall not be planted; yea, they shall not be sown; yea, their stock shall not take root in the earth."*[63]

The irony of repentance is that reconciliation with God most often occurs in the midst of distress. Why do we test his patience, delay our service to him and wait till it's too late since *"then they call me, but I answer not; they seek me, but find me not, because they spurned all my reproof."*[64] As in the days of old, do we need to see the hand of God writing on a wall that we are found wanting in the balance or hear someone like Daniel say *"You have lifted up yourself against the Lord of heaven, and the God who has your breath and all your ways in his hand, you have not glorified."*[65]

No longer can we push our iniquity to the limit because we have already crossed the line for many punishments and we must seek any mercy God might grant. This grace can only come by our contrition as *"My guilt have I not hid, I said, I will confess my faults to the Lord, and you forgave the guilt of my sin."*[66] While there is still occasion to find favor with him, then *"today if you will hear his voice: Harden not your hearts. Seek you the Lord while he may be found, call upon him while he is near. In an acceptable time have I heard you, and in a day of salvation have I helped you."*[67]

An inclusive metaphor of end times prophecy is likened to the labor pangs of a woman with child whose travail ushers in the watches of redemption. The frequency and intensity of labor pangs will increase, but we must discern the separate periods of labor that will produce dire casualties. These pangs and sorrows of the church apply to apocalyptic wars while her voice of travail, anguish and woe plead for mercy in the appointed times of deliverance. Seasons of those periods are similar with cries for peace and security met by violence and then sudden perilous destruction.

Analogy of this travail applies specifically to references in the prophets that relate to the captivity of Israel in WWIV, yet with general respect to the three watches *"Like as a woman with child who draws near the time of her delivery is in pain and cries out in her pangs, so have we been in your sight, O Lord. The wicked will not behold the majesty of the Lord when your hand is lifted up. They shall see and be ashamed for their envy at your people. When your judgments are in the earth, the inhabitants of the world will learn righteousness."[68]* These judgments are plural and involve global wars.

True significance of Zionism is trust in God and his Son whose throne is in heaven for he said *"I have set my king upon my holy hill of Zion, and I will give him the nations for an inheritance and the ends of the earth for his possession. Be wise, O kings, take warning, you rulers, lest you perish when his anger blazes suddenly."[69]* The curses of war have a double timeframe in what Jesus described as the beginning of sorrows.[70] Those who forsake Christ will be counted among the wicked for *"such as turn aside to crooked ways, the Lord will lead them forth with the workers of iniquity."[71]*

Controversy of our Lord with the nations of earth is not only against persecutors of his people, but it is against his people themselves who have fallen away from his truth as *"Let them all be turned back that hate Zion."[72]* This hatred is against the divine life that comes from God in Christ. A fixed axiom of justice is *"the rod of the wicked shall not rest upon the lot of the righteous, lest the righteous put forth their hands unto iniquity."[73]* God rules with Christ and *"If his children forsake my law and walk not in my ordinances, then I will visit their transgression with the rod, and with stripes."[74]*

Statistics plainly show that the number of Christians who regularly attend church has drastically fallen in recent decades while the total of priests and religious is only a small fraction of what it was. Dissension from established doctrines is common and resentment against authorities who maintain these principles has grown. Many children are no longer brought up in religious schools and do not have the example from their parents to pray, keep the Sabbath and live holy lives. Spirituality has generally become a matter of vain personal opinion, not an ongoing communion with the living God.

Why do the heathen rage or where is our faith? The spreading spirit of atheism will bring ruin to our world, yet the voice of divine mercy still pleads, *"Create in me a clean heart, O God, and renew a right spirit within me. Cast me not away from your presence, and take not your holy spirit from me."[75]* To humble hearts will *"The Lord hear and strengthen you out of Zion, he will hear him from his holy heaven with the saving strength of his right hand."[76]* Security is in discovering foreseen omens since *"wisdom and knowledge shall be the stability of your times, and the strength of salvation."[77]*

Very detailed information is provided in Scripture and it would be foolish to dismiss these predictions as hearsay or maintain they have no place in our theology. Of this instruction for present and future conflicts, *"the wise man's heart discerns both times and judgments, yet it is misery for man that he is ignorant of what is to come, for who will make known to him how it will be."*[78] No one can teach anyone who is unwilling to learn, nor can sloth be of any comfort for *"when hands are lazy, the rafters sag; when hands are slack, the house leaks."*[79] Why be lax in teaching God's prophetic word?

Knowledge is in works of faith in him whom all things exist as *"the just, the wise, and their deeds are in the hand of God. Remember your Creator, before the evil days come, before the sun is darkened, the day when keepers of the house tremble and the doors to the street are shut."*[80] We need to study and understand the bible since *"To every thing there is a season, and a time to every purpose: a time to plant, and a time to uproot; a time to break down and a time to build up; a time of war and a time of peace; a time to weep, and a time to laugh, a time of silence and a time to speak."*[81]

In ancient history Abraham armed and led his servants to slay armies who plundered his family. Moses, Joshua and many just rulers of the Israelites were helped by God to defeat their enemies for *"The Lord is a man of war: your right hand, O Lord, has dashed the enemy in pieces."*[82] Prudence in war is to *"Execute judgment and justice, deliver the spoiled out of the hand of the oppressor."*[83] Further, *"Blessed be the Lord my strength who trains my hands for battle and my fingers for war. Rid me and deliver me from strangers who swear falsehood and their right hands are raised in perjury."*[84]

Revenge is vindicated by God alone, but along with great signs he acts through his people to carry out his will to help those who suffer from affliction and defend those who have fidelity toward him from harm. This is not a time to play politics with public desire for peace, nor sit back in pretext of piety while people die from acts of genocide. We cannot take both sides of the fence or sugarcoat our position on war in some fantasy that distorts our reality. Our place is to carry our own cross and have compassion for others. We certainly need to make spiritual amends, but terror threats are real.

Military reprisals against acts of war and oppression are justified in the sight of God as even now *"Awake, awake, put on strength, O arm of the Lord; awake as in the ancient days, in the generations of old. Hearken unto me, O my people: for a law shall proceed from me, and I will make my judgment to rest for a light of the nations."* This prophecy is to people of today who live in fear, but God will rise them up since *"I, even I myself, will comfort you. Fear not the reproach of men, and be not afraid of their blasphemies. Have you not struck the proud one, and wounded the dragon?"*[85]

When the baby Jesus was brought into the temple to dedicate him to God by custom of the law, a prophet then spoke *"Behold, this child is a sign that shall be contradicted."*[86] Rejection of Christ is the heart of indignation in divine justice and *"when the enemy shall come in like a flood, the Spirit of the Lord shall lift up a standard against him."*[87] This banner concerns the power of Christ for *"Behold, your Savior comes, his reward is with him, and his work before him. Go through, go through the gates, prepare the way of the people, make plain, extol the highway, pick out the stones, lift up the standard."*[88]

The sign we are to lift up is the Mother of God, the ark of salvation and Queen of Heaven.[89] She is the apocalyptic sign of hope, refuge, light and power over evil. What standard could be more complete than she who first felt the heartbeat of immortal life and brought forth Emmanuel, the Incarnate Word meaning God with us? She is the Lord's right hand of his heavenly host and as his handmaid she represents the gates we enter and highway we travel to rapture in heaven. We must remove the obstacles, be ready for this reward and join her passion with him as *"your own soul a sword shall pierce."*[90]

Our Lady shares the joy of salvation for those who abide in Christ, but she is united also with them in persecution as *"The sorrows of death compassed me, and the pains of hell seized upon me. I will take the cup of salvation and call upon the name of the Lord. O Lord, truly I am your servant, and the son of your handmaid."*[91] God helped ancient Jews by angelic miracles and he would do so now for those who attend to his word. Our Lady is a great warrior for *"Gird your sword upon your thigh, O mighty one! In your majesty ride on triumphant in the cause of truth and for the sake of justice."*[92]

Long ago, Joshua led the Jews to victory because he obeyed the command to *"Keep this Book of the Law on your lips, observe carefully all that is written in it, then you will make your way prosperous."*[93] Fortitude we need is in the rosary and the Eucharist for *"Give unto the Lord the glory due unto his name, show forth his salvation from day to day, strength and beauty are in his sanctuary."*[94] It is here in the daily Liturgy of the Mass that *"though war should rise against me, in this will I be confident, that I may dwell in the house of the Lord, and my head shall be lifted up above my enemies."*[95]

Nations are being brought into the biblical lines of great battle expressed in the second seal. Since the fall of Soviet communism and the carnage of 9/11, there are some aspects of prophecy about WWIII that have already or are now being fulfilled. This scenario is of the present tense and what is speculative in narration of military ventures when written may have happened by the time of readership. Since we may have entered this stage of turmoil, prophetic events during this period can rapidly transpire into a fully engaged world war and nobody can determine that exact timing of divine providence.

Relative calm in global peace will change quickly since biblical passages point to a sudden peril of wars before the end. Once the sword is fully drawn out, it is a moot question to curb God's anger. Unless we admit and change the moral errors of society, its foundation will crumble under the weight of sin. We have no true conscience or sanity if we cannot even discern the gross evils of abortion and homosexuality as well as other insults to our dignity. The penitent message of Scripture to turn from iniquity for the favor of divine mercy or incur curses for apostasy does not change.

Efforts toward diplomacy have been vigorously sought on multiple fronts to achieve lasting treaties to stop confrontations before they begin or end them. It would be ideal if peace could be reached by dialogue, but experience has taught that this tactic only delays more bloodshed while terrorist bands rearm and regroup. There is little or no hope for compromise with radical Islamic militants whose propaganda instills hatred and hostility against Israel, its allies and any nation that does not conform to their agenda. This ideology seeks to dominate all cultures by an oppressive form of Islamic state.

Objectives of misled radicals are more than an assault on western societies since these extremists have infiltrated many countries including moderate Moslem regimes in order to overthrow their governments. There is a conflict occurring within Moslem states that raises the question of who is the real occupation. This perplexity only adds to sectarian battles between Sunni and Shiite Moslems. Some political and clerical Islamic leaders see terrorists as crusaders against their rule and have disgraced them as apostates who falsely come in the name of God to kill, imprison and displace their own sheep.

Calls for conciliation, order and truces have fallen on deaf ears while deep internal military struggles continue among Moslems to fight terror along with international forces. The strategy of radical jihad to recruit the whole Moslem world to join in this scheme has failed as *"they that plow iniquity, and sow wickedness, reap the same."*[96] Most Islamic authorities are not willing to give up their sovereignty, prosperity and values to an enemy they view as hypocrites. The evil plan to enroll all Moslems in a war of hatred and greed has backfired for *"The heathen are sunk down in the pit they made."*[97]

If there is any solution to the problems we face, it is not in appeasement of persistent fascist forces but rather in instruction of the word of God. Our dialogue should focus on prophetic truth to refute delusions about the end times. The only recourse to mitigate the horror of nuclear war is in understanding divine will and making amends in our sinful lives. By opening our hearts to his pending justice, even radicals can recognize error, remove deception about the prophets and perceive our reality with soundness of doctrine. We need to count the costs of rejecting that wisdom from above.

Solving the puzzle of prophecy requires sorting out of biblical passages according to the signs of Jesus' gospel and thereby gain a sense of both timing and character of each unique season. Of the present, we are headed toward the period he said *"nation shall rise against nation."*[98] What becomes obvious in studying this and other stages leading to the end is that many ancient names of nations are recorded in relation to their opposing military roles. Which nations these unfamiliar names refer to in our current world is of utmost importance. Research and reason are essential in determinations.

Most people have an idea of the power of a nuclear bomb, but few realize the bible predicts this weapon of mass ruin. God instructs the seed of Abraham whom he has taken from the ends of the earth to *"be not dismayed, for I am your God: I will strengthen you, yea, I will help you; I will uphold you with the right hand of my righteousness."* Abraham's lineage in Christ is our righteousness without respect to race. It is to this faithful seed that *"Behold, I will make you a new sharp threshing instrument having teeth: you shall thresh the mountains, and shall make the hills as chaff."*[99]

Countless people wondered and asked if the event of 9/11 had any connection to the bible. This act of war reflects a prophecy by an enemy leagued to destroy the State of Israel and its allies. Psalm 83 lists a group of nations located near or adjacent to ancient Israel from which a confederacy arises within them to *"take for ourselves the dwelling place of God."* Their intent is to control Jerusalem and the Holy Land, but these motives are called an affront on God himself for *"Be not silent, O God, and be not still! For they have consulted together with one consent: they are confederate against you."*

History has not seen the occasion when such an enemy described in Psalm 83 emerged until now. This confederacy involves terrorists with a united purpose who are native to the Middle East region. They have said *"Come, let us destroy their nation so that the name of Israel be remembered no more!"* It is no secret terrorists have sought to plunder Israel and its allies as *"Against your people they plot craftily, they conspire against those you protect. For behold, your enemies raise a tumult, and they who hate you lift up the head."* This lifting up of their head was the violent act of war in 9/11.

Demands for the destruction of Israel among militant groups from surrounding areas have existed ever since this new state was created, but an organized confederacy of these extremists, especially against the U.S., was not fully apparent until the shock of 9/11. Their goal is clearly one of political power over the holy places, but the psalmist's prayer of their defeat is for the glory of God and for the conversion of sinners since *"O my God, make them like chaff before the wind, as a flame sets the mountains ablaze, let them be put to shame, and perish, that men may seek your name, O Lord."*

Ancient names of nations recorded in Psalm 83 as the central recruitment areas for this insurgency date to the 10th Century B.C. Analysis of these countries proves they existed in close proximity to Israel and also shows that not until the time of recent history has such a particular broad band of peoples allied together as their enemy. Application of this prophecy is yet present tense and these diverse nations include *"The tents of Edom, and the Ismaelites; Moab, and the Hagarenes; Gebal, and Ammon, and Amalek; the Philistines with the inhabitants of Tyre; Assur also is joined to them."*

Psalm 83 describes a confederacy whose threat goes beyond Israel itself to all who are sheltered by divine protection. This oracle of old points to an enemy of God that has global as well as regional ambitions to plan and conquer by military force. The nature of this confederacy consists of a conspiracy within a wider system of governance that aptly relates to the method used by terrorist cells in the Middle East. Ongoing conflict has divided political and religious objectives among the leaders of their own nations posing a power struggle against extremist networks that has surfaced in war torn zones.

Civil war caused by practical and ideological splits is a major factor in the overall circumstances of prophecy in quelling the rebellion of violence, but this inward unrest is also part of the divine plan to inhibit and defeat a much greater army gathered against the State of Israel and its allies in WWIII. From the start of the U.S. led war against terrorist camps in Afghanistan, local tribal leaders assisted through intelligence sharing and fought with coalition troops. The internal battle of warring fronts continues as it reflects a central biblical prediction that brother will raise his sword against brother.

While the insurgency rooted in Psalm 83 takes hold in other places of the world, the logical question after years of intense fighting is whether or not this complicated conflict will develop into a much broader and more deadly war. There is strong evidence of the resilience of radical forces to rebound from routs or setbacks in any places of warfare so what end or exit strategy is in sight? Can this enemy be stopped before their expansion grows into a global war? Only time can tell if our collective conscience in civilization will heed warnings of God to reconcile with his love and life in divine law.

Control over Jerusalem is a dominant issue of diplomatic endeavors to end continuing strife, but how can Israel negotiate with those who want to annihilate it? This inherent deadlock in the peace process will at some point turn into great disaster of world war for *"Behold, I will make Jerusalem a cup of trembling unto all the people round about when they shall be in the siege both against Judah and against Jerusalem. And in that day I will make Jerusalem a burdensome stone: all that burden themselves with it shall be cut in pieces, though all people of the earth are gathered together against it."*[100]

Scholars have consistently misinterpreted this passage of Scripture as a war in which every nation will rise against Israel and have mistakenly linked it to the end of the world when the Messiah comes to establish justice and peace. The siege against Judah and Jerusalem is not only against Jews but it must be considered in a broader context of the whole church since Jesus was born of the tribe of Judah and his cities span the Christian world. Also, the Hebrew word 'gowy' for the people who gather against Jerusalem denotes a group of heathen warriors, not every Gentile nation on earth.

The most crucial element of this war is despite a great enemy *"In that day shall the Lord defend the inhabitants of Jerusalem, and he that is feeble among them at that day shall be as David; and the house of David as that of God, as an angel of the Lord in their sight."* No army can alter the providence of God to shield the Jews who will look like

David who slew Goliath and led in great conquest. Christian bond to Jews is in faith of their conversion as *"the governors of Judah shall say in their heart: Let the inhabitants of Jerusalem be strengthened for me in the Lord of hosts, their God."[101]*

Support for Israel is still strong among its allies and as the onslaught against Jerusalem and Judah develops, God explains *"I will make the governors of Judah like a hearth of fire among the wood, and they shall devour all the people round about, on the right hand and on the left: and Jerusalem shall be inhabited again in her own place."* These governors of Judah are Israel's allies as *"The Lord shall save the tents of Judah first, that the glory of the house of David and inhabitants of Jerusalem do not magnify themselves against Judah."[102]* Tents of Judah and house of David are not the same thing.

Metaphors have a major role in Scripture and it is necessary to study key phrases and their relation to the wider prophetic context. With respect to the siege against Judah and Jerusalem as including the allies of Israel, King David was of the house of Judah so how can the house of David brag that it is better than itself? This distinction then applies to the governors of Judah as plural allies of Israel joined in a fight for their own security. In the wisdom of God, Christians who watch and are ready in spirit will be saved first in rapture as a sign to Jews and Gentiles alike of the power of Christ and his word.

Victory is relative in nearly all wars as it is a matter of proportion to the damage done by opposing forces and the terms of surrender. There is no doubt that WWIII will cause untold catastrophe, but God's intent for this time is clear and firm since *"it shall come to pass in that day, that I will seek to destroy all the nations that come against Jerusalem."* Conclusive proof in this passage from Zechariah is part of a cohesive warning by other prophets of defeat to those who war against Jerusalem. The divine word does not waver as they will be cut in pieces referring both to their armies and boundaries.

Intrinsic details about an impending global war fit together in an intriguing reality of the present and future. A noteworthy prediction is *"In that day says the Lord, I will smite every horse with astonishment, and his rider with madness, and I will open my eyes upon the house of Judah."[103]* God will open his eyes for conversion of the faithful, but that conflict will be a state of bedlam as most of modern warfare depends on computer and satellite technology that will become impaired or useless. These linked networks can be destroyed by missiles or broken by computer malware and cutting cyber optic lines.

Events predicted in the bible about great wars of the last days largely revolve around whether the Jews keep or lose their returned statehood, but an obvious question in this war is what function does the U.S. military have in relation to Jews? Is this superpower named in Scripture and if so for what purpose? The answer is in identifying a repeated reference to a nation called the islands or isles whose location to the ancient world lies beyond the sea or far away.[104] We cannot ignore these citations and the U.S. is the only country that fits this location with a diverse alliance of forces to defend Israel.

Intelligible calls are made by God to the U.S. as a leader of all nations who receive his prophetic guidance for *"Keep silence before me, O Islands; and let the nations take new strength. Let them come near, and then speak, let us come near together to judgment."* This drawing of grace is to his word so he can help us overcome an evil threat to the structure and very soul of our civilization. He speaks to all nations who will hear as *"The isles saw it, and feared; the ends of the earth were astonished, they drew near, and came. They helped everyone his brother, and said: Be of good courage."[105]*

Jews have returned to their ancient homeland not by chance, but their survival through severe hardships over many centuries to come back is due to the divine plan of the bible. Similar to ancient history, they have again become the center of prophecy now being revealed for the same reasons as before. In that time when pagan worship was rampant everywhere, God led the Jews out of slavery in Egypt into the Promised Land to make himself known and prove his glory above all other gods, but Jews are not his stooges since the promise to them of land and harmony with him remains undone.

Surely the Israelites were judged in the past for their iniquity and biblical predictions also show they will fall into the same fate before the Messiah comes in glory. There is no partiality in divine justice, but we must determine from the prophets what circumstances does judgment apply to the State of Israel. Those nations who recognize the design of God's word to defend the Jews in this current period will obtain wisdom and at least some protection, while those who pervert his plan will conversely find grim penalties. These matters are not subject to evasion so all should consider and do the math.

Divine intervention in the birth of Christ for our eternal salvation by his death and resurrection is an immutable fact of prophetic history. This is the crux of God's purpose for humanity as *"I, even I, am he that blots out your iniquities for my own sake, and I will not remember your sins. Put me in remembrance, and let us plead together: declare you, that you may be justified."*[106] Church history has seen much bloodshed, but of present dangers, *"I have long time held my peace: I have been still and refrained myself: now will I cry like a travailing woman: I will destroy and devour at once."*[107]

Truth in historical prophecy about Christ is that he rose from the dead and ascended back into heaven whence he came. We know from his words, confirmed by the prophets and apostles, that he will come again to rescue his servants and also save the remnant of mankind. This testimony of him who is the eternal Alpha of God's creation and firstborn of his children in resurrection now beckons us to proclaim he is also the timeless Omega of creation and that chosen seed. We must grasp intricacies of end things and realize God will destroy before he devours, but these wars are not an end to suffering.

End times lead to a transition from an old to a new reality. God is constant in time yet, *"Hearken to me, O Jacob and Israel, my called: I am he; I am the first, I am also the last. My hand also has formed the earth, and my right hand has measured the heavens: I shall call them, and they shall stand together."* This end is the joining of heaven and earth, but it is by God's hand of Christ who will come again for *"yea, I have called him, I have brought him, and he shall make his way prosperous. From the time before it was done, I was there, and now the Lord God has sent me, and his spirit."*[108]

In these times we must distinguish between the dispensation of grace upon Gentiles and Jews. Jesus explained that the first would be last and the last would be first.[109] The gospel was first preached to Jews, but seeing they rejected it, Christianity came to the Gentiles. There is a strong purpose to reveal Christ to the Jews as *"through your mercy they also may obtain mercy."* This mercy of Gentile believers is their support of Jews in war at which time a measure of grace will be complete for Gentiles in the first watch of rapture. This sign will convert many Jews who will then spread the gospel.

Elements of time and season are decisive in the course of events in the last days. The word Israel is used in the bible to describe all Christians as *"In the Lord shall all the seed of Israel be justified, and shall glory."*[110] This grouping is separated as it applies to Jew or Gentile in order to instruct and chasten since *"For Jacob my servant's sake, and Israel my elect: I have surnamed you.*" The term Jacob refers only to Jews while Israel often relates to Gentiles yet of these both "*you have wearied me with your iniquities, return to me, and I will give you hidden treasures and concealed riches.*"[111]

Regarding the place of America as a leader of allied forces in defense of Jews, "*Give ear, you islands, and hearken you people from afar: The Lord has called me from the womb. You are my servant, O Israel, in whom I will be glorified.*" This call from the spiritual womb of Our Lady is in context of war to spur partial conversion of Jews for "*It is a light thing that you should be my servant to raise up the tribes of Jacob, and to restore the preserved of Israel. He has made my mouth like a sharp sword, he protected me and made me as a chosen arrow, in his quiver he has hidden me.*"[112]

Instruction to the U.S. and its allies in this battle is plain since "*the Lord formed me to be his servant, to bring Jacob again to him. Though Israel is not gathered, yet I shall be glorious in the eyes of the Lord, and my God shall be my strength.*" This verse exhibits an obligation to the Jews and speaks of gathering the spiritual Israel in separate watches which at the time of Jewish conversion not all Christians will yet be gathered. Despite criticism of this mission "*Then I said, I have labored in vain, I have spent my strength for naught, yet my judgment is with the Lord, and work with my God.*"[113]

Political and public support for an offensive war against terror has dwindled in the U.S. and its allies because many want to isolate themselves from the threat, but "*Behold, all they that were incensed against you shall be ashamed and confounded: they shall be as nothing, and they that strive with you shall perish.*"[114] God has many faithful in the U.S. and has chosen our nation to guide others in fighting his enemies as "*the islands shall wait upon me, and in my arm shall they trust.*" The U.S. is still a Christian nation and in the overall balance among nations "*the islands are as a little dust.*"[115]

Continuing battles in Afghanistan, Iraq and in other countries against the confederacy listed in Psalm 83 reflect a smaller scale of a developing world war. Security in these battlegrounds remains fragile as unexpected resurgence in terrorist raids and bombings prolongs a fight that most leaders thought would be finished. NATO commanders in Iraq uselessly resisted calls for troop withdrawal saying any improvements are reversible and the exit strategy of soldiers deployed in Afghanistan is vulnerable to default as terrorists prepare for long range offensives in safe tribal areas of neighboring Pakistan.

Critics recognize the dangerous situation in the Middle East that is on the verge of regional war driven by extremists and sectarian divisions in Islamic nations. What military advisors have failed to see is a much more powerful enemy rising from Russia and its allies. When Soviet communism fell apart, a pervasive viewpoint emerged that the cold war was completely over and that Russia no longer posses a threat to the U.S. or its growing NATO alliance. This deception stems from enduring prejudice and short-sighted views that Russia would not recover or challenge western nations.

After the Berlin wall collapsed and former Soviet nations gained their independence, the U.S. and European countries gloated over a victory that was an act of God. Instead of welcoming a confused and fledging Russian democracy, this powerful nation has been battered with insults, pushed aside by military incursions and hindered from alliance with the West. Who would have thought after the Cuban missile crisis when many Americans cried 'Better Red than Dead' that Russia would repeatedly come to the U.S. asking for financial help only to be turned down and sent away empty handed?

Russia has been needlessly humiliated, ignored and treated as if it suddenly had lost its military might and exists in a remote corner of the earth. Jesus taught *"What man is of you, whom if his son ask bread, will you give him a stone? Therefore all that you wish men to do to you, even so do you also to them."[116]* The U.S. has stifled opportunities to build a partnership with Russia and obvious rifts have tested any real trust these nations shared. Money talks and when the U.S. invaded Iraq, what happened to the billions of dollars of debt Iraq owed to Russia and its huge oil contracts with Russia?

Ignorance, pride and isolation in U.S. relations with Russia have renewed antagonistic Cold War attitudes of the past. The exclusion of Russia from monetary foreign aid at a period of critical need and failure to cooperate in military actions against genocide in places like Croatia, Bosnia-Herzegovina and Kosovo have costly repercussions that our policymakers did not consider. This unilateral approach to world problems and disregard for Russia as a fallen foe rather than a new found friend were diplomatic errors largely seen by critics as a struggle for supremacy, not a humanitarian act of charity.

Compassion for and fair diplomacy with Russia has been lacking since the Soviet era ceased. As a result, the Kremlin has moved to a more centralized government and state control over its media, natural gas and oil industries. Russia has flexed economic muscle on countries that depend on it for trade exports and vital energy imports. Marxist atheism still lingers in Russia and few would deny its desire to gain control over enormous energy resources of former states. Russian leaders view U.S. military bases in Central Asia and its building of a missile defense shield in Eastern Europe as encroachment.

When the U.S. announced its initiative to place missile interceptors in Poland with a radar defense system in the Czech Republic, Russian authorities denounced the move as directed against Russia, not at Iran's nuclear activities. They claim the action violates agreements that the U.S. would not base its troops in former Soviet bloc states and in response these security installations would become targets for Russia's missile arsenal. The U.S. stifled joint oversight, began phased NATO plans including sea based capacity with radar in Turkey and more ships with land sites in Romania and in Poland.

Now that Russia has regained its economic footing and become a major player in the global energy market, it no longer must take a back seat in world politics. Beside its rank among the top producers of oil and natural gas, Moscow has secured a firm position over an expanded market that could pose a serious threat to supply and pricing, particularly for the heavily dependent European Union. The Russian people have come to a new sense of unity and support for their leaders who have improved their livelihoods and boldly shown they will use armed force to protect their national interests and guard their allies.

Patriotism grew significantly among Russians with their economic rebound, but the revival of national pride greatly solidified as a result of their crushing defeat of Georgian aggression. This resurgence of self-respect signals a new domestic spirit in Russia that it is again a big superpower able to stand up to western nations. Its disposition regrettably reflects a deeper resentment against the U.S. as a dominant threat whose push for NATO expansion and other exploits has now given it a status of suspicion. A return to the covert Cold War tactics of defense is a reality the U.S. has brought upon itself.

Unfortunately, the bottom line for Russia is readiness to exact military and economic pressure to serve or defend its security. The unexpected reversion to Soviet era hardball has firmly generated a widespread desire among Russians to expand Moscow's political influence, especially in former borderland republics whom they maintain good relations.

Either by using a financial or armed approach, it is clear that the Russians intend to shift the balance of global power in their favor. Negative opinions of American foreign policy as a bully have grown and it is no surprise they will make the most of it.

With the major assault of Georgian troops in the summer of 2008 to regain power over separatist provinces that broke from their government in the 1990's, a new tense era with NATO began as Russia responded with a swift and decisive military invasion. Georgia soon became the center of a defense and economic dispute between Russia and the West. This relatively obscure nation that borders the Black Sea north of eastern Turkey is a strategic geographical link to a land based invasion of Israel and also is a host country for a key Caspian Sea oil pipeline operated by the British from Azerbaijan.

Like Georgia, the Azerbaijani nation lies on the southwestern flank of Russia and has its own problems of conflict with neighboring Armenian separatists whom they claim are armed by Russia. These nations are critical crossroads as transit corridors for pipelines and railroads to transport energy to Europe and could provide a flashpoint for a biblical world war. The interethnic and political conflict that took place in Georgia is not to be ignored as a passing event because Russia claims the U.S. instigated the war and covertly supported the secession of Georgian regions that want integration into Russia.

Making amends with Russia over indifferent U.S. foreign policies of the past seems a debatable prospect, especially when Iran's nuclear capability poses a threat to U.S. and Israeli security. Russia has commercial and defense interests in Iran so any aggression against this strategic client would not be taken favorably. Further discussion of Iranian and Syrian concessions to the U.N. along with other hotspots of contention are made in the final chapter of my book, but a decision by the Kremlin to manipulate the terrorist agenda for material and political gain would be its worst disaster in history.

Analysis of Scripture presents a scenario of our present day reality where Russia leads its allies against Israel and its allies in a world war that ends in utter futility for Russian pursuits. These warnings constitute a very grave judgment directed at Israel's enemies in order to glorify God and protect the Jews in their homeland. This security, albeit for only a limited period or time of testing, is dependent on Jewish obedience to divine law. The main issues for Russian hostility are money and to regain regional dominance, but these motives to assert its power are against the principles and providence of God.

Connecting issues of prophecy in the bible about the sword of the second seal when nation rises against nation involves details that can be found in chapters 38 and 39 of the prophet Ezekiel. Many scholars agree that these warnings apply to Russia and its allies in warfare aimed at the destruction of Israel, but they miss the timing of this war by placing it with the final battle of Armageddon. This perception does not consider the real nature of the Second Advent, nor account for other prophetic events. These benchmarks include prior world wars that will profoundly alter our global political landscape.

The literal earth shaking prophecy of Ezekiel describes a broad group of nations by their ancient names that unite by Russian control to annihilate Israel. Logic concerning our political realities as well as geographical clues given about the movement of these armies is essential in identifying what peoples these ancient names refer to in our modern world. Ezekiel's prophecy is directed at God's communication to a ruler of Russia who will obtain supreme command over this diverse multitude as *Thus says the Lord God, Behold, I am against you O Gog, the chief prince of Meshech and Tubal."*

Apart from tracing the ancient lineage and location of the Meshech and Tubal nations, who descended from Noah's son Japheth and settled in the east Black Sea region, the important link of these ancient cultures to Russia is in prophecy for *"You shall come from your place out of the northern parts, you and many people with you. And you shall come against my people of Israel, as a cloud to cover the land: it shall be in the latter days."* These verses clearly indicate that the chief prince will come from a homeland in areas north of Israel and specify the timeframe of his invasion in the last days.

Strong rebukes are made to this Stalin-type ruler as if he knew about his doomed role in warfare, but spurned the word of God since *"Are you he of whom I have spoken in old time by my servants the prophets of Israel, who prophesied in the days of those times that I would bring you upon them?"* The prophecy focuses on the return of Jews and predicts their survival as *"in the latter years you shall come into the land that is brought back from the sword, and is gathered out of many people, against the mountains of Israel: it is brought forth out of the nations, and they shall all of them dwell securely in it."*

Admonishments to this leader of forces will prove fruitless for *"In that day projects shall enter into your heart, and you shall conceive a mischievous design. And you shall say: I will go up to the land which is without a wall, to take spoils, and lay hold on the prey, to turn your hand upon them that had been wasted and afterwards restored, which have begun to possess and to dwell in the midst of the earth."* This plot to subvert even its allies by an appeasing attack against Israel whose territory is now in dispute will fail as *"Shall you not know, in that day, when my people shall dwell safely?"*

Ezekiel's prophecy has already started in context of Jews regaining sovereignty and although the Soviet Union developed into an oppressive union of republics, God foretold *"set your face against Gog, the land of Magog. And I will turn you about, and I will put a bit in your jaws, and I will bring you forth."* Gog is a surname for the chief prince of Russia while Magog is its land boundary. Before Russia engages in war due to events such as an air strike on Iran's nuclear facilities, this nation was first to be turned around which refers to the fall of Soviet communism and loss of former states.

Several different nations are named who will align with Russia in a great company and mighty army. These are *"Persia, Ethiopia, Libya with them; Gomer and all his bands; the house of Togarmah of the north quarters and all his bands, and many peoples with you."* Persia is Iran while ancient nations of Ethiopia and Libya extended from the Horn of Africa into Sudan and into Algeria. Togarmah and Gomer who descended from Japheth settled south and west of the Black Sea and refer to Kurds and to native Cossacks in the Ukraine.[117] Many other peoples are sympathetic nations and extremists.

Besides strategic location in the north quarters of Kurds and their bands to Russia's military circle, the Kurdish people have long sought nationalism but still live in a region including parts of Turkey, Iraq, Iran and Syria. Their ambition supports the idea that they will join Russia for their own goals. Kurds have fought in eastern Turkey and northern Iraq and then in Syria for independence. Including militias of Dagestan and Armenia, this geographic area completes a route from war-torn Georgia and Chechnya to invade Israel with additional aggression from Syria, Lebanon and the Gaza Strip.

Question of the Ukrainians applying to ancient Gomer as a member of Russian forces must be answered in light of historical ties between these countries. Despite contrary aims of the Orange Revolution, eastern and southeastern provinces of Ukraine are mostly pro-Russian and these neighboring sections provide a buffer zone as well as an extended land and sea launch pad against western nations. With its own coastline and occupation of the Georgian ports of Abkhazia, the Russian Black Sea naval fleet is based in Crimea, a Ukrainian province which opted by vote to join Russia in a formal treaty.

Plans to sign an Association Agreement with the European Union were postponed by the Ukraine due to Moscow's monetary bailout and discount on gas. Security concerns grew in Kiev due to overthrow of the president and his protégés who took this package to avoid bankruptcy. Deep division in public opinion caused huge protests in a deadly tug of war that could end in ceding of more territory by politics or violence. The new regime that signed a trade pact with the EU in a prelude to membership is scoffed by many as an Orange Plague. Exclusive bilateral relations are not a road to peace.

Painful discord in the Ukraine dates back centuries to its roots in prior domains of Lithuania, Poland, Hungary, Austria and Russia. The cultural split is evident by one third of the population speaking Russian with strong reasons to look at Moscow as their main motherland. On the other side, European neighbors have a long chronicle of intermixed families considered largely as their fatherland. Seeds of biblical unrest within this huge country grows in a EU push to replicate its enlargement policy with Eastern Partnership offers to enlist more states by the promise of more commerce, jobs and loans.

Ethnic and economical bonds of a post Soviet era Iron Curtain between Russia and the West cannot be dismissed. This reality of a renewed arms race for control over energy and global political power is revealed in Scripture. The ancient people of Gomer along with their bands form a military front that extends north of the Ukraine to Belarus whose alliance to Russia is reinforced by its partnership in an oil pipeline to Europe. Russians are resolved to protect their Ukrainian friends and similar proximate districts. Warnings by Russia against further NATO expansion have proven potency to strike.

Exactly how far the Russian alliance will stretch might be partly determined by new members of its Customs Union that started with Belarus and oil-rich Kazakhstan. The southern border states of Russia geographically form a sort of bit in a horse's bridle and stand in line to join the trade bloc. It is guesswork to say what will trigger a full-scale world war, but aside from conflict with Iran, any upheaval in these nations or in Caucasia could draw military reprisal from Russia. The biblical bit in Russia's jaws that brings it into war seems to be a sudden adverse event somewhat like the attack of 9/11.

Conspicuously left out of bible prophecy about WWIII is the place of China who now ranks among the world's top industrial and military powers. This great nation is named in Scripture with its neighboring allies in the next world war, but the Chinese dilemma of choosing sides in the apocalyptic war of the second seal is a matter of trust and economic stability. How China responds to Russian plans for regional dominance or any threats to its global energy assets is an uncertainty. China has invested heavily in Kazakhstan oil fields and must consider its vital stake in commercial trade with western nations.

Although China held joint anti-terrorism military exercises and signed big natural gas contracts with Russia and also restrained U.S. efforts for UN sanctions on its energy allies in Sudan and Iran, this powerful nation must weigh the monetary and defensive consequences of yielding to Russian goals of head supremacy. The massive wealth that China has gained to finance its industrial prosperity is mostly the result of record trade surpluses with the U.S. and European Union. Without provocation by U.S. allied forces, there is little reason for China to break its economic ties by striking the West.

Issues concerning the Chinese military posture in a developing world war involve the safeguarding of China's reliance on Persian Gulf oil and the planned expansion of its transnational pipeline in Kazakhstan to pull oil directly from the Caspian Sea. There are no simple answers of whom China regards as an enemy or how much of a role it would have in a global war, but it has shown a major buildup of armed forces especially in naval strength. China's investments and military influence stretch to parts of Africa and Latin America and it will likely defend itself against rebels who want more power.

Civil wars and outbursts of terrorism are apparent in much of the mixture of nations predicted to align with Russia. Disturbances in North Africa and from Somalia to Darfur have produced great tragedies beyond the UN's capacity to stop. Piracy in trade routes off the Horn of Africa in the Gulf of Aden rose and threat in black market sale of nuclear bomb-making material is real. At a time when diplomacy turns to a Cold War mode, unity is needed among our global leaders to fix these problems and diffuse tensions in places like North Korea, Ukraine, Afghanistan, Iraq, Yemen, Syria and Gaza.

Suspicions of America's fight for freedom as an excuse for colonialism has reinforced negative feelings about U.S. allied military actions. The humanitarian crisis in varied nations has divided political and public opinion of who is to blame and how to restore order. Moscow's direct role in unfolding strife with naval, air and land bases in Syria projects its footprint in a tactical move that puts a new spin on force and leadership. This abrupt buildup of weapons and soldiers in the heart of intense rivalry shows firmness to boost its grip and coerce arbitration. Their intervention is not a training practice.

Hatred for Israel and its U.S. allied forces has certainly spread farther than the Middle East confederacy of Psalm 83. As terrorist networks solidify and connect with other nations, they are laying the foundation for a great army described in Ezekiel. Whatever instigates Russia's ruler to command Israel's enemies for a supposed tradeoff, he will lead them as *"Prepare and make yourself ready, and all your multitude that is assembled about you, and be you commander over them."* After secret operations to make a war plan with complying patrons, these nations will swear allegiance to him.

Motives of this tyranny are not to set up some kind of greater Islamic state, but they include a subversive ploy to placate extremist sentiment against Israel to obtain regional control. It is clear from prophecy that the intent is not only to take spoils, but also to take prey which means governing rule over tributaries. This evil scheme contrived with diverse generals is for raw power, not for religious or moral principles. The radical jihad forces involved in planning this unholy war will know its objectives, yet continue on a path that undermines their own people for selfish political reasons.

Notwithstanding the size, strength and composition of forces not seen in history, *"it shall come to pass at that time when Gog shall come against the land of Israel, says the Lord God, that my fury shall come up in my wrath. And I will call for a sword against him in all my mountains: every man's sword shall be against his brother."* We have seen strife in Afghanistan, Pakistan, Iraq, Lebanon, the Gaza Strip, Africa and vast regions of the so-called Arab Spring, but this force of brother against brother within the Russian alliance will create chaos and bloodshed that no one will be able to restrain.

Judgments against this anti-Israeli army are similar to ancient history when God sent his angels to curse the enemies of Jews since *"I will judge him with pestilence, and with blood, and with overflowing rain, and great hailstones: I will rain fire and brimstone on him, and on his army, and on the many nations that are with him."* God will use powers of nature, epidemic disease and the nuclear armor of men to breakdown and defeat this enemy. An atomic missile exchange between the U.S. and Russia appears inevitable for *"I will send fire on Magog, and among them that dwell carelessly in the islands."*

Devastation will overwhelm Russian forces as *"I will break your bow in your left hand, and will cause your arrows to fall out of your right hand."* God is against them for *"You shall fall upon the mountains of Israel, you and all your bands, and the nations that are with you."* In fact, *"I will give Gog a noted place for a sepulcher in Israel, and they shall call it the valley of Hamongog."* It is there that *"the house of Israel shall bury them for seven months, they shall seek out them that were remaining upon the face of the earth, that they may cleanse the land. And the name of the city shall be Hamonah."*

Following the war's end, another migration of Jews will take place from other lands to Israel. At some point during the war *"in that day there shall be a great shaking in the land of Israel, so that the fishes of the sea, and the fowls of the air, and the beasts of the field, and all men that are upon the face of the earth shall shake at my presence, and the mountains shall be thrown down, and the steep places shall fall, and every wall shall fall to the ground."* This massive destruction will suddenly affect everyone on earth and it seems to be the result of a huge earthquake, not from nuclear bombs.

Consequences of WWIII will be our world's worst nightmare and a bitter lesson of divine justice for enemies of Israel and for those who have forsaken the way of God in Christ. The purpose of God in defeating these armies is his glory *"that the nations may know me, when I shall be sanctified in you, O Gog, before their eyes. Thus will I magnify myself, and sanctify myself; and I will be known in the eyes of many nations, and they shall know that I am the Lord."* As we emerge from war *"all nations shall see my judgment that I have executed, and my hand that I have laid upon them."*

Only God could have predicted precise details of a devastating war in a correlating prophetic time when Jewish people have come back and begun to possess their homeland. We should know that all nations will see both his judgment and his hand in this battle which applies to the defense of Israel and rapture in the first watch. These are separate but closely connected matters. The comprehensive nature of Ezekiel's prophecy does not end with WWIII, but extends to Christian conversion among Jews, their acquisition of great spoils, their ensuing captivity and final return from enemy lands.

Future events beyond this war are described in the bible and discussed in subsequent chapters, but the passage in Ezekiel about Russia and its allies states Jews *"shall make a prey of them whom they had been a prey, and they shall rob those who robbed them."* They will know God gave victory for *"I will make my holy name known in the midst of Israel: and I will not let them pollute my holy name any more."* After the Jews gain prosperity and fall into sin, *"All nations shall know that the house of Israel was made captive for their iniquity, and I gave them into the hands of their enemies."*

Similar to ancient history, Jews will forsake God and he will abandon them since *"I have dealt with them according to their uncleanness and wickedness, and hid my face from them. Now will I bring again the captivity of Jacob, and will have mercy upon the whole house of Israel."* The key word for a second captivity is again, but God will have mercy and fulfill the promise of inheritance for Jews *"After they have borne their shame, when I have brought them again out of their enemies lands, then I will hide my face no more from them, for I have poured my spirit on the house of Israel."*

Information given in Ezekiel after WWIII points to security for Jews *"When they dwelt safely in their land, and none made them afraid."* Material desires rather than spiritual wealth will result in their captivity. God's justice is equal, but his promises are sure and the Messiah will restore the ruins of this kingdom and of all nations left on earth. The timeframe of these things is within the span that Jesus said *"This generation shall not pass, till all these things are fulfilled."*[118] Despite parallels for Jews of the ancient past and the present, God is not now going to plead with them for centuries.

Counterparts of biblical passages relating to the present threat of global war show an affiliation of Iran with the Russian alliance in Ezekiel. This link together with Iranian ties to the confederacy of Psalm 83 place Iran in the middle of a regional and world conflict. Thus, hostility against Iran or conversely their aggression toward Israel and its allies seems to be a major factor in fomenting an all-out cataclysm. Iran's hostile stance against Israel is well known and its ambition to expand regional power is of great concern to other regimes in the area. Diplomacy has resulted in repeated failure.

Proliferation of nuclear weapons endures despite efforts to halt the number of nations known to possess this kind of arsenal. With respect to Iran's vigorous nuclear program, negotiations aim to restrict and monitor its capabilities in exchange for lifting sanctions. The main concern of the U.N. is to insure its technology is used for civilian purposes. If Iran develops a nuclear bomb or else invites military retaliation from the ranks of highly armed Arabic rivals and from Israel who would confront any threats to their security, the attack on Iran's military and nuclear facilities could spiral into world war.

Clues provided in Ezekiel indicate widespread anarchy due to brother against brother, but also name surrounding Middle East nations who are threatened by invading armies with Russia for *"Sheba, and Dedan, and merchants of Tarshish, with all the young lions thereof, shall say unto you, Are you come to take spoil? Behold, you have gathered your multitude to take prey, to take silver, and gold and to carry away goods and substance, and to take rich spoils."* These nations form a strategic and formidable force as danger comes upon them. They include Turks who stand against separatism of Kurds.

Persian Gulf sheikdoms of the oil-rich Arabian Peninsula have much to loose in a war aimed at control over global energy demand and dominion over power producing nations. The extreme luxury of these countries primarily comes from consumers in America, Asia and Europe. They are known as the Gulf Cooperation Council and contain Saudi Arabia, Kuwait, Bahrain, Qatar, the United Arab Emirates and Oman. Their location in the Gulf region provides a hedge from Russian forces in Africa while a large Saudi-led military coalition embracing Egypt and Jordan unified to confront hazards from Yemen.

Close-minded views regarding terrorism can only increase abusive resolve for more intense attacks to create chaos and separate our civil authorities. The extensive financial failings of banking and business brought a global confidence factor that applies to the fight against terror, not only to economy. Many have become discouraged as if they are boxed in a no win situation. There is a pervasive lack of hope giving way to ambivalence toward acts of injustice and reports of corruption. Retrenchment in troop withdrawal and problems of risky diplomacy open a power vacuum to further oppression.

For the most part, American people have not understood the Iraqi war and are caught in an isolationist deception that we can retreat from the Middle East without incurring greater harm. The prior dictator of Iraq proved his ruthless ambition to extend power by military incursions, financing terrorism against Israel and building an army to conquer

Jerusalem. If the Iraqi government falls prey to Iranian and terrorist interests, it would become more powerful than before. Iraq is not another Vietnam, but it is a symptom of another world war. We must grasp this threat and prepare ourselves.

Orders for a hurried retreat of armed forces from Iraq by the U.S. administration fail to calculate depths and scope of terrorism. Both Iraqi and U.S. officials wanted to end the tragic bloody saga of freedom from dictatorship, but the withdrawal of foreign troops and transfer of security to Iraq does not insure any civil liberty already won. Arbitrary measures with little flexibility are superficial and they can defeat their purpose. Radical groups still based within or outside Iraq have consistently defied its army, police and government in a determined effort to cash in on vast oil reserves.

Education is sorely needed on all sides about the magnitude of this war since *"The revelation of your words sheds light; it gives understanding to the simple."* The answers are in Scripture for *"It is time for you, Lord, to work: for they have made void your law."* That divine work is to reveal his word and fulfill his judgments. Many of us are guilty of failing to love God and to love our neighbor as our self. This pride and selfishness has brought us to the grave problems we face as *"Rivers of water run down my eyes, because they kept not your law."[119]* Seeing truth can lessen danger of false hopes.

Human suffering reached pathetic levels in most of Iraq displaying a violent mixture of brothers killing their own brothers. Who is responsible for this disgusting slaughter of innocent people who rejoiced over the toppling of a tyrant and were happy to vote for officials of a new government? The U.S. had no intention to occupy Iraq and would have left sooner if not for a terrorist insurgency whose sole aim is power. Their devious plans are being found out, derided and repulsed by their brethren who see their false piety since *"so they shall make their own tongue to fall upon themselves."[120]*

Internal discord is a critical warning to those who vainly seek their own profit as *"The wicked have drawn out the sword, and have bent their bow, but their sword shall pierce their own hearts, and their bows shall be broken."[121]* What began with 9/11 has become a sinister rally for global power driven by the idea of holy war yet *"O God, the proud are risen against me, and the assemblies of violent men have sought my soul, and have not set you before them."[122]* It is the Lord who *"frustrates the tokens of liars, makes diviners mad, turns wise men backward, and makes their knowledge foolish."[123]*

Waning conviction of NATO leaders in fighting this war due to casualties and funding is sending a strong message of defeat among its enemies. This weakness has caused a loss of credibility that is a swaying factor in the spread of terrorism since *"my enemies speak against me, and take counsel together saying, God has forsaken him: pursue and seize him, for there is none to rescue him."[124]* These designs suggest a rise of aggression as also *"My ravenous enemies beset me; their steps even now surround me, crouching to the ground, they fix their gaze, like young lions lurking in hiding."[125]*

Proficient onslaughts of hostility have demonstrated the skill and reach of an evil force intent on the breakdown of U.S. allied nations. Major damage occurred in a brazen attack on India's financial center to disrupt its foreign trade ties and renew rivalry between nuclear armed states of India and Pakistan. Small cells of militants have caused deadly carnage in Europe while new recruits within the West are enlisted and trained to target their own countries. Identified numbers of these suspects grow with much alarm while law enforcement tracking and raids to stop these plans have never been so tense.

Deep scars have been left in the minds of entire regions as a result of the terrorist agenda. Grave problems of dispersion, death and destruction have clouded the fight for human rights as fear and anarchy persist. Displaced citizens of Iraq and Arab nations like Syria reflect another record high refugee crisis that already existed in sections of Africa. Breached areas in Somalia and Yemen are havens for insurgency where security is frail or collapsed. Ongoing treachery has stepped up an intense offensive chain in multiple battlegrounds seeking an armed or parliamentary coup of governing bodies.

Complex and volatile civilian uprisings have spread from Tunisia and Egypt to places like Algeria, Bahrain and Libya. These shocking open revolts against old-guard regimes exemplify the widespread internal discord among many nations where brother is rising up against brother. This wave of anger displays how public revolutions can quickly take place. The continuing struggle for freedom and democracy in and beyond Arab countries indicates deep divisions and strong potential for public rebellion. Political and economic stability is an uncertainty that involves diverse opposing factions.

Contrary to all the bad news occurring on a daily basis, a climate for compromise still exists for our world leaders to draw them together rather than extending the course of enmity and doubt. No civilized nation wants war if it can avoid it or solve it by another means. The serious impact of global recession and overall political abhorrence of terror present a combination of economic need and human reason that could benefit all peoples. Despite errors in American diplomacy stretching back to the dissolution of Soviet Russia, most sensible rulers are eager for improved relations with Washington.

Previous U.S. administrations never fully abandoned Cold War policies of the past, but with a frank look at our reality there is an opportunity to heal wounds mainly caused by excessive American pride. In the midst of growing conflicts, financial problems have ironically highlighted the inter-dependency of nearly all sovereign societies. This unique medicine of divine justice has tempered harsh international attitudes by an urgent matter to maintain means of commerce for the common good. The sudden state of budgetary poverty has brought a sense of humility sorely needed in foreign relations.

Desire for change in global affairs to achieve peace and security is evident throughout humanity, but unless we recognize the teachings of Jesus and abandon our selfish ways, no treaty or economic package will stand the test of time. Almost all sectors of business are still reeling on a worldwide scale in a doubtful mode of slow recovery. The obvious conclusion to this web of despair and to the straits of terror wherever it strikes is we are in it together and no nation is immune from the dangers. Governing powers will soon have to devise a path to see eye to eye or else sink into an awful abyss.

Reconciliation must be made to deal with compelling humanitarian, industrial and security issues and any methods have a required spiritual dimension for success. The beatitudes described by Jesus in his Sermon on the Mount include the proverb that *"Blessed are the peacemakers: for they shall be called the children of God."*[126] This virtue of love to make amends has its basis in God and by his spirit true harmony abides. He alone is good and from him all goodness proceeds. We must ask ourselves whose children we are and what purpose we serve for only his kingdom will last.

The continuing message of Scripture against sorrows of violence is in our awareness and conversion since *In you O Lord do I put my trust: let me never be put to confusion. You are my strong habitation where I may continually resort. My mouth will show forth your justice and your salvation all the day for I know not the numbers thereof. Deliver me, O my God, out of the hand of the wicked, out of the hand of the unjust and cruel man."*[127] Penance from sin to restore the zeal of faith is a condition for any hope against the plague of war and although its signs are here no person knows when.

Transition from terrorist war to global conflict may involve lulls due to diplomacy and force, but if there is any major profit toward peace, it is in a critical time when all people will have an opportunity to consider the prophetic word of God. This advance of his voice and grace in an acceptable time of salvation to reveal his providence in the affairs of mankind provides an option. It seems in his perfect timing out of love and truth of his existence who gave us an eternal inheritance with him in his Son, he wants us to see the great perils that lie ahead and console us with hope this world cannot offer.

Reproofs of Scripture are happening in reality because iniquity abounds and the love of many has grown cold. With respect to these warnings *"Be not unwise, but understand what the will of the Lord is."*[128] Too often we turn our heads the other way when it comes to justice as if it were none of our business, but *"the mouth of the righteous speaks wisdom, and his tongue talks of judgment."*[129] Gross human rights violations, attempts at genocide and terrible plagues are occurring while few care or can even cope. What can we expect if we don't discern our own evils and turn our hearts from God?

Jerusalem is more than a place on earth since it reflects all people of faith who have divine law in their hearts. Great wars of the end times including Armageddon involve conflict against this physical and spiritual city so the broader struggle is between good and evil over the whole of humanity. God is not finished with outpouring his grace to draw souls into his kingdom, nor has the time come when mankind will face his final wrath and judgment. We need to perceive these stages and awake to the great hope of escaping the full measure of his anger in the watches of rapture into heaven.

Even now, the Lord has set up watchmen over his house for *"I have set watchmen upon your walls, O Jerusalem: you that make mention of the Lord, keep not silence."* Of the spiritual nature of this city *"they shall call them the holy people, the redeemed of the Lord: and you shall be called, Sought out, A city not forsaken."*[130] All children of God in Christ are citizens of this city that has its base in heaven as *"he shall build my city, and he shall let go my captives, not for price nor reward."*[131] That freedom from sin and damnation cannot be bought with money or goods, but it is obtained by faith.

Keeping silent about signs of our times violates an obligation to Christ as he declared, *"the word I have spoken, the same will judge you."*[132] We must hear and respond to the omens since *"whoever hears the sound of the trumpet, and takes not warning, his blood shall be upon his own head. But he that takes warning shall deliver his soul."*[133] To those whose seed is in pride, lust and deceit *"Hear you indeed, but understand not; and see you indeed, but perceive not."*[134] There is no peace to the wicked as *"they can never have enough, they all look after their own gain, from the first to the last."*[135]

Debauchery has its roots in atheism regardless of any perverted vanity someone may profess toward God since *"you have found the life of your hand and you fear me not, your works shall not profit you."*[136] No person can sustain life nor substitute the path of Christ but *"they hear your words and do them not for they turn them into a song of their own mouth, and their heart goes after covetousness."*[137] Of this way to perdition *"this is a people robbed and wasted; they are all of them snared in holes, hid in prison houses: they are for a prey and none delivers, for a spoil and none say, Restore."*[138]

Forms of evil tyranny do not want to negotiate peace, but are bound by lusts to their ruin for *"the forgers of errors are gone together into confusion: they are all confounded and ashamed."*[139] Yet for the faithful *"Let integrity and uprightness preserve me. My eyes are ever toward the Lord, for he shall pluck my feet out of the net."*[140] This promise of redemption into heaven is in context of global end time wars that will prove the words of the prophets and manifest the unprecedented mercy and power of God since *"when he makes inquisition for blood, he forgets not the cry of the humble."*[141]

Secrets about the last days will no longer be hidden from our theology or withheld from our reality. World wars will bring tremendous damage and cost innocent lives as *"some of them of understanding shall fall to try them, and to purge, and to make them white; they shall fall by the sword, and by flame, by captivity, and by spoil, many days, even to the time of the end."*[142] Christians must realize that some will die before the watches occur as Jesus bluntly taught *"the hour is coming for whoever kills you to think he is offering worship to God, because they knew not the Father, nor me."*[143]

The work of God in Christ must reach conversion among Jews and others as *"yet will I gather others to him, besides those that are gathered unto him."*[144] He will continue to lead his flock for *"my horn shall you exalt like the horn of a unicorn: I shall be anointed with fresh oil. Those that be planted in the house of the Lord shall still bring forth fruit in old age."*[145] In this old age, the church will receive a fresh anointing of grace while the metaphor of a unicorn conveys mystery since *"Deliver me, O God, out of the hand of the wicked, cause me to escape, and save me. I am a wonder unto many."*[146]

Lessons to be drawn from Scripture in the present consistently project divine help for the State of Israel and a calling to its allies for defense against a mutual enemy. What any nation should consider is God's current favor with Israel for *"I will bless them that bless you, and curse them that curse you."*[147] This great trial will draw a myriad of souls to join with the church for a holy union with God and in his timing they will be gathered in rapture into heaven. The awesome miracle will cause more conversion and renewal in expectation of the other watches that yet occur during another global war.

Terrible destruction looms over our world due to hatred, greed and absence of faith, but this plague will bring spiritual amends for many as the voice and grace of God's word spreads *"that they may know from the rising of the sun, and from the west, there is none besides me. Drop down, you heavens from above, and let the skies pour down justice: let the earth open, and let them bring forth salvation: I the Lord have created it."*[148] The thought and misery of a war so detailed in prophecy that we already can actually see its formation, purpose and end passes our intellect to faith in the Almighty.

Until humanity accepts unity of God with his Son Jesus and the universal love in his Holy Spirit, it will continue the path of bloodshed to the end when the final battle will be fought against Christ himself. Of these dangers and yet hope in divine mercy *"the preacher was wise, he still taught the people knowledge: yea, he gave good heed, and sought out, and set in order many proverbs. The preacher sought to find out acceptable words: and that which was written was upright, even words of truth."* This is not an abstraction, but it is a concrete writing of a complex prophetic reality.[149]

Holy scholars, even bishops of the church, will scrutinize this message as the writing itself and its confirmation are both portents of prophecy for *"The words of the wise are as goads, and as nails fastened by the masters of assemblies given from one shepherd."*[150] That good shepherd is Jesus and the masters are those whom he has given responsibility to lead his people in all truth, especially now in these difficult times as *"The coppersmith striking with a hammer encouraged him that forged at that time, saying: It is ready for soldering. And he strengthened it with nails, that it should not be moved."*[151]

[1] Mark 13,8; Luke 21,9-10; II Timothy 3,1-9
[2] James 3,14-18
[3] Isaiah 13,3-13; 24,20; 34,4; Mathew 24,29-30
[4] James 4,1-5
[5] Hebrews 5,11-14
[6] Psalm 12,2
[7] James 4,7-12
[8] Isaiah 5,18-24
[9] Mathew 24,43; Luke 12,39
[10] I Corinthians 6,2-3
[11] Proverbs 31,8-9
[12] Luke 12,56-57
[13] John 5,30
[14] Revelation 12,7-9
[15] I Corinthians 11,31-32
[16] Isaiah 44,24-26
[17] Jeremiah 13,15-16
[18] Psalm 32,9
[19] Isaiah 42,23
[20] Psalm 32,8; 34,15
[21] Psalm 40,3; 119,33&105
[22] Deuteronomy 30,11&14; Romans 10,5-8
[23] John 14,26-29
[24] Isaiah 42,16
[25] John 9,39-41
[26] Isaiah 42,8&19
[27] Isaiah 42,9-13
[28] Zephaniah 1,14-16
[29] Luke 9, 28-35; Acts 1,1-9; 2,1-4; 7,55-59
[30] Psalm 68,9-11&33
[31] Psalm 29,3-9; 92,10-14
[32] Isaiah 40,5&10-11
[33] Job 37,1-7
[34] Isaiah 40,13-18
[35] Psalm 94,8-11
[36] Proverbs 1,20-23; 2,6-12; 3,13-18; 13,13-18
[37] Romans 5,20
[38] Romans 8,37-39; Philippians 4,6-7
[39] John 5,5-14
[40] John 14,12&26
[41] Isaiah 41,18
[42] Isaiah 43,5-7
[43] Joel 2,27-32
[44] Isaiah 43,8-9
[45] Isaiah 14,24&27; 46,9-11

[46] Isaiah 41,21-22
[47] John 10,33-36
[48] Genesis 1,27; 3,22-24; Hebrews 12,7-8
[49] Psalm 82; Hebrews 12,9-10
[50] Genesis 1,26-30; 2,8-15; Joel 2,1-3
[51] Isaiah 41,23
[52] Isaiah 40,9
[53] Amos 3,7
[54] Mathew 10,18-20; Mark 13,9-10
[55] Psalm 2,10-12; 119,46; Isaiah 52,15
[56] I Timothy 6,10
[57] Psalm 119,97-112
[58] Jeremiah 17,9-10; John 10,27; 18,37
[59] Mathew 23,13-33; Luke 11,52
[60] Romans 6.11-14; Ephesians 3,14-19
[61] II Peter 2,17-19
[62] Jeremiah 17,5; Luke 6,43
[63] Isaiah 40,24
[64] Proverbs 1,22-31
[65] Daniel 5,5-6&22-27
[66] Psalm 32,5-6
[67] Psalm 69,13; 95,7-8; Isaiah 49,8; 55,6
[68] Isaiah 26,1-20; I Thessalonians 4,13-18; 5,1-9
[69] Psalm 2,6-12
[70] Mark 13,8
[71] Psalm 125,5
[72] Psalm 129,5
[73] Psalm 125,3
[74] Psalm 89,30-32
[75] Psalm 51,6-12
[76] Psalm 20,2-6
[77] Isaiah 33,6
[78] Ecclesiastes 8,5-7
[79] Ecclesiastes 10,18
[80] Ecclesiastes 9,1; 12,1-4
[81] Ecclesiastes 3,1-8
[82] Genesis 14,12-16; Exodus 15,3-11
[83] Jeremiah 22,3
[84] Psalm 144,1-11
[85] Isaiah 51,4-13
[86] Luke 2,34
[87] Isaiah 59,18-21
[88] Isaiah 62,10-11
[89] Psalm 45,9; 118,16-20; Revelation 12,1
[90] Isaiah 26,1-2; 35,8-10; 40,3; Luke 2,35
[91] Psalm 86,14-16; 116,3&13-16
[92] Psalm 45,2-5
[93] Joshua 1,8-9
[94] Psalm 96,2-9
[95] Psalm 27,2-6
[96] Job 4,8
[97] Psalm 9,9-16
[98] Mathew 24,7; Mark 13,8; Luke 21,10
[99] Isaiah 41,8-16
[100] Zechariah 12,1-3

[101] Zechariah 12,5&8
[102] Zechariah 12,6-7
[103] Zechariah 12,4&9
[104] Isaiah 40,15; 41,1; Jeremiah 25,22; 31,10; Ezekiel 39,6
[105] Isaiah 41,1-6
[106] Isaiah 43,21-26
[107] Isaiah 42,14
[108] Isaiah 48,12-17
[109] Mark 10,29-31; Romans 11,23-31
[110] Isaiah 45,21-25
[111] Isaiah 43,21- 24; 44,21-22; 45,2-5
[112] Isaiah 49,1-6
[113] Isaiah 49,4-5; Romans 11,21-28
[114] Isaiah 41,8-14
[115] Isaiah 40,15; 51,4-5
[116] Mathew 7,9-12; Luke 11,11-13
[117] Genesis 10,1-3
[118] Mathew 24,34; Mark 13,30; Luke 21,32
[119] Psalm 119,126&130&136
[120] Psalm 64,1-10
[121] Psalm 37,12-15
[122] Psalm 86,14-17
[123] Isaiah 44,24-25
[124] Psalm 71,10-17
[125] Psalm 17,8-12
[126] Mathew 5,9
[127] Psalm 71,1-4 &14-15
[128] Ephesians 5,13-17
[129] Psalm 37,30
[130] Isaiah 62,6-12
[131] Isaiah 45,11-13
[132] Luke 12,2-5; John 12,48; 14,26; 15,16; 16,13
[133] Ezekiel 33,4-5
[134] Isaiah 6,8-9
[135] Isaiah 56,9-11; 57,20-21
[136] Isaiah 57,10-12
[137] Ezekiel 33,31-32
[138] Isaiah 42,22-23
[139] Isaiah 45,15-16
[140] Psalm 25,14-15 &19-22
[141] Psalm 9,9-14
[142] Daniel 11,33-35
[143] John 16,1-4
[144] Isaiah 56,8
[145] Psalm 92,10-14
[146] Psalm 71,2-7
[147] Genesis 12,3
[148] Isaiah 45,6-8
[149] Ecclesiastes 12,9-10
[150] Ecclesiastes 12,11
[151] Isaiah 41,7

Chapter Five/Part Two
THE FIRST WATCH

"I saw a great multitude which no man could number, out of all nations and tribes and tongues, standing before the throne and before the Lamb, clothed in white robes, and with palms in their hands." Revelation 7,9

The kingdom of God is more than a place in heaven or on earth since it refers to a state of being whereby we commune through Christ in his spirit. Paradise certainly has a physical form in the outward makeup and order of things, but the idea of obtaining peace and plenty on earth or extreme delight and beauty in heaven stems from the condition of our hearts in relation to our Creator. He is the origin of life and source of good pleasures for only by him does anything exist. Our inheritance of his bounty and everlasting life is a by-product of actively knowing him in our inner spirit through simple faith.

Revelation of God's word is foremost directed at our forgiveness and eternal salvation in the atonement of Christ. By our belief in his death and resurrection we receive graces to overcome our sinful nature and thus pass from a culture of death into the way of a new and unceasing life. Those who abide in the Son of God have entered his risen life and by his spirit we are his own children. The divine intervention of Jesus in his word and deeds revealed the separate yet connected worlds of heaven and earth. Communion with him is our only link between these realities in a timeless covenant established by God.

Despite the threat of apocalyptic world wars, mankind now dwells at a great threshold of hope unseen in its entire history. The divine principles underlying this amazing truth are the infinite power and compassionate sympathy of the Father who wants to rescue his people and reveal himself to a civilization on the brink of self-destruction for *"O Lord, I have heard your speech and was afraid, revive your work in the midst of the years, bring it to life, you shall make it known: when you are angry, you will remember mercy. You went forth for the salvation of your people, even for salvation with your Christ."*[1]

Various expressions in Scripture either clearly describe or by subtle allegory indicate a mystery that stimulates our imagination and tests our faith. This very pervasive teaching defies our human mortality and transcends scientific reasoning since *"Behold, I show you a mystery: we shall not all die, but we all shall be changed."*[2] The odd concept of human beings instantly taken alive into heaven has a broad biblical basis in the last days. There is an inherent and miraculous theme of deliverance for God's people in the midst of trials. Modern debate has not considered these distinct seasons and times of redemption.

Many Christians have become familiar with the thought of rapture into heaven, but it has been commercialized with the misleading claim that the faithful will not suffer any great tribulation. The main fallacy of this reasoning is the failure to recognize the world wars foretold before the end wrath of God. If we refuse to accept his purpose to purge the church from its sin, finish the work of salvation and lead us on the road to Calvary, how can we prepare to meet the Lord? We must encounter our dismal reality with reason that nobody can benefit from attempts to pacify them with a diluted gospel.

Diverse matters concerning rapture need to be clarified and the glaring issue must be defined in our theology and openly taught in catechesis. The word rapture is not used in the bible, but other terms are found that identify this tri-fold event. These multiple language examples applied to rapture include recognizable concepts such as gathering, harvest, appearing, coming, revelation, birth and watches. Further phrasing denotes divine action to spare, to reward, to save, to redeem, to wed and to hide or escape. Other forms of diction allude to opening of the immortal doors or gates of heaven.

Biblical citations about rapture are numerous and related verses explain the general aspects of its meaning, timing, design and spiritual instruction. The most basic difficulty of discerning this intricate topic is difference between the proximate and final coming of Jesus since verses referring to what is near the end period imply an earlier point in time. It is imperative to separate things that happen prior to the end from the end itself as *"Let no ill speech proceed out of your mouth, grieve not the holy Spirit of God, whereby you are sealed unto the day of redemption."*[3] That certain day has a unique timeframe.

After noting signs of world and regional wars that have occurred in the last century, Jesus said *"for these things must first come to pass, but the end is not by and by."* These stages of the by and by are following world wars of nations and of kingdoms he spoke of as *"the beginning of sorrows."* He indicated a context for watches of rapture in the day of redemption as *"when these things begin to come to pass, then look up, and lift up your heads for your redemption draws near."*[4] His focus on the timing of rapture is during a specific period of wars he called the beginning, not on things predicted at the end.

Doctrine relating to rapture was formed by the prophets and apostles but delineated also by Jesus who warned of the snare to come upon the whole earth and plainly urged us to *"Watch, therefore, that you may be accounted worthy to escape all these things that shall come to pass."* The snare of idolatry is in the Antichrist when he takes control over humanity. It is from this evil we can escape since *"there will be two on one bed: one will be taken and the other will be left. Two will be in the field: one will be taken and the other will be left. Two will be grinding together: one will be taken, the other left."*[5]

Accounts given by Jesus of his people literally vanishing from earth are unexplained in fields of science, but not beyond the supernatural power of God who asks us *"Is my hand shortened at all, that I cannot redeem? Or have I no power to deliver?"*[6] He wants faith from us in regard to his word for *"I have declared, and have saved. I have made it heard, when there was no strange god among you: Remember not former things, and look not on things of old. Behold I do new things, and now they shall spring forth, verily you shall know them. I will make a way in the wilderness, and rivers in the desert."*[7]

Redemption or salvation in Christ applies to the whole family of God regardless of when someone came into his grace because he is omnipotent and in his foreknowledge those works were complete from the foundation of the world.[8] These simple terms for reconciliation and adoption into his eternal house have a special meaning for the last days as he will both make known and perform new things in regard to his children that have not been manifest in the past as *"I have showed you new things from this time, even hidden things, and you did not know them. They are created now, and not of old."*[9]

Issues dealing with the mystery of rapture are puzzling and some ignore its complexity as if it does not exist in Scripture or just skip it as too absurd to believe or teach, but *"the vision is yet for an appointed time, and at the end it shall speak, and not lie: though it tarry, wait for it; for it will surely come, and it will not be slack."*[10] This vision in few emphatic words shows *"we shall not die."* Similarly, *"the voice of victory is in the tents of the just: the Lord has struck with power, I shall not die, but live, and declare the works of the Lord. He has chastened me sore, but has not given me over to death."*[11]

With respect to the power of God, he is able to do far more than we can ask or even think as *"men have not heard, nor perceived by the ear, neither has the eye seen, O God besides you, what things you have prepared for them that wait for you."*[12] We have not seen a freedom from death that transports us right into heaven, but we can grasp these things for *"God has revealed them to us by his Spirit: for the Spirit searches all things, yea, even the deep things of God."*[13] The apostles separated the idea of rapture from final judgment as *"we made known to you the power and coming of our Lord Jesus."*[14]

Distinctions in circumstances and purpose between Christ's proximate and glorious return have largely been forgotten or distorted through ignorance and desire for personal gain. We need to examine the basis and details of this important subject since it was taught to the early church *"We beseech you, brethren, by the coming of our Lord Jesus Christ, and by our gathering to him."*[15] Christ's gathering of his flock into heaven is before the end period and battle of Armageddon. This difference is in timing and intent for Jesus *"will judge the living and the dead by his coming and by his kingdom."*[16]

No one can be judged more than once because any person has only one life to give an account of as *"it is appointed unto men once to die, but after this the judgment."*[17] Those who are ready to meet the Lord in the times of watch will not die, but they will change into a resurrected form with the dead who in spirit stand in grace before God.[18] Timing of resurrection of the faithful into eternal life precedes the damnation of apostate souls either alive or dead at the consummation of the end. Yet a remnant of the church will survive the last days to inherit the earth and obtain the promises of God's kingdom.

Warnings were made to the early church by the apostles that *"we ought to give heed to the things we have heard, lest at any time we should let them slip."* This admonition is given in the prophetic context of the Lordship of Christ for God *"crowned him with glory and honor, and did set him over the works of his hands."* The kingdom of Jesus in his universal church and Eucharistic reign on earth is a doctrine set forth by the apostles in certainty for God gave to him *"subjection of the world to come, whereof we speak."*[19] He *"gave himself for our sins, that he might deliver us from this present evil world."*[20]

There is a host of references in the bible showing the divine plan to establish the new covenant in Christ with an elect remnant of humanity. We must not lose sight of this objective at the end of our troubled world *"For it has pleased God the Father that by him he should reconcile to himself all things, whether on the earth or in the heavens, making peace through the blood of his cross."*[21] Jesus has been appointed the heir of all things, but until then *"now we see not all things put under him."*[22] Likewise, *"we, according to his promise, look for new heavens and a new earth, wherein dwells righteousness."*[23]

Deliverance in a final sense is from evil itself for the powers of hell shall be broken and bound. For now these evil works will continue to inspire a willful apostasy and bring much destruction. It is God's desire to spare us from the full measure of those sorrows and not commit us to his ending wrath. For this reason *"Gird up the loins of your mind, be sober, and hope to the end for the grace that is to be brought unto you at the revelation of Christ."* This prophecy is before the end and applies to the hope of rapture as *"when the chief Shepherd appears, you will receive the unfading crown of glory."*[24]

Understanding the day of redemption as being separate from and prior to the great day of Christ is central to the gospel for *"I pray your love may abound yet more and more in knowledge and in all judgment, that you may be upright and without offense till the day of Christ."*[25] This preparation is until that day of wrath and judgment of the wicked, not during that period. All saints in heaven will already be changed into immortal life before the end time and we need to be ready *"waiting for the appearance of our Lord Jesus Christ, who shall confirm you unto the end, unimpeachable in the day of Christ."*[26]

Critical lessons on the nature and timing of rapture are written in St. Paul's epistles that urge us to *"stand firm, and hold the teachings that you have learned."*[27] He plainly set apart this hope from the end as *"the day of the Lord is to come as a thief in the night, but you, brethren, are not in darkness, that that day should overtake you as a thief."*[28] Jesus will come as a thief to destroy his enemies by several final curses defined as *"the seven last plagues, for in them is filled up the wrath of God."*[29] These are a series of disasters from which we can be saved *"For God has not appointed us to wrath."*[30]

Attention should be drawn to the fact that Jesus said *"of that day and hour knows no man, take heed for you know not when the time is."*[31] Predicting the time of watches or the day of wrath and hour of judgment is not given to us, but we know *"you are all the children of light, therefore let us not sleep, but watch and be sober."*[32] Jesus spoke of *"the day when the Son of man is revealed"* and also of *"the day of judgment."*[33] These are separate times as we are to be ready and look for the signs of redemption, but from the final wrath *"take heed to yourselves, lest that day come upon you unawares."*[34]

Only God the Father knows his appointed timing of the watches, yet Jesus provided us with visible events of those seasons and times for *"when you see these things come to pass, know that it is nigh, even at the doors."*[35] He thus indicated certain omens we can recognize and these things relate to the progression of events that will take place as he opens the doors to his heavenly kingdom since *"Blessed are those servants, whom the lord when he comes shall find watching. And if he shall come in the second watch, or come in the third watch, and find them so, blessed are those servants."*[36]

Stages of the day of redemption correspond to apocalyptic world wars Jesus foretold would happen before the judgment day. Certain clues he gave allow us to comprehend the overall scope of timings of rapture since *"whoever perseveres to the end, he shall be saved."*[37] This applies to those in the third watch who are taken up to heaven just before the end period when the Antichrist conquers the world. The Lord also told us *"when these things begin to come to pass, your redemption draws nigh."*[38] That hope is at the start of immense sorrows when nation rises against nation, the sign of the first watch.

Verifying the threefold aspects of rapture cannot be separated from the trials of wars due to the astonishing number of people who have left the path of Christ. Nobody can point to a calendar or clock to say when the watches will take place, but we can gain much insight by sorting out relevant truths. St. Paul specified that *"the Lord himself shall descend from heaven with a shout, with the voice of archangel, and with the trumpet of God: and the dead in Christ will rise first, then we who are alive and who remain will be caught up together with them in the clouds, to meet the Lord in the air."*[39]

Multiple sounds St. Paul gave for the call to rapture indicate three distinct moments in time, not a chorus of heavenly songs. This tri-form sequence of commands was also told by the ancient prophets for *"he shall appear to your glory, and they shall be ashamed: A voice of noise from the city, a voice from the temple, a voice of the Lord that renders recompense to his enemies."* These separate voices reflect different watches of which the last signals God's end wrath. He asks us of that day *"Who has ever heard such a thing? And who has seen the like to this? Shall the earth bring forth in one day?"*[40]

The testimony of rapture can be traced to when Jacob summoned his sons to inform them of *"what shall befall you in the last days."* Divine revelation was given to the tribe of Judah from whom Jesus descended and founded the church papacy: *"The scepter shall not depart from Judah, nor a lawgiver from between his feet, until Shiloh come; and unto him shall the gathering of the people be."* This reference is to Christ's redemption into heaven as *"Judah is a lion's whelp: from the prey, my son, you are gone up: he stooped down, he crouched as a lion, and as an old lion; who shall rouse him up?"*[41]

Intricate mysteries of the Messiah, the Lion of Judah, were known long ago as Jacob spoke of his crouching to gather his people to himself. Judah's tribe reflects those born spiritually of Christ who fasten to him as the vine and wash in the wine of his blood for *"Binding his ass to the vine, and his ass's colt to the choice vine; he washed his garments in wine, and his robe in the blood of grapes."* These are the Gentiles first and then Jews whom the Lord takes up *"to give them a crown for ashes, the oil of joy for mourning, a garment of praise for the spirit of grief: they are called the planting of the Lord."*[42]

When Jesus spoke of the watches of rapture, he explained that this reward would be granted in due season. He told the apostles *"It is not for you to know the times or the seasons, which the Father has put in his own power."*[43] They did not live through these things, but much is given for us to learn such as distinct parables that correspond to three different visions of rapture listed in the Apocalypse.[44] Parables Jesus gave about Noah's time and Lot's time were periods of pervasive sin, violence and judgment. These signs conclude when the door to the marriage feast is shut in the story of the ten virgins.[45]

Visions recorded in the Apocalypse reflect three separate gatherings of the watches in rapture. St. John revealed the first of these groups was made up of *"a great multitude, which no man could number, out of all nations, and tribes and tongues, standing before the throne and before the Lamb."* Instruction was given about them that *"These are they which came out of great tribulation."* They came out of terrible distress in WWIII from all nations as *"There is no speech nor language where their voice is not heard. In them he has set a tabernacle for the sun, as a bridegroom coming out of his chamber."*[46]

We should understand the context of the watches is in deliverance from global wars unprecedented in history, yet we don't know exactly how much suffering will be endured before those times are fulfilled. A certain clue in Ezekiel connects the Lord's presence as a catalyst for an apparent great earthquake during the course of or at the end of WWIII that may pinpoint the first watch, but science cannot determine these types of predictions. It is noteworthy to study this event as *"all men that are upon the face of the earth shall shake at my presence."*[47] If meant literally, his presence may signal rapture.

Before St. John wrote the seven trumpet judgments of the Apocalypse which happen after the first watch and include a fourth world war, he saw an angel holding a golden censer offer much incense *"with the prayers of all saints upon the golden altar which was before the throne. And the smoke of the incense, which came with the prayers of the saints, ascended up before God."* These united prayers seem to include the pleas for mercy by those who yet on earth comprise the great multitude of the first watch for then *"there were voices, and thundering, and lightning, and an earthquake."*[48]

Regardless of the sincere efforts of Christians to bring stability and peace to our world by their example, missions or military conflicts, we must realize that only Jesus not the church itself will establish peace and security we seek since *"we have been in pain, we have not wrought any deliverance in the earth, neither have the inhabitants of the earth fallen."* The prophets foretold our redemption from this madness for *"Your dead men shall live, together with my dead body shall they arise. Come, my people, enter into your chambers, and shut the doors; hide yourself until the indignation pass away."*[49]

Our hope for the end times is not in armed conquest or in some fleeting form of peace, but it is from heaven for *"We have a strong city. Open you the gates, so the righteous nation which keeps the truth may enter in."*[50] We who dwell in Christ are dead to the lusts of our flesh so *"that all we who have been baptized into Jesus Christ were baptized into his death."*[51] The faithful who are alive in the flesh are part of his dead body and those who wait for the Lord in the times of watch will enter the doors of their heavenly chambers. At a set time these will arise in resurrection with all the souls in heaven.

St. Paul revealed a mystery concerning when the children of God will be transformed into immortality since *"In a moment, in the twinkling of an eye, at the last trump: for the trumpet shall sound, and the dead shall be raised incorruptible, and we shall be changed."*[52] This immutable fact of theology is an ultimate reward that all servants of God will receive. The signal of the last trumpet in the Apocalypse marks the third watch and starts divine indignation against the wicked, but we who love God are told *"to wait for his Son from heaven, even Jesus, who has delivered us from the wrath to come."*[53]

The difference in Scripture between the miraculous harvest of Christians into heaven and the harvest of wicked people *"into the great winepress of the wrath of God"* needs to be recognized.[54] These are separate periods aimed primarily at either the salvation or damnation of those who embrace or reject the gospel of Christ. There are distinct times of ripeness for each to be reaped and as to the overall span of watches for the just who live by faith, *"Let us now fear the Lord our God, who gives rain, both the former and the latter, in his season, he reserves unto us the appointed weeks of harvest."*[55]

Thought of a former and latter rain as a symbol of grace being poured out in appointed seasons of harvest has great significance in the bible. St. James urged to *"Be patient, brethren, unto the coming of the Lord. Behold, the husbandman waits for the precious fruit of the earth, and has long patience for it, until he receive the early and the latter rain."*[56] This analogy relates to faith among Gentiles before some Jews believe and the watches reflect these seasons as *"his going forth is prepared as the morning light, and he will come to us as the rain, as the early and the latter rain to the earth."*[57]

In regard to Gentile conversion preceding that of Jews, St. Peter said to his fellow apostles: *"We believe that through the grace of the Lord Jesus Christ we shall be saved, even as they."* The apostle James then agreed with him about this prophecy saying Peter *"has declared how God at the first did visit the Gentiles, to take out of them a people for his name."*[58] The new covenant revealed by Jesus has not been accepted in mainstream Jewish theology, but the apostles ardently taught that this veil of disbelief will be lifted for *"when they turn in repentance to God, the veil shall be taken away."*[59]

Conversion of Jews to Christ applies to the latter rain of grace when an elect segment of all Jewish tribes will be empowered by the Holy Spirit to preach the gospel. Context of this mystery is in the period after the first watch and before the end wrath. It involves their affiliation to the church, not a political conversion of their state. The Lord *"will bring a seed out of Jacob, and out of Judah an inheritor of my mountains, for my people who have sought me."*[60] Of this renewal in faith, *"He shall cause them that come of Jacob to take root: Israel shall blossom and bud, and fill the world with fruit."*[61]

Jewish conversion to Christianity as well as their ministry to the Gentiles must be seen in a partial sense before Jesus comes in glory to establish their nation and all mankind in truth according to promise. Yet this revival gives credence to the multiple meaning of harvest in a latter season of grace to Jews beyond Gentiles as *"the Redeemer shall come to Zion, and to them that turn from transgression in Jacob."*[62] Even now we can understand these things since *"O God, who has showed me great and sore troubles, shall quicken me again, and shall bring me up again from the depths of the earth."*[63]

Scrutiny of biblical prophecy yields an abundance of information about the hope of redemption as *"Before dawn I come and cry out: My eyes greet the night watches in meditation on your promise."*[64] That blessed assurance of the Lord is in succession for *"My spirit that is upon you, and my words which I have put in your mouth, shall not depart out of your mouth, nor out of the mouth of your seed, nor out of the mouth of your seed's seed, from henceforth and forever."*[65] He delivers us so *"I may plant the heavens, and lay the foundations of the earth, and say to Zion: You are my people."*[66]

Phases of the watches in relation to wars and divine actions to rescue the faithful are consistently repeated in the course of redemption since *"At the noise of the tumult the people fled; at the lifting up of yourself the nations were scattered. Now will I rise, says the Lord, now will I be exalted, now will I lift myself up. Hear you who are far off what I have done and you who are near acknowledge my might."*[67] These verses apply to the Calvary of the church in the time of WWIV and its crucifixion at the third watch when Christ is exalted in a remnant of his mystical body taken up into heaven.

Scriptural metaphor of the lifting up of the Lord's body in those who commune with him has implicit meaning for the Liturgy of the Mass. The identity we have in the Lord's death at the consecration of the bread and wine is also of his risen life and faith in his return as Messiah. During the sacred tradition of the ringing of the bells, many Catholics were taught from their childhood to beat their heart with their hand in sorrow three times when the priest lifts up the Host and then once when he lifts up the Blood. This act of reverence is in foresight of rapture and for those who survive the end.

Ceremony of ringing the bells has deep rooted teaching dating to the early church. These prophetic mysteries need to be known as we proclaim our Lord's death until he comes in glory since we both preach and live out his passion in promise of redemption and forgiveness of sins in a new world. Our heritage contains the ritual of Advent where four candles are lit each week before Christmas. Advent is a form of Latin that means an arrival from the Greek word parousia used in Catholic theology for rapture. The four candles reflect the three watches and those left who wait for a new dawn on earth.

Awesome instruction is written in the Apocalypse regarding hope in the last days as a loud voice in heaven declared *"Now is come salvation, and strength, and the kingdom of our God, and the power of his Christ."*[68] These are different times in salvation of the first watch, strength and kingdom of other watches and when the blood of martyrs will lead to the judgment of Christ. Of this sequence in watches, *"Fight the good fight of faith, lay hold on eternal life, until the appearing of our Lord Jesus Christ, who in his times shall show who is the only Potentate, the King of kings, and Lord of lords."*[69]

Places of renown in ancient Israel such as Lebanon, Carmel and Sharon are used to mirror the watches of rapture for *"the glory of Lebanon shall be given to it, the beauty of Carmel and Sharon, they shall see the glory of the Lord, and the excellency of our God. Be strong, fear not: he will come and save you."*[70] We must see the plurality in the signs of our times and *"abide in him: that when he shall appear we may have confidence, and not be ashamed at his coming."[71]* There is mercy in our Calvary as *"He will send from heaven, and save me from the reproach of him that would swallow me up."[72]*

In contrast to the panic and fear that stems from affliction, we need to strengthen our hearts by the exercise of faith. Virtues that lead to holiness are traits we must practice and live out in the manner set forth in divine law. The urgent spiritual battle we are in is for our lives and souls as Jesus encouraged us to pray and be ready, then *"unto them that look for him shall he appear the second time without sin unto salvation."[73]* It is in our total submission to him that *"when he shall appear, we shall be like him: for we shall see him as he is."[74]* In other words, *"I will know even as also I am known."[75]*

Allegories of rapture made in the bible stimulate our imagination because *"they that escape shall be on the mountains like doves of the valleys, all of them mourning for his iniquity."[76]* Similarly, *"Oh, that I had wings like a dove! For then would I fly away, and be at rest. He has delivered my soul from the battle against me: for there were many with me. Cast your burden upon the Lord and he shall sustain you."[77]* Like coming out of a dream, *"I will behold your face in righteousness: I shall be satisfied, when I awake, with your likeness."[78]* And by our trust in the Lord, *"we are risen, and stand upright."[79]*

Escape from the calamities of our times will become more pressing and while many try to pacify themselves in sinful pleasures and hide in their vanity, some will repent and turn to God in truth since *"Fear not: for I have redeemed you, when you pass through the waters, I will be with you, and through the rivers, they shall not overflow you, when you walk through the fire, you shall not be burned."[80]* They will wait and expect divine favor for *"the Lord delivered them so they might go to a city of habitation. He brought them out of darkness and the shadow of death, and broke their bonds asunder."[81]*

Understanding God's overall anger in the last days is first against a growing apostasy in the church so *"judgment must begin at the house of God."[82]* The reproof of his word reveals this reality *"For in the hand of the Lord there is a cup, and the wine is red, it is full of mixture, and he pours out the same, but the dregs thereof, all the wicked of the earth will wring them out, and drink them."[83]* These trials for the church prior to the end are evident in *"Behold, I have taken out of your hand the cup of trembling, you shall no more drink it again: But I will put it into the hand of them that afflict you."[84]*

In a purely practical sense of reason, how can God promise that his people will not suffer catastrophic punishments of the end? As difficult as it is to comprehend, that final period will in some way afflict everyone living on earth. This mystery is explained in the unfathomable ascension of Christians into heaven before Jesus comes in glory to judge an evil kingdom of the Antichrist. St. Paul asked, *"Do you not know that the saints shall judge the world?"[85]* The just will return from heaven *"blameless in holiness before God, even our Father, at the coming of our Lord Jesus Christ with all the saints."[86]*

Study and discussion of the Apocalypse has been somewhat of a taboo subject since its nature reveals the rebellion and hypocrisy in the church and outright blasphemy of the world. A cloud of secrecy has kept us from discerning many truths of prophecy since we don't want to publicly admit our faults or proclaim things that are offensive and out of the ordinary yet *"Let the redeemed of the Lord say so, whom he redeemed from the hand of the enemy, and gathered them out of the lands."[87]* These events are more than theory concerning faith and we need sound dialogue about critical issues of those times.

Prophetic usage of the Lord's visitation is both to save his people and to punish those who reject him with severe plagues. Hence it is written *"O Lord, you know: remember me, and visit me, and revenge me of my persecutors."*[88] Also, *"the day of your watchmen and your visitation comes, my God will hear me, when I fall, I shall arise, when I sit in darkness, the Lord is my light, he will bring me forth to the light and I shall behold his righteousness."*[89] This revelation is in oppression and war for *"I will deliver you out of the hand of the wicked, and I will redeem you out of the hand of the terrible."*

Persecutions against the church are due to infidelity and it must restore penance and work toward conversion in light of dangers that surround us since *"I will bear the indignation of the Lord because I have sinned against him, until he plead my cause, and execute judgment for me."*[90] In tears Jesus said *"the things that belong to your peace are hid from your eyes. You knew not the time of your visitation."*[91] Consider *"Who shall ascend into the hill of the Lord? Or who shall stand in his holy place? He who has clean hands and a pure heart will receive the blessing from the Lord."*[92]

At the final battle of Armageddon the faithful will come back from heaven with Jesus and his angels to judge the wicked, but before then great plagues of the wrath of God will come upon the Antichrist's kingdom in the time of the end as *"Shame shall cover her who said to me, Where is the Lord your God?"* The mother of evil and idolatry is the great whore of the Apocalypse and of this deceit *"Rejoice not against me, O my enemy: my eyes shall behold her; now she is trodden down as the mire of the streets."*[93] Thus, *"O you most proud, your day is come: in the time of visitation they shall perish."*[94]

Although the church will continue in missions and fight for its survival, we should not have any delusion about the limits of its ministry toward global justice for *"The way of peace they knew not, and there is no judgment in their goings: we wait for light, but behold obscurity; for brightness, but we walk in darkness."*[95] The fact is *"evil men and seducers shall wax worse and worse, deceiving, and being deceived."*[96] God's promise of redemption is before that evil takes full control over the world as *"I have declared, and have saved, and I have shown, when there was no strange god among you."*[97]

Falsehood will dominate all political and religious systems in the end leaving those of the faithful remnant subject to execution and imprisonment. History shows brutality of Christians, Jews and others in periods of the past, but in the global scale of God's end wrath *"I have forsaken my house, I have left my heritage: I have given the dearly beloved of my soul into the hand of her enemies."*[98] Likewise in fury, *"he forsook the tabernacle of Shiloh, the tent he placed among men; and delivered his glory into the enemy's hand. He gave his people to the sword and was wroth with his inheritance."*[99]

The living passion of Christ is a great mystery for the church as he cried out *"My God, My God, why have you forsaken me?"*[100] This is a reality we also must face because *"the enemy has done wickedly in the sanctuary. They roar in the midst of your congregations, they set up their ensigns for signs, they have defiled by casting down the dwelling place of your name to the ground and burned up all the synagogues of God in the land."*[101] To both Jew and Gentile, *"The earth is defiled under the inhabitants thereof, because they have changed the ordinance, and broken the everlasting covenant."*[102]

Predictions prior to the end include apostasy that forms a false church and false Christ for *"that day shall not come, except there come a falling away first, and that man of sin be revealed, the son of perdition."*[103] This rebellion is in those who leave the church or corrupt it with falsehood and acceptance of grave sins such as abortion so *"Your hands are defiled with blood and your fingers with iniquity, your lips spread lies and mutter perversity."*[104] Even as it is now, *"Many pastors have destroyed my vineyard, they have trodden my portion under foot and made it a desolate wilderness."*[105]

Rather than calling for contrition and intercession in our times, many stay aloof in lack of virtue thinking *"all things continue as they were from the beginning of creation."* St. Peter warned *"there shall come in the last days scoffers, walking after their own lusts, and saying, Where is the promise of his coming?"* Sadly, the proof they seek is in people like themselves who are careless about our reality as in the time of Noah when *"the world that then was, being overflowed with water, perished."*[106] It is by this deception of sinful ego that *"truth has fallen in the street, and equity cannot enter."*[107]

Most of us are not familiar with the biblical details of the day of redemption, but God will make his word manifest for how can we prepare ourselves if we don't know what signs are coming or the path he expects us to take to be ready? It is hope in the heavenly mountain of Zion he is asking us to look and wait on as *"he commanded the clouds from above, and opened the doors of heaven."* In the same manner, *"Lift up your heads, O ye gates: and be ye lifted up, ye everlasting doors, and the King of glory shall come in."*[108] So too, *"they that wait upon the Lord shall mount up with wings as eagles."*[109]

Several passages from Scripture speak of a new song and describe its meaning to the faithful in the last days since *"Sing to the Lord a new song, for he comes; for he comes to rule the earth."*[110] This verse separates his coming to redeem from his coming to judge as *"he will beautify the meek with salvation"* and they will return with him in glorious victory showing *"this honor have all his saints."*[111] The new song is a liberating cry to *"Bow your heavens, O Lord, and come down: reach out your hand from on high, deliver me and rescue me out of great waters, from the hand of strange children."*[112]

Readings of prophecy reveal God's centerpiece of mercy and power over evil before the end, but we must have faith to obtain this gift since *"Such knowledge is too wonderful for me, it is high, I cannot attain unto it."*[113] Episodes of rapture will be marveled at by *"All you inhabitants of the world, and dwellers on earth, see you when he lifts up an ensign on the mountains, and when he blows a trumpet, hear you."*[114] In these appointed times *"The Lord has made his salvation known: he has revealed his justice in the sight of nations: all the ends of the earth have seen the salvation of our God."*[115]

Independent watches for Gentile and Jew is a constant prophetic theme as *"You that fear the Lord, praise him; all you seed of Jacob, glorify him, and fear him, all you seed of Israel. He has not spurned nor disdained the afflicted in his misery, but when he cried out to him, he heard them. Your heart shall live forever."*[116] Although Gentiles will yet receive the grace of conversion after the first watch, many Jews will then be saved for *"Hearken to me, my people; and give ear to me, O my nation: for a law shall proceed from me, and I will make my judgment to rest for a light of the people."* [117]

All who dwell on earth will observe the mystery of rapture and while some explain it with falsehood others will know it was an act of God. His intent is to affirm this doctrine in its proper context since *"Praise the Lord, O Jerusalem: praise your God, O Zion. For he has strengthened the bars of your gates; he has blessed your children within you. He showed his word to Jacob, his statutes and his judgments unto Israel."*[118] The church will rebound and the Lord will be magnified as *"the inhabitants of the world stand in awe of him. For he spoke, and it was done; he commanded and it stood fast."*[119]

111

Events of the last days reach a decisive juncture for the church and world in retrospect of the first watch. The spiritual Israel of Christ's new covenant as it applies to Jews has yet to be realized so even then *"thus says the Lord that created you, O Jacob, and he that formed you, O Israel, Fear not: for I have redeemed you."* Jacob who was later called Israel shall be last as *"we all, reflecting as in a mirror the glory of the Lord, are being transformed into his very image from glory to glory."*[120] Hence it is written, *"My glory was fresh in me, unto me men opened their mouth wide as for the latter rain."*[121]

The church will be inspired with new hope as an anointing of profound grace comes upon a chosen seed of Jacob who will labor in a great harvest of souls while *"I will hope continually, and will yet praise you more and more. You will increase my greatness and comfort me. My tongue will talk of your justice all the day long."*[122] To this redemption *"you have beset me behind and before, and laid your hand upon me."*[123] Similarly, *"You visited the land, and watered it: the dwellers at the earth's ends are in fear at your marvels, you make the outgoings of the morning and evening to rejoice."*[124]

Enemies of the church will be ashamed that their prey escaped in the first watch and some will likely deceive explaining it by an alien invasion from outer space. Whatever the reasons for not believing Christ *"they received not the love of the truth, that they might be saved. And for this cause God shall send them strong delusion, that they should believe a lie: that they all might be damned who believed not the truth, but had pleasure in wickedness."*[125] That delusion is the Antichrist *"whose coming is after the working of Satan with all power and signs and lying wonders to them that perish."*[126]

Who or what is obstructing the Antichrist from being manifest has somehow been lost in our theology as St. Paul asked *"Remember you not that I told you these things?"* The critical question of when this evil tyrant will be revealed rests in the mystery of the first watch for *"now you know what restrains him, that he may be revealed in his proper time, provided he who is restraining, does still restrain, until he is taken out of the way. And then that wicked one will be revealed."*[127] This male pronoun pointing to *"he who is restraining"* refers to the name Israel as it applies to Gentiles taken up before Jacob.

Pertinent questions are posed to Gentile and Jew about the return of Christ to redeem as *"Who may abide the day of his coming? And who shall stand when he appears?"*[128] The choice of doing good and evil will be even more contrast than our present with the Antichrist's influence in the world for he *"opposes and exalts himself above all that is called God, or that is worshiped."*[129] Mankind will be subject to an ugly human figure of its own pride and lust, but of the Lord's harvest *"Be converted to me with all your heart. And the floors shall be full of wheat and the presses overflow with wine and oil."*[130]

Spiritual meaning in metaphors relating to the church is often missed because we see only the physical aspects of these analogies. The wheat, wine and oil of Christ's harvest pertains to the watches we need to prepare for in holiness. Many parables give deep insights of prophecy like *"Fear not, O land: be glad and rejoice; for the Lord will do great things. He will make the early and latter rain to come down to you, as in the beginning, for the tree bears her fruit, the fig tree and the vine do yield their strength."*[131] This message is about the reaping of souls, not edible food from the fields.

Expectant hope in the watches must embrace the light of Our Lady since from the start of the human race God revealed the seed of this new Eve who is at enmity with those of the Devil. She is the beginning of our new covenant in Christ as she conceived him by the Holy Spirit in her virgin womb. Moreover, she is a tree of life and Queen of Heaven whose royal fruit are her children. It is by Jesus that she will bear the fruit of redemption in a measure of Gentile fullness as the fig tree yields its strength in the first watch before the vine in Jewish conversion yields its strength of harvest in the other watches.[132]

Jesus gave a parable of the fig tree in his discourse of end things to indicate a sign of his coming in the watches for *"when its branch is yet tender, and puts forth leaves, you know that summer is nigh: So likewise you, when you see these things come to pass, know that it is near, even at the doors."*[133] The State of Israel is a central background to the course of prophetic events, but it has an underlying spiritual dimension in preparing Gentiles and then Jews for their redemption. Omens to our generation in uncovering the gospel and Apocalypse will prompt the early and latter rain for great harvest.

A remarkable calling to conversion is made in prophecy that has yet to be fulfilled for *"Blow the trumpet in Zion, sanctify a fast, call a solemn assembly: Gather the people, sanctify the congregation, assemble the elders, gather the children, and those that suck the breasts."*[134] This urgent summons is to penance and prayer for divine mercy against the apostasy and bloodshed in our world. It is a serious wakeup notice of the perils and redemptive hope in our times to bishops, clergy, religious orders, lay ministers and all laity, especially those who are devoted to Our Lady and to praying the rosary.

Plain language indicates the command for a historic church council is prior to the first watch because *"Gather together, O nation not desired. Before the decree brings forth, before the day pass as the chaff: Seek the Lord, you who have wrought his judgment, seek the meek, seek the just, if by any means you may be hid in the day of the Lord's wrath."*[135] The nation not desired is in the church that wakes up to judgment before the decree of deliverance and the day of redemption passes in the chaff of destruction. God's desire is for us to confront evil designs and proclaim his victory over the gates of hell.

Approaches to evangelization must espouse the new song in the covenant of Christ. This is not to preach the end of the world as if it were now, but to teach his deliverance from devastating wars before then as *"My times are in your hand: deliver me from the hand of my enemies, and from them that persecute me. Blessed be the Lord: for he has showed me his marvelous kindness in a strong city."*[136] Out of dire need *"the priests, the Lord's ministers shall weep, and shall say: Spare, O Lord, spare your people, and give not your inheritance to reproach, that the heathen should rule over them."*[137]

Discipleship is dependent on teaching Scripture since it is in the word of truth that we are sanctified. Countless souls in our world hunger to know if and how our reality fits into this design. Let us not be deceived about the last days or ignore the signs now taking place. A critical opportunity still exists for the church to grasp these things and rally the public in solidarity against great evil that threatens our civilization. Our Lady revealed at Fatima that Marxist atheism would spread from Russia bringing even greater wars and annihilation of some nations unless we repent and consecrate Russia to her.

Speculation exists among some about whether or not Pope John Paul II fulfilled all the details concerning the temporary peace that Our Lady predicted. This reasoning is based on his consecration of the whole world to Our Lady's Immaculate Heart rather than the specific mention of Russia itself. The premise of extending peace relies on a renewal of consecration of Russia in particular by the Pope done in unity with all bishops who are united to him. Both the summons of a solemn assembly and the provision by St. Paul that the church *"does still restrain"* may support this hope of sustaining peace.[138]

The outpouring of God's spirit is connected to prophecy whether it applies to the past, present or future. What began in the early church with Pentecost reached the start of end times with Fatima during WWI. Our freewill determines the extent of divine mercy and it seems if the church hierarchy responds to the divine call for a solemn assembly, *"Then will the Lord be jealous for his land, and pity his people."*[139] It is up to us to adhere to the prophets since *"rend your hearts, and not your garments, and turn to the Lord your God: for he is gracious and merciful, and ready to repent of the evil."*[140]

Similar to the plagues and captivity of ancient Israelites for their sins, the church has gone through persecutions from the start as they were reproved for *"having begun in the Spirit, are you now made perfect by the flesh?"*[141] How many people claim to be holy when in fact *"they have forsaken the Lord, they have provoked the Holy One of Israel, they are gone away backward?"*[142] This backsliding reflects the warnings of Fatima, yet there is a sure sign of hope in Our Lady and her instructions for us to cease from sinful ways, pray the rosary, do penance and receive the Eucharist in purity.[143]

Our Lady's place at the right hand of Jesus as Queen of Heaven and archenemy of evil is for us to honor as her children. We must ask for grace in virtue and protection that her powerful intercession is able to provide. Joyous mystery is revealed in the Apocalypse about this devotion since *"the earth helped the woman, and swallowed up the flood which the dragon cast out of his mouth."*[144] This victory is in our hearts to believe in her and dispel heresies about her as *"to the woman were given two wings of a great eagle, that she might fly into her place for a time, and times, and half a time."*[145]

Profound truth amid times of the watches before the end is that *"Our God shall come, that he may judge his people. Gather my saints together unto me, those that have made a covenant with me by sacrifice."*[146] This covenant is in the daily Liturgy of the Mass as *"show forth his salvation from day to day, bring him an offering. Honor and majesty are before him: strength and beauty are in his sanctuary."*[147] His power of redemption is in the altar from which we receive the Eucharist for *"his brightness was as the light: he had horns coming out of his hand, and there was the hiding of his power."*[148]

To all who seek salvation and believe in the promise of redemption, we must embrace the real presence of Christ in the Eucharist and follow this path to perfect communion with him. By means of the priests who minister in remembrance of Jesus, his word and his spirit unite upon the altar in divine blessing of his body and blood whereby we obtain true knowledge of God. As the Liturgy applies to our readiness to meet the Lord, *"They have seen your goings, O God, even the goings of my God, my king, in the sanctuary. Bless you God in the congregations, even the Lord, from the fountain of Israel."*[149]

Sanctity comes first by hearing and accepting the word of God, but we are saved by our practice of that word. The irony of truth is that those who seek it must also obey it regardless of cost for *"Search me, O God, and see if there be any wicked way in me, and lead me in the way of everlasting."*[150] Making changes in our lifestyles and beliefs may prove difficult for those who must turn from their routine habits in conversion, but there is no contradiction to the Eucharist except falsehoods from the Devil and to this *"They overcame him by the blood of the Lamb, and by the word of their testimony."*[151]

Notions that spirituality can be obtained apart from its very source lead many people to live in the deception of their pride. It is foolish to act as if we had another life to live or to think we are not accountable to the word of God for *"salvation is in the tabernacles of the righteous: I shall not die, but live, and declare the works of the Lord. This is the* day the Lord has made; we have blessed you out of the house of the Lord: bind the sacrifice with cords, even to the horns of the altar."[152] That sacrifice is the Eucharist and the cords we are told to use in binding ourselves to the Lord's altar is the rosary.

Judgment concerning who will be taken up in the watches relies on our participation in the church, especially in the Eucharist as "you are come to God the Judge of all, and to Jesus the mediator of the new covenant, and to the blood of sprinkling."[153] Our baptism is lived out and redemption sealed at the altar that "the offering up of the Gentiles might be acceptable, being sanctified by the Holy Spirit."[154] This common identity of the first watch is in daily ministration of the Holy Spirit in our Communion.[155] Thus, "I will give you thanks in the great congregation: I will praise you among much people."[156]

Attendance at church and belief in the Eucharist are not optional since "we shall not escape if we turn away from him that speaks from heaven."[157] Jesus taught us: "The Sabbath was made for man, and not man for the Sabbath."[158] We are not lords over what we do on the Sabbath, but he is Lord over us. It is in offering the Last Supper "he has perfected forever them that are sanctified. By a new and living way, that he has consecrated for us, through the veil, that is his flesh." Let us draw near "not forsaking the assembling of ourselves, and so much more, as you see the day approaching."[159]

Virtues we need to overcome our sins are obtained in the process of actively seeking and asking for those graces. There are elements of training and discipline in the course of salvation that we must accept with obedience and faith, but "if our gospel be hid, it is hid to them that are lost, that they should not see the gospel of Christ, concerning the knowledge of God shining on the face of Jesus."[160] We cannot separate his spirit from his word since in the Liturgy these identities form the being of Christ in the Eucharist who will "Send you help from the sanctuary, and strengthen you out of Zion."[161]

With all reason for a holy life, prosperity on earth and hope of resurrection, we are instructed to "work out your own salvation with fear and trembling."[162] Humility is a key factor in favor of God since it allows him to work in us. With respect to watches, Jesus is coming to "present to himself a glorious church, not having spot or wrinkle, but that it should be holy and without blemish."[163] We are given a standard as "straight is the gate and narrow is the way that leads to life, and few there are that find it."[164] These patterns are in the way of Christ and example of Our Lady as the gate.

When Jesus contemplated his mission of Calvary in agony at Gethsemane, he prayed "Father, if you are willing, remove this cup from me: nevertheless not my will, but yours be done."[165] He chose to suffer and die for us to accomplish the will of God the Father as in everything he did "he that sent me is with me: for I do always those things that please him."[166] Jesus is more than a model as he said "I am the way, the truth, and the life: no man comes to the Father, but by me."[167] Yet his birth in our hearts is transmitted by her who gave birth to him as he told his disciple John "Behold your mother!"[168]

Affirming the biblical role of Our Lady to influence our lives and surroundings in the battle against evil is central to our success. None of us can even imagine her closeness to God at the right hand of his Son or the power she can use if we call upon her to help and defend us. She is the gate that we must enter and as our spiritual mother she nurtures our maturity in Christ.[169] His servants need to imitate her perfect obedience to God as she said "Be it done to me according to your word."[170] We must turn to her and pray the holy rosary to intercede for lost souls and the dangers threatening our world.

Evangelization took on a new form with the messages of Fatima since it was then that the first war of Christ's gospel took place and the biblical sign of the Queen of Heaven was manifest to call us to repentance and warn us of great wars even past those of the last century. Newness of the church's mission is not only in a comprehension and teaching of our times, but it is a revelation of Our Lady as spiritual mother and our leader against the apostasy that is destroying our world. Of this vision *"your people shall be willing in the day of your power, in the beauties of holiness, from the womb of the morning."* [171]

One of the most poignant metaphors of Our Lady's vital role with Jesus in salvation relates to the spiritual life within us and the great signs of God's kingdom in the watches as he pointedly asks *"Shall I bring to the birth, and not cause to bring forth? Shall I cause to bring forth and shut the womb?"* This passage refers to Christ's coming to save us from persecutions as *"he shall appear to your joy, and they shall be ashamed."* His redemption is portrayed in Our Lady's motherhood during the analogy of birth pangs in times of war *"for as soon as Zion travailed, she brought forth her children."* [172]

Similarities between this description of Our Lady in the writings of the prophet Isaiah and St. John's vision of her in the Apocalypse are unmistakable. Isaiah taught that she brought forth more than one child, but he also specified *"she was delivered of a man child."* The same man child of the Apocalypse who was caught up to heaven before the Devil could devour him indicates the first watch. [173] Since there are physical and spiritual aspects to the watches, we must realize that her motherhood is in her strength to protect and in graces she bestows no matter how forceful or tender loving that may be.

The integral part of Our Lady in our spiritual and corporal state is in her being the womb of God's kingdom and mother of his seed *"That you may suck, and be satisfied with the breasts of her consolations, that you may milk out, and be delighted with the abundance of her glory."* She has an eminent place in these times as *"Behold, I will extend peace to her like a river, and the glory of the Gentiles like a flowing stream: then shall you suck, you shall be born upon her sides and dandled upon her knees; and your heart shall rejoice, and the hand of the Lord shall be known to his servants."* [174]

Devotions to Our Lady as the handmaid of the Lord are not abstract because she is a mother who communicates with us on a personal level since *"Your hand shall guide me and your right hand hold me fast. Truly you have formed my inmost being: you knit me in my mother's womb. Your eyes did see my substance, and in your book all my members were written, which in continuance were fashioned."* [175] Purely by divine choice are we to honor her royal power for *"You are my hope, O Lord God. By you have I been held up from the womb: you are he that took me out of my mother's bowels."* [176]

Peace comes to our world through the mediation granted by God through Christ, but Our Lady acts by means of his grace to quell evil and triumph over it. Jesus is at the right hand of the Father, but Our Lady is at Christ's right hand to act as his right hand. It is his orders coming from the Father that she in the power of his spirit carries out even at the watches when he returns to deliver us since in response to the refrain of *"his mercy endures forever"* said in a thrice, it is also written three times in reply that *"The right hand of the Lord has struck with power."* [177] Our love to her yields great reward.

Truths concerning Our Lady are embedded deep within the bible from its start to end. She was part of the divine plan before creation: *"The Lord possessed me in the beginning of his way, before his works of old. I was set up from everlasting, from the beginning, or ever the earth was."* She shares in his redemption as *"When he prepared the heavens, I was there: when he set a compass upon the face of the depth; when he gave to the seas his decree, when he appointed the foundations of the earth, then I was with him, as one brought up with him, daily his delight, rejoicing always before him."[178]*

As we make ready for the Lord, he also is preparing for our abode with him in heaven since he said *"I go to prepare a place for you, I will come again, and receive you unto myself: that where I am, there you also may be."[179]* Our Lady is with him in completing salvation and of her encompassing light and purity at Fatima, *"Out of Zion, the perfection of beauty, God has shined."[180]* While she awaits his decree for our rapture, *"Wisdom has built her house, she has hewn out her seven pillars, she has spread her table: Come, eat of my bread, and drink of my wine, forsake the foolish, and live."[181]*

Pillars of the church are its seven sacraments by which we obtain the cardinal virtues of faith, hope and charity as well as the theological virtues of prudence, fortitude, justice and temperance. Our Lady builds the Lord's house in our hearts and invites us to partake in his Eucharistic table. Her authority as Queen calls us from his tabernacle as *"She stands in the top of high places, by the way in the places of the paths. She cries at the gates, at the entry of the city, at the coming in at the doors."* In these harsh times she *"will lead in the way of righteousness, in the midst of the paths of judgment."[182]*

Denial of doctrine concerning Our Lady as the true gate we must enter to the door of eternity is a serious error since *"Blessed is the man that hears me, for whoever finds me finds life, and shall obtain favor of the Lord. But all they that hate me love death."[183]* Those who inherit God's kingdom are her children for *"Give me wisdom, the attendant at your throne for I am your servant, the son of your handmaid."[184]* More than thought, wisdom is Our Lady's person who enters the desert of our souls to guide us as *"Prepare you the way of the Lord, make straight in the desert a highway for our God."[185]*

From ancient history Jacob prophesied about the heavenly blessings of Our Lady *"by the God of your father, who shall help you, and by the Almighty who shall bless you with the blessings of heaven above, blessings of the breasts, and of the womb."[186]* Messianic promises are certainly based in the divinity of Christ and his atonement, but his order in the heavens and in the church on earth are his means of fulfilling it. If we separate our lives from these instruments, we forsake his grace for *"She that has born seven is become weak, her soul has fainted away, her sun is gone down while it was yet day."[187]*

Seven is sometimes used as a symbolical number that only God can determine and of our times in this day of redemption, it is obvious that Our Lady has feelings for us in her function to defend the church.[188] Her ability to lead and protect her children has been made weak by all their sins, divisions and lack of faith. The analogy of her sun going down in daytime illustrates impiety toward her and deceit of so many who feel they are fine with God when in fact they have forsaken him. If we want to be ready, then *"Be diligent that you may be found of him in peace, without spot and blameless."[189]*

Divine justice of gloom and doom predicted by the prophets in times of old was not well received by most people, but God still provided an escape for a remnant of Jews that survived and flourished. Those who feared the Lord knew these plagues would come and responded to his warnings. We need to pray and let Our Lady fill our arid souls with her pure love and faith as *"The desert shall rejoice, and blossom as the rose. Strengthen you the weak hands, and confirm the feeble knees. Be strong, fear not: behold your God will bring the revenge of recompense; God himself will come and save you."[190]*

Immortality in the presence of God is a state beyond anyone's grasp, but by reason of Scripture we can have the assurance in his spirit of that hope in the risen Christ for *"He will swallow up death in victory. And it shall be said in that day, Lo, this is our God: we have waited for him, and he will save us: this is the Lord, we have waited for him, we will be glad and rejoice in his salvation."[191]* These verses apply to stages of the watches and to resurrection that will take place at the sound of the last trumpet as *"the path of the just is as the shining light that shines more and more unto that perfect day."[192]*

Much like newborns who come into this world, those that are chosen in the watches will suddenly awake in heaven and be considered by all its citizens as if they were born there since *"Glorious things are spoken of you, O City of God. And of Zion it shall be said, This and that man was born in her: The Lord shall count, when he writes up his people that this man was born there."[193]* The wonders of God's making will cause great rejoicing for *"I will ransom them from the power of the grave: I will redeem them from death: O death, I will be your plagues; O grave, I will be your destruction."[194]*

This is a day of decision for the lives and souls of everyone who dwells on earth since *"God the Lord has spoken and summoned the earth, from the rising of the sun to its setting. Before him is a devouring fire, around him is a raging storm."[195]* The context of choosing and of saving his people is in periods of ruin, yet the metaphor of daylight in the morning to the sunset of these times reflects divine grace. Counsel to repent is prior to the end as *"Cut off your hair, O Jerusalem, and cast it away, and take up a lamentation on high places: for the Lord has forsaken the generation of his wrath."[196]*

Examination of conscience is needed by those who claim freedom of choice so *"Will you steal, murder, commit adultery, swear falsely, and walk after other gods, and come and stand before me in this house, which is called by my name, and say, We are delivered to do all these abominations?"[197]* Do we want vain excuses for errors we profess or the sacrileges we commit? Why lie to God? Can we try to make a fool out him and not be held accountable? Count the cost as *"the destruction of the transgressors and the sinners shall be together, and they that forsake the Lord shall be consumed."[198]*

An urgent SOS is made in the Psalter from the servants of God who see the vanity of this dying world since *"Help Lord, for the godly man ceases, for the faithful fail from the children of men who have said, With our tongue we will prevail, our lips are our own: who is lord over us?"* They don't realize their slavery to sin whose lord is their belly, but in these times of hatred for those who follow and promote the statutes of truth *"now will I arise says the Lord: I will set him in safety from him that puffs at him. You shall keep them O Lord: you shall preserve them from this generation forever."[199]*

Old-fashioned preaching of fire and brimstone has lost its spark in most sermons we hear, but the bible remains as a testament of the source of life: *"Hear, O my people, and I will speak; O Israel, and I will testify against you: I am God, even your God. Think you that I am like yourself? I will reprove you. Now consider this, you that forget God, lest I tear you in pieces and there be none to deliver."[200]* God is not corrupt and his warning is to those who have lost his way and fail to treat the sickness in his church. Many have abandoned the Sabbath, the need for confession and focus of daily prayer.

Relevance of prophecy is all around us and awareness of these things can bring about conversion as *"In a dream, in a vision of the night when deep sleep falls upon men in slumbering upon a bed: then he opens the ears of men and seals their instruction that he may withdraw man from his purpose and hide pride from man."[201]* This passage reveals

God's desire to wake us up to our sins and show us his plan for *"He looked upon men and if any say, I have sinned and perverted that which is right, and it profits me not: He will deliver his soul from going down to the pit and his life shall see the light."*

Challenges we face are practical ones since we can influence divine justice by our zeal to intercede through works of devotion and evangelization. It is our business to share our faith in Jesus with those who say *"I do not know this man"* or *"We will not have this man rule over us."*[202] The prophetic call to blow the trumpet in the church and assemble its elders and people is to correct those who abandon the articles of our faith, but also to address the signs of our times and our deliverance in light of Scripture. We must turn to Our Lady and heed the warnings of Fatima against the spread of Marxist atheism.

Religious freedom is a commodity we will lose if we don't use. This axiom applies on a personal and social level since the vacuum we create by apathy toward God will most certainly be filled with oppression and debauchery. Jesus told us to *"Let your loins be girded about and your lights burning: And you yourselves like unto men that wait for their lord, that when he comes and knocks, they may open to him."*[203] We need to make time for him and *"set your affection on things above, not on things on the earth. When Christ, who is our life, shall appear, then you shall appear with him in glory."*[204]

Reflection on Jesus' agony at Gethsemane is pertinent to our present trial since *"being in agony, his sweat became as great drops of blood falling to the ground."*[205] His pain and sweating of blood was not only for himself, but he felt sorrow of all who suffer for his kingdom, even immolation of those in the time we now live. This period is unlike the past since heaven will open in the midst of great bloodshed and it will pave the way for the Antichrist who will eventually prohibit the Eucharist and briefly conquer the entire world. In allegory, the church has entered a parallel passion of Christ.

While Jesus contemplated his purpose to die for the remission of sins in the world, his apostles slept and deserted him. This same response is going on today as people slumber in their lack of contrition and walk away in disbelief. Yet in his loneliness, an angel of God appeared during his agony to comfort him. Jesus urged his disciples to watch and pray not to fall into temptation and we should seek Our Lady's help from him for *"Send her forth from your holy heavens and from your glorious throne dispatch her that she may be with me and work with me, that I may know what is pleasing to you."*[206]

Affluence among Christian peoples has sorely weakened their faith and ability to see the signs of our times in relation to divine justice. They don't have enough humility and reason to discern how lax our laws have become and how far we have drifted from the God we claim to serve *"Because you say, I am rich and increased with goods and have need of nothing, but know not you are wretched and blind and naked."* Materialism and hedonism prevent us from knowing Christ and his disdain for our lusts so *"because you are lukewarm and neither cold or hot, I will vomit you out of my mouth."*[207]

God is not the author of confusion, divisions and neglect which are choking the true breath of life from the church. The road to perdition has not changed, but the number of those who travel it have surely crowded a wide street *"For the wicked man glories in his greed and the covetous blaspheme. Your judgments are far from his mind and all his foes he scorns. He says in his heart, I shall not be moved: for I will never see adversity, God has forgotten, he never sees, he will not avenge it."*[208] With technology that has proven man's intelligence, why do people distort God's word to condone their sin?

Perversion of divine law and denial of its justice are psychological illusions of our reality that are perpetuated by demonic forces. Those who are bound in their lusts to this world and think they are morally upright or not responsible are living a lie *"For rebellion is as the sin of witchcraft, and stubbornness is as iniquity and idolatry."*[209] These many wicked works that separate us from God include *"Adultery, fornication, uncleanness, lasciviousness, idolatry, witchcraft, hatred, variance, emulations, wrath, strife, seditions, heresies, envying, murders, drunkenness, reveling, and such like."*[210]

Prevalence of sin in society results in divine retribution, but even the worst examples of decadence are being justified as civil liberty and honored by some as Christian values. Let us not be deceived about the vile affections of men and women who oppose nature or the killing of innocent unborn human life. Abortion and homosexuality are examples of a wider array of other common profane actions that will not escape judgment for *"O that my people had hearkened to me, and Israel had walked in my ways! I should soon have subdued their enemies, and turned my hand against their adversaries."*[211]

Unless a broad and penetrating change comes about to restore our traditional role in serving Christ and keeping the Sabbath, we can be sure our world will fall into an all-out war. Most people are looking for better days, but refuse to deal with the source of our problems in their own sins. Prophecies concerning the last days are not a fictional story or fantasy of what could be, but they contain a realism very apparent for those who are willing to *"live soberly, righteously, and godly in this present world, looking for that blessed hope and the glorious appearing of our Savior Jesus Christ."*[212]

Morality is more than a code of cannon law since holiness comes by grace as we open our hearts to commune with God. Although the bible is precise about precepts of faith, we don't need to be experts, but to love God is a relationship with him in knowing and doing his will as *"Cleanse you me from my secret faults. Keep back your servant from presumptuous sins, and I shall be innocent from the great transgression."*[213] Faith comes by him who searches our hearts for *"let God be true, but every man a liar."* Also, *"If we say we have not sinned, we make him a liar, and his word is not in us."*[214]

The onus for unfolding dangers is upon every God fearing person to respond to events of prophecy now evident. If we don't love God enough to amend our lives and thank him on the Sabbath, how can we show his love to others? Our spiritual life is in the Eucharist since *"send out your light and your truth: let them lead me unto your holy hill, and to your tabernacles, then I will go to the altar of God, unto God my exceeding joy."*[215] Thus we prepare for *"unto you that fear my name shall the Sun of righteousness arise with healing in his wings: and you shall go forth, and grow up as calves in the stall."*[216]

Unity of faith is in the acceptance of Scripture as the true word of God. Most people believe in the prophets, but are bewildered because the Messianic story of how things end has been neglected, confused and distorted by those who should decipher these mysteries. Nothing is covered that will not be known or revealed and it is in this context *"you shall return, and discern between the righteous and the wicked, between him who serves God and him who serves him not. And they shall be mine, in that day when I make up my jewels; and I will spare them as a man spares his own son who serves him."*[217]

Bible students, scholars and other readers may find it surprising that there are so many references to the topic of rapture, but these appointed times are in bloody trials to arrest our awry ways and purify our souls. Whether the present terrorist war abates or erupts into a third world war depends on each of us as individuals, but also on how leaders of the church and of sovereign nations respond to doctrine of the prophets. That decision is pressing since the political state of our global society is in great jeopardy and the solution to our problems must be quickly based on turning to God for his mercy.

Faith is not abstract, but it is a familiar force to everyone. All of us are innately given a measure this divine gift, but we must yield to it with a pure heart. Divine law is not far from any of us if we are honest with God. Our world is at a precipice that excludes any more pretense and we must know the Lord's anger, even for America as *"According to their deeds he will repay; to the islands he will repay recompense."*[218] Yet our recourse is simple for *"If my people, who are called by my name, shall pray and seek my face, and turn from their wicked ways, then I will forgive their sin and will heal their land."*[219]

Destruction resulting from the sword is the most serious curse any nation brings upon itself due to its iniquity. There have been many recent plagues upon the earth intended by God to bring us to repentance, but thought of a conventional world war spinning into nuclear battle is a near prospect we must admit with dreadful fear or lasting hope. Yet clemency of Christ dictates *"At what instant I shall speak concerning a nation to pluck it up, and to pull it down, and to destroy it; if that nation, against whom I have pronounced, turn from their evil, I will repent of the evil that I thought to do unto them."*[220]

History offers a prime example of the efficacy in heeding the penalties of divine justice since a prophet named Jonah was sent to the ancient city of Nineveh with a notice of its ruin in being overthrown in just forty days *"so the people of Nineveh believed God, and proclaimed a fast, from the greatest of them to the least."* When the king heard the news, he published a decree of public mourning to *"cry mightily unto God: turn everyone from his evil way, and from the violence in their hands."* In his mercy, *"God saw their works, and repented of the evil he had said he would do, and he did it not."*[221]

Everyone seems to want to know how long it will be until the end of our world, but they don't consider terrible curses that will occur before the final battle of good and evil. It is in these intermediary times we must realize the immense perils we now face and be ready to meet the Lord. Only God can determine the balance of world peace and when prophecy about the sword of the second seal will be fulfilled. We should take courage in the fact that no man could number the people from all nations, tribes and tongues that St. John saw in the first watch. Our chances may be better than we think.

---

[1] Habakkuk 3,2&13
[2] I Corinthians 15,51-52
[3] Ephesians 4, 29-30
[4] Mark 13,8; Luke 21, 9-10&28
[5] Mathew 24,40-42; Luke 17,26-36; 21,35-36
[6] Isaiah 50, 2
[7] Isaiah 43,12&18-19
[8] Ephesians 1,4; 3,9; Hebrews 4,3
[9] Isaiah 48,3-7
[10] Habakkuk 1,12; 2,1-4

[11] Psalm 118,15-19
[12] Isaiah 64,4; Ephesians 3,20
[13] I Corinthians 2,9-10
[14] II Peter 1,16
[15] II Thessalonians 2,1
[16] II Timothy 4,1-5
[17] Hebrews 9,27-28
[18] Philippians 3,20-21
[19] Hebrews 1,2-3; 2,1-8
[20] Galatians 1,3-4
[21] Colossians 1,19-20
[22] Hebrews 2,8
[23] II Peter 3,13
[24] I Peter 1,13; 5,4
[25] Philippians 1,6-10
[26] I Corinthians 1,5-8
[27] I Corinthians 1,10; II Thessalonians 2,15
[28] I Thessalonians 5,2-6; I Peter 4,17
[29] Revelation 15,1; 16,15
[30] I Thessalonians 5,9
[31] Mark 13,25-37; Luke 12,35-46
[32] I Thessalonians 5,5-8
[33] Mathew 10,15; Mark 6,11; Luke 17,30-36
[34] Luke 21,34-36
[35] Mathew 24,33; Mark 13,29; Luke 21,28&36
[36] Luke 12,35-38
[37] Mathew 10,22; 24,13-14; Mark 13,13
[38] Luke 21,28
[39] I Thessalonians 4,15-17
[40] Isaiah 66,5-9
[41] Genesis 49,8-11
[42] Isaiah 61,1-3
[43] Acts 1,7; I Thessalonians 5,1
[44] Revelation 7,9-17; 14,1-5; 15,2-4
[45] Mathew 24,37-44; 25,1-13; Luke 17,26-37
[46] Psalm 19,1-5&9-11
[47] Ezekiel 38,20
[48] Revelation 8,2-6
[49] Isaiah 26,16-20
[50] Isaiah 26,1-4; Hebrews 11,16
[51] Romans 6,1-6; Galatians 2,20; 5,24-25
[52] I Corinthians 15,51-52
[53] I Thessalonians 1,9-10; 5,9
[54] Revelation 14,14-19
[55] Jeremiah 5,24; Mark 4,26-29
[56] James 5,7-8
[57] Hosea 6,3
[58] Acts 15,7-14
[59] II Corinthians 3,14-18
[60] Isaiah 65,8-9
[61] Isaiah 27,6
[62] Isaiah 59,20
[63] Psalm 71,20
[64] Psalm 119,146-149
[65] Isaiah 59,20-21

[66] Isaiah 51,14-16
[67] Isaiah 33,2-3&10&13
[68] Revelation 12,10-11
[69] I Timothy 6,12-15
[70] Isaiah 35,1-4
[71] I John 2,28
[72] Psalm 57,1-3
[73] Hebrews 9,28
[74] Colossians 3,4; I John 3,2
[75] I Corinthians 13,12
[76] Ezekiel 7,16
[77] Psalm 55,6&18&22-23
[78] Psalm 17,4&15
[79] Psalm 20,7-8
[80] Isaiah 43,1-2
[81] Psalm 107,6-7&13-14
[82] I Peter 4,17-18
[83] Psalm 75,8
[84] Isaiah 51,21-23
[85] I Corinthians 6,2-3
[86] I Thessalonians 3,12-13
[87] Psalm 107, 2-3&30
[88] Jeremiah 15,15-21
[89] Micah 7,4-9
[90] Micah 7,9-10
[91] Luke 19,40-44; I Peter 2,12
[92] Psalm 24,3-8
[93] Micah 7,9-10; Revelation 17,1-6
[94] Jeremiah 50,31; 51,17-18
[95] Isaiah 59,8-10
[96] II Timothy 3,13-15
[97] Isaiah 43,11-13
[98] Jeremiah 12,6-7
[99] Psalm 78,1-8&56-62
[100] Mathew 27,46; Mark 15,34
[101] Psalm 74,3-8
[102] Isaiah 24,1-6
[103] II Thessalonians 2,2-4
[104] Isaiah 59,2-3
[105] Jeremiah 12,10
[106] II Peter 3,3-6
[107] Isaiah 59,14
[108] Psalm 24,6-10; 78,23
[109] Isaiah 40,31
[110] Psalm 96,1&13; Isaiah 42,9-16
[111] Psalm 149,1-9;
[112] Psalm 40,1-3; 144,5-7
[113] Psalm 139,5-13
[114] Isaiah 18,3-7
[115] Psalm 98,1-4&9
[116] Psalm 22,1-6&23-26
[117] Isaiah 51,4-5
[118] Psalm 147,12-13&19
[119] Psalm 33,3&8-12
[120] Isaiah 43,1; II Corinthians 3,15-18

[121] Genesis 32,28; 35,9-12; Job 29,19-25
[122] Psalm 71,14&21-24
[123] Psalm 139,5-6&16
[124] Psalm 65,8-9
[125] II Thessalonians 2,10-12
[126] II Thessalonians 2,8-9
[127] II Thessalonians 2,2-7
[128] Malachi 3,2
[129] II Thessalonians 2,4
[130] Joel 2,12-13&24
[131] Joel 2,22-24
[132] Proverbs 3,18; Revelation 12,5&17
[133] Mathew 24,32-34; Mark 13,28-30
[134] Genesis 49,25; Isaiah 66,11; Joel 2,15-16
[135] Zephaniah 2,1-3
[136] Psalm 31,15&19-21
[137] Joel 2,17
[138] Joel 2,15-17; II Thessalonians 2,6-7
[139] Joel 2,18; John 17,17
[140] Joel 2,13
[141] I Corinthians 15,34; Galatians 3,3
[142] Isaiah 1,4&27
[143] Isaiah 1,16-19; Revelation 12,16
[144] Psalm 45,9; Revelation 12,15-16
[145] Revelation 12,14
[146] Psalm 50,3-5; I Peter 4,17-19
[147] Psalm 96,2-9
[148] Habakkuk 3,4
[149] Psalm 68,24-26
[150] Psalm 139,23-24
[151] Revelation 12,10-11
[152] Psalm 118,15-27
[153] Hebrews 12,22-25
[154] Romans 15,14-16
[155] Acts 2,40-42; 6,1-3; II Corinthians 3,7-9
[156] Psalm 35,17-18&23-24
[157] Hebrews 12,25
[158] Mark 2,27-28
[159] Hebrews 10,14&19-25
[160] II Corinthians 4,2-7
[161] Psalm 20,1-2&7-8
[162] Philippians 2,12-16
[163] Ephesians 5,26-27&31-32
[164] Matthew 7,13-14
[165] Matthew 26,39; Mark 14,36; Luke 22,42
[166] John 8,28-29
[167] John 14,6
[168] John 19,27
[169] Psalm 86,16; 118,15-20; Isaiah 28,6
[170] Luke 1,28-38
[171] Psalm 110,3
[172] Isaiah 66,5-9
[173] Isaiah 66,7-8; Revelation 12,4-5&17
[174] Isaiah 66,10-14
[175] Psalm 139,10-16

[176] Psalm 22,9-10; 71,4-7
[177] Psalm 118,2-4&15-16
[178] Proverbs 8,20-32
[179] John 14,3
[180] Psalm 50,1-2&15-20; Jeremiah 31,21-23
[181] Proverbs 9,1-6
[182] Proverbs 8,1-5&20-21
[183] Proverbs 8,32-36
[184] Wisdom 9,4-6
[185] Isaiah 40,3-5; Revelation 12,14
[186] Genesis 49,25-26
[187] Jeremiah 15,9-11
[188] Psalm 119,164
[189] II Peter 3,14
[190] Isaiah 35,1-8
[191] Isaiah 25,8-9; I Corinthians 15,51-57
[192] Proverbs 4,18
[193] Psalm 87,3&5-6
[194] Hosea 13,14
[195] Psalm 50,1-7
[196] Jeremiah 7,27-30
[197] Jeremiah 7,8-11
[198] Isaiah 1,27-28
[199] Psalm 12,1-7
[200] Psalm 50,7&21-22; Isaiah 1,6
[201] Job 33,14-18&27-28
[202] Mathew 26,69-75; Luke 19,12-14
[203] Luke 12,34-36
[204] Colossians 3,2-6
[205] Luke 22,44
[206] Wisdom 9,10-11
[207] Revelation 3,15-20
[208] Psalm 10,3-6&11-13
[209] I Samuel 15,23
[210] Galatians 5,19-21; I Corinthians 6,9-10
[211] Psalm 81,11-16
[212] Titus 2,11-13
[213] Psalm 19,12-13
[214] Romans 3,3-4; I John 1,8-10
[215] Psalm 43,3-4
[216] Malachi 4,2
[217] Malachi 3,16-18; Luke 12,2-3
[218] Isaiah 59,18-20
[219] II Chronicles 7,14
[220] Jeremiah 18,6-8
[221] Jonah 3,3-10

Chapter Six
OPENING OF THE THIRD SEAL
THE BLACK HORSE

"When he opened the third seal, I saw a black horse and he who sat on it had a balance in his hand, and I heard a voice say: A measure of wheat for a denarius and three measures of barley for a denarius. Do not harm the wine and the oil."
Revelation 6,5-6

Our earthly reality reflects a direct and detailed relationship to the dire warnings yet great promises of hope set forth in the biblical end times. These prophecies are intriguing since they reflect present day events in a manner that we can see the future of our world with reason and truth despite the severity of divine justice and inability to explain the power of redemption in finite terms. There is much for us to learn in our journey toward God's kingdom and his plan to unite mankind in his love, but the ongoing grasp of prophecy in the mission of the gospel is one to be revealed in his appointed times. Signs given in each seal relate to this transition.

Those who are left on earth after WWIII will awake from a nightmare that most did not expect. They will have seen God's strength to save his people in rapture and either believe in his holy word or look to the blind falsehoods of their own affairs. Christian scholars have largely ignored the promise of land to the Jews who survive an awesome onslaught yet go into captivity by a dreadful forecast of events before they obtain it. Many specific matters of famine and war relating to Messianic hope in saving the church and Christ's universal reign are seen as forgotten history, but the sequence of these things is made clear to anyone who will listen.

From the time of God's oaths to Abraham that promised an inheritance to Hebrew people and a holy seed from all nations, the overall concern of the patriarchs and prophets was what will happen in the latter days. The central theme of these prophecies is he whom Jacob spoke of and Moses preached would come after him to shepherd the faithful. This Messiah who is called the Son of David and Son of God has been revealed not only in his human yet divine person, but in his resurrection so we may be certain about his apocalyptic teachings concerning our human existence and eternal life in heaven. To him every soul will account for their deeds.

History has proven the cruelty and injustice of man's search for power and wealth. Although the prophetic outlook is disturbing and even sickening in regard to morality and destruction, we have come to a time when these things actually make sense as we consider our global military structure and the growing rebellion against Christ by whom grace is given to follow divine law. A great irony about end times is the resemblance between modern and ancient Israel since they will again be forced into cruel captivity while a portion will escape by redemption and a remnant reserved to come back from their dispersion to inherit the promise of lasting prosperity.

The fact that Jews have returned to their homeland sets a scenario for all sacred visions to be fulfilled. As in the past they will rise to a secure kingdom and once they attain it their fall will be trust in earthly goods and pursuit of sinful lusts. These spiritual and political aspects of their nation were revealed by Moses who plainly said *"evil will befall you in the latter days, because you will do evil in the sight of the Lord to provoke him to anger by the work of your hands."*[1] He warned of things still hidden under the terrible sanction of the curse that would be looked back upon by *"the generation to come of your children who will rise up after you."*[2]

Theologians who study the book of Revelation have not understood the future timeframe or context in opening of the third seal and its connection to the prophetic word of God. They have missed the primary intent in this very broad plague of famine by him who sits on the black horse holding a balance in his hand and not perceived the meaning of favor toward those who are symbolized by wine and oil. There are many instructions made in the bible to explain these issues in regard to the phase of events following WWIII and the spiritual struggle for the church. In this period of trial, Jews will have a critical role in that balance of divine justice.

When Jesus was brought to the temple at the time of his circumcision, the prophet Simeon had been foretold he would see the Lord's Christ and then said *"this child is set for the fall and rising again of many in Israel, and for a sign that shall be contradicted."*[3] Similarly, God revealed to Moses that *"I will raise them up a Prophet among their brethren, like unto you, and whosoever will not listen to my words he speaks in my name, I will require it of him."*[4] The Christ in whom all nations are blessed has been manifest and they are without excuse who reject the holy promise of him who Jacob called the *"the Shepherd, the Rock of Israel."*[5]

It is necessary to review some of the biblical verses in this chapter already discussed in prior sections that form a basis or outline of things to come. The preview of these prophecies applying to the captivity of Israel and the watches of redemption was provided as a general sketch of the separate phases in the end times. Further details of the Jewish people and political changes in the world that will lead to another global war are presented herein. God is not a respecter of persons or nations who refuse the atonement of Christ and oppose the moral order of his law, but he said to him *"Sit at my right hand until I make your enemies your footstool."*[6]

One of the core readings relating to hardness of human hearts in believing in Jesus asserts *"The stone which the builders refused is become the headstone of the corner."*[7] And again it is written, *"Behold, I lay in Zion for a foundation stone, a tried stone, a precious cornerstone, a sure foundation: he that believes shall not make haste."*[8] These references are made specifically to the builders of an actual third Jewish temple, but the headstone applies to the spiritual temple in Christ of whom *"he shall be as a sanctuary, but a rock of offense to both houses of Israel. And many among them shall stumble, and fall, and be broken, and snared, and be taken."*[9]

As in ancient history, the promise of land and prosperity for Jews are conditional since *"If you return, O Israel, return unto me: and if you will put away your abominations out of my sight, then you shall not remove."*[10] Likewise, *"If you thoroughly amend your ways and your doings, then will I cause you to dwell in this place, in the land that I gave to your fathers, forever and ever."*[11] The curses of the law are subject to man's free will for *"If they had stood in my counsel, and had caused my people to hear my words, then they would have turned them from their evil way."*[12] So too *"because you have rejected knowledge, I will reject you."*[13]

Science in a pure sense is truth and that knowledge is revealed in Christ by whom we have our very being let alone our awareness and technology of bodily elements around us. We have much reason to believe in him not only by the historical facts recorded of his life, death and resurrection that were seen beforehand by holy men of God, but because of his spirit bearing witness in our hearts since *"Not by might, nor by power, but by my spirit says the Lord."*[14] We cannot play God or substitute our vanity for his righteousness *"For he has made him to be sin for us who knew no sin that we might be made the righteousness of God in him."*[15]

Apostasy is the integral cause for divine vengeance upon Israel and the whole world as *"Who has directed the Spirit of the Lord, or being his counselor has taught him?"*[16] Scripture was not made by human intellect, nor can anyone pervert the divine grace of him who is Savior of mankind as Jesus proclaimed *"I am come in my Father's name, and you receive me not. For had you believed Moses, you would have believed me, for he spoke of me."*[17] As our mediator before

God, *"If you believe not that I am he, you shall die in your sins."[18]* Nobody can bypass his role in our atonement or his authority as *"he who hates me, hates my Father also."[19]*

Persecution of Christian Jews in the early church by their own brethren was rampant since religious leaders spurned the gospel due to envy and feared the apostles would take over their rabbinical rule.[20] The blindness to Christ was in their pride of being justified by Mosaic Law for *"they have a zeal for God, but not according to knowledge. For they being ignorant of God's righteousness and going about to establish their own righteousness, have not submitted themselves to the righteousness of God."[21]* All people have sinned and need divine mercy granted through Jesus who taught *"It is the spirit that gives life, the flesh profits nothing."[22]*

Moses instructed about the dissension of Jews against Christ and his church as God told him *"I will move them to jealousy with those who are not a people, and I will provoke them to anger with a foolish nation."[23]* The Gentiles from many peoples who receive Jesus are one nation in the unity of faith and in his spirit as *"I am found of them that sought me not: I said, Behold me, behold me, to a nation not called by my name."[24]* Moses prophesied of the end times as *"O that they were wise, that they understood this, that they understood their latter end. You were unmindful of the Rock that begot you, you forgot the God who gave you birth."[25]*

After decades of conflicts and useless attempts to reach a lasting peace accord that result in WWIII, the State of Israel will survive *"For of old time I have broken your yoke, and burst your bonds."[26]* Against great odds, God will defend their nation in a war of unimagined bloodshed as *"I drew them with bands of love and was to them as they who take off the yoke on their jaws, and I laid meat to them."[27]* In context of the last days after that yoke is broken, their wealth and military will increase for *"Their land is full of silver and gold, neither is there any end to their treasures; their land is also full of horses, neither is there any end of their chariots."[28]*

Numerous citations of prophecy indicate a period of prosperity for Israel and the rebuilding of their temple, but these predictions are mixed with corruption and idolatry that bring the fury and wrath of God. It will take seven months just to cleanse the land from dead bodies and seven years to recycle all the military hardware left behind by invading armies so *"This is the day whereof I have spoken. They shall spoil them who spoiled them."[29]* Concerns of building riches in their new kingdom will lead them into ruin as *"they are become great, and waxen rich. Your children have forgotten me, and when I fed them to the full, then they committed adultery."[30]*

Profuse affluence usually induces a state of spiritual depravity because material possessions become an exclusive ambition in life as Jesus explained *"No servant can serve two masters. You cannot serve God and mammon."[31]* This excessive desire for social status and money inhibits our pure motives toward faith for *"I caused you to multiply and you increased and grew great. You were decked with gold and silver, and did prosper into a kingdom. Your renown went forth among the heathen, but you did trust in your own beauty and prostituted yourself to every passenger, to be his."[32]* Most of us know that covetousness is the root of all evil.[33]

Creation is given to us to have dominion over, but many have exploited it through selfish lusts and closed their hearts to the God who created it and saved us from our own destruction. With respect to Israel, *"I brought you into a plentiful country, but when you entered, you defiled my land."[34]* Warnings by the prophets will prove of no avail for *"she that was great among the nations, how is she become tributary! She remembered not her last end."[35]* The Lord disputed with them that *"they were filled, and their heart was exalted, and they have forgotten me. As they increased, so they sinned against me: therefore I will turn their glory into shame."[36]*

Thoughts of inheriting the Promised Land have permeated the minds of Israelites ever since ancient times, but God will test their faith for *"You have brought a vine out of Egypt: you have* cast out the heathen, and planted it. She sent out her boughs unto the sea, and her branches unto the river."[37] Projections of an extensive expansion of Jewish rule involve the advent of sorrows as "they shall be as the early dew that passes away."[38] Their reign will be lost since "The crown of pride shall be trodden under feet, and the glorious beauty shall be as a fading flower."[39] Likewise, "in the morning it springs up, but by evening it wilts and fades."[40]

An eminent dichotomy exists in the spiritual and physical inclination of Jews during the rebuilding of their temple. A portion of them from all tribes will zealously embrace the gospel and as living stones will open themselves to the cornerstone of Christ in ministry. Those who believe in the new covenant are the temple of God who dwells in us in his spirit.[41] Although ample references are made to a third Jewish temple made by human hands, many Jews who are architects of this house of worship will not accept salvation in the house of their hearts, nor see the consequences of their materialism and persecution of their Christian brethren.

Precise dimensions for the construction of a third temple were given to the prophet Ezekiel by a heavenly messenger. This angelic being revealed exactly how this massive structure is yet to be made, including its outward and inner courts as well as its chambers and Holy of Holies.[42] The timeframe for this physical temple to be rebuilt in Jerusalem is prior to the Messiah's return to establish his earthly reign because "the majesty of the Lord came into the house by way of the gate that looked to the east. And he said to me, Son of man, the place of my throne and the soles of my feet, where I will dwell in the midst of the children of Israel forever."[43]

Predictions of and references to the third temple recorded by the prophets are marred by the rebellion and stubborn idolatry of its keepers for "you have brought strangers into my sanctuary, uncircumcised in heart and in flesh, to pollute it, even my house. They have defiled my holy name by their abominations, wherefore I consumed them in my anger." This rebuke is found in the very chapters that describe the pattern of the temple as "You have not kept charge of my holy things. The Levites who are gone away far from me when Israel went astray: they ministered to them before their idols, and caused the house of Israel to fall into iniquity."[44]

Distinctions between the spiritual and corporeal teachings as they relate to Jerusalem and the temple need to be recognized. There is a unique parallel of this physical location with that city and place in our hearts expressed by the universal church. Concurrent theme of prophecy in the temporary restoration of these things is revealed as a renewed evangelization emerges among Jewish tribes for conversion to Christ while outward construction of the temple is done since "He is my shepherd and he shall build my city, saying to Jerusalem: You shall be built, and to the temple: your foundations shall be laid, and I will raise up the decayed places thereof."[45]

Permanence of the inheritance of land and the temple for Jews can only take place after all matters of God's word are fulfilled. Many scholars recognize that a rebuilt temple is a major landmark of the last days, but they don't admit "In the day that your walls are to be built, in that day shall the law be far removed."[46] Idolatry in the temple is a sign of the timing of divine justice "For both prophet and priest are profane, yea, in my house I found their wickedness: I will bring evil upon them, even the year of their visitation."[47] Similarly, "The end is come upon my people of Israel. And the songs of the temple shall be wailings in that day."[48]

Great deception will cover the hearts of many priests and prophets when they reach a peak of power and wealth "For they have healed the hurt of the daughter of my people saying: Peace, peace, when there was no peace. They shall fall among them that fall: in the time of their visitation, they will be cast down."[49] Their hypocrisy is evident as "the word of the Lord is a reproach to them, they have no delight in it."[50] This denial of prophetic justice could not be more outspoken *"for they know not the way of the Lord, nor the judgment of their God. They have belied the Lord saying: It is not he, neither shall we see sword nor famine."*[51]

How can anyone explain the unscrupulous acts of those who will bring civilization to near extinction? Pervasive secularism in our world has stifled conscience and perverted the divine word. Iniquities of Jews found in the bible are not exclusive to their own people, but reflect a stigma that will reach all nations. If we cannot discern what sin is, then we are also unable to see its outcome since *"Your prophets have not discovered your iniquity, to turn your captivity. They are prophets of deceit who think to cause my people to forget my name, as their fathers forgot me for Baal."*[52] It is absurd to suppose we can stop God from being our ultimate judge.

Idolatry has many forms, but the sacrilege of defaming the Lord's house is an extreme kind of blasphemy as *"the time is come, the day of trouble is near, and not the sounding again of the mountains. They shall pollute my secret place, and robbers shall enter it to defile it."*[53] These verses refer to a time after WWIII when the temple is profaned and give warning of the day when Israel will fall. The prophet Ezekiel verified that abomination when he was brought in visions *"to the door of the inner gate toward the north, where was the seat of the image of jealousy. They worshiped the sun toward the east and put a branch to their nose."*[54]

Defiance of God in the temple is against Christ who will destroy and judge the Antichrist's world kingdom as *"I have raised one from the north, and he shall come from the rising of the sun. He shall call upon my name, and make princes to be as mortar, as the potter treading clay."*[55] In delusion of sin, they will think *"The Lord has forsaken the earth, and the Lord sees us not."*[56] They will believe they are in control of their destiny saying *"Get you far from the Lord: unto us is this land given in possession. Abraham was one, but we are many; this land is given to us for inheritance."*[57] That promise is not based on occupation, but on obedience.

Blatant mockery in the temple by those who worship the rising sun and put a branch to their nose is of him *"whose name is The Branch, and he shall build the temple of the Lord, and he shall sit and rule upon his throne, and he shall be a priest upon his throne."*[58] This is Jesus of whom *"I will raise unto David a just Branch, and a king shall reign and prosper, and execute judgment and justice in the earth, and he shall be called: The Lord Our Righteousness. He shall smite the earth with the rod of his mouth, and slay the wicked with the breath of his lips."*[59] It is clear that they who ridicule know the Scripture of him whom they oppose.

In the study of God's word we must see the dire straits of the last days before the dawn of peace on earth since *"Woe to you that desire the day of the Lord! To what end is it for you? The day of the Lord is darkness, and not light."*[60] It is in this setting of apathy and rebellion that *"Woe to them who are at ease in Zion, and you that put far away the evil day, and cause the seat of violence to draw near. You have borne the tabernacle of Mo-loch and Chi-un your images, the star of your god."*[61] They will invite anger of the Antichrist and not believe the signs of their times showing *"the Lord has rejected and forsaken the generation of his wrath."*[62]

References to the judgments of Israel repeatedly specify a framework of the end *"For it is the day of the Lord's vengeance, and the year of recompenses for the controversy of Zion."*[63] The plagues foreseen by the prophets reveal *"the day of your watchmen and your visitation comes."*[64] In regard to the temple, *"Our adversaries have trodden down your sanctuary. Our holy and beautiful house, where our fathers praised you, is burned up with fire."*[65] This tragedy of ruin and their demise is in the future tense for *"The Lord has not pitied the daughter of Judah: he has cast down Israel, and given her palaces into the hand of the enemy."*[66]

Many harsh prophecies toward Israel indicate a generation called the daughter of my people as this leap in time is marked by the return of their kingdom. A poignant comparison to their ancient fate is made in the proverb *"As is the mother, so is her daughter."*[67] Possession of land or even of the temple itself is not an indemnity. With respect to fulfillment of divine promise, *"Behold, I will bring back again the captivity of Jacob's tents, and have mercy on his dwellings, and the city shall be built on her own heap, and the temple shall remain after the manner thereof."*[68] God will have mercy on them and again bring them back from captivity.

The defeat of Israel and severe damage to the holy temple of Jerusalem do not negate the promise of land with a restored temple in accordance with the new covenant. It may boggle our minds that after centuries of banishment, the Jews will again go into captivity despite their gracious blessings and counsel of the Lord. Not in our power or timing, but in his spirit and word the divine plan will be accomplished. Most of us have not thought about WWIV or its consequences of an evil world empire led by the Antichrist and subsequent wrath of God. Christ will triumph in his redemption and judgment to usher in the kingdom of God.

Details of WWIV and final curses of end wrath are subjects of following chapters, yet some preliminary discussion is made in this chapter to provide a background for revealing these phases of the Apocalypse. Topics examined in the third seal of Revelation include iniquity of Israel, an extreme famine on earth and obvious arrival of the Antichrist in the early stage of his mischief. During this period of events an elect segment of males from the tribes of Israel will awake to the gospel with a great anointing and passion, enter the priesthood and lead the church in growing persecution and diverse plagues until they are redeemed in the second watch.

God's design to reconcile all nations to himself by the atonement of Christ will take place when his enemies are destroyed and removed even unto eternal damnation. As for Israel, *"I will destroy it from off the face of the earth, saving that I will not utterly destroy the house of Jacob. All the sinners of my people shall die by the sword, which say: The evil shall not overtake or prevent us."* After the end of these things and the final wrath and Second Advent of Christ in his glory, then a holy seed will be restored as *"In that day will I raise up the tabernacle of David that is fallen, and I will raise up his ruins, and I will build it as in the days of old."*[69]

If we want to know how and when mankind will stop its warfare and learn to live in the grace of divine love, then we must acknowledge the day of the Lord for *"Yet once, and I will shake the heavens and the earth, and the sea, and the dry land. And I will shake all nations, and the desire of all nations shall come: and I will fill this house with glory. The glory of this latter house shall be greater than the former."*[70] Humanity has never seen the magnitude of damage caused by the forces of nature in the end wrath of God, but his purpose in Christ is not to annihilate mankind but rather save it from doom. As for the ruins of the temple, it will again be rebuilt.

Jesus spoke about those who refuse to repent of their path to perdition for *"If they hear not Moses and the prophets, neither will they believe even if someone rises from the dead."*[71] Although he rose from the dead and appeared to many people to show his eternal salvation, neither his warnings nor those recorded by Moses and the prophets will change the evils to befall our world. To Jews it is written, *"I have spread out my hands all the day to an unbelieving people, who walk in a way that is not good, after their own thoughts. I will bring their fears upon them, because when I called, none did answer, when I spoke, they did not hear."*[72]

Mysteries of the end times will be made public despite the tendency of people to think these things won't happen in their lifespan through lies to hide their fear. This spiritual battle against deceit will continue to save souls and lives as *"Your watchmen shall lift up the voice, together shall they sing: for they shall see eye to eye when the Lord shall convert Zion."*[73] These priestly converts from Jacob's tribes will communicate with each other and preach about his word since

"In the latter days, you shall understand his counsel."[74] They will warn their brethren of war saying *"Hearken to the sound of the trumpet. But they said: we will not hearken."*[75]

Obsessive pride in their earthly goods and obstinate vice will delude them for *"They have cast off the law, and despised the word of the Holy One of Israel. They have forsaken the Lord, the fountain of living waters."*[76] To them who believe in false divination and trust in oppression, *"This iniquity shall be to you as a breach ready to fall, whose breaking comes suddenly at an instant."*[77] God will not extend his mercy as in the centuries of ancient times, but they will be confounded of this generation since *"There shall none of my words be prolonged any more: for in your days, O rebellious house, will I say the word, and will perform it."*[78]

Messages of the last days are in order of succession and the foresight of these things is given to us to expect and preach in continuance of the gospel as *"In measure, when it shoots forth, you will debate with it."*[79] What is current news in a future tense is still to be lived out by many who come to realize the appointed seasons and times in their conversion to Jesus as their Savior. In the third seal, a great famine and inner discord will arise in Israel while affliction grows against the church *"For the Lord takes away from Jerusalem and from Judah the stay of bread and of water. And the people shall be oppressed, everyone by another, and by his neighbor."*[80]

Conflict between Jews over issues of faith was predicted by Jesus who said *"they will deliver you up to the councils, and they will scourge you in their synagogues. Brother shall deliver up brother to death. And a man's foes shall be of his own household."*[81] The natural bond of family units will break down because of greed, envy and refusal to repent or hear the warnings of prophecy since *"their works are works of iniquity, and the act of violence is in their hands. Their feet run to evil, and they make haste to shed innocent blood. They trust in vanity, and speak lies. The way of peace they know not, and there is no justice in their goings."*[82]

Injustice of political and religious leaders is the primary reason for the curses of famine and war contained in Scripture because *"Hear, O heads of Jacob, and princes of the house of Israel, that abhor judgment, and pervert all equity. They build up Zion with blood, and Jerusalem with iniquity. The heads thereof judge for reward, and the priests teach for hire, and the prophets divine for money."*[83] This corruption of a renewed kingdom after WWIII is compared to the days of old for *"Are you polluted after the manner of your fathers? As I pleaded against your fathers, even so will I judge you. And I will purge out the rebels from among you."*[84]

Israel's backsliding in the last days is well documented and reveals *"we and our fathers, from our youth even to this day, have not obeyed the voice of the Lord our God."*[85] This parallel to the past is consistent as *"you have done worse than your fathers. Therefore I will cast you out of this land into a land you know not, neither you nor your fathers. I will forsake you and the city I gave to you and to your fathers."*[86] These verses refer specifically to another generation that is returned who worse than their fathers *"sacrificed unto devils, not to God: to gods whom they knew not, to new gods that came newly up, whom your fathers feared not."*[87]

What happens to the Jewish nation in the last days will be known to the faithful for *"I will chastise them as their congregation has heard. Though I redeemed them, yet they spoke lies against me. They return, but not to the most High."*[88] Their governors will follow vanity as *"O my people, they who lead you cause you to err, and destroy the way of your paths."*[89] Despite those who speak out in truth *"They hate him who rebukes in the gate, and they abhor him who speaks uprightly."*[90] Hence it is written, *"You are become guilty in the blood you shed and idols you made, and caused your days to draw near, and brought the time of your years."*[91]

Some kind of evil design will develop in Israel since *"there is a conspiracy of her prophets, they have devoured souls, they have taken riches for hire. Her priests put no difference between the holy and profane. Her princes are like wolves, to shed blood, and to destroy souls, to get dishonest gain."*[92] The practice of extortion will become common for *"the prophets make my people to err, and him that puts not into their mouths, they even prepare war against him."*[93] This type of corruption and oppression has existed in nations throughout history and in response to the growing tyranny *"the prudent will keep silence: for it is an evil time."*[94]

Rebellion against Christ and persecution of his servants will not happen overnight, but *"You will revolt more and more. How is the faithful city become a harlot! It was full of judgment, and righteousness lodged in it, but now murderers."*[95] It will take time for Israel to acquire wealth and build status, yet as they do many will afflict those who believe in Jesus as *"I am become a stranger to my brethren, and an alien to my mother's children. The reproaches of them that reproach you are fallen on me."*[96] Oppression will spread for *"your enemies roar in the midst of your congregations, the tumult of those who rise up against you increases continually."*[97]

Division and strife among Jews in the time called Jacob's trouble are symptomatic of a global trend toward evil *"for the dark places of the earth are full of the habitations of cruelty."*[98] Like an epidemic disease, injustice will be accepted by world leaders as a normal way of business. During this period *"A conspiracy is found among the men of Judah, and among the inhabitants of Jerusalem. They are turned back to the iniquities of their forefathers."*[99] In the midst of spreading idolatry *"according to the number of your cities are your gods, O Judah. Your own sword has devoured your prophets, in your skirts is found the blood of poor innocents."*[100]

Similar to vile persecution of the early church when Christ was first preached in Jerusalem, *"My people shall know my name: they shall know in that day that I am he that does speak. They that rule over them make them to howl, and my name is continually every day blasphemed."*[101] Their leaders will become vain in their pride saying *"We are lords, we will no more come unto you. Yet they have said: I am without sin and am innocent, surely his anger will turn from me."*[102] Almost as a choir among the nations whose song is met with delight *"they set their mouth against the heavens, and their tongue walks through the earth."*[103]

In reflection of the last days Jesus foretold *"the time comes that whosoever kills you will think he does God's service."*[104] Not only will they outwardly profess to be doing him a favor, they will believe it. This mask of religious deception to justify lusts for power and greed has served as a cloak for many since civilization began, but Jesus prophesied to the scribes and Pharisees saying *"You are the children of them who killed the prophets. Fill up then the measure of your fathers. Behold, I send you prophets, and wise men, and scribes: some of them you will kill and some you will scourge in your synagogues, and persecute them from city to city."*[105]

No mistake should be made in understanding what Jesus said about the generation of the end times with respect to Israel *"For these are the days of vengeance that all things which are written may be fulfilled. In those days, there shall be great distress in the land, and wrath upon this people. They shall fall by the edge of the sword, and be led away captive into all nations and Jerusalem shall be trodden down by the Gentiles."*[106] Those days of vengeance in which all of prophecy is fulfilled clearly refer to the last days, not a point in history. Before the captivity of Israel from WWIV, great distress will fall upon the land due to violence and famine.

Although a period of peace and prosperity will occur in Israel following WWIII, the harmony and joy among Jews in gratitude to God will turn into rivalry for *"the daughter of my people is become cruel. We watched for a nation that could not save us. They hunt our steps: we cannot go in our streets."*[107] This internal civil struggle and strife against those who follow the gospel will become bitter as *"All that hate me devise my hurt. Yea, my own friend in whom I trusted, has lifted up his heel against me.*"[108] Of this treachery in division of their people, *"it was you, my companion and friend, at whose side I walked in company in the house of God."*[109]

Salvation in Christ will be preached among the Jews since *"I will declare your name to my brethren: in the midst of the congregation will I praise you."*[110] They will not only realize and accept Jesus as their Lord, but also will know and proclaim his judgments written of old in his word for *"The Lord's voice cries to the city, and the wise men shall see your name: hear you the rod and who appointed it."*[111] Religious freedom will be cut off and those who speak out in truth will be shut up as *"Prophesy you not, say they to them who prophesy: they shall not prophesy to them that they shall not take shame. My people are risen up as an enemy."*[112]

Repentance will be far from them who are bound in iniquity *"for they proceed from evil to evil, and they know not me, says the Lord."*[113] Despite the callings to divine grace and mercy to avoid tragic plagues *"They have blown the trumpet, even to make all ready, but none goes to the battle."*[114] Instead of the contrition and prayer needed to appease the anger of God *"Woe to the foolish prophets who follow their own spirit, who see vanity and lying divination. You have not gone into the gaps, nor made up the hedge for the house of Israel to stand in the battle in the day of the Lord."*[115] They will trust in their own strength and not see omens of that period.

Opposition to the new covenant that God made in Christ will increase as Israel and the whole world falls into great transgression of divine law since *"you have made void the covenant of your servant, you have profaned his crown and brought his strongholds to ruin, you have set up the right hand of his enemies."*[116] They will seek help from the Antichrist as terrible famine grips their land yet *"We looked for peace, but no good came, and for healing, but behold trouble."*[117] In their affliction, the faithful will pray *"O Lord, how long shall I cry to you, for spoiling and violence are before me, and those who raise up strife and contention."*[118]

The passion of Christ is reflected in a prophetic Calvary of the church when *"for your sake we are being slain all the day, we are counted as sheep for the slaughter."*[119] Slander and threat of execution will encompass the faithful while a cruel enemy tries to eliminate them and stop the practice of their belief so *"Lord, how long will the wicked triumph? They attack the life of the just and condemn innocent blood."*[120] They will target those who trust in the Lord as prey and spoil out of greed and fear that their evil ways will be exposed for *"they covet fields and houses, and take them by violence. Even so they oppress a man and his heritage."*[121]

Warning was given by Moses to ancient Hebrews and to their seed who would return to the Land of Promise *"If your heart turn away, so you will not hear, but be drawn away to worship other gods, you shall surely perish, and not prolong your days in the land that the Lord swore to your fathers."*[122] Even though Christ has been manifest and his power will be seen in the first watch *"they have forsaken me, and burned incense to other gods, whom neither they nor their fathers have known."*[123] In allegory of their loss of faith *"I planted you a noble vine, wholly a right seed: how then are you turned into a degenerate plant of a strange vine?"*[124]

Transition from a place of honor among the nations to one of shame will again take place for the Jewish kingdom since *"Israel has cast off the thing that is good. They have set up kings, but not by me: of their silver and gold they have made idols to themselves."*[125] Sorcery will become customary as *"they shall say to you: seek unto them who have familiar spirits, and to wizards that peep, and that mutter."*[126] Rather than obeying divine law, they will profane it by turning to such things as astrology for *"they have burned incense unto all the host of heaven, and poured out drink offerings to other gods."*[127] These falsehoods were strictly forbidden.

Animosity will progress against the Eucharistic altar of the new covenant because it is the center of Christian worship and the primary object of dissension in the rabbinical priesthood. To those responsible for teaching the law, but that same clergy who only see what they want to see, *"O priests, who despise my name and say the table of the Lord is contemptible: you are departed out of the way, you have caused many to stumble at the law; you have corrupted the covenant of Levi."*[128] Morality will be based on personal choice, but *"Woe to them that call evil good, and good evil, who are wise in their own eyes, and prudent in their own sight."*[129]

Jewish claim to the Holy Land is a matter of faith in him who without sin was sent by God to die in atonement for everyone's sin and *"You shall make his soul an offering for sin: the Lord has laid on him the iniquity of us all, by his knowledge shall my righteous servant justify many, because he has poured out his soul unto death."*[130] This is the heart of Scripture as Jesus is the chosen one whom God plainly said *"I will beat down his foes before his face, and plague them that hate him. I will make him my firstborn. His seed shall endure forever, and his throne as the sun before me."*[131] How can any literate person deny his death and rising from the dead?

Religious leaders were confronted by Jesus for their pretense of being God's children when he told them *"If God were your Father, you would love me, for he sent me."*[132] It is in him that God forgives sin and we become his people and living temple. Not according to the measure of our works or ability to keep Mosaic Law, nor by reason of human bloodline but *"I will make a new covenant with the house of Israel, and the house of Judah. I will put my law in their hearts, and I will be their God, and they shall be my people."*[133] That covenant was sealed in the blood of Christ and in his resurrection, but its bond will regretfully come by judgment.

Severe famine is the evident plague in the opening of the third seal of the Apocalypse. This devastating dearth will extend far beyond the borders of Israel, but the main prophetic focus on exhausting drought concerns enmity among Jews against Christ and his church seeing *"you have forgot the God of your salvation, and not been mindful of the rock of your strength, and therefore the harvest shall be a heap in the day of grief and desperate sorrow."*[134] The theme of rebellion and divine justice of famine before war in the last days permeates the prophets so that *"the glory of Jacob shall be made thin, and the fatness of his flesh shall wax lean."*[135]

In a parable that describes the new rebuilt Israel as the vineyard of the Lord of hosts *"he looked for it to bring forth grapes, and it bought forth wild grapes. And now, I will tell you what I will do to my vineyard. I will lay it waste and command the clouds that they rain no rain on it: their honorable men are famished, and their multitude dried up for thirst."*[136] This curse against iniquity was set forth among others in divine law before the horror of war and there is no doubt about the cause and effect since *"you have polluted the land with whoredom and wickedness: therefore the showers are withheld, and there has been no latter rain."*[137]

Prophetic warnings of famine in Israel clearly point to the coming day of the Lord and great destruction from the Almighty. There will be much mourning and grief *"because the harvest of the field is perished. The vine is dried up, and even all the trees of the field are withered. Yea, the flocks of sheep are made desolate, for the rivers of waters are dried up, and the fire has devoured the pastures."*[138] Punishment from above is evident for *"How has the Lord cast down the beauty of Israel, and remembered not his footstool in the day of his anger. Lift up your hands to him for the life of your children who faint in hunger in the top of every street."*[139]

With respect to the lack of wisdom about the reality of prophetic plagues Jesus said *"Many false prophets will arise, and they shall deceive many."*[140] They will thwart the conscience of those who are lost in sin by affirming their actions and denying the justice of the Lord since *"The prophets prophesy lies in my name: I sent them not, yet they say sword and famine shall not be in this land. But by sword and famine shall those prophets be consumed."*[141] Contrary to a public sense of false hope *"I will surely consume them, and the things I gave them shall pass away."*[142] Of the severe famine *"the vintage shall fail, the gathering shall not come."*[143]

Desperation from drought will suddenly strike because *"you are the land that is not cleansed, nor rained upon in the day of indignation."*[144] Extreme dearth will signal the final downfall of Israel in siege when *"They who were brought up in scarlet will embrace dunghills. The hands of pitiful women sodden their own children: they were their meat in the destruction of the daughter of my people."*[145] Sorrows of hunger are meant to shed light on their blindness to judgment of war and cause repentance from ways of iniquity, but instead *"They shall fall and be hungry. And when they are hungry, they will be angry, and curse their king and their God."*[146]

Correlation of ancient Hebrew history to their prophetic future needs to be understood since they will again go into captivity, but this time it will be swift and counted in one generation. The perils are grave for *"These two things are come unto you: desolation and destruction: the famine and the sword. Who shall be sorry for you or comfort you?"*[147] They will themselves be the only blame *"for the daughter of my people is broken with a great breach, with a grievous blow."*[148] The course of nature will turn against them and many others in this time as *"they came to the pits, and found no water: the ground is cracked, for there was no rain in the earth."*[149]

Major events of the end times involve the person called the Antichrist because he will succeed in taking global power before the final battle of Armageddon. He is the main political figure of an ultimate blasphemy of God and Christ or any other religious beliefs since he will profess himself to be God and demand worship as such. Speculation has risen for many years about who he is and how he will obtain control, but that reign will come by much bloodshed. This so-called son of perdition will not appear or be known until after the first watch and end of WWIII and his *"coming is after the working of Satan with all power and lying wonders."*[150]

The prophet Daniel revealed the Antichrist's kingdom as a dreadful beast *"which shall devour the whole earth, and shall tread it down and break it in pieces."* In this vision of the beast *"it had ten horns, and there came up among them another little horn, before whom three of the first horns were plucked up by the roots."*[151] These ten horns are European kingdoms where the Antichrist will arise and conquer the resistance in three of these kingdoms thereby setting up a new power base that Scripture clearly indicates is centered upon the city of seven hills which is Rome.[152] Even from the start of his plans he will form and command armed forces.

Political fortunes will change in the aftermath of WWIII as a cold war develops between new western and eastern superpowers in the remaining world society. Nobody can predict exactly how much damage will result from nuclear war, but it is apparent that the U.S. and Russia will suffer great losses in a battle of their opposing militaries over the security of Israel.[153] Borders of other countries defeated in the war will be redrawn and amid a vacuum of leadership some kind of a greater Europe will emerge with the Antichrist as its head while China expands its control over neighboring nations to polarize these dominant military arsenals in an arms race.

Discord of a fourth world war involves an alliance of nations surrounding China under its dominion against the evolving empire of the Antichrist from a united Europe. A power struggle will occur among the ten horns described by Daniel when the Antichrist solidifies his reign over a new Europe since *"he shall subdue three kings."* He is the little horn who rises in a military coalition to rule this vast region by force *"And he shall speak great words against the High One, and crush the saints of the Most High, and think himself able to change times and laws."*[154] Regardless of his demonic powers, only God controls time or physics of the universe.

Human vanity will reach its climax in the Antichrist for *"he shall exalt himself, and magnify himself above every god, and shall prosper, until the wrath be accomplished."*[155] He is the epitome of pride in all people who reject the family of God founded in Christ and his Eucharistic presence as *"he opened his mouth in blasphemy against God, to blaspheme his name, and his tabernacle, and them who dwell in heaven."*[156] Mankind will become subject to utter madness of this impostor because *"they received not the truth that they might be saved. Therefore God will send them strong delusion, that all may be damned who refused the truth."*[157]

While most scholars admit the Antichrist is a human person who will rise to global power, they don't perceive when he will come or understand the fact that his conquest will be with armed forces in a state of world war. During the time he begins the military base of this new Roman empire, there is another biblical figure called the false prophet who plays a decisive role in bringing about the fall of Israel and final wrath of God. There is a distinction between these characters since the Antichrist is the chief political leader appearing as the supreme false Christ, while the religious high priest who heads the false church is the false prophet.

Little attention has been given in teachings about last days regarding who the false prophet is or his function to assist the Antichrist in ruling the world but *"he causes the earth and them who dwell therein to worship the beast. And he deceives them by means of miracles which he had power to do, saying they should make an image to the beast."*[158] Like the Antichrist, the false prophet will possess demonic powers and work miracles to persuade people to worship this truly insane person possessed by the Devil and his image for *"Every man is brutish in his knowledge, for his molten image is falsehood: in the time of their visitation they shall perish."*[159]

Israelites were strictly forbidden to worship false gods or make images of idolatry and Moses plainly warned them to *"Take heed to yourself, lest you make a covenant with the inhabitants of the land, and do sacrifice unto their gods, and one call you, and you eat of his sacrifice."*[160] This prophecy of someone who would lure them into deep idolatry has direct application to the last days since *"There is one come out of you that imagines evil against the Lord, a wicked counselor."*[161] Instead of abiding in the new covenant God gave to us in Christ, this wicked counselor will lead them into making an unholy covenant that results in their captivity.

Several prophecies relate to Jewish officials who guide their nation on a destructive course until the Messiah comes to judge and restore their kingdom as *"You, profane wicked prince of Israel, whose day is come, when iniquity shall have an end. Remove the diadem, and take off the crown: and it shall be no more, until he come whose right it is."*[162] This political evil prince is led by one of the corrupt priesthood who will be more interested in his own lusts than serving his people for *"O you priests, if you will not hear to give glory to my name, I will corrupt your seed, and one shall take you away with it: for one covers violence with his garment."*[163]

Due to the devastating famine that will adversely affect the social and physical welfare of its people, Israel will seek help from other nations *"for she said I will go after my lovers that give me my bread and water, my wool and my flax, my oil and my drink."*[164] Whatever alliances are made to bolster their economy and insure their security, they will not stand since *"Say you not a confederacy. Associate yourselves, O you people, and give ear all you far countries: take counsel together, and it will come to nothing."*[165] They will not trust in the Lord who asks *"Will you pollute me among my people for handfuls of barley and pieces of bread?"*[166]

At some point before the start of WWIV, their leaders will turn to the Antichrist in a compact they think will protect them from growing global tensions as *"you sons of the sorceress, the seed of the whore, upon a lofty and high mountain have you set your bed. Behind the doors and the posts have you set up your remembrance, and made a covenant with them. And you went to the king and sent your messengers far off, and did debase yourself even unto hell."*[167] Depravity will seal their fate for *"Judah has dealt treacherously, and an abomination is committed in Israel and in Jerusalem: for Judah has married the daughter of a strange god."*[168]

Descriptive language of the evil nature and manifest deception in the making of a contract that will result in divine vengeance is clearly written since *"You scornful men who rule over my people in Jerusalem, you have said: We have entered into a league with death, and we have made a covenant with hell, when the overflowing scourge shall pass through, it shall not come upon us."*[169] It is a wonder how they believe they can beat the Devil at his own game, but that agreement is misfortune as *"Hell has enlarged herself, and opened her mouth without measure, and their glory, and their pomp, and their multitude shall descend into it."*[170]

Rejection of the saving grace in Christ will reach gravely into the hands of darkness and the treaty with the Antichrist meant to insure peace will spell disaster. The perplexing question for the political and religious rulers of Israel is why they don't perceive outward signs of their times and the related warnings of the prophets who said *"Your league with death will be abolished, and your covenant with hell will not stand: when the overflowing scourge passes, then you will be trodden down by it."*[171] Refuge in their lies is vain for *"They have spoken words, swearing falsely in making a covenant: thus, judgment springs up as hemlock in the field."*[172]

By its very nature to protect the security of Israel, an alliance with the Antichrist indicates it will be formalized in a time of rising political turmoil among nations but *"they have seduced my people, saying Peace, and there was none. Therefore I will break down the wall you made with non-tempered mortar, and you will be consumed in the midst thereof."*[173] Whether the pact is an evil ploy to bide time in order to improve Israeli defenses with other nations or seen as a real deterrent of war, *"Destruction comes: they shall seek peace, and there will be none. For I have heard from the Lord of hosts a consumption, even determined upon the whole earth."*[174]

The security pact made by Israel with the Antichrist will have the opposite effect of what it was intended since *"From the time that it goes forth, it shall take you: for morning by morning, by day and by night, it will be a vexation to hear the report."*[175] Their former friends will become enemies and fear of the scourge of war will become a reality as God said *"I will bring the worst of heathen, and they shall possess their homes. Trouble will come upon trouble, and I will do to them after their own way, and judge them according to their judgments."*[176] The news of Israel's reliance on foreign nations will be seen as weakness and opportunity for spoil.

Prospects for peace will turn into bitterness as friends and foes alike take actions against a nation once known for its integrity and respect in the global community for *"I will gather all your lovers, with all them that you hated, and give you into their hand, and they shall leave you naked and bare."*[177] Foreign affairs will become a nightmare and their economy will fall apart *"And from the daughter of Zion all her beauty is departed: all that honored her despise her, all her friends deal treacherously with her, they have become her enemies."*[178] Similarly, *"Though you clothe with crimson and gold, your lovers will despise you and seek your life."*[179]

Deplorable corruption and repulsive iniquity of the last days will grow and be accepted as a normal way of life, but these traits will lead to WWIV wherein the Antichrist obtains ruthless control over the earth. It seems fitting that gross injustice will be met with the same before the end wrath and battle of Armageddon. Prior to that end time the gospel will be preached in all parts of the world as the church strives against falsehood and looks to the hope of redemption. An elect segment of Jewish males will be chosen by God and their conversion will transpire in a decisive second Pentecost to carry out the missionary work of evangelization.

WWIV is the primary subject of the fourth seal of Revelation discussed in the next chapter. Within the timeframe of a generation, it will take numerous years or several decades for mankind to recover from immense destruction in WWIII and then arrive at another global military crisis. Detailed analysis of the great mystery of a holy anointing of many among the tribes of Israel and their ministry in the Catholic priesthood is provided in the following section. This event marks the final periods of watches for the church in times of increased persecution, unusual plagues and plight of the sword before the wrath of God and his judgment of the wicked.

[1] Deuteronomy 31,29
[2] Deuteronomy 29,14-15&21-29
[3] Luke 2,25-34
[4] Deuteronomy 18,15-19
[5] Genesis 49,10-12&24
[6] Psalm 110,1
[7] Psalm 118,22
[8] Isaiah 28,16
[9] Isaiah 8,13-15
[10] Jeremiah 4,1-2
[11] Jeremiah 7,5-7
[12] Jeremiah 23,22
[13] Hosea 4,6
[14] Zechariah 4,6
[15] II Corinthians 5,20-21
[16] Isaiah 40,13
[17] John 5,43-46
[18] John 8,23-24
[19] John 15,23-24
[20] Acts 4,14-17; 8,1-3; 13,45; 17,5; 22,3-5
[21] Romans 10,1-3
[22] John 6,63
[23] Deuteronomy 32,20-21
[24] Isaiah 55,5; 65,1
[25] Deuteronomy 32,18&29
[26] Jeremiah 2,20-21
[27] Hosea 11,4
[28] Isaiah 2,7-12
[29] Ezekiel 39,8-14
[30] Jeremiah 5,7&23-31
[31] Mathew 6,24; Luke 16,13
[32] Ezekiel 16,7&13-15
[33] I Timothy 6,10
[34] Jeremiah 2,7-9
[35] Lamentations 1,1&9
[36] Hosea 4,1&7; 13,6
[37] Psalm 80,8-13
[38] Hosea 13,2-3
[39] Isaiah 28,1-4
[40] Psalm 90,5-8
[41] Jeremiah 31,31-34; II Corinthians 6,16-18

[42] Ezekiel 40,3-49; 41,1-26; 42,1-20
[43] Ezekiel 43,4-7
[44] Ezekiel 43,8; 44,6-12
[45] Isaiah 44,24-28; 45,11-13
[46] Micah 7,11
[47] Jeremiah 23,9-12
[48] Amos 8,2-3
[49] Jeremiah 6,13-14; 8,7-12; 23,16-20
[50] Jeremiah 6,10-13
[51] Jeremiah 5,4&12
[52] Jeremiah 23,26-27
[53] Ezekiel 7,7&22-25
[54] Ezekiel 8,3&16-17
[55] Isaiah 41,2&25
[56] Ezekiel 8,12; 9,9
[57] Ezekiel 11,15; 33,24
[58] Zechariah 3,8; 6,12-13
[59] Isaiah 11,1-5; Jeremiah 23, 5-6
[60] Amos 5,18-26
[61] Amos 6,1-3
[62] Jeremiah 7,29
[63] Isaiah 34,8
[64] Micah 7,4
[65] Isaiah 63,18; 64,11; Jeremiah 7,11-14&30
[66] Lamentations 2,1-7
[67] Ezekiel 16,44
[68] Jeremiah 30,3&18
[69] Amos 9,8-11
[70] Haggai 2,6-9
[71] Luke 16,31
[72] Isaiah 65,2-7; 66,4-5
[73] Isaiah 52,6-8; 62,6-7
[74] Jeremiah 23,19-20; 30,23-24
[75] Jeremiah 4,5&19-20; 6,17-19; Ezekiel 7,14-15
[76] Isaiah 5,24-25; 48,17-19; Jeremiah 17,13
[77] Isaiah 30,9-13
[78] Ezekiel 12,22-28
[79] Isaiah 27,8
[80] Isaiah 3,1-5
[81] Mathew 10,17-22&36
[82] Isaiah 59,3-8
[83] Micah 3,9-12
[84] Ezekiel 20,30-39
[85] Jeremiah 3,25
[86] Jeremiah 16,12-13; 23,36-40
[87] Deuteronomy 32,17
[88] Hosea 7,10-16
[89] Isaiah 3,12-14
[90] Amos 5,10
[91] Ezekiel 22,4
[92] Ezekiel 22,25-27
[93] Micah 3,1-5
[94] Amos 5,13
[95] Isaiah 1,2-5&21-25
[96] Psalm 69,7-12

[97] Psalm 74,3-4&23
[98] Psalm 74,18-22; Jeremiah 30,7
[99] Jeremiah 11,9-10
[100] Jeremiah 2,28-34
[101] Isaiah 52,5-6
[102] Jeremiah 2,31-35
[103] Psalm 73,6-9
[104] John 16,2-3&21-22
[105] Mathew 23,29-39
[106] Luke 21,22-24
[107] Lamentations 4,3&16-18
[108] Psalm 41,5-9
[109] Psalm 55,9-14
[110] Psalm 22,22-24
[111] Micah 6,9-13
[112] Micah 2,6-9
[113] Jeremiah 9,2-6
[114] Ezekiel 7,14
[115] Ezekiel 13,3-7
[116] Psalm 89,27-29&38-43
[117] Jeremiah 8,15; 14,19
[118] Habakkuk 1,2-3
[119] Psalm 44,22
[120] Psalm 31,11-13; 35,14-20; 94,3&21
[121] Micah 2,1-2
[122] Deuteronomy 30,15-20
[123] Jeremiah 19,4
[124] Jeremiah 2,11&20-22
[125] Hosea 8,3-4
[126] Isaiah 8,19
[127] Jeremiah 7,17-18; 8,1-2; 19,13
[128] Malachi 1,6-7; 2,7-9
[129] Isaiah 5,20-23
[130] Isaiah 53,5-12
[131] Psalm 89,18-27&35-37
[132] John 8,37-44
[133] Jeremiah 31,31-34
[134] Isaiah 17,10-11
[135] Isaiah 17,4
[136] Isaiah 5,1-6&13
[137] Jeremiah 3,2-5
[138] Joel 1,10-19
[139] Lamentations 2,1&19
[140] Mathew 7,15; 24,11
[141] Jeremiah 14,11-15
[142] Jeremiah 8,13
[143] Isaiah 32,10-13
[144] Ezekiel 22,13&24
[145] Lamentations 4,4-5&9-10
[146] Isaiah 8,20-22
[147] Isaiah 51,19
[148] Jeremiah 14,17
[149] Jeremiah 14,1-6
[150] II Thessalonians 2,3-10
[151] Daniel 7,8&23-24

[152] Revelation 17,8-9&18
[153] Ezekiel 39,1-2&6
[154] Daniel 7,24-25
[155] Daniel 11,36
[156] Revelation 13,4-8
[157] II Thessalonians 2,9-12
[158] Revelation 13,11-14
[159] Jeremiah 10,14-15
[160] Exodus 34,12-17
[161] Nahum 1,9-11; 2,1-2
[162] Ezekiel 21,25-27
[163] Malachi 2,1-3&16
[164] Hosea 2,5
[165] Isaiah 8,9-15
[166] Ezekiel 13,19
[167] Isaiah 57,3-9
[168] Malachi 2,11-12
[169] Isaiah 28,14-15
[170] Isaiah 5,14-16
[171] Isaiah 28,18
[172] Hosea 10,4
[173] Ezekiel 13,10-15
[174] Isaiah 28,22; Ezekiel 7,25-27
[175] Isaiah 28,18-19
[176] Ezekiel 7,24-27
[177] Ezekiel 16,35-39
[178] Lamentations 1,2-8
[179] Jeremiah 4,27-31

Chapter Six/Part Two
THE SECOND WATCH

"I looked and saw a Lamb stand on the mount Zion, and with him a hundred and forty four thousand having his Father's name written in their foreheads. These were redeemed from among men, the first fruits unto God and to the Lamb."

Revelation 14,1-5

A great awakening to the gospel news in the last days within the Jewish community is clearly professed in Scripture. The context of this conversion follows the end of WWIII when the mystery of rapture is revealed in the first watch as a sign of divine power in the redemption of Christ. St. John recorded a vision in the Apocalypse of 144,000 virgin Jewish males of all the tribes of Israel who were marked by angels in their foreheads with the seal of God.[1] There are 12,000 from each of the twelve tribes who have a special purpose in the priesthood, except for some unexplained reason the tribe of Dan is replaced by the half-tribe of Manasseh.

Expectation of the early apostles that salvation in Jesus would come to the Jews will occur when they see the miracle of redemption and their nation spared in a great war as *"in that day, I will pour upon the house of David, and upon the inhabitants of Jerusalem, the spirit of grace and of prayers. And they shall look upon me, whom they have pierced, and they shall mourn for him as for an only son, as for the death of the firstborn. And the land shall mourn, all the families that remain, every family apart, and their women apart."*[2] Their eyes will open in every tribe to the word and spirit of God as they realize their chosen place in leading his church.

Old Testament prophecies correspond to the sealing of an elect segment of Jews seen in the book of Revelation. Great plagues including famine will disrupt the world's livelihood, but an angel cried *"Hurt not the earth, neither the sea, nor the trees, till we have sealed the servants of God in their foreheads."*[3] The gospel mission will be given to them since *"they that dwell in the land of the shadow of death, upon them has the light shined. The Lord sent a word into Jacob and it lighted upon Israel."*[4] Likewise in this anointing, *"He shall cause them that come out of Jacob to take root: Israel will blossom and bud, and fill the face of the world with fruit."*[5]

Those who believe in Jesus are his fruit and they who come out of Jacob in zeal will make disciples of the spiritual Israel throughout the world. What the prophets described in metaphor as the latter rain of his grace was known to the early church for *"Be patient, brethren, unto the coming of the Lord. The husbandman waits for the precious fruit of the earth, until he receive the early and latter rain."*[6] In this latter time the seed of faith will be revealed *"As the new wine is found in the cluster, I will bring forth a seed out of Jacob, and out of Judah an inheritor of my mountains: and my elect shall inherit it, and my servants shall dwell there."*[7]

The new covenant in Christ will be accepted by certain Jews who carry on the work of saving souls as *"He established a testimony in Jacob, and appointed a law in Israel."*[8] This testimony is of redemption and the law is of the church in keeping its sacraments. They will know the Lord and his judgments since *"Among the tribes of Israel I have made known that which shall surely be."*[9] These chosen ones will spread truth in signs of their times for *"Bind up the testimony, seal the law among my disciples. Behold, I and the children whom the Lord has given me are for signs and wonders in Israel from the Lord of hosts, who dwells in mount Zion."*[10]

Conversion of God fearing Jews to Christ in the last days relates to only some of their nation, but when he restores their kingdom they who are left will know him as Lord. The latter rain of grace extends until the time of the end as *"the Lord of hosts shall be for a crown of glory, and a diadem of beauty, unto the residue of his people.*"[11]   They are told in distress of persecution, famine and war to *"Hearken unto me, O house of Jacob and all the remnant of Israel who are borne by me, even to your old age and to your grey hairs I will carry you, and deliver you."*[12] He will *"raise up the tribes of Jacob, and restore the preserved of Israel."*[13]

In a startling vision of the end times describing divine vengeance upon Israel for its iniquity, Ezekiel saw an angel with a writer's inkhorn *"And the Lord said to him: Go through the midst of the city, through the midst of Jerusalem, and set a mark upon the foreheads of the men who sigh and mourn for all the abominations that be done in the midst thereof."* This prophecy offers a direct comparison to those marked by angels with the seal of God in Revelation and each one of these men who abhor the sins of their brethren and gross apostasy in the world will be protected by him from slaughter for *"come not near any man whom is the mark."*[14]

Specific references from the prophet Ezekiel when an elect holy priesthood is sealed by an angel of God are in context of a city and of Jerusalem including idolatry committed within chambers of the rebuilt temple. This passage does not suggest, nor is it logical that every male seed of Jacob marked with the seal of God resides in Jerusalem. The places where they live are both in the spiritual city of the church on earth and Jerusalem itself, but rebellion in their nation against divine law will be widespread since *"The iniquity of the house of Israel and Judah is exceeding great, and the land is full of blood, and the city full of perverseness."*[15]

Jesus established a new priesthood at the Last Supper and the clergy of this sacred rite will include an influx of Jews for *"he shall purify the sons of Levi that they may offer unto the Lord an offering in righteousness."*[16] These priests have an identity with the ancient priesthood of the tribe of Levi, but these sons who apply to all those marked with the seal of God will be purified by the blood of Christ and have an important role in ministry as *"they that be of you shall build the old waste places: you shall raise up the foundations of many generations, and you shall be called, The repairer of the breach, The restorer of paths to dwell in."*[17]

Biblical references indicate a renewal of Christian faith confirmed by unique sealing of those chosen by God as it is written, *"Arise, O Lord, into your rest, you and the ark of your strength. For the Lord has chosen Zion: I will clothe her priests with salvation, and her saints with joy. In her, I will make the horn of David to bud."*[18] The horn of David is the gospel of Christ who was born of God to raise up an immortal seed in his heavenly kingdom and inherit the throne of David over Israel and all the earth. Jesus rests in our hearts in his spirit, but also is present with us in the ark of Eucharist tabernacles by that same spirit where he dwells with us.

The apostles of Jesus knew God was not finished with his plan for redemption of Jews as St. Peter taught them to *"Repent and be converted, in order that when the times of refreshment shall come from the presence of the Lord, he may send him who has been preached to you, Jesus Christ."*[19] These times of refreshment include the latter service of an elect clergy sealed by angels of God and the ensuing revival to the ends of the earth for *"He shows his word unto Jacob, his statutes and his judgments unto Israel."*[20] The seasons of this outpouring of grace culminate with the Lord coming to redeem in the second and third watches.

Although Christianity has been rejected by dominant Judaic theology since the early church, *"there remains a rest to the people of God, and they to whom it was first preached entered not because of unbelief."*[21] This future rest is in conversion to the Lord within and beyond the Jewish community. It will happen after the first watch and they also have promise since *"You are a God who works wonders; among the peoples you have made known your power. With your strong arm you redeemed your people, the sons of Jacob and Joseph."*[22] These sons of Jacob and Joseph will look forward to redemption in their own respective watches.

Terminology used in the bible to explain aspects of the future often relates to teachings of the past, even to the very beginnings of ancient times. St. Paul plainly wrote about a conversion of Jews and a revealing to them of prophetic mysteries put forth by Moses for *"even unto this day, when Moses is read, the veil covers their hearts, but when they turn in repentance to God, the veil shall be taken away."*[23] They will turn to Jesus among the tribes of Jacob as *"He was king in Jeshurun when the heads of the people and tribes of Israel were gathered together."*[24] Moses and Isaiah used the term Jeshurun to refer collectively to the sons of Jacob sealed of God.

Building blocks of prophecy transpire over periods of time and numerous parables to events of ancient history have a vital function in learning their meaning. For instance *"in the time appointed, he ordained in Joseph for a testimony, when he went out through the land of Egypt: where I heard a language that I understood not."*[25] There is a parallel here to Jewish conversion in Christ because the wisdom that Jacob gave to his son Judah and to his son Joseph involves the evolution of the church from the start of its scepter to the time of the end.[26] These visions of the last days include salvation among the Jews and others as well their rapture.

Great mysteries are hidden in the blessings of Jacob to his sons and also in the blessings Moses gave to the tribes of Israel. Jacob spoke of Christ as the Shepherd and Rock of Israel when he foretold that *"Joseph is a fruitful bough, even a fruitful bough by a well, whose branches run over the wall."* These boughs apply to Gentiles and then to Jews whose branches reach souls all over the world in the latter rain of grace. The transition is in times of war and persecution for *"The archers sorely grieved him, shot at him, and hated him: but his bow abode in strength, and the arms of his hands were made strong by the mighty God of Jacob."*

Instructions to both Judah and Joseph contain the most ancient reference to rapture as Jacob told Judah that the Messiah would come and gather the people unto himself in heaven. He described the Lord as the Lion of Judah who stooped down, then couched and again leaned down to take up his body in the church. Similarly, Jacob revealed to Joseph that *"the God of your father shall help you, and the Almighty shall bless you with the blessings of heaven above, unto the utmost bound of the everlasting hills."* He knew this promise of the Messiah is of heaven itself since he said these blessings surpass earthly oaths to his forebears.

Despite rebellion against the papacy, Jesus ordained this authority upon St. Peter as a rock which his church would be built. Jacob confirmed this governance to Judah from whom Christ the Lion was born for *"the scepter shall not depart from Judah, nor the staff from between his feet, until he come to whom it belongs."* This scepter of the Gentiles' papal power from God in Christ will be given to the staff of a Jew before Jesus comes in glory to his kingdom. The office long held by Gentiles will be filled by a Jewish Pope as Jacob told Joseph *"the blessings of your father shall be upon the head of Joseph, and on the prince among his brethren."*

St. Paul's ministry was to the Gentiles but he cautioned them not to be wise in their own conceits because he compared Jesus to an olive tree saying of Jews *"They also, if they abide not still in unbelief shall be grafted in for God is able to graft them in again."*[27] It may seem novel to some that a holy Jewish Pope will serve as the Vicar of Christ, but what can only be described as a second Pentecost will happen to an elect priesthood sealed of God. Even as they spoke in other tongues at the first, in the time appointed to Joseph as he travels through the symbolical land of Egypt *"with stammering lips and another tongue will he speak to this people."*[28]

Understanding the parallel of prophecy in Joseph who hears the tongue of God's spirit in a world of idolatry relates to the story of Joseph being a hero since the Pharaoh selected him as magistrate over the land and he saved his family from dire famine. Loathing between Jews and others who deny Christ against those who are saved in conversion will lead to persecution in a type of global spiritual Egypt. Moses praised Joseph in the work for souls in God's kingdom for *"Blessed of the Lord be his land, and the precious fruits brought forth by the sun, and the precious things put forth by the moon, and the favor of him who dwelt in the bush."*

Metaphors articulated by Moses in his blessings to the tribes of Israel confirm aspects of prophecies given by Jacob to his sons. The priesthood of Jeshurun will have the favor of God who spoke from a burning bush while the sun and moon reflect the light of Jesus and Our Lady shining in their ministry. Moses spoke very plainly about the change in papacy from Gentile to Jew and its subsequent world mission since *"Let the blessing come upon the head of Joseph, and upon the head of him who was separated from his brethren. His horns are like the horns of unicorns, with them he will push the people together to the ends of the earth."[29]*

Since the sealed priesthood of God is guided by his providence and is fairly large in number, they have an unusual capacity for outreach as *"Jeshurun grew fat, and kicked: you are become fat, you are grown thick. The Lord alone did lead him, and there was no strange god with him. He made him ride on the high places of the earth."[30]* These verses apply to the growth in discipleship and wealth, but these servants will kick against wickedness and hatred for *"they shall be as mighty men, that tread down their enemies in the mire of the streets in the battle. Out of him came forth the corner, the nail, the battle bow and workmen together."[31]*

Effects of a second Pentecost show remarkable success in the struggle between good and evil as *"The Lord of hosts has visited his flock, and I will strengthen the house of Judah, and I will save the house of Joseph. I will multiply them as they were multiplied before and will hiss for them and gather them for I have redeemed them."[32]* Many will convert and be saved while these priests earnestly father the faith for *"Sing, O barren, you who did not bear: Enlarge the place of your tent, stretch out your tabernacles. All your children shall be taught of the Lord, and great will be their peace. No weapon that is formed against you shall prosper."[33]*

Deep irony exists in the prospect of building a third Jewish temple and restoring its ancient rites since *"If perfection were by the priesthood of Levi, what further need was there that another priest should arise after the order of Melchizedek and not called after the order of Aaron? If the first covenant had been faultless, then no place would be found for the second."[34]* Jesus is that high priest whom David called Lord, but strife will develop over the new covenant as Jacob told his sons Levi and Simeon *"Weapons of violence are in their swords. Cursed be their anger and wrath: I will divide them in Jacob, and scatter them in Israel."[35]*

Inside the temple's Holy of Holies, the Ark of the Covenant holding the Ten Commandments and Book of the Law was center-place but in front of it were kept a golden pot with manna and the budded rod of Aaron.[36] These things were meant as signs about the last days to those who build the temple as *"when many evils and troubles befall them, this song shall testify against them as a witness, for it shall not be forgotten out of the mouth of their seed."* The song of Moses shows the latter end of idolatry in those who reject Christ *"For the Lord shall judge his people when he sees that their power is gone, and there is none shut up or left."[37]*

The faithful lives of those on earth and their intercession for conversion or corporal needs holds back divine justice on others who offend God, but after that power is gone due to the redemption of his people in rapture, his final wrath and judgment will come. Moses taught the hope for believers, *"Happy are you, O Israel: who is like you, O people saved by the Lord! There is none like the God of Jeshurun, who rides the heavens in his power, and rides the skies in his majesty. He spread out the primeval tent, he extended the ancient canopy."[38]* This explicit and powerful prophecy applies to opening of the heavens to save his people.

Severe famine in the third seal of Revelation described as a measure of wheat for a denarius and three measures of barley for a denarius may signify a day's wages for a loaf of bread. It indicates a famine price, but its cause is scorning prophetic warnings as *"the days come, that I will send a famine in the land of hearing the words of the Lord."*[39] Irony of those times is they will reject its signs and builders of the temple will oppose the cornerstone of Christ taught by Jeshurun. The rod of Aaron that miraculously sprouted with blossoms and yielded almonds reflects a Jewish priesthood that minister the sacred manna of the Eucharist.

Moses reminded the priestly tribe of Levi of rebellion and taught about division that would take place among them. He referred to the place of the waters of Meribah where they rose up against him and mocked the Lord to quench their thirst, but he also said of true priests *"Let your Thummim and your Urim be with your holy one, for they kept your word and upheld your covenant. He acknowledged not his brethren nor knew his own children. They shall teach Jacob your judgments and Israel your law. Smite them who rise against and hate him so they rise not again."*[40] The pastors of Jeshurun will not marry, nor be like their corrupt brethren.

Emblems of truth and light were reflected in the Thummim and Urim on the breastplate of the high priest. This sanctity was given by Moses to a priestly order of the Holy One of Israel who will be manifest in a new Levite priesthood *"for a spirit of judgment to him who sits in judgment, and a strength to them that turn the battle to the gate."*[41] They will turn to the Queen of Heaven who is its gate during oppression while Jesus directs difficult decisions of the papal seat which apparently will be chosen from the tribe of Gad since *"He saw that the best should be his when the princely portion was assigned, while the heads of the people were gathered."*[42]

Affliction of Christians will spread but those of Jeshurun will fight back in military operations led by divine power and wisdom as *"every tongue that shall rise against you in judgment, you shall condemn."*[43] Self-defense among the faithful will result from persecution for *"the people who know their God shall be strong and do exploits."*[44] They will revolt in civil and armed conflict against cruelty because it is God who *"bent Judah for me as a bow, and I will raise up your sons, O Zion, against your sons, O Greece, and I will make you as the sword of a mighty man."*[45] They will have assurance of his word in their vengeance and his salvation.

Extraordinary events will accompany the ministry of Jeshurun in their lead of the faithful's exodus into heaven from an evil slavery since *"According to the days of your coming out of Egypt will I show unto him marvelous things."*[46] This is a chosen seed set apart from the world with the promise of their and the church's redemption as *"Awake, awake: put on your strength, O Zion: put on your beautiful garments, O Jerusalem, the holy city. Loose yourself from the bands of your neck, O captive daughter of Zion."*[47] They will be *"full of power of the Lord's spirit of judgment and might to declare to Jacob his transgression and to Israel its sin."*[48]

In the midst of spiritual darkness and gross iniquity *"your watchmen will lift up the voice."* They will know the way of the Lord and his anger toward the nations and Israel for *"Cry aloud, spare not, lift up your voice as a trumpet, and show my people their transgression, and the house of Jacob their sins."*[49] Their voice of repentance and hope of redemption will bring many to conversion since *"Be you clean who bear the vessels of the Lord. My covenant was with him of life and peace. The law of truth was in his mouth, and iniquity was not found on his lips: he walked with me in peace and equity, and did turn many away from iniquity."*[50]

The gospel message to watch and pray to be accounted worthy of deliverance from evil and escape from the wrath of God will be announced in all the earth as *"The Lord has proclaimed unto the end of the world, Say to the daughter of Zion: Behold, your salvation comes. And you shall be called: A city sought out, and not forsaken; the holy people, the redeemed of the*

Lord."[51] As bride of Christ, the church will expect and prepare itself to meet the Lord for *"Their line is gone out through all the earth, and their words to the end of the world. In them he set a tabernacle for the bridegroom and rejoices as a strong man to run a race."*[52]

Turmoil will prevail in Israel despite its efforts to retain peace and prosperity in a weakened nation, but the faithful will trust in the promise of Christ since *"we have heard the voice of trembling, of fear, and not of peace: It is the time of Jacob's trouble, but he shall be saved out of it. Fear you not, O my servant Jacob, neither be dismayed, O Israel. I will save you from afar and your seed from the land of their captivity."*[53] This trouble is a sign to the church and *"The Lord hears you in the day of trouble. He will hear from his holy heaven with saving power of his right hand. They are brought down and fallen, but we are risen and stand upright."*[54]

In times of further hardship and suffering, the faithful *"will lament and say we are utterly spoiled. The Lord has changed the portion of my people, removed it far from me and divided our land. My people are risen up as an enemy. Arise you, and depart for this is not your rest since it will destroy you, even with a sore destruction."*[55] To those sanctified priests of God and to any of the believers who remain until the end, *"I will surely assemble all of you O Jacob, and I will gather the remnant of Israel. They shall divide and pass through the gate, and shall come in by it, and their king shall pass before them, and the Lord at the head of them."*[56]

Theology about the second and third watches has a crucial place in teaching since it shows the continuing grace and mercy to the church, but it also is a test of faith to believe in the power of God who will be glorified for *"Rejoice greatly, O daughter of Zion: shout, O daughter of Jerusalem. The Lord their God shall save them in that day: for they shall be as the stones of a crown, lifted up as an ensign upon his land."*[57] Any study of the last days must deal with these times when *"Turn you to the strong hold, you prisoners of hope. As for you also, by the blood of your covenant I have sent forth your prisoners out of the pit wherein is no water."*[58]

Various descriptions of the daughters of Zion and of Jerusalem must be interpreted in the physical or spiritual context of their usage, but as they apply in this period to faith in the church *"Praise the Lord, O Jerusalem: praise your God, O Zion. For he has strengthened the bars of your gates, he has blessed your children within you."*[59] These verses point to the strong zeal of anointing grace in Jeshurun and the following conversion of souls who will seek to be delivered from death as *"The Lord takes pleasure in them who fear him, in those who hope in his mercy. He does build up Jerusalem and he gathers together the outcasts of Israel."*[60]

Zionism concerns the new covenant of God in his people since Jesus is both with us in his tabernacle and in us in his spirit as *"Remember your congregation, this mount Zion, wherein you have dwelt. For God is my king, working salvation in the midst of the earth."*[61] This salvation extends beyond human life because it is based on the immortal lineage of Christ and *"They who trust in the Lord shall be as mount Zion, which is immovable, and abides forever."*[62] By faith in him we become citizens of a heavenly Jerusalem where *"The Lord shall reign forever, even your God, O Zion, unto all generations. I will extol and bless your name forever and ever."*[63]

Truth of biblical prophecies in redemption and harsh judgments of war, divine wrath and the Second Advent will circulate in the world despite great apostasy so *"Behold you, and regard and marvel: for a work is done in your days that you won't believe when it is told."*[64] A great number of souls will be converted by the works and example of Jeshurun because God *"will pour my spirit upon your seed, and my blessing upon your offspring."*[65] Many people will seek the wisdom and path of these priests as *"I will go unto the great men, and will speak unto them; for they have known the way of the Lord, and the judgment of their God."*[66]

Due to their anointing of divine grace and obedience to their election in the priesthood, the Lord said *"unto the eunuchs who keep my Sabbaths, and choose the things that please me, and take hold of my covenant: I will give them an everlasting name that shall not be cut off."*[67] They will lead a multitude to practice their faith whose *"feet shall stand within your gates, O Jerusalem: where the tribes go up, the tribes of the Lord, according to the decree for Israel, to give thanks to the name of the Lord."*[68] These holy men will draw lost souls to eat and drink of his Eucharistic table which is *"the bread of the elect, and wine springing forth virgins."*[69]

Division among Jews regarding the new covenant, persecution of the church and watches in redemption before the destruction of their nation that Jesus foretold would happen in the last days have not been perceived in the physical reality of his gospel. Conversion in the tribes of Israel to the priesthood will bring discipleship to other Jews and to *"sons of the stranger who join to the Lord to serve him and take hold of my covenant. Even them will I bring to my holy mountain and make them joyful in my house of prayer. The Lord who gathers the outcasts of Israel will yet gather others to him besides those who are gathered to him."*[70]

Modern eschatology involves conflicting doctrines that have omitted or distorted major events of the last days leaving a sense of confusion, apathy and discord but *"Arise, shine, O Jerusalem: darkness shall cover the earth, and gross darkness the people, but the Lord shall arise upon you, and his glory shall be seen in you."*[71] Mankind will reap unthinkable destruction due its selfish lusts that reject the unity of God's spirit in Christ yet *"the Redeemer shall come to Zion, and unto them who turn iniquity in Jacob. My spirit that is upon you, and my words that I have put in your mouth, shall not depart from you, nor your seed or your seed's seed."*[72]

Phases of the last days will be realized as these things are taught and transpire according to the divine plan of salvation for *"Rejoice, O children of Zion, and joy in the Lord your God, because he will make the early and latter rain to come down to you as in the beginning. And the floors shall be full of wheat, and the presses shall overflow with wine and oil."*[73] This pouring out of his saving grace as in the early church has not reached its potential in the stage of a latter renaissance following a second Pentecost. Harvest of souls expressed by wheat, wine and oil is in the watches. That oil and wine spoken of in the third seal will be preserved.

What Jacob revealed to Judah about the Messiah's gathering of his people was confirmed by the prophet Balaam who said *"there shall come a Star out of Jacob, and a Scepter shall rise out of Israel. Out of Jacob shall come he who shall have dominion."* Balaam was paid to curse the ancient Israelites by Balak, king of Moab, but the Lord blessed them and Balaam foretold *"There is no sorcery against Jacob, nor omen against Israel. It shall yet be said of them, 'Behold what God has wrought!' He couched, he lay down as a lion, and as a great lion: who shall arouse him?"*[74] This Lion of Judah will shock many by his work of redemption.

Belief in rapture is a hope beyond all hope never experienced in history and this event of the watches will certainly bewilder those who remain in the world. Some may try to explain it by the falsehood of an alien invasion, but many will know the expectation of those who believed in Christ. The testimony and law sealed in the hearts of the tribes of Israel at a second Pentecost are embedded in Scripture and those who seek truth will find it since *"Hear me, O Lord: I will keep your statutes. I cried unto you: save me, O Lord, quicken me according to your judgment. Concerning your testimonies, I have known of old that you founded them forever."*[75]

Whether it be in the present dispensation of grace or that to be revealed in the conversion among Jews, the public in general are blind to the signs of our times and stubbornly profess all things continue as they were from the beginning of creation. The fact is that some major issues of prophecy have already happened in the last century while others are taking place before our eyes. St. Peter wrote about the end times, *"we have not followed fictitious fables when we made known to you the power and coming of our Lord Jesus Christ, but were eyewitnesses of his majesty. We have also a more sure word of prophecy that you do well to take heed."*[76]

Reaction to events of redemption must be considered in the climate when the Antichrist will be made known after the first watch and his rising military and political might until his conquest in the end time. Besides instilling fear of any resistance to his forces, both he and the false prophet will possess demonic powers to deceive the nations. Iniquity will grow worse and if history provides any lessons neither the ancient Egyptians nor the Israelites repented of idol worship in the face of divine miracles. The same can be said of Christ who was crucified and so too the prophets and his apostles who were seen as apostates by their religious leaders.

The third seal of the Apocalypse indicates a severe famine in the earth, but the angelic voice that commanded this plague clearly said *"Hurt not the oil and the wine."*[77] This symbolism of those elements applies to the great anointing of Jeshurun in a new Pentecost and to the faithful who are branches of the vine of Christ. Despite the hatred and persecution of the church, all members of this holy priesthood will live to see their reward in the second watch and the lives of many believers will also be upheld by divine providence, yet *"Some of the learned shall fall to try them, and to purge, and to make them white, even to the time of the end."*[78]

Oil is an analogy of those sealed of God because it is used for light in lamps and for a sign of sanctity as *"I will triumph in the works of your hands. O Lord, how great are your works! My horn shall you exalt like the horn of a unicorn. I shall be anointed with fresh oil."*[79] This horn of newness in love for Jesus and hope of triumph in his redemption will cause them to watch and pray that *"You, O Lord, are our father, our redeemer. Return for your servants' sake, the tribes of your inheritance."*[80] It is also written of these priests *"Is not this a brand plucked out of the fire? They are men wondered at: for I will bring forth my servant the Branch."*[81]

Jeshurun's ministry correlates to the timeframe of a rebuilt Jewish kingdom in the aftermath of WWIII until another tragic world war begins to form. The global recovery of nations from an extremely war torn civilization will perish in battle and in curse. There are some apocalyptic plagues of the trumpet judgments that happen in addition to great famine during transition of the third and fourth seals before the end phase wrath. Of the seven trumpets recorded by St. John, the first five coincide with the earthly lives of those sealed of God since they are seen in writing of the fifth trumpet and somehow stay immune to the piercing pain of its effects.[82]

Direct causes of the mysterious trumpet judgments that begin in the later stage of the third seal most likely are either man-made or due to great disruptions in nature. It is conjecture to grasp what produces these calamities, but the signs will be made known and are plainly written to know their outcome. The wildfires covering a third part of the earth in the first trumpet exemplify how intense the drought will be. Any number of reasons could be offered to explain the spoil of creatures and ships spanning a third part of the sea in the second trumpet or the contamination of a third part of the earth's rivers and lakes in the third trumpet.

Expansive darkness that blocks the light of day and night over a third part of the world in the fourth trumpet may result from fires, volcanic ash or dust storms. This type of curse where the sun and also air are darkened is in the fifth trumpet showing God's justice against the spiritual darkness of humanity. The focus of the fifth trumpet, however, is *"that they should not kill them, but they shall be tormented five months, and their torment was as that of a scorpion."* This scourge could be some form of chemical or biological warfare which does *"not hurt any green thing, but only those men who have not the seal of God in their foreheads."*

150

Timing of the second watch is a matter of study and reason since a key signal appears to be an urgent warning by Jesus who taught *"When you see the Abomination of Desolation, spoken of by the prophet Daniel, stand in the holy place, then let them who are in Judea flee to the mountains. Pray that your flight be not in winter, or on the Sabbath day."*[83] This abomination is an idol image of the Antichrist that will be set up at the very summit of the Holy See for *"arms shall stand on his part, and they shall pollute the sanctuary of strength, and shall take away the daily sacrifice, and they shall place the abomination that makes desolate."*[84]

Nobody can predict exactly when the second watch will occur, but demonic control over the central place of the papacy would seriously disrupt the function of a final holy Pope and his brethren sealed of God. It seems rational that the priesthood of Jeshurun will be taken into heaven shortly before the Antichrist forcibly takes over the Vatican and prohibits the daily sacrifice of the Mass. Before the Antichrist obtains world control *"his heart shall be against the holy covenant and he shall have indignation against the holy covenant."*[85] Jesus spoke about this disturbing and visual event as an eminent sign of war forming against Israel.

Plagues of the first five trumpet judgments were summarized by Jesus as outward physical events that would precede the fall of Israel since *"There shall be signs in the sun, and in the moon, and in the stars; and upon the earth distress of nations, with perplexity, the sea and the waves roaring."* It is in this context of early turmoil that he warned about the abomination of desolation to be set up against the holy covenant in the sanctuary of strength so *"when you shall see Jerusalem compassed with armies, then know that the desolation thereof is near. Then let them in Judea flee and depart out, and let not them in the countries enter therein."*[86]

Widespread political instability will develop and result in massive bloodshed that most of the public will think ended with WWIII. Since the main issue of the abomination of desolation is so pivotal with respect to WWIV, it should be understood that this particular act does not refer to the Jewish temple because it will already be profaned by those who *"Behind the doors and the posts you have set up your remembrance, and you made a covenant with them."*[87] This prior abomination of the temple is not by force but by consent at *"the door of the inner gate, that looks to the north, where was the image of jealousy, which provokes to jealousy."*[88]

Scholars have largely dismissed the significance of those marked in their foreheads with the seal of God. These servants of his are not to be passed off as an abstraction, but they have a vital purpose in spreading the gospel to the ends of the world in the midst of worsening apostasy and threatening circumstances. Conversion of these Jews even to the priesthood and its hierarchy in the church is documented in many verses of Scripture. We cannot deny this elect darling called Jeshurun *"sung as it were a new song before the throne, and no man could learn that song but the hundred and forty four thousand who were redeemed from the earth."*[89]

Few people have thought about humanity after the devastation of WWIII because most think it will end in annihilation or there will be little to nothing left for anyone to rebuild. The truth is a substantial portion of mankind will survive and what is most important concerns the work of salvation. There is no question that sinful lusts will lead to the path of self-destruction and judgment, but God has all power *"And except that the Lord had shortened those days, no flesh would be saved."*[90] He has a plan to establish his covenant on earth and we must examine the intricacies of his word in the final seasons of the Apocalypse to see how it will unfold.

[1] Revelation 7,2-8; 14,1-5
[2] Zechariah 12,9-14
[3] Revelation 7,2-3
[4] Isaiah 9,2&8
[5] Isaiah 27,6
[6] Jeremiah 5,24; Hosea 6,3; James 5,7
[7] Isaiah 65,8-9
[8] Psalm 78,5-6
[9] Hosea 5,8-9
[10] Isaiah 8,16-20
[11] Isaiah 28,5-6
[12] Isaiah 46,3-4
[13] Isaiah 49,6
[14] Ezekiel 9,3-6
[15] Ezekiel 8,3-5&16; 9,8-9
[16] Malachi 3,2-4
[17] Isaiah 58,12-14
[18] Psalm 18,2; 89,24; 132,8-17
[19] Acts 3,18-20
[20] Psalm 147,19
[21] Hebrews 4,6-9
[22] Psalm 77,13-15
[23] II Corinthians 3,11-18
[24] Deuteronomy 33,4-5; Isaiah 44,1-3
[25] Psalm 81,3-5
[26] Genesis 49,8-12&22-26
[27] Romans 11,1-5&17-28
[28] Isaiah 28,11-12
[29] Deuteronomy 33,13-17
[30] Deuteronomy 32,9-15
[31] Zechariah 10,1-5
[32] Zechariah 10,6-8
[33] Isaiah 54,1-3&13-17
[34] Jeremiah 31,31-34; Hebrews 7,11; 8,7
[35] Genesis 49,5-7; Psalm 110
[36] Exodus 16,31-34; Numbers 17,1-10
[37] Deuteronomy 31,19-29; 32,29-36
[38] Deuteronomy 33,26-29
[39] Isaiah 6,9-10; Amos 8,11
[40] Numbers 20,1-13; Deuteronomy 33,8-11
[41] Isaiah 28,5-6
[42] Deuteronomy 33,20-21
[43] Isaiah 54,17
[44] Daniel 11,32
[45] Zechariah 9,13
[46] Micah 7,15
[47] Isaiah 52,1-2
[48] Micah 3,8
[49] Isaiah 58,1
[50] Isaiah 52,6-11; Malachi 2,4-7
[51] Isaiah 62,11-12
[52] Psalm 19, 2-11
[53] Jeremiah 30,5-10
[54] Psalm 20,1-9
[55] Micah 2,1-10

[56] Micah 2,12-13
[57] Zechariah 9,9&16
[58] Zechariah 9,11-12
[59] Psalm 147,12-13&19
[60] Psalm 147,2-5&11
[61] Psalm 74,2&12
[62] Psalm 125,1
[63] Psalm 145,1&10-13; 146,10
[64] Habakkuk 1,5&12; 2,1-4
[65] Isaiah 44,2-4
[66] Jeremiah 5,5
[67] Isaiah 56,3-5
[68] Psalm 122,1-5
[69] Zechariah 9,17
[70] Isaiah 56,6-8
[71] Isaiah 60,1-2
[72] Isaiah 59,20-21
[73] Joel 2,23-24
[74] Numbers 23,20-24; 24,5-9&14-19
[75] Psalm 119,146-152
[76] II Peter 1,16-19; 3,1-4
[77] Revelation 6,6
[78] Daniel 11,33-35
[79] Psalm 92,4-10&13-14
[80] Isaiah 63,16-17
[81] Zechariah 3,2&8
[82] Revelation 8,6-13; 9,1-5
[83] Mathew 24,15-20; Mark 13,14-18
[84] Daniel 11,31
[85] Daniel 11,28-31
[86] Luke 21,20-25
[87] Isaiah 57,8
[88] Ezekiel 8,3
[89] I Corinthians 15,20-24; Revelation 14,1-5
[90] Mathew 24,21-22; Mark 13,19-20

Chapter Seven
OPENING OF THE FOURTH SEAL
THE PALE HORSE

"I saw and behold a pale horse: and his name who sat on it was Death, and Hell followed with him. Power was given to them over the four parts of the earth to kill with the sword, with hunger, with pestilence and with beasts of the earth."
Revelation 6,7-8

How many people in this modern age of communication and literacy have earned degrees in everything under the sun, but have not bothered to study the Holy Bible, nor understand the reality of its spiritual and practical lessons for this life and promise of immortality? Even for clergy and those who teach catechism, the book of Revelation is mainly an ignored subject or distorted and obscure topic but the Apocalypse is a word that reflects discovery in the meaning of its content. In that sense we need to be honest with ourselves concerning moral law and open to the prophetic judgments that may stir our conscience and alter our views.

There is no unfair bias in the light of truth and we must realize what has been neglected or not understood will be made known for *"Call unto me, and I will answer you, and show you great and mighty things, which you knew not."*[1] Many events of the last days were taught by the apostles as St. Paul said *"we write nothing to you than what you read or acknowledge. I trust you shall understand even to the end."*[2] They relied on the gospel of Jesus and writing of the prophets who also faced oppression for the word of God *"But as for me, my prayer is to you O Lord in an acceptable time, in your mercy hear me in the truth of your salvation."*[3]

Predictions of growing corruption and persecution following the recovery of civilization from WWIII are indeed shocking since *"it is a shame even to speak of those things which are done in secret. See then that you walk prudently, not as fools but as wise because the days are evil."*[4] The divine word is not written in vain as *"Who is wise and he shall understand these things? For the ways of the Lord are right, and the just shall walk in them, but transgressors shall fall therein."*[5] An inherent yet puzzling question of prophecy is *"Who will give ear to this? Who will hearken for the time to come?"*[6] Hearing and doing good advice are different matters.

Profound warnings of great disasters and massive destruction of global wars in the end times are meant to lead us to repentance from sins so that we can be forgiven and be ready for the promise of redemption. It is beyond our grasp to know how much God loves us and would refrain from his vengeance if mankind served his covenant in Christ. Jesus wept in pity as he pondered the judgment of Jerusalem and in this respect, *"Give glory to the Lord your God, but if you will not hear it, my soul shall weep in secret places for your pride, and my eye shall weep sore, and run down with tears because the Lord's flock is carried away captive."*[7]

Dire forecasts are made in Scripture that many scholars see as past tense or fail to separate these sorrows from the end wrath, but *"I announced your justice in the vast assembly, I did not restrain my lips. I have not hid your righteousness within my heart. Your salvation I have spoken of, I made no secret of your kindness or your truth."*[8] The prophet Micah wrote with robust zeal: *"I am filled with the strength of the spirit of the Lord, with judgment and power to declare unto Jacob his wickedness, and to Israel his sin."*[9] Musing on these unnerving matters of justice and iniquity proves surprising and piercing as *"Whoever hears, his ears shall tingle."*[10]

Hypocrisy is rooted in deception since it involves a perverted conscience of what is right and wrong. Its motive is selfishness for *"the children of your people speak one to another saying,*

154

Come and hear the word of the Lord. They hear your words, but they will not do them for their heart goes after their lusts."[11] Of this curious flirtation and fleeting knowledge of divine law that turns into apostasy *"Why say my people, we are lords: we will no more come to you, yet you say I am innocent, surely his anger will turn from me?"[12]* Moses warned about calamity due to this falling away because *"they are an obstinate generation, children with no faith."[13]*

Transition from great famine and starvation in much of our planet to a full scale world war is a primary topic of this chapter. Nearly all those left in the world will suffer an ill fate because *"The Lord of hosts has purposed it, to stain the pride of all glory and to bring into contempt all the honorable of the earth."[14]* It is difficult to compare outcomes of the next world wars since both have nuclear capacity to cause untold horror, but in WWIV *"Hear all you people, hearken O earth and all that is therein: let the Lord God be witness against you and I will execute vengeance in anger and fury upon the heathen, such as they have not heard."[15]*

The opening of the fourth seal of the Apocalypse indicates a plurality of terrors on humanity for *"The Lord will send upon you cursing, vexation and rebuke you in all that you do, until you are destroyed and perish quickly, whereby you have forsaken me."[16]* These plagues are plainly defined in Mosaic Law and warnings of the fourth seal are repeated by the prophets *"when I send my four sore judgments upon Jerusalem: the sword, famine, pestilence and mischievous beasts."[17]* In that dreadful time, *"a fire is kindled in my anger: it will burn to the lowest hell and consume the earth with her increase, and the foundations of its mountains."[18]*

Theologians do not generally recognize the State of Israel's captivity in the last days although Jesus made references to that tragedy such as *"the days come that your enemies will lay you even with the ground."[19]* In the same way of linking Old Testament prophecies of the end times to the ruin of the first Jewish temple, they miss the point by teaching Jesus was talking about the Romans who destroyed the second Jewish temple in the first century. Despite confusion and deceit that exists about the Antichrist forming a one world government by peaceful means, we must realize his vicious tyranny will result from military force in WWIV.

References to the sequence of Christ's gospel about when kingdom will rise against kingdom prior to the end period focus on the depravity and captivity of the Jewish nation, but there are plenty details of how this consuming battle takes place and its widespread casualties for *"the mighty man shall cry there bitterly: A day of the trumpet and alarm against the fenced cities, and against the high towers. I will bring distress upon men, because they have sinned against the Lord, and their blood will be poured out as dust, and their flesh as dung. The whole land will be devoured by the fire of his jealousy."[20]* This distress will cover the entire earth.

While examining the wording of the fourth seal in each of the bible versions used in my text, it is noteworthy that a translation discrepancy was found between these two bibles. Even slight distinctions in the phrasing of translation can lead to major issues of accuracy in interpreting the truth of God's word. This discovery is a critical link in the dimension of conquest expressed by killing of the sword and may help to explain why the seven seals have not been put in the right place of mainstream theology. The variation of a particular phrase in these versions reflects vastly different conclusions about a partial or global extent of evil power.

Reading of the fourth seal speaks of St. John's vision of *"a pale horse: and his name who sat on it was Death, and Hell followed with him."* These names refer to Satan and to the demon Baal who respectively possess the Antichrist and the false prophet.[21] It is written of Christ that through his death *"he might destroy him who had the power of death, who is the devil. The last enemy to be destroyed is death."[22]* The inconsistency of an older Catholic edition with the King

James Version is in regard to the dominion of Death and Hell since the Catholic writing states power over *"the four parts of the earth"* versus *"the fourth part of the earth."[23]*

Either the fourth seal reveals a complete takeover of evil forces over the whole earth or the outcome of its four different curses to kill which include the sword only affects a much smaller part of it. In view of the numerable accounts of prophecy that signify the same kinds of plagues listed in the fourth seal as a precursor to the end wrath and judgment at Armageddon, it is reasonable to discern this seal describes excessive ruin to any society who remains in that stage of divine justice. The sword of the fourth seal involves great conflict to erupt that will draw all rulers into an astonishing war ending in victory by the armor of the Antichrist.

WWIV is a complex sequence of military actions as many nations, cities and lands specified in the prophets have a role in this flood of tumult as *"I will call for a sword upon all the people of the earth. An uproar shall come even to the ends of the earth: for the Lord has a controversy with the nations, he will contend with all flesh and give the wicked to the sword."[24]* There is no question that prophecies relating to this war apply to civilization before Armageddon and *"My sword shall go forth out of its sheath against all flesh from south to north. Every heart will melt, all hands will be feeble and knees weak. It comes and will be brought to pass."[25]*

Never in mankind's history has such a line-up of races named in the bible come against each other in a massacre that will lead to ruthless reign of the Antichrist and institution of a global church to worship him headed by the false prophet. In the beginning of the war, *"evil will go forth from nation to nation, and a great whirlwind will be raised up from the coasts of the earth. And the slain of the Lord will be in that day from one end of the earth even to the other end of the earth."[26]* This massive army from the coasts of the earth is a league of nations around China who team with it to rise up against the Antichrist's growing Roman empire.

Lines of battle in a broad sense are divided by a combat build up between new superpowers of the east and west due to the severe damage that Russia and the U.S. will suffer in WWIII. This new balance of power will clash for *"Behold, a people shall come from the north, and a great nation, and many kings will be raised up from the coasts of the earth."[27]* These are two opposing forces as those of the north are from Europe and the coastal kings who ally with China *"shall roar like the sea, everyone in array to battle against you, O daughter of Babylon."[28]* This daughter of ancient Babylon is a synonym for the Babylon of Revelation.

Similitudes of the ancient Hebrew captivity used in the prophets to explain events of the last days must be determined in their proper context and in light of clues such as daughters of any peoples of the past. In regard to opposition of the Antichrist, *"I will raise up a destroying wind against Babylon, and them who dwell in its midst who rise up against me. Fanners will be sent to Babylon that will fan her and empty her land. The daughter of Babylon is like a threshing floor, it is time to thresh her: yet a little while and the time of her harvest shall come."[29]* Final demise of this wicked kingdom is in the end wrath and at the Second Advent.

Severe damage and loss of wealth will take place in lands controlled by the Antichrist as the Lord declared *"I am against you, O destroying mountain, which destroys all the earth: blow the trumpet among the nations, prepare the nations against her. Call together against her the kingdoms of Ararat, Minni and Ashchenaz. Appoint a captain against her with the kings of the Medes and all the rulers thereof."[30]* These diverse nations are of Eastern Asia or the Far East and include India and Pakistan. They once formed the farthest eastern border of ancient time and will yield to the command of China then known as Elam on their southern flank.

Countries listed and described as coastal peoples who form a military treaty under sway of China contain a strategic force in WWIV. These old land based nations spread from around the

Caspian Sea south to the Persian Gulf Sea became our modern world of the East surrounded by oceans. Congeneric nature of the rulers of the Medes refers to Indochina and Indonesian tribes from Vietnam, Cambodia, Laos, Thailand, Malaya, Burma, Indonesia, Philippines, Japan and Korea. Taiwan is part of China in this mix while the remaining fourth ethnic region that joins it in armed revolt appears to be from a newly formed Mongolia with access to the sea.

The size and power of this army is like an infestation of caterpillars or locusts that come up as a hurricane since *"Make the arrows bright, gather the shields. Set up the standard upon the walls of Babylon, make the watch strong, prepare the ambushes: the Lord will fill you with men as with caterpillars, they shall shout against you and the land shall tremble and sorrow."*[31] This army is truly of biblical proportions in the scope of its members and intent. Of the multitude of warriors and their ensuing harvest of treasure, *"Your spoil will be gathered like the gathering of caterpillars, as the running to and fro of locusts shall he run upon them."*[32]

Historians seem to have failed in tracing ancient migration of the far eastern peoples before Persians conquered Babylon. Many people wonder what China will do with its military and economic might or how it fits into the biblical scheme of the end. That nation once called the sleeping giant is a major player in world affairs and Moses told of its role in the last days as *"The Lord will bring a nation against you from far, from the end of the earth as swift as the eagle flies, a nation whose tongue you do not understand, a nation of fierce countenance. He shall besiege all your gates, until your high and fenced walls come down in all your land."*[33]

Other prophets affirmed teachings of Moses about the generation of those who return from the captivity of old and they reveal a startling scenario of the awesome breadth and depth of God's word for *"I will bring a nation upon you from far, O house of Israel. It is a mighty nation whose language you know not. Their quiver is an open sepulcher: they will impoverish your fenced cities with the sword. O daughter of my people, make mourning and lamentation for the spoiler will suddenly come upon us. Because my people forsake me to make their land desolate and a hissing, I will scatter them with an east wind in the day of their calamity."*[34]

False prophets will arise in Israel to deny its reality since *"surely you have greatly deceived this people and Jerusalem saying, you will have peace but the sword reaches to their soul. My bowels are in pain, my heart has heard the sound of the trumpet, the cry of war: Destruction upon destruction, and all the earth is laid waste."*[35] The overall impact in WWIV of the allied eastern armies starts with the carnage of those linked with China, but ends in triumph for the Antichrist because *"Israel is a scattered sheep, the lions have driven him away: first the king of Assyria has devoured him, and last this king of Babylon has broken his bones."*[36]

Resemblance of WWIV to ancient captivity of Hebrew kingdoms of Samaria and Judah are remarkable in the way things happen and the terminology that refers to the future. Decisive incursions of the eastern offensive and responding defense of a growing Roman empire come separately in which *"the whirlwind goes forth with fury, a continuing whirlwind."*[37] Unlike the ancient past, this double blow of bloodshed will come quickly for *"Behold, a whirlwind of the Lord is gone forth in fury, even a grievous whirlwind."*[38] Key instructions are made in the path of the wind in that *"he stays his rough wind in the day of the east wind."*[39]

In metaphor, the Assyrian king of an expansive new empire is Chinese since they and their allies will have great influence in building areas of ancient Assyria for economic reasons. In the war *"The Lord will blow the trumpet, and go with the whirlwinds of the south."*[40] Although this kingdom is from the east, trade routes have long been established from the Gulf of Aden into the Red Sea and from the Persian Gulf. Therefore, *"as whirlwinds in the south pass through, so it comes from the desert, from a terrible land. Go up, O Elam: besiege, O Media. My loins are filled with pain; pangs have taken hold of me as of a woman who travails."[41]*

Prophecy is determined by whether or not what is spoken has been fulfilled and thus its application is to the past, present or future. We cannot change the wisdom of God but we can learn the matters of our times, even things that have not been part of our dialogue since *"Turn you at my reproof: behold, I will pour out my spirit upon you. I will make known my words to you."[42]* It is difficult to put in order intricate details of WWIV because of the manifold names of nations and cities which are part of divine justice. This maze of knowledge can be seen by study of how these events unfold as a result of the whole picture in that chaotic epoch.

A major factor in the pattern of battles is the great onslaught from the east *"For it is a day of slaughter, and of treading down and of perplexity of breaking down the walls and crying in the mountains. Elam bare the quiver with chariots of men and horsemen. And Kir uncovered the shield."* No historical record exists of the league of eastern nations who come against Israel and the city of Jerusalem, but *"I will weep bitterly for the spoiling of the daughter of my people. You have seen the many breaches of the city of David. The covering of Judah is discovered and you looked to the armor of the house of the forest."[43]* This forest is south of their borders.

Israel will not expect the crushing forces of both smaller nations and regional kingdoms as *"now shall be their perplexity. Although the land will be desolate for the fruit of their doings, in that day also he will come to you from Assyria, and from the fortified cities and from the fortress to the river, and from sea to sea and from mountain to mountain."* This plan of attack is from the Persian Gulf and from the Red Sea in the Arabian Peninsula. Defense by people who live in this area will fail to help the Jews for *"Feed your people with the rod, as in the days of old. The nations will be confounded at all their might and dread the Lord our God."[44]*

Trumpet judgments of the Apocalypse are intermixed with various predictions of the last days and five of these plagues briefly discussed in the last chapter start with great famine of the third seal. Some of these disasters apparently involve strife between nations in early turmoil and in progress of other later events to when the whole world is engulfed in war. Most theologians confuse the pervasive sixth trumpet trial with the battle of Armageddon thereby omitting a paramount season of cleansing and redemption of the church along with a deadly sentence of the wicked and captivity of all nations. This trumpet has its own purpose and time.

When the angel sounded the sixth trumpet, St. John heard a voice from the golden altar before God to loose the four angels at the great river Euphrates, *"And the four angels were loosed who were prepared to slay the third part of mankind."* Whatever the total population of the world is at that moment, the toll of human life will be enormous. No military has ever reached the size of the monstrous one recorded here and it is clear that the weapons of mass destruction used by it are nuclear because *"The number of the army of horsemen was two hundred thousand times a thousand and by fire, by smoke and by brimstone was the third part of men killed."[45]*

Practical sense dictates that only those who inhabit eastern countries in and around China have the capacity to develop such a huge group of troops who stand at two hundred million. Countries of the eastern alliance are the most populous nations on earth and this vision of the future is conceivable. Nuclear arsenals will continue to expand in these nations, but no wonder the prophets used examples of grasshoppers and caterpillars to describe this immense army. We must interpret this passage literally and put it in the proper perspective as St. John wrote *"I heard the number of them."* It is a serious error to trifle or misuse the bible.

Analogies used by prophets have an essential function in discerning the divine word. One such parable concerns the wealth and power of China whose head is captain of a military host not seen in the past. Harbors and exchange centers of trade in what was ancient Assyria may have regional princes, but China will have a hold on their reigns as *"the Assyrian was a cedar in Lebanon and his height was exalted above all the trees of the field. His boughs were multiplied and became long for his root was by great waters. Thus was he fair in his greatness and an assembly of many nations dwelt under his shadow. All the trees of Eden envied him."*[46]

China's eminent status in commerce and defense will prompt an unholy pride of loftiness that contradicts God's grace for *"His heart is lifted up in his height. Therefore I have delivered him unto the mighty one of the heathen: he will surely deal with him, I have driven him out for his wickedness. Strangers and the most cruel of the nations shall cut him down, and cast him away upon the mountains, and in all the valleys are his branches fallen, and his boughs are broken by all the rivers of the land. The people of the earth are gone down from his shadow, and have left him."* These waterways are the Tigris, the Euphrates and the Nile rivers.

Retaliation of the Antichrist against momentous damage and spoil by the eastern army will be swift and decisive as *"Upon his ruin, none of the trees by the waters exalt themselves for they are delivered to death. The nations shook at the sound of his fall, when I cast him down into hell with them who descend into the pit. They who were slain by the sword went down into hell with him, they who were his arm under his shadow in the midst of the heathen."*[47] Most people shun the thought of damnation, while others deny there is a hell or think little about the cost of grave sins but *"It is a fearful thing to fall into the hands of the living God."*[48]

Realizing China's role in the mysterious title of a new Assyria to lead an assembly of eastern nations is an essential part of the puzzle since *"O Assyrian, the rod of my anger and the staff in their hand is my indignation. I will send him against a hypocritical nation to take spoil, to take prey and to tread down like mire of the streets. It is in his heart to destroy and cut off nations, not a few. I will punish his stout heart who says: By my own hand and wisdom I have done it. The glory of his forest will be consumed and he will run away for fear. The rest of his trees will be few."*[49] What happens to Israel and the Middle East extends to global war.

Unrest and turmoil will prevail in much of our world prior to an assault from the east. An example of this disorder stemming from a lack of food, money and repentance of iniquity will occur when *"I set the Egyptians against the Egyptians and they will fight every one against his brother and against his neighbor: city against city, and kingdom against kingdom."*[50] Middle East uprisings including attacks against Israel are symptoms of widespread revolt for *"Woe to the multitude of many people who roar like the sea. The nations shall rush like many waters, but God will rebuke them and they shall flee far off before the wind, and the whirlwind."*[51]

Several verses of Scripture describe the major forces in WWIV with very few words. In regard to Jerusalem, *"You have stricken them, but they have not grieved; you have consumed them, but they refused correction."*[52] It is a pity that people do not repent at the signs of prophecy so the Lord's rage will be kindled against his people as *"he has smitten them, the hills trembled and their carcasses were torn in the streets. But his anger is not turned away and his hand is outstretched still."*[53] In the conflict *"they will go out from one fire, and another fire will devour them, and you will know I am Lord when I set my face against them."*[54]

Suffering from plagues in the fourth seal of the Apocalypse will affect all of mankind and the Israelites are no exception despite the fact they have returned to the Land of Promise: *"As the thief is ashamed when he is found so is the house of Israel ashamed. They have turned their back to me and not their face. Your own sword has devoured your prophets like a destroying lion."*[55] Their iniquity and falsehoods will not profit them or go unpunished since *"All our enemies have*

159

opened their mouths against us. You have made us as outcasts and refuse, a desolation and destruction. The stones of the sanctuary are poured out in every street."[56]

Deceit will cover the minds of people who think they are not liable for their evil ways, but *"Hearken not to the prophets who make you vain and to them who blaspheme me that say no evil will come upon you, as their fathers forgot my name for Baal."*[57] Israel will become an object of hatred to their neighbors and to all nations for their debauchery and devious foreign policy for *"I have made you a reproach to the heathen, and a mocking to all countries. Those who are near and those who are far from you shall mock you. And I will scatter you among the heathen, and disperse you in the countries to consume the wickedness out of you."*[58]

Border line nations in the Middle East will rise up against the Jewish nation as *"I will bring fear upon you from all those round about you, and you shall be scattered everyone out of one another's sight."*[59] They will be a prime target not only for what's left of their wealth from the famine, but for their location in the center of commerce so *"Woe to them who are at ease in Zion, they will go captive with the first that go captive. The eyes of the Lord God are on the sinful kingdom, and I will destroy it from the face of the earth, saving I will not utterly destroy the house of Jacob, but sift them among the nations like corn is sifted in a sieve."*[60]

Vengeance of God against humanity is for its refusal to accept his covenant in Christ and walk in his spirit of love. We cannot blame God whose desire for us is to live in peace, security and abundance of goods. The basis of his judgments is in ourselves because it is simple fact we reap what we sow and most adversities in our lives are the result of our own doing. The divine plan is to instill harmony with our Creator, our families, our community and our society. He has not changed, but *"I beheld the earth, and it was without form and void, and the heavens had no light. The Lord said: The whole land will be desolate, yet I will not make a full end."*[61]

Signs of the end times are inclusive for all people, but many intricacies of prophecy revolve around Israel *"For death is come up into our windows, and is entered into our palaces. I will punish all them who are circumcised with the uncircumcised: Egypt, Judah, Edom, Ammon, Moab and all who are in the utmost corners that dwell in the wilderness."*[62] The nations between and around the Nile and the Euphrates rivers will serve as a decisive battleground of the eastern kings and also all those in league with the Antichrist. Extensive spoil and carnage from the eastern kings will take place before the full force of his Roman empire.

Timing of these things within this vital trade region for many commodities is clearly stated in future tense since *"The spoiler shall come upon every city, he will fly as an eagle and spread his wings over Moab. The calamity of Moab is near to come and its captivity again in the latter days. Concerning Edom, his seed is spoiled and his brethren, and his neighbors, and he shall not be. Alarm of war is heard in Rabbah of the Ammorites, and her daughters burned with fire. Then Israel will be heir to them who were his heirs. An east wind will come up from the wilderness: he will spoil all the pleasant vessels and Samaria will become desolate."*[63]

Firm consistency of the prophets permits us to piece together great mysteries of the inspired word, but *"Who is the wise man that may understand and declare it?"* Sorting out of events fits into a rational wisdom of our reality. As for Israel, *"they will fall among them who fall: in the time of their visitation, they will be cast down. I take up weeping for the mountains and wailing for the wilderness, because they are burned up. I will open Moab from the cities on his frontiers to the men of the east with the Ammonites in possession. I will cut off Edom from Teman, and Dedan will fall. I will rebuke the Philistines and destroy them of the sea coast."*[64]

Men of the east named in Scripture and referred to by metaphors have an intrinsic role in this day of vengeance and their assault of the Middle East is well defined as *"the riches of Damascus and the spoil of Samaria will be taken away by the king of Assyria. The Lord brings upon them the waters of the river, strong and many. He shall come up over all his channels, and go over his banks, and pass through Judah and fill the breath of your land.*⁶⁵ Logically this land based attack is from east of the Euphrates River to transport a colossal army beside any air or sea offensives, and he will also *"lead the Egyptians prisoners and Ethiopians captive."*⁶⁶

Study of the overall conflict of WWIV indicates an abrupt wave of spoil from the east before the concluding blitz of the Antichrist for *"the virgin daughter of my people is broken with a great breach, with a grievous blow. I will scatter them with a fan in the gates of the land. I brought upon them a spoiler at noonday and cast terror suddenly upon the cities."*⁶⁷ We might ask how an army of millions could startle anyone given our satellite systems, but *"Write it in a table, and note it in a book that it will be in the latter days for a testimony forever. This iniquity will be to you as a breach ready to fall, whose breaking comes suddenly at an instant."*⁶⁸

Considering the number of eastern allied troops, the only element of shock and terror would be the fire and brimstone described in the sixth trumpet of Revelation. Reliance on military air forces together with long range sea and land missile launching pads is basic to modern warfare. Before movement of troops, this barrage is supported in that *"There shall be an adversary round about the land, he will bring down your strength and your palaces spoiled. I destroyed some of you as God overthrew Sodom and Gomorrah, yet you returned not to me. The virgin of Israel is fallen, she shall no more rise, she is cast down and none to raise her up."*⁶⁹

An interesting question about the extent of Jewish rule and spreading of its territories after WWIII is *"O Lord, you have planted them, they have taken root, they prosper and bring forth fruit, but prepare them for the day of slaughter. If you have been secure in a land of peace, what will you do in the swelling of the Jordan? The spoilers are come upon all the high places through the wilderness: for the sword will devour from one end of the land to the other. No flesh shall have peace."*⁷⁰ This concept of swelling of the Jordan has far reaching implications for the limited expanse of power by the Jews in some form of a greater Samaria.

Certain passages of the Old Testament either directly or by inference refer to the growth of wealth, land and influence of Israel. Some of these writings have already been discussed, but of occupation of areas on the other side of the Jordan River *"Why glory you in the valleys, your flowing valley, O backsliding daughter who trusted in her treasures saying: Who shall come to me? Has Israel no heir? Why then does her king inherit Gad, and his people dwell in his cities?"*⁷¹ Any Jewish control over this large place once called the lands of Jazer and of Gilead which the tribes of Gad and Reuben received in ancient time will come to ruin.

Spoiling and destruction will engulf the world, but areas in and around Israel will become a forgotten center of commerce whose wasting will leave a great void in means of global trade as *"The earth mourns and pines: Lebanon is ashamed and hewn down, Sharon is like a wilderness, Bashan and Carmel shake off their fruits. Fear has surprised the sinners in Zion."*⁷² Direction of the eastern army and its main military objectives include the Middle East as they *"shall come up like a lion from the swelling of the Jordan against the strong: Damascus is waxed feeble, Hemath and Arpad are confounded. There is sorrow on the sea, it cannot rest."*⁷³

Sea ports in the Mediterranean at the Nile River and in Lebanon at the ancient cities of Tyre and Zidon will become focal points for world trade and essential centers in the exchange of goods. Jesus told the people of cities where he performed miracles *"if the mighty works were done in Tyre and Sidon that were done in you, they would have repented. But it will be more tolerable for Tyre and Sidon at the day of judgment than for you."*⁷⁴ We need to contemplate what he said because *"Tyre built herself a stronghold and heaped silver and gold as dust, but the Lord will cast her out, and smite her power in the sea, and devour her with fire."*[75]

Vital importance of a future Tyre as a port to global livelihood is clearly documented in the prophetic scheme of the last days since *"your borders are in the midst of the seas, your builders perfected your beauty. Your wares went forth out of the seas and filled many people. You enriched the kings of the earth with the multitude of your riches and your merchandise."*[76] Tyre's renown for enhancing industrial growth will be tied to commerce from Egypt as it is called *"the crowning city, whose merchants are princes of the earth, and by the seed of the Nile in many waters, the harvest of the river is her revenue and she is a mart of nations."*[77]

Traders from all directions will have a hand in the making of Tyre and in running its business. China will be a main investor in improving this harbor to welcome traffic going in and out of the Nile River and the Persian Gulf for trade with the west. Ironically these attributes will help rebuild Europe before relations turn sour in that *"the land of the Chaldeans was not until the Assyrian founded it for them who dwell in the wilderness: they set up the palaces thereof."* But the Lord commanded *"against the merchant city, to destroy the strongholds thereof. He stretched out his hand over the sea, he shook the kingdoms, and brought it to ruin."*[78]

This city of merchants is a pivotal factor in divine justice for *"I am against you O Tyre and will cause many nations to come against you. They will destroy her walls and towers. It will be for the spreading out of nets in the midst of the seas and a spoil to the nations. They filled the midst of you with violence by the iniquity of your traffic. I will bring a fire from the midst of you, it will devour and bring you to ashes on the earth."* There will be piracy and conflict on the seas due to widespread corruption and greed. Dishonest gain will cause sharp divisions that turn into hatred and violence until *"the east wind has broken you in the midst of the seas."*[79]

At the sound of the second trumpet of the Apocalypse *"a great mountain burning with fire was cast into the seas, and a third part of sea creatures died and a third part of the ships were destroyed."*[80] Rather than natural disaster this mountain of fire appears to result from war on the seas to sink many ships and probably damage shoreline oil rigs that would cause gushing oil spills to destroy life in vast regions of the sea. Nuclear weapons used in that war would in itself cause profuse loss of life to anything that lives in the sea and also have the power to destroy complete brigades of naval ships or any other ships in range of the bombing.

Rebuilding and demise of the sea ports of Tyre and Zidon which still exist like relics of the past is a vision to be fulfilled and we need to think about what the world will look like after the nightmare of WWIII, especially in light of lessons we can learn from the bible. What remains to be seen will far surpass their ancient glory or adversity before Jesus spoke about them in his gospel. Mariners will weep and get off their ships on land saying *"What city is like Tyre that became silent in the midst of the sea? Your riches, your goods, your sailors, your men of war, and all the company with you shall fall into the sea in the day of your ruin."*[81]

Our world's fate will be known to the church in expectation for they will be taught about the signs of their time and live to see when these things happen since *"As we have heard, so have we seen in the city of our God. The kings were assembled, they passed by together. They saw it, and were stunned, terrified and routed. Anguish seized them there as an east wind shattered the ships of Tarshish."*[82] Location of this ancient city is disputed, but in practical reality it refers to the Asia Minor port of Tarsus in Turkey. After Tyre is fallen, *"O daughter of Tarshish, there is no more strength, for it is laid waste so there is no house, no entering in."*[83]

Main parts of warfare between the new east and west are defined as times of calamity and of visitation in which the later end is an evil captivity. This sequence is expressed by various events but China will enter a quagmire with Egypt as they *"Declare in Egypt and say, Stand up and prepare you for the sword will devour all around you. The mighty man has stumbled against the mighty, and both are fallen together. They are turned back and fled away: they did not stand in the day of their calamity, and in the time of their visitation. The daughter of Egypt will be confounded, and she will be delivered into the hand of the people of the north."*[84]

Strife among nations at the very start of WWIV will prompt China and its allies to defend their sweeping interests, especially in the Middle East. Concerning Egypt who will be perplexed by ethnic and political turmoil of the region, *"You are like a young lion of the nations and as a whale in the seas. You pushed with the horn in your rivers, troubled the waters with your feet, and fouled their rivers."*[85] The Egyptians will contrive a fiendish plan to expand their power as *"Egypt rises up like a flood, and he says, I will go up and cover the earth. I will destroy the city and its inhabitants. Let the valiant men rage: the Ethiopians, Lybyans and Lydians."*[86]

These prophecies about an Egyptian alliance, including Lydia whose people are Turks, reveal a failed attempt to conquer Tyre and control its trade routes but *"their mighty ones are beaten down, fled and turned back: they stumble and fall toward the north by the Euphrates. They said, Arise and go back to our land from the oppressing sword."*[87] Routing of their armies and many other nations by the east will likely cause the third trumpet sign which results in fouling of many rivers and lakes so *"the sword will come upon Egypt, Ethiopia, Libya, Lydia, Chub, the men in league with and they who uphold Egypt and the tower of Syene will fall."*[88]

Egypt will develop into a great kingdom whose influence affects a wide range of peoples, but of its pride and lust for power *"The Lord God is against you, Pharaoh, king of Egypt, the great dragon that lies in the midst of his rivers who has said, My river is my own and I made it for myself. I will spread out my net over you with a company of many people, I will lay your flesh upon the mountains and the valleys, the land where you swim and the rivers. The hearts of many people will also be vexed among the nations when I shake my sword upon them."*[89] This net involves the invasion from the east and then military response of the Antichrist.

Ideas about the future are often expressed in brief phrases or singular words that are hidden in meaning without knowing the context. One such cliché relates to Israel's location in the middle of two chief trade routes as *"Tyre has said against Jerusalem, Aha she is broken who was the gates of the people."*[90] This reference to the gates is central to pathways of the armies of the east and of Europe because the term refers to harbors at the mouth of the Nile River and at Tyre. Therefore, *"the kings of the earth and people of the world would not have believed that the adversary and the enemy would have entered the gates of Jerusalem."*[91]

The time of the heathen is not one of dancing and joy, but instead it is a season of chaos and horror for *"My soul is among the lions, and I lay among them who are set on fire."*[92] Incursion of Egypt and its alliance to spoil the wealth of Tyre and control its merchants will set off a massive offensive from the east. Israel will find itself at the center stage of conflict when *"the children of Noph and Tahapanes have broken the crown of your head."*[93] The Egyptians will be *"a staff of reed to the house of Israel. When they took you by the hand, you did break and rend all their shoulder, and you weakened their loins when they leaned on you."*[94]

Pride in self and reliance on riches or in the might of phony friends can lead to a deceptive and harmful conceit of egomania which darkens our ability to see reality or respect the rights of others. This attitude results in oppression and envy whereby divine law is a byword. In regard to Jerusalem, *"all who honored her despise her: she remembered not her last end. The heathen entered her sanctuary: All you who pass by, the Lord has set fire into my bones, and it prevailed against them. He spread out a net, turned me back and trod the daughter of Judah as a winepress. The sword destroys abroad, and at home alike there is death."*[95]

Mankind's own haughtiness will bring it to ruin. There is reason in divine law that shows us the way to peace and prosperity, but due to delusions of grandeur and pretense of dignity *"they prepared a net for my steps, and they dug a pit before me, into the midst thereof they are fallen themselves."*[96] The greed of Egypt will blind it to other powers and China likewise will think they are invincible, but in the meantime *"The Lord has burned against Jacob like a burning fire that devours round about. He swallowed up Israel, destroyed his strongholds, took away his tabernacle, caused the feasts and Sabbaths to cease, her gates are sunk to the ground."*[97]

Hebrew people were chosen to be separated from idols and iniquities of other nations, but after their modern return *"You prospered into a kingdom, trusted in your own beauty and played the harlot with everyone who passed by. Because of your whoredom and the idols of your abominations by the blood of your children whom you gave to them, I will gather all your lovers with all them you hated against you, and I will judge you in fury and jealousy. I will give you into their hand and they will destroy your brothel house, break down your high places and leave you bare."*[98] These demonic rituals of the high places date from ancient time.

In this parable about the creation, building and defeat of Israel *"You decked the high places and made images of men. Your sons and daughters, you sacrificed unto them. Is this a small matter that you slay my children to cause them to pass through the fire?"* This prophecy is not a misprint nor only applies to the past, but it unveils an aberration worse than the process of partial-birth abortion even now condoned in our society. The holy and profane will become ambiguous, but of corrupt dealings by the Jews, *"You fornicated with the Egyptians, you also played the whore with the Assyrians and multiplied fornications unto Chaldea."*[99]

Trust in wealth and power is worthless without faith in God. It is not only for economic concerns of hardship, but also for military assistance that Israel will seek and make compacts with other nations. Analogy of two sisters describes Israel similar to that of old for *"Samaria is Aholah, and Jerusalem is Aholibah."* These names of an enlarged yet divided kingdom imply tents of idolatry linked to being defiled by treaties with other nations as *"They did whoredom in Egypt, Aholah doted with the Assyrians and they both took one way. Aholibah sent to the Babylonians who came to her in a bed of love, she was polluted with them."*[100]

Covenants with Egypt and the major powers of China and the Antichrist will lead to all kinds of idolatry for *"you have gone whoring after the heathen and are polluted with their idols. I will bring your lovers against you on every side: The Babylonians and all the Chaldeans, all the Assyrians and with them Pekod, Shoa and Koa. I will set judgment before them, and they will judge you according to their judgments. They will deal furiously with you, take your children and burn you with fire. I will do these things because you have cast me behind your back. When they had slain their children to their idols, they came into my sanctuary to profane it."*[101]

God's design of justice is given to prepare and save us from the void of immorality that continues to grow into the abyss. The line of evil will reach its tragic end, but what use is it to justify sin and commit sacrilege since *"They walked after the imagination of their own heart, and after Baal, which their fathers taught them. You children of Israel, there is no truth, mercy nor knowledge of God in the land. Will you steal, murder, perform adultery, swear falsely, burn incense to Baal, walk after other gods and stand before me in the house called by my name saying, We are delivered to do all these abominations?"*[102] This is self-serving drama.

Should we try to hide the unseemly aspects of truth or misuse its principles by twisting right from wrong? To what purpose does this kind of deception serve except to lose your soul *"for you have kindled a fire in my anger that shall burn forever. The sin of Judah is written with a pen of iron, and with the point of a diamond: it is graven on the table of their heart, and upon the horns of your altars. You have done worse than your fathers and defiled my land. They have filled my inheritance with the carcasses of their detestable and abominable things.*"[103] We can either close our eyes to these awful things or see the reality of God's word.

Demonism and occult practices will become more common while humanity falls into a spiritual vacuum that can only be satisfied by submission to divine grace. We must realize that *"evil men and seducers shall wax worse and worse, deceiving and being deceived."*[104] Great strides of apostasy have already transgressed many cultures with a perverted sense of approval in this bane vanity yet, *"My people have consulted their stocks and their staff declares to them. They sacrifice flesh for the sacrifices of my offerings and eat it. I will visit upon her the days of Baal when she went after her lovers, and take the names of Baal out of her mouth."*[105]

Since Christ came as an eternal offering for sin we have no alternative to following this way of salvation so *"To the law and to the testimony: if they speak not according to this word, it is because there is no light in them. What has my beloved to do in my house seeing she wrought lewdness with many, and the holy flesh is passed from you. The Lord called your name, A green olive tree, fair and of goodly fruit. But they said, Let us destroy the tree with the fruit thereof and let us cut him off from the land that his name may no more be remembered."*[106] The irony of their scorn of the Eucharist and the church is that they themselves will be forgotten.

Jesus did not shy from rebuking hypocrites nor refrain from warnings of the last days that started with world wars of the last century and progressed to the doorway of a catastrophic third world war. He told the church *"blessed are you when men hate you and cast you out as evil for the Son of man's sake."*[107] It is his name and his holy flesh in the Eucharist that the gates of hell work to destroy and the savage oblation of human sacrifice and cannibalism are the ultimate blasphemy of his holy altar. These satanic rites are against *"your Redeemer the Holy One of Israel: I have given him for a witness, a leader and commander of the people."*[108]

This witness proclaimed by God the Father is his *"holy one, and I have exalted one chosen out of the people. In my name shall his horn be exalted. I will make him my firstborn, higher than the kings of the earth. His seed will endure forever and his throne as the days of heaven. You profaned his crown and brought his strongholds to ruin. You set up his adversaries, and made his enemies to rejoice."*[109] Who is so feeble minded to believe they can succeed against God or his Christ who explained *"I know whence I came, and where I go. I am one who gives witness of myself, and the Father also who sent me confirms witness of me."*[110]

He is the Messiah who *"was in the beginning with God, and was made flesh and dwelt among us. He came to his own, and his own received him not. But as many as received him, he gave power to become sons of God, even to those who believe on his name, who were born not of blood, or the will of man but of God."*[111] This rebirth is not of our race or righteousness, but of faith and *"Cursed be the man who obeys not the words of this covenant, which I commanded your fathers in the day I brought them out of Egypt from the iron furnace."*[112] Many Jews will convert after the iron furnace of WWIII, but their brethren will despise them.

Covenants with heathen nations are forbidden by Mosaic Law due to the seduction of idols and strange gods, but materialism and desire to follow trends of occult doctrines will prevail as their kingdom grows. These agreements, especially with the Antichrist, will spell disaster when Israel becomes an enemy of the church *"because the Lord has been witness between you and the wife of your youth whom you dealt treachery, since you regard not the offering anymore, or receive it with goodwill. I will be a swift witness against the sorcerers, adulterers, liars, those who oppress and fear not me.*"[113] Their espousal to Christ will be short lived.

If we don't embrace the foundation of God's kingdom, how can we obtain his promises or withstand his anger against those who scorn his word as *"everyone that loves him who begot loves also him who is begotten of him. This is the witness of God that he testified of his Son. Whoever believes not makes God a liar."*[114] Let no mistake or lie be made about *"Jesus Christ who is the faithful witness, the first begotten of the dead, the prince of kings of the earth who loved us and washed us from our sins in his own blood. He has made us kings and priests unto God and his Father, to him be glory and dominion forever and ever. Amen."*[115]

Key points of battles in WWIV concern the idol worship and foreign policy of the Jews for *"the people of Samaria will fear because of the calves of Bethhaven: the nations shall be gathered against them when they bind themselves in their two furrows. They sin more and more saying, Let the men that sacrifice kiss the calves. Israel and Ephraim will fall in their iniquity, Judah also shall fall with them."*[116] These furrows are places of idolatry in Samaria, while also in Judah *"they built the high places of Tophet to burn their children in the fire, and in their cities burned incense to the host of heaven and poured out drink offerings to other gods."*[117]

Political dealings will fail for Jewish leaders who *"go down into Egypt to trust in the strength of Pharaoh, for his princes were at Zoan, and his ambassadors came to Hanes. They will be ashamed of a people that could not profit them nor be a help, but a shame and also a reproach."*[118] Instead of seeing the signs of their times and turning from sin, *"you forsake the Lord your God when he led you by the way, and now what have you to do in the way of Egypt or in the way of Assyria?"*[119] They will seek food in the famine and military aid since *"we got our bread with the peril of our lives because of the sword of the wilderness."*[120]

Overwhelming drought and disregard of human rights will instill a social climate of unrest and survival of the fittest in much of our world. In this season of distress, *"the pride of Israel testifies to his face: they call to Egypt, they go to Assyria. When they shall go, I will spread my net over them. They shall be wasted for they have fled from me. The calf of Samaria will be broken in pieces. Israel has forgotten his Maker, and Judah has multiplied fenced cities, but I will send a fire on his cities and it shall devour his palaces."*[121] Their pleas for help from the wealth and military power of China and Egypt will result in calamity.

Researching the outbreak of conflicts shows that Israel will not only suffer from aggression from around its borders, but there will be internal strife among factions as it will be *"a land of trouble and anguish: for spoiling and violence are before me, and them who raise up contention. Those who revolt are profound to make slaughter, the prophet is a snare of ruin and hatred is in the house of God."*[122] Christians will sorrow because *"the daughter of my people is become cruel. They hunt our steps so we cannot go into our streets. Keep me O Lord from the hands of the wicked and from violent men who purposed to cast down my goings."*[123]

Religious persecution will be common among the nations, but vice is an internal force that consumes itself since *"The earth is defiled under the people thereof: they have transgressed the laws, changed the ordinance and broken the everlasting covenant."*[124] The rising power of the Antichrist and influence of false prophets or others who glorify demons will adversely affect humanity. Lack of charity and faith of Jews is a reflection of evil to come all over the globe and *"Take heed for every brother will supplant, and every neighbor will walk with slanders. They lie and commit iniquity to speak peace to a friend, but lay in wait for him."*[125]

Civil wars and isolated battles will extend far beyond the land of Israel. These symptoms of hatred and greed will affect many who know not or turned from Christ so *"The rich men are full of violence with their treasures of deceit. Your casting down will be in the midst of you and I will give you to the sword. The holy man is perished out of the earth for they lie in wait for blood, everyone hunts his brother to death. Let the mountains and strong foundations of the earth hear the justice of the Lord for he will judge his people and plead against Israel. The man of wisdom will fear your name, and know the rod and who appointed it.*"[126]

Specific movements of military aggression told by the prophets can be traced by certain phrases that refer to the general timeframe of major events such as *"the day of rebuke" or "the day of battle, with a tempest in the day of the whirlwind."*[127] This period of uprising and strong rebuke is when they *"Publish in the palaces of Ashdod, and in the land of Egypt saying, Assemble yourselves upon the mountains of Samaria, and behold the great tumults in the midst thereof and the oppressed in its midst. They do not right who store up violence and robbery in their palaces."*[128] These riots and killings for spoil are from within and without.

Intricacies of the armed offensives by various ethnic groups who abide near a greater Israel or its tributaries include *"The Syrians before, and the Philistines behind, and they will devour Israel with open mouth."*[129] Ancient peoples of the Middle East will maintain their identity and relative proximity to homelands, but the boundaries of these nations will change after WWIII in favor of large Jewish occupation. Regardless of the exact names and borders that apply to Syria, Gaza, Iraq, Lebanon, Jordon and others, they will spoil Israel before they become captive. This turmoil will set the stage for much greater invasions by Egypt and nations of the east.

Examples of festering hatred against Jews stemming from ancient history and disputes that occurred after they returned to their homeland seem to solidify after WWIII when Israel is weak from famine since *"I have heard the reproach of Moab, and the rivalry of the children of Ammon whereby they magnified themselves against their border. Wickedness burns as fire and will kindle in the forest."*[130] Regarding other neighbors, *"Remember the children of Edom in the day of Jerusalem who said, Raze it, raze it even to the foundation thereof. The Philistines dealt by revenge to destroy it. Damascus threshed Gilead with iron chariots."*[131]

Demolition of Israel will come in waves of revolt and attack from all sides, but the forces of Egypt have a distinctive place in spoiling Middle East countries while China and the Antichrist have a much wider consequence of spoil, ruin and captivity. In relation to Israel: *"Woe to you rebels who trust in the shadow of Egypt. Behold, they are gone in destruction, Egypt will gather them up, Memphis shall bury them. The end is come upon my people Israel, it will come as a flood cast out and drowned, as by the flood of Egypt."*[132] Egypt will plunder many people but their plans will be foiled so they also will be pillaged and then taken captive.

Subtle hints of Scripture expose critical turning points in this series of invasions for *"The Assyrian shall smite you with a rod, and lift up his staff against you after the manner of Egypt. Yet a very little while and the indignation shall cease, and my anger in their destruction."*[133] The flood of warfare to cast out and also to drown Israel like the flood of Egypt refers to separate but similar attacks by the eastern alliance and those with the Antichrist. Like the manner of Egypt whose forces will make their way to the Euphrates River, eastern forces will spoil and scatter that whole region, but then suffer defeat from European armies.

Instead of communion with Christ and faith in his deliverance, the Jews will look to idols and other nations for security, but *"Woe to you who are wealthy in Zion and trust in the mountain of Samaria: you great men, heads of the people who go in state with the house of Israel. Ephraim follows after the east wind, and they make a covenant with the Assyrians, and oil is carried into Egypt."* It seems Israel will have some control over oil reserves in Iraq but their treaty with

China involves fraud in trade relations as *"The balances of deceit are in his hand, he loves to oppress. Their princes will fall by the sword for the rage of their tongue."*[134]

Ephraim is used as a term for Jewish leaders who join a confederacy of peoples that *"Take counsel together, and it shall come to nothing. Associate yourselves, O you people, and you will be broken in pieces. Give ear, all you far countries: gird yourselves and you will be broken in pieces."*[135] This counsel of countries relates to trade and to bolster security, but *"The fortress will cease from Ephraim, and the kingdom from Damascus. Behold, Damascus will be a ruin. The crown of pride, the drunkards of Ephraim, will be trodden down."*[136] This fortress or crown of pride refers to Tyre for *"Ephraim, as I saw Tyre, is planted in a pleasant place."*[137]

Like other parables of prophecy similar to riddles that have confused theologians, the new confederacy foretold in prophecy somewhat parallels a time in ancient history when Syria was confederate with the tribe of Ephraim and Pekah, king of the house of Israel in Samaria, against the house of Judah to conquer Jerusalem.[138] This plot did not succeed, but Samaria was taken captive by Assyria shortly thereafter. Unlike the past, the future Assyria is comprised of eastern nations in a different context of the last days with apocalyptic signs that have not happened in the past. References to that Assyrian alliance have an evident part of a time yet to come.

Egypt's ambition to enter and quench the tumult against Israel for their advantage to rule the trade routes of Tyre will be foiled for *"Hear now house of David, the Lord will bring upon you days that have not come from the day Ephraim departed from Judah, even the king of Assyria: A burning wind of the high places in the wilderness toward the daughter of my people not to fan, nor to cleanse. Even a full wind, and I will give sentence against them. A voice declares from Dan, and affliction from mount Ephraim. Watchers come from a far country against the cities of Judah."*[139] Egypt and Judah will not withstand those from the east or the north.

Judgment coming from eastern allies will devastate *"them who swear by the sin of Samaria saying, Your god lives O Dan and the manner of Beersheba lives. They shall fall and never rise up again. The daughter of my people cry out due to them who dwell in a far country. His horses were heard from Dan, the whole land trembled for they devoured it"*[140] These armies will show no mercy on those who spoil their investments. For those who trust in the temple of Jerusalem *"go now to Shiloh and see what I did to my people Israel. I will do to this house as I did to Shiloh, and cast you out as your brethren, even the whole seed of Ephraim."*[141]

Individual governorship of lands in ancient Samaria appears to again take place among Jews, but for the throne of David *"You are Gilead unto me, and the head of Lebanon: yet surely I will make you a wilderness, and cities that are not inhabited."*[142] Distinct from history when it took decades between the fall of Samaria and of Judah, these perils will transpire in quick succession since *"my confusion is continually before me, and shame has covered me for the voice of him who reproaches and blasphemes, by reason of the enemy and the avenger. You have sore broken us in the place of dragons, and covered us with the shadow of death."*[143]

Catastrophe will develop in the throes of WWIV and what happens in the Holy Land sets the pace of a global design. For Jews who do not flee and escape, but listen to the false prophets that deny warnings of the divine word and wisdom of those who proclaim it *"O Israel, you have destroyed yourself, but in me is your help. I will meet them as a bear that is bereaved of her whelps, and will rend the caul of their heart, and there I will devour them like a lion, the wild beast shall tear them. I will cause them to eat the flesh of their children and their friends in the siege where their enemies who seek their lives shall straiten them."*[144]

Graphic scenes of divine justice are appalling and it is indeed a pity to read *"They who are slain with the sword are better than they who die of hunger. Their visage is blacker than coal, their skin cleaves to their bones like a stick."*[145] Many who do not flee will seek shelter in vain because they will be trapped inside hideouts without food or water and in that time *"The cities of the south shall be shut up, and none will open them. Blow the cornet in Gibeah, and the trumpet in Rammah: cry aloud at Bethaven, behind your back O Benjamin. Ephraim shall be desolate in the day of rebuke. Let us enter the defended cities and be silent there."*[146]

Detailed military affairs of the Assyrian are truly awesome since many cities and countries are listed in his path of spoil and ruin. These mysteries of prophecy confirm the existence of an omnipotent God who will fulfill his purpose in Christ. The Chinese leader has a symbolical name meaning adversary as *"the sin of Ephraim and Samaria was discovered for they commit falsehood: the thief comes in, the troop of robbers spoil without. Ephraim is oppressed and broken. When he saw his sickness and Judah saw his wound, then Ephraim went to the Assyrian and sent to king Jareb, yet he could not heal, nor cure you of your wound."*[147]

Whatever kinds of fraud are committed to swindle the Chinese and others, their own doings will beset them about for *"you shall conceive chaff, you will bring forth stubble: your breath will devour you as fire and the people will be like the burnings of lime, as thorns in the fire. The highways lie waste, the wayfaring man ceases. He has broken the covenant and despised the cities, he regards no man. Who among us will dwell with the devouring fire? Who among us will dwell with everlasting burnings?"*[148] These burnings of lime suggest nuclear explosions that leave radioactive fallout for those left alive, but many also will be condemned to hell.

To students who seek to discern prophetic times, we are asked a very simple question about how the last days are distinguished from history: *"Has this happened in your days, or in the days of your fathers? Awake, weep and howl for a nation is come upon my land, strong and without number whose teeth are of a great lion. As the morning spread upon the mountains, a great people and strong, there has not ever been the like, neither shall be any more after it. A fire devours before them, and behind a flame burns. All faces will gather blackness. The earth will quake before them, the heavens will tremble. The sun, moon and stars will be dark."*[149]

Omens of the time when men of the east open fire with missiles that include nuclear warheads followed by an army like the sun rising over the horizon are marked by darkness over the third part of earth and a more extreme darkness found in the fourth and fifth trumpet plagues of the Apocalypse since *"In that day they shall roar against them like the roaring of the sea, and if one looks unto the land, behold darkness and sorrow, and the light is dark in the heavens thereof. By the anger of the Lord is the land dark, and the people will be as fuel for the fire: no man shall spare his brother."*[150] Bombing of oil fields may contribute to this darkness.

Aspects of the prophets written long ago that show things yet to come correspond to the book of Revelation and to the gospel of Jesus who said *"There will be signs in the sun, the moon, the stars and distress of nations with perplexity, the sea and the waves roaring."*[151] These events primarily relate to the impact of WWIV with numerous warnings such as *"Give glory to the Lord your God before he cause darkness, and he turns it into the shadow of death, and make it gross darkness. Behold trouble and darkness, dimness of anguish and they will be driven into darkness. I clothe the heavens with blackness, and make sackcloth their covering."*[152]

Exact reasons for roaring seas and growing darkness that spreads over the air of the whole earth may be explained from natural disasters and bombing. Geological impacts of nuclear weapons are capable of producing earth quaking traumas like volcanoes and tsunamis, but *"darkness will cover the earth, and gross darkness the people. I will cause the sun to go down at noon, and darken the earth in the clear day."*[153] Some of this might result from massive wild fires in the earth at the first trumpet, an example shown *"against the forest of the south, and it will devour every green and dry tree. The flaming fire shall not be quenched."[154]*

Nuclear barrages between superpowers of a new east and west will create a crescendo as warfare is directed over the seas. Many ships and creatures of the sea will be destroyed in this exchange, but armies of the east will be scattered and defeated for *"Be not afraid of the Assyrian. The Lord will stir up a scourge against him, and as his rod was upon the sea, so shall he lift it up after the manner of Egypt."[155]* The Antichrist also will attack the Middle East and retaliate with power of his own nuclear rod *"for the sea has spoken, even the strength of the sea. As the report concerning Egypt, so shall they be sorely pained at the report of Tyre."[156]*

Identity of the Antichrist has baffled many people but the mystery of when he will be made known is after WWIII and his path to a global empire is bloodshed. His home base is in Europe *"And the ten horns of this kingdom are ten kings. These have one mind, and shall give their power and strength to the beast."[157]* His throne will be in Rome from which he launches an armed outreach as *"out of the north an evil will break forth, all the families of the kingdom of the north shall come, and each one will set his throne at the entering of the gates of Jerusalem, and against all the walls round about, and against all the cities of Judah."[158]*

The gates of Jerusalem along the sea coast at opposite borders of the Israelite nation will be central places of battle for Egypt first, then China and last the Antichrist. These global ports will suffer great spoil and final ruin after European armies close the gap of war since *"you who put far away the evil day, and cause the seat of violence to draw near. You who lie on beds of ivory and stretch themselves on their couches, I abhor the excellency of Jacob and hate his palaces. The banquet of them will be removed: Behold, I will raise up a nation against you, and they will afflict you from the entering in of Hemath unto the river of the wilderness."[159]*

Once this apocalyptic war begins, it seems the progression of warfare will be at a rapid pace. No one can predict how long it will take from its start to end because there are several phases in this process of spoiling and ruin, but *"The Lord comes out of his place to punish the people of the earth for their iniquity. He called to contend by fire, and it devoured the great deep, and did eat up a part. The lofty city, he lays it low, even to the ground, he brings it even to the dust. Thus shall the sins of Jacob be purged. In that day the Lord will strike from the channel of the river even to the torrent of Egypt."[160]* This sea coast will come to great destruction.

Various names or analogies are given to the Antichrist who leads a new Roman empire in complete conquest when battles rage in the Middle East. Of the main power struggle, *"Blow the trumpet, gather together and go into the defensed cities. Set up the standard in Zion: retire, stay not for I will bring evil from the north and great destruction. The lion is come up from his thicket, and the destroyer of the Gentiles is on his way."[161]* This lion is the Assyrian whom the Antichrist as a destroyer will defeat for *"they will waste the land of Assyria with the sword, and the land of Nimrod in the entrances thereof when he comes into our land."[162]*

Strategy of the Antichrist to disrupt and destroy his enemies involves a trap that is already set for spoil since to Egypt *"I will spread out my net over you with a company of many people, and they will bring you up in my net."[163]* This net forms when eastern armies begin their land assault and they too become entangled with the Egyptians and other countries in an area ripe for slaughter as *"A sword, a sword is sharpened, and also furbished to give it into the hand of the slayer. Let it be doubled the third time, the sword of the slain condemns the rod of my son."[164]* The slayer is the Antichrist who will annul all religions, particularly Christianity.

Believers who know the gospel and others who see threats to their security will exodus out of Israel and its borders. Jesus warned *"when you see Jerusalem compassed with armies, know its*

170

desolation is near." His instruction to flee Judea applies to tumult before China enters the fray and to the sign of emergency he gave *"when you see the Abomination of Desolation stand in the holy place."* It is then the Antichrist will prepare to waste Jerusalem and all his enemies when *"they who forsake the holy covenant will pollute the sanctuary of strength and take away the daily sacrifice."*[165] This sanctuary is in the Vatican, not the Jewish temple.

Outward functions of the church will cease because freedom of any religion will be turned into a pledge of worship to the Antichrist after he destroys his enemies *"For the king of Babylon stood at the parting of the way, at the head of the two ways to use divination: he consulted with images, he looked in the liver to appoint battering rams against the gates, to cast a mount and build a fort. Appoint two ways that the sword may come to Rabbah of the Ammonites and to Judah in Jerusalem, to them who have sworn oaths, he will call to mind their iniquity whose day is come. I will give them to the hand of brutish men, skillful to destroy"*[166]

Visions of the prophets about the day of Jacob's trouble revolve around the captivity of Israel and redemption of the faithful as Jesus taught *"You will be hated of all men for my name's sake, but he who endures to the end shall be saved."*[167] It is like splitting hairs to grasp some verses pertaining to the end, but *"unto the land of Israel: an end is come, the end is come. An evil, a whole evil is come. The time is come, the day of trouble is near, and not again the sounding of the mountains. The sword is without, the pestilence and famine within."*[168] These ends are the onslaughts of Egypt, the east and north distinguished from the sounding of WWIII.

Treaties made by Israel with China and especially with Egypt will betray the covenant that Jerusalem makes with the Antichrist for *"The king of Babylon is come to Jerusalem, and he led the king and princes to Babylon who made a covenant with him and took an oath that their kingdom might be base and not lift itself up, but by keeping of his covenant it might stand. But he rebelled against him by sending ambassadors to Egypt that they might give him many horses and people. Seeing he broke the covenant, he shall not escape."*[169] It seems obvious that Israel will attempt to secure itself by deals that conflict with other prior agreements.

Underhanded accords with chief rulers will result in captivity when the Antichrist *"shall pass over the strait of the sea with affliction, and will smite the waves in the sea and all the depths of the rivers will dry up. The pride of Assyria will be brought down and the scepter of Egypt will depart away."* This particular prophecy was made during the Persian kingdom after the former Assyrian and Babylonian empires ended so the warning is made in a future tense to *"Come forth, and flee from the land of the north. Deliver yourself, O Zion, who dwells with the daughter of Babylon."*[170] The theme of a new Assyria and Babylon is basic to the last days.

Instruction of the divine word is given to reveal the true God and know the matters of his loving mercy and abiding justice, but *"To whom shall I speak and give warning that they might hear? They have dealt treachery against me. Thus I have hewed them by the prophets: I have slain them by the words of my mouth, and your judgments will go forth as the light. O you children of Benjamin, gather yourselves to flee out of the midst of Jerusalem. This is the city to be visited. Oppression is in her midst, violence and spoil is heard in her. Blow the trumpet in Tekoa and in Bethhaccerim for evil appears out of the north, and great destruction."*[171]

Elements of history are critical in learning the wisdom of prophecy since the Jews of ancient time were told to go out and serve the king of Babylon in order to save their lives as *"I set before you the way of life and death. He that stays in this city shall die, but he who goes out and falls to the Chaldeans shall live."*[172] This is in stark contrast to the future when they are urged to flee Judea but also to run away from lands of the new daughter of Babylon and its idolatry. Jesus did not refer to the Roman invasion of the first century when he surely specified *"those days will be affliction, such as was not from the beginning of creation, neither shall be."[173]*

Precise facts of things not yet seen are amazing as only our Creator could know and relate all these mysteries but despite apathy or scorn, *"This gospel of the kingdom will be preached in all the world for a witness to all nations, and then the end will come."[174]* Biblical theology clearly reveals unpleasant issues and points to a satanic global reign of the Antichrist. It is *"He who smote the people in wrath with a continual stroke and he that ruled the nations in anger: this is the purpose upon the whole earth, and this is the hand that is stretched out upon all nations. I will break the Assyrian in my land, and tread him under foot upon my mountains."[175]*

Despite the mighty army of the east, it is the Lord's purpose to submerge all nations in the fruit of their evil doings and China is no exception. This nation and its eastern allies will do incredible harm to the world, but *"I will break the bow of Elam, the chief of their might. Upon Elam I will bring the four winds from the four corners of heaven, and scatter them toward those winds, and there will be no nation where the outcasts of Elam will not come. I will cause Elam to be dismayed before their enemies and bring my fierce anger upon them with the sword after them till I have consumed them."[176]* Revenge of many will change their course.

In response to overall damage done by eastern forces, they will garner wrath of people from every direction. This complex conflict cannot be fully explained, but in that time of nightmare the Antichrist will step with rage to subdue and *"He will go forth with great fury to destroy, and utterly to slay many. For lo, I raise up the Chaldeans marching upon the breath of the earth. They are terrible and dreadful: they all come to take the prey, sup up as a burning wind and gather the captivity as the sand. Their prince will triumph over kings and princes. His desire is as hell and death, and he gathers all nations and heaps all people unto him."[177]*

Bitter destiny awaits all sovereign states for contempt of divine law sealed in the blood of Jesus. They will lose their reign to the Antichrist and to the enemies of Israel: *"Because they have made you desolate and swallowed you on every side, in the fire of my jealousy I have spoken against the residue of the heathen, and against all Idumea who have appointed my land into their possession. Surely the heathen who are about you will bear their shame."[178]* That disgrace is conclusive since: *"How long, Lord? Why should the enemy say where is their God? Pour out your wrath upon the kingdoms that have not called upon your name."[179]*

Those who take part and rejoice in the fall of Israel will suffer defeat for *"All your lovers forgot and seek you not for I wounded you with an enemy and chastened you with a cruel one, but all who devour you and all your enemies, every one of them shall go into captivity."[180]* Pride and deceit will cover the hearts of many, but *"Woe to you who spoil and were not spoiled, and you who deal treachery: when you cease to spoil you will be spoiled, and when you make an end of treachery, they will deal treachery to you."[181]* There will be no winners in this war of massive ruins except the Antichrist who will have little left in the world to brag about.

Although many nations will spoil and kill the Jews in blasphemy against God who promised them an inheritance, he will bring them back to the Holy Land as *"The Lord says against all my evil neighbors who touch the inheritance I caused my people to inherit, I will pluck them out of their land and pluck the house of Judah from among them. And they shall be in all the earth: two parts therein shall be scattered and perish, but the third part left. I will bring the third part through the fire, and refine them as silver and gold. They will call on my name and I will hear them. I will say, you are my people and they will answer, The Lord is my God."[182]*

Leagues with Egypt and China will prove fatal for the Jewish nation who chose not to obey and trust in the Lord, but think they will stand by arms and pacts since *"In returning and rest shall be your strength, but you would not. The Lord has rejected your confidences, and you will not prosper in them. You will be ashamed of Egypt as you were ashamed of Assyria.*"[183] These nations will turn against Jews and each other before they fall by the Antichrist who will "*Arise, go up to Kedar, and spoil the men of the east. Egypt will be desolate, and Edom destroyed for their violence against Judah for they shed innocent blood in their land.*"[184]

Doomsday is a concept that has captured countless minds and we must grasp the affliction to come before the Second Advent. The battle of Armageddon follows a period of brief despotic reign of the Antichrist where his kingdom will be far less from the glory we might expect when "*the Lord has turned away the excellency of Jacob, as the excellency of Israel for the spoilers have emptied them out. He makes the earth empty and waste, turns it upside down and scatters its people abroad. The land shall be utterly emptied and spoiled: the curse has devoured and they that dwell therein are desolate and burned so that few men are left.*"[185]

Nuclear annihilation of some nations is unlike the fire of Christ's glory to end iniquity, but "*Come near you nations, let the earth hear, the world and all things that come forth from it. For the Lord's anger is upon all nations and his fury upon all their armies: he has utterly destroyed them. The Lord has a sacrifice in Bozrah and great slaughter in the land of Idumea for the streams thereof shall be turned into pitch, the dust into brimstone and the land burning pitch. The smoke thereof will go forth forever from generation to generation it shall be laid waste.*"[186] This stunning sacrifice is from bombing yet there is hope for survival of humanity.

Total chaos in the Middle East caused by the Antichrist's military allies reflects the timing of his vanquish toward all his enemies. There is no doubt that other regions of the world will also be turned into ghost towns and it will be hard to find a place of refuge so "*Flee, turn back and dwell deep O people of Dedan for the time I will visit you. Mt. Seir will be desolate and all Idumea. All the cities of Bozrah will be perpetual wastes. Edom will be desolate like Sodom and Gommorrah and no man shall abide there. The earth is moved at the noise of the fall of Edom and those of Teman. The noise of their desolation was heard in the Red Sea.*"[187]

Final demise of Egypt is connected to an all-out offensive against many nations. It seems beyond our comprehension to visualize the mass destruction of WWIV, but in this massacre "*I will make the land of Egypt desolate in the midst of the countries that are desolate, and scatter the Egyptians among the nations. I will make strong the arms of the king of Babylon and put my sword in his hand. The daughters of nations will lament and wail for the multitude of Egypt. Cast them down, even her and the daughters of famous nations. Destroy Noph, make Pathros desolate, set fire in Zoan, cut off No, Sin, Aven, Pibeseth and Tehaphnehes.*"[188]

Among the strongholds of Egypt that are listed in the path of its ruin are nations of Asshur, Elam, Meshech, Tubal, Edom, the Zidonians and all the princes of the north. This vast takeover extends far beyond the Middle East to include Russia and all the countries around it as well as China whose many allies of the Far East will also be defeated and go into captivity. As for fate of a wealthy Egypt, "*The princes of Zoan are become fools and the princes of Noph are deceived for they have seduced Egypt to err, even them who are the stay of the tribes thereof. I will give the Egyptians to the hand of a cruel lord, a fierce king will rule over them.*"[189]

Closely associated with the dispersion and destruction of Egypt are judgments of seacoast harbors of Tyre and Zidon. Rebuilding of these cities into a commerce metropolis appears to be part of a concurrent plan to create an inland trade center in the ancient city of Nineveh once known as a major merchant crossing between traffic routes of the Mediterranean Sea and the Indian Ocean. This place along the Tigris River is now populated by the adjacent city of Mosul in northern Iraq and holds great promise of expansion due to its central location and prospect of economics in continued development of the huge oil fields of neighboring Kirkuk.

Logic plays a vital role in considering a new reality of the end times that is explained by teachings of issues which have not yet been resolved. Nineveh has not seen the glory of old and scholars look to the past to explain its ruin, but forecasts about this place are in the future and *"This is the rejoicing city that said in her heart: I am and there is none besides me. How is she become a desolation? You have multiplied your merchants as the stars of heaven. Woe to her that is filthy and polluted, to the oppressing city. The Lord will famish all the gods of the earth, he will stretch out his hand to destroy Assyria and make Nineveh a desolation."*[190]

Context of this judgment plainly states certain signs that *"The great day of the Lord is near, a day of calamity and misery. Nineveh shall flee away, she is empty and void and waste. The heart melts, the knees smite together and much pain in all loins, the faces of them all gather blackness. Her chariots will burn in the smoke, the sword will devour your young lions and your prey cut off from the earth. There is a multitude of slain and she was carried into captivity. The land shall be wide open to your enemies as the sword cuts you off and the fire will devour your bars. Your shepherds slumber, O King of Assyria, your nobles dwell in the dust."*[191]

Modern architects have likely dreamed about the lucrative enterprise in construction of seaports at Tyre and Zidon with a luxury trade post that has access to tributaries of the Tigris and Euphrates rivers, but the main problem is persisting political turmoil of this region. Grand cities have been swiftly built in rich areas of the Middle East and once the opportunity presents itself, contractors will seek the great profits from these investments but rewards will be short-term as *"I will bring upon Tyre a king of kings from the north and he will set engines of war against your walls. Then will all the princes of the sea come down from their thrones."*[192]

Aside from specific clues about the latter times and Tyre's resistance to ancient Babylon, it stands to reason the earth shaking events of fire and brimstone do not apply to history but they are predictions not yet seen *"When I shall make you a desolate city, when I bring up the deep upon you and great waters will cover you. When I bring you down into the pit with the people of old time and set you in the low parts of the earth. The isles will tremble in the day of your fall: yea, the isles that are in the sea will be troubled. I will make you a terror and you will be no more, though you shall be sought for, yet you shall never be found again."*[193]

Concluding battles of WWIV involve the amazing plunge of Tyre into the sea when *"waters rise up out of the north, and overflowing flood in the land and all that is therein. The day comes to spoil all the Philistines, and cut off from Tyre and Zidon every helper who remains. You will no more rejoice, daughter of Zidon, for I will send upon her pestilence and the sword on every side. Woe to the people of the sea coast for Gaza will be forsaken. O Canaan, the land of the Philistines, I will destroy you that there be no inhabitant."*[194] This overflowing flood from the Mediterranean Sea may be caused by an earthquake due to nuclear bombs.[195]

Dismal prophecies of the bible form a shocking reality we must contemplate and decide whose side we are on as immorality grows to stifle the breath of truth. Do we not know the story of Christ or *"Should I give my firstborn for my transgression, the fruit of my body for the sin of my soul?"*[196] Where do we draw the line between right and wrong or can we subject divine law to our own lusts without being held accountable? God has not changed, nor the way of his salvation or path to perdition. Why do people profess a faith they do not follow for *"You are near in their mouth, but far from their reigns. You have turned judgment into gall."*[197]

Jerusalem will no longer be a tourist attraction or place where people want to go to see and walk in the noted places where Jesus stood, but it will become a place of anguish and destruction because *"They forsake me and burn incense to other gods whom they nor their father's knew. They have built the high places to burn their sons with fire for burnt offerings to Baal. Thus this place will no more be called Tophet, nor the valley of Hinnom, but the valley of slaughter. And Jerusalem will be defiled as Tophet, and this city will be desolate and a hissing even as Tophet. They will bury the carcasses in Tophet till there be no place to bury them."*[198]

Incidents mentioned in Scripture display unique events of deep rebellion and deceit against the risen Christ and his word since *"My people know not the judgment of the Lord. The pen of the scribes is in vain. Why are these people slid back by a perpetual backsliding? At that time, they will bring out the bones of the kings of Judah and of his princes, and of the priests, and of the prophets, and of the people out of their graves. They will spread them before the sun and the moon and the host of heaven whom they have sought, and served and worshiped. They shall not be gathered, nor buried but they shall be for dung upon the face of the earth."*[199]

Numbers are given by the prophets to get an idea of the wreckage and how many people will be slain as *"The city that went out by a thousand will leave a hundred and that which went forth by a hundred will leave ten to the house of Israel."*[200] Whether they remain or go captive, there is a promised remnant who will return to inherit their land but first *"The Lord will carry you away with a mighty captivity and violently turn and toss you like a ball in a large country. Weep day and night for the daughter of my people. I will make Jerusalem heaps and a den of dragons, and make the cities of Judah desolate."*[201] How is it they do not know their God?

Whatever the head count of slaughter is in the world as a result of its iniquity, we should know there is a worse end for the souls of those who defy their Creator. As much as we would like to think otherwise, *"Hell has enlarged herself, and opened her mouth without measure and their glory, their multitude, their pomp and him who rejoices shall descend into it. The mean man will be brought down, the mighty and the eyes of the lofty shall be humbled but the Lord of hosts will be exalted in judgment and God who is holy will be sanctified in righteousness. I have cut off the nations: their towers, their streets and their cities are destroyed."*[202]

Nations and groups of peoples in several different regions that comprise most of the globe are listed by the prophet Jeremiah in a clash of warfare described as a wine cup of fury at the Lord's hand. In summary of the inclusive conflict, this drink was given to *"all the kingdoms of the world which are on the face of the earth, and the king of Sheshach shall drink after them. Howl, cry, and wallow yourselves in the ashes, for the days of your slaughter are accomplished. Their land is desolate because of the fierceness of the oppressor and his furious anger."*[203] This king of Sheshach is the Antichrist whose appointed time is at the Second Advent.

Civilization will fall and disperse under the height of a war never seen in its history but the terrible plagues of conflict, hunger, disease and pests of this period are not an end of misery for the remnant who survive since *"The people of the prince who will come will destroy the city and the sanctuary. And at the end thereof shall be a flood, and unto the end of the war desolations are determined, even until the consummation and that determined will be poured out upon the desolate."*[204] The spoil, ruin and captivity explained in this chapter will be followed by what is called the consummation, which involves edicts of final wrath in the Apocalypse.

Prevailing theology has somehow come up with the idea that humanity will be annihilated in nuclear war leaving nobody alive on earth or that Jesus will come back in glory to stop that war, judge the wicked and allow the meek to inherit the earth. Neither of these assumptions are true because the battle of God Almighty is separate in itself between his heavenly army against those of the Antichrist. Some scholars have perpetuated the idea that this is the end of time, but there is no such wording in the bible or clear indication that time is going to end. We all have an end to our human existence, but the time of the end is not the end of time.[205]

Misuse of Scripture in isolating certain verses out of their overall context confuses its intent and abrogates many other lessons as if it were not written or not to be interpreted as literal. There are many metaphors that need to be understood, but we cannot change the basic foundations upon which they are built. What St. Peter and St. Jude spoke of as the last time is the time of the end *"when the mystery of God should be finished, as he declared to his servants the prophets."*[206] This is when he will *"destroy them who destroy the earth"*, but for others who are not part of this evil *"the people who dwell therein will be forgiven their iniquity."*[207]

During the finale of the fourth seal of Revelation, there seems to be an ending battle for *"I will gather all nations and bring them down into the valley of Jehoshaphat and plead with them there for my people Israel whom they have scattered and parted my land. You have sold them to the Grecians to remove them far from their border. Let all the men of war draw near, let them come up. Assemble and gather yourselves together. Multitudes, multitudes in the valley of decision: I will sit to judge all the heathen round about for their wickedness is great."*[208] This slaughter is in a valley near Jerusalem, not Megiddo where Armageddon will take place.

Issues of divine prophecy are complex yet stages of these seasons and times are presented in my book in an orderly way. Many have sought to know the mysteries of the last days and it is time for us to evaluate our perceptions since *"The Spirit of truth will guide you into all truth. There is nothing covered that shall not be revealed, and hid that will not be known. What you whispered in the inner chambers will be preached on the housetops."*[209] This is not a question of if, but of when we know and declare the reality of our times. The next section deals with the third watch and following chapters explain the end wrath and Second Advent.

---

[1] Jeremiah 33,3
[2] II Corinthians 1,13
[3] Psalm 69,9-13
[4] Ephesians 5,11-16
[5] Hosea 14,9
[6] Isaiah 42,23
[7] Jeremiah 13,16-17; Luke 19,41-44
[8] Psalm 40,7-11
[9] Micah 3,5-8
[10] Jeremiah 19,3-6
[11] Ezekiel 33,30-32
[12] Jeremiah 2,31-35
[13] Deuteronomy 32,19-20&35
[14] Isaiah 23,9
[15] Micah 1,2-9; 5,10-15
[16] Deuteronomy 28,20-46
[17] Ezekiel 14,13-21
[18] Deuteronomy 32,22
[19] Luke 19,42-44

[20] Zephaniah 1,14-18
[21] Isaiah 25,7-8; 46,1; Jeremiah 50,2; 51,44
[22] I Corinthians 15,24-26; Hebrews 2,14
[23] Revelation 6,7-8
[24] Jeremiah 25,29-31
[25] Ezekiel 21,2-7
[26] Jeremiah 25,32-33
[27] Jeremiah 6,22-24
[28] Jeremiah 50,41-42; Revelation 17,5
[29] Jeremiah 51,1-2&33
[30] Jeremiah 51,25-28
[31] Jeremiah 51,11-14&29-32
[32] Isaiah 33,4
[33] Deuteronomy 28,49-58
[34] Jeremiah 5,15-18; 6,23-26; 18,15-17
[35] Jeremiah 4,9-10&19-21
[36] Jeremiah 50,17
[37] Jeremiah 30,23-24
[38] Jeremiah 23,16-20
[39] Isaiah 27,8
[40] Zechariah 9,14
[41] Isaiah 21,1-5
[42] Proverbs 1,5-6&23-28
[43] Isaiah 22,4-9
[44] Micah 7,4&12-17
[45] Revelation 9,13-21
[46] Ezekiel 31,3-9
[47] Ezekiel 31,10-17
[48] Hebrews 10,26-31
[49] Isaiah 10,3-19
[50] Isaiah 19,2
[51] Isaiah 17,11-14
[52] Jeremiah 5,3
[53] Isaiah 5,24-25
[54] Ezekiel 15,6-8
[55] Jeremiah 2,26-30
[56] Lamentations 3,45-48; 4,1&11-13
[57] Jeremiah 23,16-17&26-27
[58] Ezekiel 22,4-5&15
[59] Jeremiah 49,5
[60] Amos 6,1&7; 9,8-9
[61] Jeremiah 4,21-28
[62] Jeremiah 9,19-26
[63] Jeremiah 48,8&40-47; 49,1-13; Hosea 13,12-16
[64] Jeremiah 8,12; 9,7-12; Ezekiel 25,9-17
[65] Isaiah 8,4-8
[66] Isaiah 20,3-6
[67] Jeremiah 14,17-18; 15,6-8
[68] Isaiah 30,8-13
[69] Amos 3,9-11; 4,10-11; 5,2-5
[70] Jeremiah 12,2-12
[71] Jeremiah 49,1-5
[72] Isaiah 33,9-14
[73] Jeremiah 49,19-24; 50,43-44
[74] Mathew 11,20-24; Luke 10,13-16

[75] Zechariah 9,3-4
[76] Ezekiel 27,3-4&33
[77] Isaiah 23,3&8
[78] Isaiah 23,11&13-15
[79] Ezekiel 26,3-5; 27,26; 28,16-18
[80] Revelation 8,8-9
[81] Ezekiel 27,27-32
[82] Psalm 48,3-8
[83] Isaiah 23,1&10
[84] Jeremiah 46,8-24
[85] Ezekiel 32,2
[86] Jeremiah 46,8-10
[87] Jeremiah 46,5-6&16
[88] Ezekiel 30,3-9; Revelation 8,10-11
[89] Ezekiel 29,3-5; 32,3-10
[90] Ezekiel 26,2
[91] Lamentations 4,12
[92] Psalm 57,4-6
[93] Jeremiah 2,14-16
[94] Ezekiel 29,6-8
[95] Lamentations 1,8-15&20
[96] Psalm 57,6
[97] Lamentations 2,2-9
[98] Ezekiel 16,13-15&36-39
[99] Ezekiel 16,16-29
[100] Ezekiel 23,2-5&11-17
[101] Ezekiel 23,22-39
[102] Jeremiah 7,8-11; 9,13-16; Hosea 4,1-2
[103] Jeremiah 16,12-18; 17,1-4
[104] II Timothy 3,13
[105] Hosea 2,13&17; 4,12-13; 8,13
[106] Isaiah 8,20; Jeremiah 11,15-19
[107] Luke 6,22-26
[108] Isaiah 54,5; 55,4
[109] Psalm 89,18-42
[110] John 8,14-19
[111] John 1,1-14
[112] Jeremiah 11,2-11
[113] Exodus 34,12-16; Malachi 2,11-14; 3,5-7
[114] 1 John 5,1-10
[115] Revelation 1,5-7
[116] Hosea 5,3-5; 10,5-10; 13,1-2
[117] Jeremiah 7,17-18&28-31; 19,4-5&13
[118] Isaiah 30,1-5
[119] Jeremiah 2,17-18
[120] Isaiah 30,6; Lamentation 5,9
[121] Hosea 7,10-13; 8,5-6&14
[122] Hosea 5,1-2; 9,7-8; Habakkuk 1,2-3
[123] Psalm 140,1-5; Lamentations 4,3&18
[124] Isaiah 24,5
[125] Jeremiah 9,2-8
[126] Micah 6,1-2&9-14; 7,2-6
[127] Hosea 5,9-10; Amos 1,14
[128] Amos 3,9-11
[129] Isaiah 9,12

[130] Isaiah 9,18-19; Zephaniah 2,8
[131] Psalm 137,7; Ezekiel 25,12&15; Amos 1,3-15
[132] Isaiah 30,1-3; Hosea 9,6; Amos 8,2-9
[133] Isaiah 10,24-25
[134] Hosea 7,16; 12,1&7; Amos 6,1
[135] Isaiah 8,9-12
[136] Isaiah 17,1-4; 28,1-3
[137] Hosea 9,13
[138] II Kings 16,5-9; 17,1-6&18
[139] Isaiah 7,17-20; Jeremiah 4,11-16
[140] Amos 8,14; Jeremiah 8,14-19
[141] Jeremiah 7,11-15
[142] Jeremiah 22,6
[143] Psalm 44,9-19
[144] Jeremiah 19,8-9; Hosea 13,7-9
[145] Lamentations 4,8-9
[146] Jeremiah 8,12-14; 13,19; Hosea 5,8-9
[147] Hosea 5,11-14; 7,1-2
[148] Isaiah 33,7-14
[149] Joel 1,2-6; 2,1-10
[150] Isaiah 5,30; 9,19; Revelation 8,12; 9,1
[151] Luke 21,25
[152] Isaiah 8,22; 50,2-3; Jeremiah 13,14-16
[153] Isaiah 60,2; Amos 8,9
[154] Ezekiel 20,46-48; Revelation 8,7
[155] Isaiah 10,24-26
[156] Isaiah 23,4-5
[157] Daniel 7,7-8&23-24; Revelation 17,9-13&18
[158] Jeremiah 1,13-16
[159] Amos 5,17-21; 6,3-14
[160] Isaiah 26,5&21; 27,9-12; Amos 7,4
[161] Jeremiah 4,5-7
[162] Micah 5,6
[163] Ezekiel 32,2-3
[164] Ezekiel 21,9-15
[165] Daniel 11,30-31; Mathew 24,15; Luke 21,20-24
[166] Ezekiel 21,19-31
[167] Jeremiah 30,7; Mathew 10,22; 24,13
[168] Ezekiel 7,2-19
[169] Ezekiel 17,12-15
[170] Zechariah 1,1; 2,6-7; 7,1; 10,11
[171] Jeremiah 6,1-10; Hosea 6,4-7
[172] Jeremiah 21,8-10
[173] Mathew 24,15-22; Mark 13,14-20
[174] Mathew 24,13-14
[175] Isaiah 14,5-6&24-27
[176] Jeremiah 49,34-37
[177] Daniel 11,44; Habakkuk 1,6-10; 2,2-5
[178] Ezekiel 36,1-7
[179] Psalm 79,5-10
[180] Jeremiah 30,12-16
[181] Isaiah 33,1
[182] Jeremiah 12,14-15; Zechariah 13,8-9
[183] Isaiah 30,15; Jeremiah 2,36-37
[184] Jeremiah 49,28-30; Joel 3,19

[185] Isaiah 24,1-6; Nahum 2,1-2
[186] Isaiah 34,1-10
[187] Jeremiah 49,13-21; Ezekiel 35,3-15
[188] Ezekiel 29,10-12; 30,13-26; 32,16-30
[189] Isaiah 19,3-4&13-14
[190] Nahum 3,16-17; Zephaniah 2,11-15; 3,1-4
[191] Nahum 2,8-13; 3,3-18; Zephaniah 1,14-15
[192] Ezekiel 26,7-9&15-17
[193] Ezekiel 26,18-21
[194] Ezekiel 28,21-24; Zephaniah 2,4-5
[195] Isaiah 23,4&11-12; Jeremiah 47,2-7
[196] Micah 6,1-7
[197] Jeremiah 12,1-2; Amos 6,12
[198] Jeremiah 7,30-34; 19,3-13
[199] Jeremiah 8,1-8
[200] Amos 5,3
[201] Isaiah 22,17-18; Jeremiah 9,1&11
[202] Isaiah 5,14-16; Zephaniah 3,6
[203] Jeremiah 25,15-38
[204] Daniel 9,26-27
[205] Daniel 11,35; Revelation 10,6-7; 19,11-19
[206] I Peter 1,3-5&13; Jude 14-21
[207] Isaiah 33,24; Revelation 10,6-7; 11,14-18
[208] Joel 3,2-15; Revelation 16,13-16
[209] Mathew 10,26-27; Luke 12,2-3; John 16,13

Chapter Seven/Part Two
THE THIRD WATCH

"I saw them who overcame the beast and his image and his mark and the number of his name standing on a sea of glass having the harps of God and singing the song of Moses and the song of the Lamb, for your judgments are made manifest."
Revelation 15,1-4

Secrets of the last days are not kept in some kind of vault in which only a chosen few have access and are sworn to seclusion. The veil that has covered the prophets is largely due to the complex nature of sorting out details of the separate phases foretold by Jesus in his gospel. This difficulty is compounded by the metaphors or parables used to explain certain issues and also by the keen likeness of future affairs to the past. Although the early apostles wrote about matters of the end times we seem to neglect, distort or have forgotten, only now has the world developed to the point we can more accurately grasp this divine plan for the church and for humanity.

Pertinence of prophecy starting with the profound warnings of Fatima and the creation of Israel's statehood has become more pressing than ever with serious threats to global security. It is high time we *"Study to show yourselves approved unto God, a workman who needs not to be ashamed, rightly dividing the word of truth."*[1] We should meditate on these teachings to society as *"Be mindful of the words spoken by the holy prophets, even as our beloved brother Paul has written to you of some things hard to understand."*[2] Despite its intricacy we will know for *"The vision is yet for an appointed time, but at the end it shall speak and not lie. Wait for it."*[3]

St. Paul wrote important things about the mysteries of Christ saying *"by revelation he made known to me the dispensation of grace which in former ages was not made known as it is now that the Gentiles should be fellow heirs of the same body of Christ by the gospel."*[4] This and other doctrines were big news to a Jewish community who *"declared how God at the first did visit the Gentiles to take out of them a people for his name. We believe by the grace of the Lord Jesus Christ we shall be saved even as they."*[5] To Jews *"whom it was first preached entered not in because of unbelief"* Jesus said *"So the last shall be first, and the first will be last."*[6]

Much discussion was made in prior chapters about the conversion of many Jews before the Messianic reign on earth. This tenet permeates Scripture from the time of ancient patriarchs and *"Your people shall be willing in the day of your power, in the beauties of holiness from the womb of the morning. We will go into his tabernacles, we will worship at his footstool."*[7] The day of power is redemption from hatred and war when *"my people will know my name and it is I who speak, they shall see eye to eye when the Lord converts Zion. My soul waits for the Lord more than they who watch for the morning."*[8] This hope precedes a new earth's dawn.

Watches of redemption go beyond any scientific reasoning, but so does our belief in miracles of the bible and resurrection into eternal life. None should be deceived concerning the Calvary we must endure, yet *"The Lord's hand is not shortened that it cannot save, nor his ear heavy so it cannot hear. The Redeemer shall come to Zion and unto them who turn from transgression in Jacob."*[9] Scrutiny is required to discern the ongoing signs of Scripture since *"I pray your love may abound more and more in knowledge and in judgment. Wisdom and knowledge will be the stability of your times and the strength of salvation: the fear of the Lord is his treasure."*[10]

Some readers may be surprised that the concept and seasons of rapture are so well defined in the prophets, the gospel, the epistles and the Apocalypse, but this ultimate theme to deliver is an exodus into the Promised Land of heaven as *"From the end of the earth will I cry to you. I will* abide in your tabernacle forever. The voice of rejoicing and salvation is in the tabernacles of the just: I will not die, but live. The Lord has chastened me sore, but he has not given me over to death."[11] It's a big mistake to shrug off this glorious hope which we are plainly taught by St. Paul to "Behold, I show you a mystery: we shall not all die, but we shall be changed."[12]

Three distinct visions in the book of Revelation conform to Jesus urging us to "Let your loins be girded about, and your lights burning and you as men who wait for their Lord. If he comes in the second watch, or comes in the third watch and find them so, blessed are those servants."[13] This passage has surely puzzled preachers and students of his word, but the third watch consists of those who St. John saw that "overcame the beast and his image and his mark and the number of his name. They sing the song of Moses and the song of the Lamb saying, who shall not fear you, O Lord and glorify your name: for your judgments are made manifest."[14]

When the Antichrist succeeds in securing his military power over all nations, he will begin a banking program whereby "no man might buy or sell unless he who had the mark, or the name of the beast, or the number of his name."[15] This economic order of currency will most likely start throughout his European base and in other countries in league with him. That conclusion is supported by those redeemed from the earth who avoided his purchasing identity and by the factor of time in setting up a new type of exchange. Many people will lose their souls by taking the mark of the beast before all barter of global banking is geared to the system.

Judgments of the Lord refer both to his justice and to his mercy which will be manifest to all who live in times of rapture. The song of Moses sung in the third watch is a testament against his brethren who "sacrificed to devils, not to God. O that they were wise and would consider their latter end, for the day of calamity is at hand, and the Lord will judge his people, when he sees their power is gone, and none shut up or left." This song is of victory and of promise since "Rejoice O you nations with his people: for he will avenge the blood of his servants, and render vengeance on his enemies. He will be merciful to his land and to his people."[16]

Mysteries of the gospel will be revealed in due times, but the center of faith and hope is in the Eucharist for "Gather my saints unto me, those who have made a covenant with me by sacrifice. Sing to the Lord, you saints of his, give thanks at the remembrance of his holiness."[17] To everyone who seeks redemption "in the way of your judgments O Lord, we have waited for you. The desire of our soul is to your name and to the remembrance of you. I will bring my people again from the depths of the sea. They have seen your goings, O God, even the goings of my God, in the sanctuary."[18] Let us not forget the Christ who sanctifies his altar.[19]

Despite increasing apostasy and oppression against divine law, "The Lord will increase you more and more, you and your children. Blessed are they who dwell in your house. How amiable are your tabernacles, even your altars, my King and my God. They go from strength to strength, every one of them in Zion appears before God. I will hope continually, and yet praise you more and more. You will quicken me again and bring me up again from the abyss of the earth."[20] The church will spread in these times "even to your old age I will bear, carry you and deliver you. They who do justice in your ways: in those is continuance, and we shall be saved."[21]

Circumstances engulfing humanity during the period leading to the third watch involve great plagues and persecution as Jesus warned "You will be hated by all nations for my name's sake and they will deliver you up to be afflicted and kill you. Now you have sorrow, you will weep and lament but I will see you again. Your heart will rejoice and none can take away your joy."[22] How many of us practice our precious freedom of religion or think of the devout faith it takes for those whose "enemies would daily swallow me up. My eyes fail as I wait for my God. For your sake we are killed all the day long, and counted as sheep for the slaughter."[23]

182

The church will go through a trial not seen in its history, yet mankind will reap agony from its evil and God will be exalted when *"They cried to the Lord in trouble, he delivered them out of distress that sit in darkness and the shadow of death being bound in affliction and iron. They who do business in ships see the works of the Lord and his wonders in the deep that lift up its waves. He turns rivers into wilderness and makes the fruitful land barren. They are diminished by oppression, affliction and sorrow. He delivered and brought them to their desired haven. With terrible deeds of justice you answer us, the hope of all the earth and distant seas."[24]*

Vanity will pay an enormous price in the delusions of greed and power due to overwhelming death and ruin, but the faithful look beyond that pain and mortality since *"O God, you have cast us off and scattered us. You made the earth to tremble and split it open: heal the breaches for it shakes. You showed your people hard things and astonishment, but gave a banner to them who fear you that your loved ones may escape. The captive exile hastens that he may be loosed and not die in the pit, nor that his bread should fail. You brought us into the net and men rode over our heads, we went through fire and water, but you brought us into a wealthy place."[25]*

Special benefits of divine providence extend to those who love the Lord *"For the Lord will help me. I will not be confounded, nor ashamed. Who among you obeys the voice of his servant that walks in darkness and has no light? Let him trust in the name of the Lord and stay upon his God.[26] I will instruct and teach you in the way you shall go, I will guide you with my eye. Mercy will compass all upright in heart to deliver their soul from death and keep them alive in famine. The steps of a good man are ordered by the Lord to help them, deliver them and save them. God is my portion forever. Wait on the Lord, be of good courage: wait I say on the Lord."[27]*

Who can question why God allowed the martyrdom of holy prophets, apostles and others except they were examples to us of the power of faith in the promise of eternal life in heaven. It is a harsh fact that mankind would annihilate itself *"unless the Lord had shortened those days, no flesh would be saved, but for the elect's sake he has shortened those days."[28]* There is a remnant chosen who will serve God and Christ, but until then Jesus said *"If they persecuted me, they will also persecute you."[29]* There is a balance to God's word for *"some of understanding shall fall to try them, to purge and make them white even to the time of the end."[30]*

Preparing for the terrors of the fourth seal is first a process of diligence in following the precepts of Christian faith. If we don't have spiritual communion with the Lord and fidelity to his church, just temporal profits can be gained by intelligent reactions to biblical signs. Before the start of WWIV during great famine or even in the early phase of isolated turmoil, practical decisions can be made about which countries are the safest place to move. Oppression and iniquity will vary in parts of the world so people can take notice and make ready to migrate. Apathy and false hopes can only add to their burdens while events turn from bad to worse.

Advice to abstain from sinful acts and relocate from places of persecution and eminent ruin are repeated in the prophets as *"They cried to them, Depart you, it is unclean: depart, depart, touch not when they fled away and wandered. They said among the heathen, they will no more sojourn there."[31]* To those who are aware and look for pending threats to lands controlled by the Antichrist, especially from eastern armies *"Flee out of the midst of Babylon, and deliver every man his soul: Be not cut off in her iniquity, for the Lord will render to her a recompense."[32]* The warnings are made to the wise who see the signs and make logical choices.

Similar to prevailing public opinion of today that tends to ignore the real dangers of world strife, tense military outbreaks often take place quickly and will come unexpectedly both in the present and future stages of global conflict. This is why we need to watch, pray and respond to wisdom in omens of our times as *"Go forth of Babylon, flee from the Chaldeans with a voice of* singing to declare and tell to the end of the earth that the Lord has redeemed his servant Jacob. Deliver yourself, O Zion that dwells with the daughter of Babylon. Come forth and flee the land of the north, for I have spread you abroad like the four winds of heaven."[33]

Guidance is given to Jews and Gentiles alike who abhor the evil around them. Evangelization will be silenced by imprisonment and execution so it is rational to assume some kind of network will unfold among believers to save lives. Of this emotional and bodily need, *"Oh that I had a lodging place of wayfaring men in the wilderness so I can leave my people and go from them. They are adulterers and treacherous men."*[34] Counsel is urged to *"Arise and depart for this is not your rest because it is polluted, it will destroy you even with a sore destruction."*[35] Many will face this daunting challenge to forsake evil ways and abandon their roots.

Faith is a gift given to everyone and we can either nurture that sense in our hearts or bury it with the lusts of our flesh. If we don't build on this virtue we lose it, but *"The Lord knows them who trust in him and he is a stronghold in the day of trouble. You are my rock and my fortress, for your name's sake lead me and guide me. Pull me out of the net they laid for me. You will hide them in the secret of your presence, he will conceal me in the shelter of his tent."*[36] Jesus is present in the Eucharist and our shelter in his church so *"Rejoice for your King comes to you, by the blood of your covenant I have sent forth prisoners out of the pit where is no water."*[37]

Maturity in grace comes by meditation and submission to the divine word since *"Your saints will bless you, O Lord. They will speak of the glory of your kingdom and talk of your power to make known to the sons of men his mighty acts and majesty of his kingdom. As many as are led by the Spirit of God, they are the sons of God. He has not given us the spirit of fear, but of power, of love and a sound mind."*[38] The apostles taught *"When the chief Shepherd will appear, you will receive a crown of glory that fades not away. We look for the Savior who will change our vile body like his glorious body. When he appears, you will appear with him in glory."*[39]

Many preachers who frequently talk about rapture present a false illusion that God is going to save the church and then judge the world, but St. Peter clearly wrote *"that judgment must begin at the house of God, and if it first begins with us, what will be the end of those who obey not the gospel?"* St. Paul added *"that in the last days perilous times will come"* but he specified for us in these times *"to serve God and wait for his Son from heaven, even Jesus, who delivered us from the wrath to come."*[40] Our hope is in sorrows as *"They will fight against you, but will not prevail. I will bring you again to save and deliver you, and you will stand before me."*[41]

Incredible destruction will happen from warfare before the end wrath as the church cries for mercy from above to *"Give ear O Shepherd of Israel, you who lead Joseph as a flock. Stir up your strength: come and save us. How long will you be angry while your people pray? Return O God of hosts, look down from heaven, behold and visit this vine. The vineyard your right hand planted and the branch you made strong for yourself are burned with fire, it is cut down. Let your hand be upon the man of your right hand, upon the son of man whom you made strong for yourself. Quicken us and turn us again, cause your face to shine and we shall be saved."*[42]

Pernicious forces of the wicked will overcome them in their quest for fortune and fame to the fearful end that *"I will do unto them after their way, and judge them according to their crimes. You will all bow down to the slaughter. But they who escape of them will escape and be on the mountains like doves of the valleys, all of them mourning for his iniquity. Your brethren who hated you and cast you out for my name's sake saying, Let the Lord be glorified: he will appear to your joy and they will be ashamed, a voice of the Lord to render recompense to his enemies. The hand of the Lord will be known to his servants, and his wrath to his enemies."*[43]

Deception and iniquity will prevent the public from accepting or allowing anyone to proclaim Christ since *"the proud are risen against me and the assemblies of violent men have sought my soul. In the day of my trouble you will answer me. Save the son of your handmaid. Show me a token for good so they who hate me may see it and be ashamed. They are brought down and fallen, but we are risen and stand upright. We will rejoice in his salvation, he will hear from his holy heaven with the saving strength of his right hand. I will deliver my people out of your hand and they will be no more in your hand to be hunted and you shall know I am the Lord."[44]*

Sorcery will saturate the culture of that time even as Jesus cautioned that *"False saviors and false prophets will arise and show signs and wonders to seduce, if it were possible, even the elect."[45]* Yet it is also written, *"Truth is fallen in the street and he who departs from evil makes himself a prey. The Lord saw it and his arm brought salvation and justice to him. Woe to the shepherds of Israel who feed themselves and do not feed the flock, but rule them with force and cruelty. My flock was scattered upon all the face of the earth and became a prey. I will deliver my flock from their mouth. And as for you, behold I judge between rams and he-goats."[46]*

There are no adequate words to describe the empty emotion of pity for explicit suffering of the last days, but *"I have heard the voice of anguish of the daughter of Zion who bewails herself saying, Woe is me now for my soul is wearied of murderers! Revive your work, O Lord, in the midst of years make known: in wrath remember mercy. Before him went pestilence and burning coals at his feet. He stood and measured the earth, he beheld and drove asunder the nations. The mountains trembled, the overflowing water passed by, the deep lifted up on high. You went forth for salvation of your people with your Christ, my Holy One: We shall not die."[47]*

The enigma of rapture is a consistent theme of Scripture which needs to be brought out in our dialogue of eschatology. Although this mystery creates strong zeal of enthusiasm for many who believe in this hope, it must be explained in its proper perspective for the sanctity of truth. Jesus told that *"Jerusalem will be trodden down by the Gentiles, until the times of the Gentiles are fulfilled. They will fall by the sword and be led away captive into all nations. Watch and pray always that you may be accounted worthy to escape all these things, and stand before the Son of man."[48]* Times of the Gentiles include final events of WWIV and the end wrath.

Reflection of the sacrifice of Christ on the cross in our Liturgy of the Mass parallels the real crucifixion of his mystical body in his church, *"For as often as you eat this bread and drink this cup, you proclaim the Lord's death until he comes."[49]* To proclaim means a showing forth or to bring tidings after the manner of his death in essence to display by experience. Before Jesus was crucified, he prayed *"Father save me from this hour, but for this cause I came unto this hour. Then came a voice from heaven saying, I have both glorified it and I will glorify it again."* Jesus told those who stood by, *"This voice came not for me, but for your sakes."[50]*

Why would God say he would glorify the passion of Christ again or why did Jesus indicate that the message was for us? Although he overcame death he also revealed *"And I, if I be lifted up from the earth, will draw all men unto me. Now is the judgment of this world: now will the prince of darkness be cast out."* Both he and the Father spoke of another time when judgment would take place and the Devil himself bound in the pit of hell. We will suffer his passion yet in hope because Jesus taught *"Walk while you have the light, that darkness does not overtake you. Believe in the light while it is day: the night comes when no man can work."[51]*

However we may wish or think otherwise, a type of sepulcher remains for the church, *"But you brethren are not in darkness so that day overtakes you as a thief. You are children of light and of the day."[52]* The day of darkness or what Jesus described as the night begins with the Antichrist's global reign after St. John saw those in heaven who got victory over him or his mark and also *"seven angels having the last seven plagues, for in them is filled up the wrath of God."* This is the last trumpet as *"the seventh angel sounded, the nations were angry and your wrath is come."* Of that precise time *"at the last trump, the dead will rise incorruptible."*[53]

Catastrophic prophecies of disaster and destitution are mixed with awesome hope of the third watch, but in regard to that mystery *"Gird up the lions of your mind, be sober and hope to the end for the grace to be brought to you at the revelation of Jesus Christ. Blessed be God who begot us again to an inheritance incorruptible, undefiled that does not fade away reserved in heaven for you."*[54] This is the moment of our immortal bodies with all who yet dwell in spirit in heaven: *"O Lord we have waited for you, our salvation in the time of trouble. At the noise of the tumult the people fled. At the lifting up of yourself the nations were scattered."*[55]

Consecration of the bread and wine in the Liturgy of the Mass has deep significance for the lifting up of the church and for the forgiveness of sin in a new world since *"God shall send Jesus Christ whom heaven must receive until the times of restitution of all things."*[56] Each of us must die to our selfish lusts so his love can live in us but the church has its own cross to carry as *"We have thought of your mercy Oh God in the midst of the temple, he will be our guide even to death. Sorrows of death compassed me and pains of hell got hold of me. Gracious is the Lord who delivered my soul from death. I will walk before him in the land of the living."*[57]

Fortitude in faith is essential in this struggle for survival and redemption for they will *"Be in pain and travail to bring forth, O daughter of Zion. You will go out of the city and dwell in the field. You will even go to Babylon, there you will be delivered and the Lord will redeem you from the hand of your enemies."*[58] They will flee and some will go into captivity, but *"By the rivers of Babylon, there we sat down. We hung our harps upon the willows in the midst thereof. They who carried us away captive and wasted us required a song of Zion. O daughter of Babylon who will be destroyed, happy will he be who rewards you as you have served us."*[59]

Amazing truths are found in inquiry of the last days because once we grasp the succession of overall stages of these times, all the parts of our reality fit into a systematic order. Above all things is *"The Lord will be a refuge for the oppressed in times of trouble, you lift me up from the gates of death.*[60] *Seek the Lord all you meek, it may be you will be hid in the day of his wrath. Break forth into joy, sing together you waste places of Jerusalem for the Lord has comforted his people, he redeemed Jerusalem. The eyes of all nations and all the ends of the earth will see the salvation of our God. Now will I arise, now will I be exalted, now will I lift myself up."*[61]

How is it the Lord will rise, be exalted and lift himself up in a time when the earth mourns in languish or why is it written the people had already fled from tumult at the lifting up of himself when the nations were scattered? These conditions did not exist when he was crucified, but they bear witness to the church in his gospel. The Antichrist will slaughter many nations and *"When I heard, my belly trembled that I might rest in the day of trouble. The flock will be cut off from the fold and there will be no herd in the stalls. Yet I will rejoice in the God of my salvation. He will make my feet like hinds' feet and lead me upon my high places singing songs."*[62]

Application of biblical citations to rapture varies since some speak of the plurality of times, but others are specific to each watch. Ironically, a Jewish priesthood will spread the gospel to all ends of the earth. Both they and then the rest who are ready will be saved for *"I will surely assemble all of you O Jacob, I will surely gather the remnant of Israel. The breaker is come up before them: they shall divide and pass through the gate, and are gone out by it. Their king will pass before them and the Lord on the head of them. Save me O God from my enemies. Let them be blotted out of the book of the living, but let your salvation set me on high."*[63]

186

Contrast between vanity and truth will become profound in this testing of faith as they plead *"Rid me, and deliver me from the right hand of falsehood. Bow your heavens O Lord, and come down: save me from workers of iniquity and bloody men. The wicked walk on every side when violent men say, Who is lord over us? Now will I arise, I will set them in safety, preserve them from this generation forever.*[64] *Our end is near: our days are fulfilled for our end is come. The punishment of your iniquity is finished, O daughter of Zion. Break into singing you mountains, O forest and all therein for the Lord redeemed Jacob and glorified himself in Israel."*[65]

Review of redemption of our bodies in resurrection has direct impetus for the third watch. Many passages and quotes about rapture into heaven have been examined in prior chapters. The concise summary in this section results in incorruption, but a temporary end of the scepter in the church as *"The wicked have fought against me without cause. Set a wicked man over them and let Satan stand at his right hand. Save and gather us from among the heathen, O Lord, to triumph in your praise. I have spread my hands all the day to a rebellious people who provoke me to anger that say, Depart from me, come not near me for I am holier than you."*[66]

Conditions of the end period during the final plagues of divine wrath must be distinguished from disasters before the Antichrist rules the earth in the Devil's power, *"When he is judged, let him be condemned and his plea be in vain. Let his days be few and let another take his office. May his posterity be cut off and their name blotted out in the next generation. He persecuted the poor and needy to slay the broken in heart. As he loved cursing, let it come to him. Deliver my soul from the sword, my darling from the power of the dog. You heard me from the horns of the unicorns. Help me, O Lord my God, that they may know your hand has done it."*[67]

All the seed of the Antichrist will be destroyed from the world and damned for all eternity, but *"Deliver me out of the mire and let me not sink. Rescue me from my foes and out of deep waters. Let not the flood waters overwhelm me, nor the deep swallow me up or the pit shut its mouth over me. You who dwell on the earth will see when the sign is lifted up. In that time a gift will be brought to the Lord of hosts of a people scattered and peeled, a nation meted out and trodden under foot to the place of mount Zion. The great trumpet will be blown, and they will come who were ready to perish and worship the Lord in the mount of Jerusalem."*[68]

Explosive prophecies are given to us in relationship of our spiritual dimension to our physical existence. We have the moral choice of renewal in fidelity to divine law toward making social transformation, but this revival is sorely stifled by those who lost interest in the Sabbath or are part of a growing void of vain religious profession that rejects living out our faith. Jesus did not form his church on individualism or homemade privacy. He created it as a fraternal body with the bond of his love whose mission for each of us is discipleship and primary focus is belief that *"You, O Lord, will live forever and your remembrance unto all generations."*[69]

Calamities, violence and corruption are part of the reality of our times, yet *"Strengthen the weak hands and confirm the feeble knees. Say to them who are of a fearful heart, Be strong, fear not: Behold your God will come with vengeance, even God with a recompense. He will come and save you. The Lord who created you O Jacob and he who formed you O Israel, I have called you by name, you are mine: Fear not, I have redeemed you. He sent from above, he took me and drew me out of many waters. He delivered me from them who hated me who were too strong for me. By God I leaped over a wall, he brought me forth to a place of liberty."*[70]

Immortality after death is a belief shared by people of different religious faiths. That state of being is either in eternal life or in damnation, but *"Who shall ascend into the hill of the Lord or stand in his holy place? This is the generation who seeks the face of the God of Jacob. Lift up your heads O you gates, be lifted up you everlasting doors, the King of glory will come in. The*

187

ransomed of the Lord will return and come to Zion with songs of everlasting joy.[71] They will be mine in that day when I make up my jewels, and I will spare them. The Lord God will save them as the flock of his people, as stones of a crown lifted up as an ensign upon his land.*"[72]

Affliction will continue for the faithful until the last trumpet is blown to signal the time of the end. They will know and experience the words of the prophets in unity of hope so *"Hearken to me, you who seek the Lord for a law will proceed from me and I will make my judgment to rest for a light of the people. My justice is near, my salvation is gone forth and my arms will judge the people.*[73] O Lord, for your name's sake break not your covenant with us. Therefore we will wait upon you. He put a new song in my mouth: many shall see it, fear and trust in the Lord. You will guide me with your counsel, and afterward receive me to glory."[74]*

Redemption is based in a coherent set of premises and principles that form a rational pulpit of faith. Detailed warnings of world wars still not recorded in history and the dilemma of divine justice are not conjecture for *"Rejoice not against me, Oh my enemy: when I fall, I shall rise. I will bear the indignation of the Lord until he plead my cause and execute judgment for me. Then my enemy will see it and shame will cover her who said, Where is the Lord your God? The snare is broken, we are escaped. Seek the Lord, O nation not desired, if by any means you may be hid in the day of the Lord's wrath. He prepared a sacrifice, he has bid his guests."[75]*

Everyone in life and in death must confront the witness of God who said *"he will come forth of me who will be ruler in Israel, whose goings forth have been from old, from everlasting. He will give them up until the time that she who travails brings forth, then the remnant will return to the children of Israel."[76]* This prophecy about the Incarnation of God in Christ speaks of his goings to redeem his church and then save the remnant of Jews with mankind. St. John wrote, *"Who is a liar, but he who denies Jesus is the Christ? Abide in him so when he will appear, we may not be ashamed. When he appears we will be like him, we will see him as he is."[77]*

Jacob foretold of the Messiah as the Lion of Judah to gather the people whose scepter is in the church and he also prophesied to Joseph about conversion of Jews whose branches reach outside their own people.[78] To those who endure to the third watch *"Hate the evil, love the good and establish judgment in the gate: It may be that the Lord God of hosts will be gracious to the remnant of Joseph. Hear O Lord, attend to my prayer. By your word I have kept myself from the destroyer. Keep me as the apple of your eye. Arise, deliver my soul from the wicked. Cast him down, but as for me I will behold your face when I awake with your likeness."[79]*

Intricacies of the divine word reveal the penetrating knowledge and power of God to make known his adoption of us in Christ, yet his unnerving justice to those who refuse to obey the truth of his covenant. A unique testimony of the third watch is converts of Egypt in that *"The land of Judah will be a terror to Egypt because of the Lord's counsel he determined against it. In that day five cities in the land of Egypt will swear to the Lord of hosts. There will be an altar to the Lord in the midst of Egypt and a pillar at the border thereof. It will be a sign and a witness for they will cry because of their oppressors and he shall deliver them."[80]*

What a marvel to contemplate these detailed predictions that *"The Lord is near to them who call on him in truth. He will preserve them, hear their cry and save them. Men shall discourse of the might of your terrible deeds. They publish the fame of your compassion and sing of your justice. Your word is a lamp to my feet and a light to my path. Your testimonies I have taken as a heritage forever.*[81] God will redeem my soul from the power of the grave. Praise him you heaven of heavens, and you waters who are above the heavens, for he commanded and they were created. He established them and made a decree that shall not pass."[82]*

In closing this chapter about the immeasurable death and destruction of the fourth seal, it is in that context of homily Jesus taught *"This gospel of the kingdom will be preached in all the world for a witness unto all nations, then the end will come. In my Father's house are many mansions: if it were not so I would have told you. I go to prepare a place for you. And if I go to prepare a place for you, I will come again and receive you to myself that where I am, there you may be also. Where I go you know, and the way you know. I am the way, the truth and the life. No man comes to the Father, but through me. Oh love the Lord, all you saints."[83]*

[1] II Timothy 2,15
[2] II Peter 3,1-4&13-17
[3] Habakkuk 1,12; 2,3
[4] Ephesians 1,17-20; 3,1-6
[5] Acts 15,7-18
[6] Mathew 20,16; Luke 13,29-30; Hebrews 4,6-9
[7] Psalm 110,3; 132,7-9
[8] Psalm 130,5-7; Isaiah 52,6-9
[9] Isaiah 50,2; 59,1&20
[10] Isaiah 33,5-6; Philippians 1,9-10
[11] Psalm 61,2-4; 118,14-20
[12] I Corinthians 15,50-51
[13] Luke 12,35-40
[14] Revelation 15,2-4
[15] Revelation 13,16-17
[16] Deuteronomy 32,17-18&29-43
[17] Psalm 30,3-4; 50,5&23
[18] Psalm 68,22-24; Isaiah 26,1-8&19-20
[19] Hebrews 12,22-25; 13,10
[20] Psalm 71,14-21; 84,1-7; 115,12-14
[21] Isaiah 46,3-4; 64,4-5
[22] Mark 13,12-13; John 16,19-22
[23] Psalm 44,22; 56,2-6; 69,2-9
[24] Psalm 65,5-8; 107,2-42
[25] Psalm 60,1-5; 66,10-12; Isaiah 51,14
[26] Isaiah 50,8-10
[27] Psalm 27,14; 32,6-8; 33,18-19; 37,23&40; 73,26
[28] Mathew 24,21-22; Mark 13,19-20
[29] John 15,16-21
[30] Daniel 11,33-35
[31] Lamentations 4,15
[32] Jeremiah 51,6
[33] Isaiah 48,20; Zechariah 2,6-7
[34] Jeremiah 9,2
[35] Micah 2,10
[36] Psalm 27,4-6; 31,19-21; Nahum 1,7
[37] Zechariah 9,9-12&16-17
[38] Psalm 145,10-15; Romans 8,14; II Timothy 1,7
[39] Philippians 3,20-21; Colossians 3,1-4; I Peter 5,4

[40] I Thessalonians 1,9-10; II Timothy 3,1; I Peter 4,17
[41] Jeremiah 15,15-21
[42] Psalm 80,1-19
[43] Isaiah 65,11-12; 66,5-6&14; Ezekiel 7,14-16&27
[44] Psalm 20,1-9; 86,7-17; Ezekiel 13,17-23
[45] Mathew 24,24; Mark 13,22
[46] Isaiah 59,14-16; Ezekiel 34,2-10&17
[47] Jeremiah 4,31; Habakkuk 1,12; 3,2-13
[48] Luke 21,24&36
[49] I Corinthians 11,23-26
[50] John 12,27-30
[51] John 9,4; 12,31-36
[52] I Thessalonians 5,4-5
[53] I Corinthians 15,52; Revelation 11,14-18; 15,1-4
[54] I Peter 1,3-4&13&23
[55] Isaiah 33,2-3
[56] Acts 3,18-21
[57] Psalm 48,9-14; 116,3-9
[58] Micah 4,10
[59] Psalm 137,1-8
[60] Psalm 9,9-14
[61] Isaiah 33,9-10; 52,9-10; Zephaniah 2,3
[62] Habakkuk 1,6-7; 3,16-19
[63] Psalm 69,1&14-29; Micah 2,12-13
[64] Psalm 12,3-8; 59,2&16; 144,5-11
[65] Isaiah 44,21-23; Lamentations 4,18&22
[66] Psalm 106,4-6&46-47; 109,2-8; Isaiah 65,2-5
[67] Psalm 22,20-22; 109,7-27
[68] Psalm 69,13-17; Isaiah 18,3-7; 27,13
[69] Psalm 102,12
[70] Psalm 18,16-29; Isaiah 35,4; 43,1
[71] Psalm 24,3-7; Isaiah 35,10
[72] Zechariah 9,16; Malachi 3,17
[73] Isaiah 51,4-5
[74] Psalm 40,1-3; 73,23-26; Jeremiah 14,21-22
[75] Psalm 124,7; Micah 7,7-10; Zephaniah 1,7; 2,1-3
[76] Micah 5,2-4
[77] I John 2,22-28; 3,1-3
[78] Genesis 49,8-12&22-26
[79] Psalm 17,1-15; Amos 5,14-15
[80] Isaiah 19,16-21
[81] Psalm 119,103&105&111; 145,6-20
[82] Psalm 49,15; 148,4-6
[83] Psalm 31,19-24; Mathew 24,14; John 14,1-7

Chapter Eight
OPENING OF THE FIFTH SEAL
MARK OF THE BEAST

"I saw under the altar the souls of them who were slain for the word of God and for their witness saying, how long O Lord do you not judge and avenge our blood on them who dwell on the earth?" Revelation 6,9-11

Crisis in faith toward evil apostasy will reach an epitome of theoretical and practical atheism in self sufficiency of mankind's ability to determine its own destiny and moral values. Secular materialism of society substitutes creation in place of the Creator causing the belief that people are their own gods in defiance of divine law. The road to sanctity will be replaced by the path of perdition in a global false church which glorifies human lusts and demonism. All devils act under a hierarchy in which Satan who is the prince of darkness will possess the Antichrist with deceptive extraordinary powers to blaspheme God and his holy covenant in Christ.

The bible is not an abstract odyssey or fictitious myth, but words of the holy prophets were proved in the events of ancient history and manifest in the eternal kingdom of atonement in the risen Jesus. Stages of the end times in our Lord's gospel began with global wars of the last century and continued with many regional commotions. Apocalyptic conflicts when nation rises against nation and when kingdom rises against kingdom are still to come. Distinction of great tribulation of these battles from the final end wrath is in catastrophic disorders of nature that create amazing afflictions never before seen by anyone throughout the world.

Curses of this period are against a remnant of civilization who are literally bent on hellfire. Even after the cumulative disasters of nuclear wars and wonders in divine power of the watches to redeem the faithful, *"The rest of the men who were not killed by these plagues yet repented not that they worship devils and idols. Neither did they repent of their murders, or sorceries, or fornication or thefts."*[1] It seems fitting these people will dwell in a culture of wicked disposition led by a crazed tyrant *"whose coming is after the workings of Satan with lying prodigies. God will send them a strong delusion so all might be damned who believe not the truth."*[2]

Transition from the global cataclysm of WWIV to a sequence of great natural disasters will precede judgment at the Second Advent.   Magnitude of these plagues will reveal what can only be understood in existence and anger of God as *"Then I said how long Lord? And he answered: Until the cities are wasted without inhabitant and the houses without a man and the land is utterly desolate. There will be a great forsaking and the Lord will remove men far away."*[3] It is perplexing to imagine the overwhelming damage of luxuries in our world or loss of life, but consider *"The day of the Lord is great and very terrible, and who can abide it?"*[4]

Humanity will suffer the consequence of its grave sins and refusal to accept our salvation to overcome the audacity of man's fallen nature since *"The Lord is the true God, he is the living God and an everlasting King: at his wrath the earth will tremble and the nations will not be able to abide his indignation. The gods that have not made the heavens and the earth shall perish from the earth and from under the heavens."*[5] Purpose in the divine plan to establish the new covenant of peace and prosperity is independent of the petty strength of mortal pride for *"the inhabitants of the world will learn justice when your judgments are done in the earth."*[6]

Personal vanity as a means to freedom is a paradox in its bondage to iniquity and separation from divine grace so *"walk not as others walk in the vanity of their mind, being alienated from the life of God through ignorance because of the blindness of their heart. While they promise liberty, they are servants of corruption.*"[7] The irony of rejecting divine law to obtain status, money and pleasure is *"Hell and destruction are never full: the eyes of man are never satisfied. Nothing is pure to them who are defiled and unbelieving, even their mind and conscience is marred. They disown God being abominable and worthless for any good work."*[8]

Our existence is fraught with being an individual soul divided between our inner spirit and exterior body which creates a dilemma due to our free will. We are told to *"Be not wise in your own conceits for to be carnally minded is death and is enmity against God. The way of life is above to the wise so he may depart from hell beneath. Fear the Lord and depart from evil."*[9] Vice will be an obtrusive force in the end time, but *"they are without excuse who changed the truth of God into a lie and worshiped and served the creature more than the Creator. As they refused the knowledge of God, he gave them over to a reprobate mind."*[10]

Witchcraft and idolatry will pervade the world as never before while the infinite truth of our reality asks *"To whom will you liken me, and make me equal and compare me? For I am God and there is none like me declaring the end from the beginning and from ancient times the things that are not yet done."*[11] The depravity of falsehood will cease since *"I am the Lord who makes all things, frustrates the omens of soothsayers, makes the diviners mad and turns wise men backward. Woe to him who says awake to the wood and arise to the dumb stone, it will teach. What profits the maker of idols who trust in his image? There is no breath in it."*[12]

First among the commandments of God written in stone tablets by his finger at Mount Sinai is *"You shall not have other gods before me. Turn you not to idols nor make to yourselves molten gods. You shall not bow down to them or serve them for I am a jealous God."*[13] This malaise of society debases our reason and integrity, yet *"The unjust knows no shame saying to a stock you are my father and to a stone you have brought me forth. But where are your gods that you made? Let them arise if they can save you in the time of trouble. How long will you turn my glory into a shame? How long will you love vanity and falsehood?"*[14]

Obscurity and despair will prevail over the nations as a result of widespread psychosis and terrible plagues. Human beings did not evolve from animals, but they will act like them in the most despicable ways for *"My people have not known me, they are wise to do evil but to do good they have no knowledge. They are all vanity, their works fail, their molten images are wind and confusion. None calls for justice or pleads for truth: they speak lies, conceive mischief and iniquity. They will be turned back who say to molten images, you are our gods. The Lord has poured on you the spirit of deep sleep for the wisdom of their wise men will perish."*[15]

There is no success in evil since it is usually requited by the same corruption practiced, but in the end *"The Lord will take vengeance on his adversaries and he reserves wrath for his enemies. I have shown you new things from this time, even hidden things, and you did not know them. They are created now and not of old. Before it came to pass I showed it to you lest you should say you knew them. The days come I will do judgment upon the graven images of Babylon and her whole land will be confounded, her slain will fall in her midst. Babylon has made the earth drunk, all the nations drank of her wine: therefore the nations are mad."*[16]

Many people know the biblical prediction of a vile person called the Antichrist to rule the earth by a system of commerce controlled by the mark of the beast. The false prophet or high priest of a malicious church *"does great wonders and deceives them who dwell on the earth by means of those miracles he had power to do, saying they should make an image to the beast."* This image is of the Antichrist which the false prophet will *"cause as many as would not worship the image to be killed. He causes all to receive a mark in their right hand or forehead so no man could buy or sell unless he had the mark or name or number of the beast."*[17]

Current thought and discussion of the mark or number 666 of the beast tends to generate fear because of the broad bogus idea that a world government of the Antichrist will develop through peaceful means and everybody will be caught up in this new asset or credit identity. We must realize the impact of nuclear wars and other plagues before then. Most of mankind will not be alive to make the choice of either execution or damnation, but *"If any man worship the beast and his image, and receive his mark in his forehead or his hand, the same will drink of the wrath of God, and he will be tormented with fire and brimstone forever and ever."[18]*

Extent and length of the Antichrist's reign before the final battle of Armageddon is distinctly explained in the Apocalypse. The implication of this inclusive evil kingdom for the church's viability and martyrdom of its faithful cannot be ignored as *"it was given to him to make war with the saints and to overcome them, and power was given to him over every kindred, tongue and nation. He opened his mouth in blasphemy against God and his tabernacle and them who dwell in heaven. Power was given to him to continue forty two months and all who dwell on earth will worship him, whose names are not written in the book of life of the Lamb."[19]*

Once the entire globe is ruled by an economic stranglehold and with brutal force, no nation would dare to rise up against its vicious dictator. Scholars have held an irrational fallacy that the end of this world involves all nations or kingdoms at war with each other, but the Second Advent describes a heavenly army against what's left of a savage society. Given the lack of ethics, it would seem that few if any communities will be able to keep any ample semblance of peace, but overall *"They worshiped the dragon who gave power to the beast and they worshiped the beast saying, who is like the beast? Who is able to make war with him?"[20]*

In his discourse of the last days, Jesus noted the prophets who referred to the mark of the beast *"For take heed to yourselves so that day comes not upon you unawares. As a snare it will come on all who dwell on the face of the earth."[21]* This warning of a global trap was foreseen since *"Fear and the pit and the snare are come upon you, O inhabitant of the earth. There is a bridle in the jaws of the people causing them to err. You are they who forsake the Lord, prepare a table for that troop and furnish the drink offering unto that number. He will destroy the face of the covering cast over all people, and the veil spread over all the nations."[22]*

Autocracy of the Antichrist will not happen overnight as this conversion involves restoring order from ruin, appointments of governing bodies and transfer of all business or private assets into a world bank. This period seems to occur before his forty two month reign when the Devil who is *"the dragon gave him his power, and his seat, and great authority."[23]* His seat is Rome since the great whore of the Apocalypse called Mystery Babylon *"is that great city, which reigns over the kings of the earth."* This whore is the false church that sits on a beast whose *"seven heads are seven mountains on which the woman sits."[24]* The city of seven hills is Rome.

Correlation of political evil and religious hypocrisy of the end time is in a theocracy led by Satan through his powers in the Antichrist. In homage of his demonic image, *"Every man is brutish by his knowledge: every founder is confounded by the graven image for his molten image is falsehood. They are vanity, the work of errors: in the time of their visitation they shall perish. O you who dwell on many waters, abundant in treasures, your end is come and the measure of your covetousness. Waters where the whore sits are peoples, multitudes, nations and tongues. People of the earth were made drunk by the wine of her fornication."[25]*

Physical affliction in extreme plagues of nature will be compounded by infernal clergy of the whore described as *"The Great Mother of Harlots and Abominations of the Earth arrayed in purple and scarlet color, decked with gold, precious stones and pearls having a golden cup in her hand full of abominations and filthiness of her fornication. And I saw the woman drunken*

193

with the blood of the saints and with the blood of the martyrs of Jesus."[26] People will be lining up as in an epidemic for mass vaccination of the mark of the beast and black magic worship of his image. Their choice will be survival or death causing much hardship for fugitives.

Satanism will become common while a perverted spirit of darkness covers the world, *"But draw near, you sons of the sorceress, the seed of adulterers and the whore. Are you not children of transgression, a false seed who seek comfort in idols, sacrificing children under the clefts of the rocks? They are your lot, you pour out libations, offer sacrifice to them: you set up altars to that shameful thing, even altars to burn incense to Baal. Shall not I be angry at these things?*[27] *I will cut off witchcrafts and the graven images out of the midst of you. Stand now with your sorceries and enchantments if so you may prevail. They will be as stubble.*"[28]

Visions of the Antichrist reveal a ruthless person who is so utterly insane to believe he has power over the universe with an ability to change the order of things in time itself. It is sad to ponder how anyone's pride could reach such deception for *"He will speak great words against the most high, wear out the saints and think to change times and laws. They will be given into his hand until a time, and times and half a time. He will magnify himself above every god and prosper till the wrath is fulfilled. Judgment will sit so his power is taken away, broken in pieces and perish to the end. When he finishes scattering the holy people, this will be done.*"[29]

Fidelity to truth of the gospel will require many believers to be martyred yet Jesus taught *"What will a man give in exchange for his soul? Fear not them who kill the body, but are not able to kill the soul. Fear him who is able to destroy both soul and body in hell. Whoever loses his life for my sake will save it.*"[30] The souls of them under the altar of heaven in the fifth seal of the Apocalypse are those *"who were beheaded for Jesus and the word of God, which did not worship the beast or his image, nor received his mark."* In this time *"Blessed are the dead who die in the Lord until their fellow servants are slain as they were is complete.*"[31]

Judgments of the end wrath include a mystery not explained in the prophets that is beyond conjecture since St. John *"saw a mighty angel cry as a lion roars, and seven thunders uttered their voices. Then I heard a voice say to me, Seal up those things and write them not.*"[32] These thunders may be connected to *"my two witnesses who have power to smite the earth with all plagues, as often as they will."* The ministry of these holy prophets is during the time when *"The Gentiles will tread the holy city under foot for forty two months.*"[33] This period seems to coincide with the start of turmoil against Jews before the Antichrist reigns on earth.

Who these witnesses of God are and exactly when they wreak havoc in the world present a puzzle of speculation, but the place they exert their great powers is in Jerusalem which *"the city will be taken, and half the city shall go into captivity and the rest of the people will remain in the city.*"[34] Some say these are Enoch and Elijah who *"will prophesy a thousand two hundred and threescore days. If any man desires to harm them, fire comes out of their mouth to devour their enemies."* These mighty prophets will be killed and their bodies left in the street yet *"The Spirit of life entered into them, they stood on their feet and ascended into heaven.*"[35]

Following the last trumpet that signals the third watch and military victory of the Antichrist *"the nations were angry and your wrath is come to destroy them who destroy the earth."* This fury is contained in a succession of penalties specified as *"seven golden vials full of the wrath of God."* These distinct seven plagues were given to seven angels who were instructed to *"Go your ways and pour out the vials of wrath of God upon the earth.*"[36] Many people who are left will suffer and die in this sequence of afflictions which leads to devastation of Rome and to the final battle of Armageddon. An evil society will come to its end and damnation.

Timing of the first vial appears to be after the empire and false church of Antichrist are put in place as the first angel *"went and poured out his vial upon the earth, and there fell a sore and grievous wound upon the men who had the mark of the beast and upon them who worship his image."³⁷* It is merely guesswork to attempt any scientific reasons for all of the various terrors in the seven vials. Other than an infectious disease, the first vial's painful sore may be an allergic reaction to the mark which likely is a kind of computer chip to be implanted in the right hand or forehead with a scan number used in credit or debit cards in order to buy or sell.

Outcomes of the second and third vials are very similar because these extensive disasters are directed against a primary source of human life. Putrid results reflect equity in divine justice while *"The second angel poured out his vial upon the sea, it became blood as of a dead man and every live thing in the sea died. And the third angel poured out his vial upon rivers and founts of waters and they became blood."* Atmospheric anomalies or residual radioactive fallout could account for these strange events, but *"You are just O Lord because they have shed the blood of saints and prophets so you gave them blood to drink. They deserve it."³⁸*

Environmental calamities will cause extraordinary misery as awesome conditions still get even worse. Dreadful harm of solar power will occur when *"the forth angel poured out his vial upon the sun and mankind was scorched with fire and great heat. They blasphemed the name of God and did not repent to give him glory."³⁹* This sign is probably a consequence of ozone layer disruptions in the sky or sunbursts of immense solar flares since *"the light of the moon will be as the sun, and the light of the sun will be sevenfold as the light of seven days in the day the Lord binds up the breach of his people and heals the stroke of their wound."⁴⁰*

It seems inconceivable to grasp the intensity of heat in weather multiplied by seven times its normal temperature. Countless living creatures will obviously die from exhaustion and sunburn while adequate shelter will be nearly impossible to find. Despite all of the severe chastisement, obstinacy of an evil society will continue as *"The fifth angel poured out his vial upon the seat of the beast and his kingdom became dark. They gnawed their tongues for pain and blasphemed God of heaven because of their pain and sores, and they repented not of their deeds."⁴¹* Polluted dust storms and volcanoes will likely arise to choke with a poisonous effect.

A momentous event will transpire to prepare an army of the Antichrist against the heavenly host of the Lord at the Second Advent. This is an intervening phase of ghastly demonic forces to assemble evil troops to final judgment for *"The sixth angel poured out his vial on the great river Euphrates and the water was dried up to make a way for kings of the east. Three unclean spirits like frogs came out of the mouths of the dragon, of the beast and of the false prophet as they are spirits of devils working signs which go forth to kings of the whole earth to gather them to the place called Armageddon for battle on the great day of God Almighty."⁴²*

Complete demise of the Antichrist's kingdom will happen as Jesus triumphs with his angels and saints, yet the plagues of divine wrath will severely disrupt mortal life to the point of near extinction. Before the last battle, *"The seventh angel poured out his vial into the air and there was a great earthquake such as was not since men were on the earth. Cities of the nations fell, every island fled away, the mountains were not found, there fell upon men great hail about the weight of a talent, the great city was split into three parts and Babylon came in remembrance to give her fierce wrath. Men blasphemed God for the exceeding great hail."⁴³*

Exceptional power of an earthquake and weird thunderstorms unlike any time in history will level cities, sink islands and crumble mountains. Of Rome, *"Babylon the great has fallen, she is fallen. Her sins reached into heaven, and the Lord has punished her iniquities for she says, I sit as a queen and shall see no sorrow. Kings will bewail when they see the smoke of her burning for no man buys her merchandise any more saying Woe, woe to the great city wherein all the ships were made rich out of her wealth. In one hour she is made desolate. An angel cast a great stone into the sea saying thus will the city Babylon be thrown down and found no more."*[44]

Mass confusion will spread in the world at the ruin of Rome since it will become the center of banking, trade and idolatry. There is a resemblance to prophecies about demolition of the city of Tyre, but Rome's plagues are not due to human warfare. Its iniquity and murder of the faithful or others spans the globe, *"For strong is the Lord who judges her. Your merchants were great men of the earth, by your sorcery all the nations have been led astray. In her was found blood of the prophets and of saints, and of all who have been slain upon the earth. You will be visited with thunder, earthquake, storm, tempest and flame of devouring fire."*[45]

Prophets affirm predictions in the Apocalypse of a violent and sudden fall of Rome to *"Come down and sit in the dust, O daughter of Babylon: there is no throne, daughter of the Chaldeans. Your shame will be seen so sit silent and go into darkness for you will no more be called, The Lady of the Kingdoms. When the wall is fallen, I will rend it with a stormy wind and overflowing shower and great hailstones in my fury to consume it. The wall is no more, neither they who daubed it."*[46] A huge earthquake and hail of an ancient talent near 120 pounds is clear as *"The hail will sweep away the refuge of lies and waters will overflow the hiding place."*[47]

No expert can estimate the massive scale of a tremor in the earth that will reduce cities to rubble, flatten mountains, swallow islands into the sea and to Rome *"How is Sheshach taken and how is the praise of the earth surprised? How is Babylon become an astonishment among the nations? The sea is come upon Babylon, she is covered with the waves thereof. Her cities are desolate, a dry land and a wilderness wherein no man dwells. The nations shall no longer flow together to him. I have heard from the Lord God of host a consumption, even determined upon the whole earth. I will lay judgment to the line and justice to the plummet."*[48]

Extinction of Rome and annihilation of cities on our planet will expose the useless vanity of a blind empire in denial of God and his word. Curses will devastate this demonic society since *"Every purpose of the Lord will be performed against Babylon to make the land a desolation without inhabitant. At the noise of the taking of Babylon, the earth is moved and the cry heard among the nations. A drought is upon her waters, they are dried up for it is the land of graven images and they are mad upon their idols. I will kindle a fire in his cities, it will devour all round about him. Babylon will become heaps, an astonishment and a hissing."*[49]

Stunning surprise is a continuing factor for most of the public who go through the separate stages in the gospel yet to come upon humanity. Although signs of our times will be preached in the world, people tend to dismiss them as far off while they go about their business without turning to the church in fidelity to God. This stubborn ignorance is evident for *"The day of the Lord comes as a thief in the night. You trusted in wickedness and your wisdom and knowledge perverted you. Babylon will be utterly broken, her high gates burnt with fire, the nations will go into the fire and perish. Evil will come upon you and desolation suddenly."*[50]

Divine wrath of the seven vials consists of terrors beyond human control so that those who follow evil will know these maladies are from God yet persist in blasphemy. Great fires caused by heat of the sun and by lightning strikes of incredible storms on drought stricken lands will be surpassed by melting light of Christ in his glory so *"the heavens and earth that are now have been reserved unto fire against the day of judgment and perdition of ungodly men. These are the days of vengeance for all things that are written will be fulfilled. I will avenge and no man can resist me, our redeemer the Lord of hosts and Holy One of Israel is his name."*[51]

Lunacy is a term usually made in reference to psychic pathology, but this madness in idol worship and demonism is not genetic. There is a simple answer to these faults as *"This is the condemnation that men loved darkness rather than light, nor came to the light lest their deeds would be reproved. Woe to them who are wise in their own eyes and prudent in their own sight. The light shines in the darkness, and darkness conquered it not."[52]* The issue of iniquity is our own choice and *"They who make graven images are their own witnesses. All will be ashamed, stand in fear and be confounded who pray that it deliver me for you are my god."[53]*

Comparison of inanimate things formed as idols to the craftsmen who make and venerate them is a suitable truth which incriminates those who share this vanity since *"They who make them are like unto them, so is everyone who trusts in them. They have mouths but speak not, eyes but see not, ears but hear not, noses but smell not, hands but feel not and feet but walk not."[54]* It is senseless and bane to deny the true God and believe physical objects are gods, but *"Fools despise wisdom and instruction. A fools mouth is his destruction and his lips the snare of his soul. The folly of fools is deceit and the thought of foolishness is sin."[55]*

Spiritual bondage to covetous vices fosters an impervious heart that becomes a castaway of perdition. Jesus warned *"You are from beneath, I am from above: you are of this world, I am not of this world. If you believe not that I am he, you will die in your sins. He who sent me is with me, the Father has not left me alone."[56]* The prophets asked about the end wrath *"Who can stand before his indignation? Who can abide in the fierceness of his anger? Preaching of the cross is foolishness to them who perish, but unto us who are saved it is the power of God. I dwell in the high and holy place, with them also who are of contrite and humble spirit."[57]*

Scripture supports the concept of an underground church for faithful who manage to hide from hatred and survive curses for *"The Lord is good, a stronghold in the day of trouble and he knows them who trust in him. You have been a strength to the poor, a defense to the needy in his distress, a refuge from the tempest, a shadow from the heat when the blast of the terrible ones is as a storm against the wall."[58]* They will rejoice because of *"The voice of them who flee and escape out of Babylon to declare vengeance of God, revenge of his temple to destroy her utterly, let nothing of her be left for their day is come, the time of their visitation."[59]*

Persecution of Christians who despise the false church and reject the mark of the beast will result in wholesale slaughter due to the Antichrist's brutality who *"has crushed me, he made me an empty vessel, he filled his belly with my pleasures, he cast me out. The people of Zion will say, the violence done to me and my flesh be upon Babylon and my blood upon the inhabitants of Chaldea. Therefore the Lord said, I will plead your cause and avenge you. As Babylon has caused the slain of Israel, so at Babylon will fall the slain of all the earth. You who escaped the sword: remember the Lord afar off, let Jerusalem come into your mind."[60]*

Moses told about the amends of his people during their captivity into a new kingdom not yet come as *"The Lord will bring you unto a nation which neither you nor your fathers have known, and there you will serve other gods of wood and stone. You will become a byword since they forsook the covenant of the Lord God of their fathers. When all these things come to pass, you will call them to mind among all the heathen, return to the Lord your God and obey his voice so then he will have compassion on you, gather you from all the peoples to the land of your fathers and you will possess it. He will do you good and multiply you above your fathers."[61]*

Predictions of the last days describe how the Antichrist will rise to world power, but then be confronted by God's wrath and judgment. In this time, *"The end is come upon my people Israel. I will make you pass with your enemies into a land which you know not. As you have forsaken me and served strange gods in your land, so will you serve strangers in a land that is not your own. In those days I will not make a full end of you. I will leave you a remnant who escape the sword when you are scattered through the countries. Those who escape will remember me, loathe themselves and know I am the Lord who said I would do this evil to them."*[62]

After rebuking the Jewish leaders who crucified him due to envy, Jesus foretold them of their final captivity and his coming in glory to establish the new covenant. He reminded them that *"the stone which the builders rejected has become the head of the corner. He who falls on this stone will be broken in pieces, and upon whomever it falls it will grind him to powder. The kingdom of God will be taken from you and given to a people yielding the fruits thereof. Behold, your house is left desolate. These things shall come upon this generation for I say you will not see me again until you say, Blessed is he who comes in the name of the Lord."*[63]

Challenges facing the church by an oppressive secular society and loss of faith by those who claim to be Christians are causing many who follow divine law to seek answers to this situation. Traditional values are being disputed not only by those who no longer honor the Sabbath, but among some of the clergy, religious and laity. The holy sacrament of penance has become a forgotten issue for people who fail to be honest about their sins. Our mission to make disciples has stagnated by substituting other priorities and ineffective programs. Resources need to be spent on God's temple in human hearts instead of modern buildings with empty pews.

In order to be serious and succeed in delivering the gospel it must be preached in its entirety as Jesus taught *"not one jot or one title will be lost from the law until all things have been done. Everything must be fulfilled which is written in the law of Moses and the prophets and in the psalms."*[64] Whether we choose to accept or deny the divine word in both blessings and curses does not change its effect, but *"If the Son shall make you free, you will be free indeed. Continue in my word, and then you will be my disciples indeed."*[65] Be not intimidated as *"we are not them who draw back unto perdition, but them who believe to saving of the soul."*[66]

St. Peter became an avid scribe in Scripture who admonished us to be mindful of the words of the prophets and teachings of the apostles. Like his brethren he was concerned and wrote about the end of this present world, but said *"The Lord is not slack concerning his promise. We look for new heavens and a new earth wherein justice dwells. The end of all things is at hand: be therefore sober and watch in prayer, knowing this first that in the last days there will come scoffers walking after their own lusts."*[67] The conclusive end yet new dawn for our human race at the Second Advent in the battle of Armageddon is explained in the next chapter.

---

[1] Revelation 9,20-21
[2] II Thessalonians 2,8-12
[3] Isaiah 6,11-12
[4] Joel 2,11
[5] Jeremiah 10,10-12
[6] Isaiah 26,9
[7] Ephesians 4,17-24; II Peter 2,18-19
[8] Proverbs 27,20; Titus 1,15-16
[9] Proverbs 3,7; 15,24; Romans 8,5-8; 12,16
[10] Romans 1,18-28
[11] Isaiah 46,5-10
[12] Isaiah 44,24-25; Habakkuk 2,18-20
[13] Exodus 20,1-5; 31,18; 34,1; Leviticus 19,2-4; 26,1
[14] Psalm 4,2; Jeremiah 2,26-28; Zephaniah 3,5
[15] Isaiah 29,10; 41,28-29; 42,17; 59,4; Jeremiah 4,22

[16] Isaiah 48,3-7; Jeremiah 51,7&47; Nahum 1,2
[17] Revelation 13,11-18
[18] Revelation 14,9-11
[19] Revelation 13,5-8
[20] Revelation 13,4
[21] Luke 21,34-36
[22] Isaiah 24,17-18; 25,7; 30,27-28; 65,11
[23] Revelation 13,2
[24] Revelation 17,3-5&9&18
[25] Jeremiah 51,13&17-18; Revelation 17,1-2&15
[26] Revelation 17,4-6
[27] Isaiah 57,3-7; Jeremiah 5,7-9; 11,13
[28] Isaiah 47,10-14; Micah 5,12-13
[29] Daniel 7,25-26; 11,36; 12,7
[30] Mathew 10,28; 16,25; Mark 8,34-38
[31] Revelation 6,9-11; 14,12-13; 20,4
[32] Revelation 10,1-5
[33] Revelation 11,2-6
[34] Zechariah 4,11-14; 14,1-2
[35] Genesis 5,24; II Kings 2,8-15; Revelation 11,3-13
[36] Revelation 11,15-18; 15,6-8; 16,1
[37] Revelation 16,2
[38] Revelation 16,3-7
[39] Revelation 16,8-9
[40] Isaiah 30,26
[41] Revelation 16,10-11
[42] Revelation 16,12-16
[43] Revelation 16,17-21
[44] Revelation 18,2-21
[45] Isaiah 29,6; Revelation 18,8-10&23-24
[46] Isaiah 47,1-5; Ezekiel 13,10-15
[47] Isaiah 28,15-17
[48] Isaiah 28,17-18&22; Jeremiah 51,41-44
[49] Jeremiah 50,32&38&46; 51,29&36-37
[50] Isaiah 47,10-14; Jeremiah 51,58; II Peter 3,10
[51] Isaiah 47,3-4; Luke 21,22; II Peter 3,7
[52] Isaiah 5,20-24; John 1,5; 3,17-21
[53] Isaiah 44,9-20
[54] Psalm 115,3-8
[55] Proverbs 1,7; 14,8; 18,7; 24,9
[56] John 8, 23-29
[57] Isaiah 57,15-21; Nahum 1,6; I Corinthians 1,18-23
[58] Nahum 1,7; Isaiah 25,2-8
[59] Jeremiah 50,25-28
[60] Jeremiah 51,33-37&49-50
[61] Deuteronomy 28,36-37; 29,22-27; 30,1-7
[62] Jeremiah 5,18-22; 15,14; Ezekiel 6,8-10; Amos 8,2
[63] Mathew 21,42-44; 23,32-39
[64] Mathew 5,18; Luke 24,44
[65] John 8,31-36
[66] Hebrews 10,35-39
[67] Acts 6,4; I Peter 4,7; II Peter 3,1-13

Chapter Nine
OPENING OF THE SIXTH SEAL
SECOND ADVENT

"When he opened the sixth seal there was a great earthquake, the sun grew dark and the moon as blood. Stars of heaven fell to earth, every mountain and island were moved out of their place. The great day of God Almighty and wrath of the Lamb is come, and who will be able to stand?   Revelation 6,12-17

Discernment of the divine plan stems from the beginning when God created Adam and Eve of whom the whole human race descended. Death came to all of us since they ate fruit from the forbidden tree of knowledge of good and evil, but enmity between spiritual seed of Our Lady and Satan's seed as well as the triumph of salvation were then foretold.[1] Many details about the Second Advent are explained in Scripture and the promises made to Abraham form a firm basis for jubilant hope in prophecy. These ancient oaths pertain to an everlasting covenant through his seed in Christ and a border of permanent land to his seed in the Hebrews.[2]

Many scholars do not comprehend the fullness in meaning for forgiveness of sins, nor are they concerned with the thought of a new dawn of peace on earth centered in Jerusalem with a holy Jewish nation whose leading example is in the life of Christ. The end of the world is not a total extermination of mankind or some kind of explosive big bang theory where the heavens and the earth disintegrate. Our universe is here to stay and there are multiple citations in the divine word that reflect this real theme of harmony between all nations and their Creator. We must recognize the truth of our Messiah coming in glory to reign in God's kingdom.

Issues of atonement involve our fidelity to the church and resurrection into eternal life, but some have forgotten the blessing for humanity clearly expressed by prophets of old and by the gospel. The Lord's purpose in judgment is to conquer evil as "*The Son of man will send forth his angels. They shall gather all things that offend with those who do iniquity and cast them into a furnace of fire. Then the just will shine forth like the sun in the kingdom of their father. So at the end of the world, the angels will sever the wicked from among the just. Let the heavens rejoice and the earth be glad: The Lord is king, he made the world firm not to be moved.*"[3]

Teachings of Jesus show the prospect for global society to reach lasting peace since "*Blessed are the meek for they shall inherit the earth. When the Son of man comes in his glory, he will sit on his throne and before him will be gathered all nations. He shall set the sheep on his right hand, but the goats on his left. The king will say to them on his right: Come you blessed of my Father, inherit the kingdom prepared for you from the foundation of the world. Then he will say to them on his left: You cursed, depart from me into eternal fire prepared for the devil and his angels. I am not come to destroy the law or the prophets, but I am come to fulfill.*"[4]

When Jesus was judged to be crucified, Pilate asked him if he was king of the Jews. He said "*My kingdom is not of this world. My servants would fight so I would not be delivered to the Jews, but now is my kingdom not from hence. You say I am a king. To this end I was born and for this cause I came into the world that I should bear witness to the truth.*"[5] Christ declared his heavenly kingdom and since he had to die for our sins to rule on earth, his reply was this reign had not now yet come until the end. He told the head priest he is the Christ "*and you will see the Son of man sitting on the right hand of power, coming in the clouds of heaven.*"[6]

Concept of a world without corruption and bloodshed where people follow divine law in the new covenant of Christ permeates Scripture so it is hard to consider how anyone could reason otherwise. We must look at the bulk of evidence which clearly shows the gates of hell will not ultimately prevail against the faithful *"to make all men see the mystery hid in God, unto him be glory in the church by Christ Jesus, throughout all ages, world without end."*[7] In that enduring time *"God arose to save all the meek of the earth. Evildoers will be cut off, but they who wait on the Lord will inherit the earth forever and delight in the abundance of peace."*[8]

Simple truths are written about a common bond of faith to unite mankind in divine love *"so the Lord God will cause justice and praise to come forth before all nations. You have forgiven the iniquity of your people, taken away all your wrath and truth will spring out of the earth."*[9] How can we ignore what the apostles taught of God's design to *"gather together in one all things in Christ, both which are in heaven and are on earth, even in him far above all power, principality, and name that is named not only in this world, but also in that which is to come, head over all things to the church that is his body, the fullness of him who fills all in all."*[10]

These statements are obvious to understand and they do not vary in content or limit in time. General scope of promise in Christ is with God in heaven, but we must grasp conversion of the whole world to him *"For it pleased the Father that in him should all fullness dwell through the blood of his cross to reconcile all things unto himself whether they be in earth or things in heaven. Oh Lord my God, who laid the foundations of the earth not to be removed forever: you send forth your spirit and renew the face of earth. Your glory will endure forever and you will rejoice in your works. Let the sinners be consumed and the wicked be no more."*[11]

An overall transformation of lifestyle in obedience to church doctrine and its sacraments will occur for Gentiles and Jews alike because *"All nations whom you have made shall come and worship before you, O Lord, and glorify your name. Jesus is the propitiation for our sins and not for us only, but for the sins of the whole world. Your seed I will establish forever and build your throne to all generations. The heavens shall praise your wonders and your faithfulness also in the congregation of the saints. As for the world and the fullness thereof, you have founded them. Justice and judgment are of your throne; mercy and truth go before your face."*[12]

Future generations will see the day when divine order and blessing are accomplished in the earth. This world to come is a radical change from what we have known and drastic measures will take place to form it *"when the Lord Jesus will be revealed from heaven with his mighty angels in flaming fire taking vengeance on them who know not God and obey not the gospel of our Christ. They will be punished with eternal destruction from the presence of the Lord and glory of his power. As wax melts before fire so let the wicked perish, but let the just be glad. He will be glorified in his saints and admired in all who believe in that day."*[13]

After Jesus appeared to many for forty days after the passion and ate food with his disciples in his new body risen from the dead, the apostles surely knew his preaching about resurrection from the dead. Yet why did they still ask him at his ascension into heaven, *"Lord will you at this time restore again the kingdom to Israel?"*[14] He did not deny this ancient vow, but instead replied the Father has put these times and seasons in his own power as *"Who is a God like unto you who pardons iniquity and passes by the transgression of the remnant of his heritage? He will cast their sins into the sea and perform the truth to Jacob sworn to our fathers of old."*[15]

Believers have assurance of endless life and also earthly inheritance knowing *"The Lord said to my Lord, Sit you at my right hand until I make your enemies your footstool. Unto the angels he has not put in subjection the world to come, whereof we speak. But now we see not yet all things put under his feet. God created the earth not in vain: he established it and formed it to be inhabited. Draw near you who are escaped of the nations. Look to me and be saved all the ends of the earth. Israel will be saved in the Lord with everlasting salvation world without end. Unto me every knee will bow, every tongue confess. All who resist will be ashamed."*[16]

Annihilation of human life on our planet would happen from mass destruction of nuclear wars and very extreme calamities in the order of nature, but Jesus explicitly taught *"except the Lord had shortened those days no flesh would be saved. But for the elect's sake whom he has chosen, he has shortened those days."*[17] These elect are the remnant of people who somehow evade the Antichrist and survive God's wrath for *"she shall be multiplied that was left in the midst of the earth. Then shall still be a tenth therein and they who shall stand therein will be a holy seed. The earth shall be full of the knowledge of the Lord as the waters cover the sea."*[18]

Exactly how many of this holy seed will inherit a new world is a mystery since the ten percent of global population may apply to those who enter and outlive the end wrath rather than the present total. Let us not confuse the truth of Jesus saying *"Heaven and earth will pass away, but my words will not pass away."*[19] He did not mean our physical reality will suddenly vanish, but referred to *"When the people are gathered together and the kingdoms to serve the Lord. Of old you laid the foundation of earth and work of the heavens. They shall perish, but as a vesture they will be changed. Your servants will abide and their seed continue before you."*[20]

Sorrows will be turned into joy at the judgment of Christ who comes to avenge the blood of martyrs and condemn a profane society as *"Rejoice, O daughter of Zion; shout O daughter of Jerusalem: Behold, your king comes to you and the battle bow will be cut off. He will speak peace to the Gentiles and his dominion shall be from sea to sea and from rivers to the ends of the earth. In that day, I will take away the idols, false prophets and unclean spirit out of the earth. You have destroyed the wicked and put their name out forever and ever. Destructions are come to a perpetual end. All nations who forget God will be turned into hell."*[21]

Fulfillment of the divine oath to Abraham concerning his lineage by his wife Sarah is a serene pledge that involves not only the Jews but includes all races.[22] They will be united together for *"Shout unto God with a voice of triumph. The Lord is a great King over all the earth. He will subdue the nations under our feet. He will choose our inheritance for us, the excellency of Jacob whom he loved. Judgment will return to justice and the upright in heart will follow it. I will cleanse them and pardon all their iniquities. It will be to me a name of joy, a praise and an honor before all nations of the earth for all the goodness and prosperity I procure."*[23]

Salvation of the Jewish nation reflects a deep global revival for the universal church which no longer will suffer persecution so *"It is God who avenges me and delivers me from my enemies. Great deliverance he gives to his king and his seed for evermore. They shall fear him as long as the sun and the moon endure throughout all generations. All kings will fall down before him and all nations shall serve him. Let the whole earth be filled with his glory. He will swallow up death in victory, wipe away tears and he will take away the rebuke of his people from off all the earth. God has made of one blood all nations to dwell on the face of the earth."*[24]

Return of Israel from its dispersion and captivity will again take place in humble repentance to the Messiah. Of their conversion, *"They will come again from the land of the enemy. There is hope in your end that your children shall come again to their own border. The days come that as I have watched over them to pluck up, break down, destroy and afflict so I will watch over them to build and to plant. I will put my law in their hearts and be their God and they will be my people for I will forgive their iniquity and remember their sin no more. They who escape of you will loathe themselves for the evils they committed in all their abominations."*[25]

Neither passage of time nor grave apostasy of the last days can disannul God's purpose in Christ or his promise to the Hebrew people who plead *"Do not abhor us for your name's sake,* do not disgrace the throne of your glory. Remember, break not your covenant with us. For my name's sake and my praise I will refrain not to cut you off. According to their doings I judged them, but I had pity for my holy name. I do not this for your name's sake and I will sanctify my great name you have profaned among the heathen. I will gather you out of all countries and bring you into your land. Then you will be clean and walk in my statutes."[26]

No person can glory in themselves for the creature is subject to its Creator and all of us must accept the atonement of Christ for our sins. Through him we become true children of God and to his Jewish heirs "I will cause you to pass under the rod and I will bring you into the bond of the covenant. I will purge out from among you the rebels and they will not enter the land of Israel. Many days and years you will be troubled until the spirit be poured upon us from on high. My people will dwell in peace, confidence and wealthy rest forever. I will make my fury toward you to cease and establish my covenant when I am pacified for all you have done."[27]

Protection and guidance of the meek who inherit the earth is due to divine grace despite the plagues of war, persecution of the Antichrist and awesome disruptions in nature. Hope for Jews reflects this help since "The people who were left from the sword found grace in the wilderness, even Israel, when I went to cause him to rest. Although I cast them far off, yet I will be to them a little sanctuary, gather you out of the countries and give you the land of Israel. They will come and take away all the detestable things and abominations. I will give them one heart and put a new spirit in you so they may walk in my statutes and keep my ordinances."[28]

Words of the prophets about another return of Israel from captivity are clear and consistent. Prosperity will follow judgment "As I have brought evil upon this people so will I bring upon them all the good I have promised them. I know the thoughts I think toward you of peace to give you an expected end. Again I will build you and you will be built: Shout among the chief of nations and say O Lord save the remnant of Israel. He who scattered Israel will gather him and keep him as a shepherd does his flock. I will bind up them who were broken. The iniquity of Israel and sins of Judah will not be found for I will pardon them who I reserve."[29]

Prominence of predictions in Scripture for the Jews is directed at truth in the divine word and revelation of Christ the Messiah in our hearts to bring joy for mankind. Unto their conversion, "the number of the children of Israel will be as the sand of the sea and where it was said to them, you are not my people there it will be said to them you are the sons of the living God. In that day I will break the sword and battle out of the earth and I will betroth you to me forever in faithfulness. I will make a new covenant, not according to the covenant with their fathers. They will all know me and I will have mercy on her who had not obtained mercy."[30]

Deliverance of the tribes of Jacob is an eminent prophecy which marks a new spiritual era to unite all diverse beliefs for "If you return, O Israel, return to me and then you will not remove. You will swear that The Lord lives in truth, in judgment and in sanctity. The nations shall bless themselves in him and in him will they glory. As the new heavens and new earth shall remain before me so will your seed and your name remain. It will come to pass from one new moon to another and from one Sabbath to another that all flesh will come to worship before me. Nation will not lift up a sword against nation, nor will they learn war any more."[31]

Lessons of the bible plainly indicate the good fortune of a remnant of people who survive to rebuild society in keeping with divine law. The Antichrist's kingdom will be destroyed so "The Lord will set his hand again the second time to recover the remnant of his people and gather them from the four corners of the earth. They shall come out of the land of the north to the land I gave for an inheritance to your fathers. It will no more be said The Lord lives who brought

Israel out of Egypt, but The Lord lives who brought them from the land of the north and from all the lands he had driven them. I will place salvation in Zion for Israel my glory."[32]

There is no mistake about growing apostasy that will turn into apocalyptic wars and divine wrath. It seems impossible to grasp the devastation to yet occur, but *"In the day I cleansed you from all your iniquities, I will also cause you to dwell in the cities and the waste places will be built. They shall say this land that was desolate is become like the Garden of Eden. I will settle you after your old estates and do better to you than at the beginning. The land will be tilled and I will multiply fruit of the tree, increase of the field and lay no more famine upon you. I will turn to you. Nations who are left will know I the Lord have spoken and done it."[33]*

Moses foretold the Lord would choose a place of worship for his name to dwell and it was revealed to King David where this temple would be built in Jerusalem.[34] Of this timeless vision *"the city will be built on her own heap and the palace shall remain after the manner thereof. Your eyes will see Jerusalem a quiet habitation, a tabernacle that cannot be taken down. None of the stakes shall ever be removed, nor any of its cords broken. You will be inhabited, the cities of Judah built and I will raise up the desolate places. People will cast out their graven images as a menstrual cloth. Judah will be saved and Jerusalem will dwell safely."[35]*

Although Jerusalem will be the center of conflict in world wars, this chosen city is destined to become the dominant place of divine glory as at this hollowed location *"It will come to pass in the last days, the mountain of the Lord's house will be established in the top of the mountains exalted above the hills and all nations will flow unto it. Out of Zion will go forth the law and the word of the Lord from Jerusalem. In my holy mountain there shall all the house of Israel in the land serve me. They will call Jerusalem the throne of the Lord and not walk after perversity of their evil heart. The Lord is our judge, our lawgiver, our king: he will save us."[36]*

Our spiritual condition relates to the hope of resurrection in a heavenly body which has not yet come, but the physical reality of prophecy is meant to be interpreted literally rather than a figurative sense. We should examine our theology and motives in these errors which ignore explicit judgments of the end times as ancient history and deal with corporeal issues in awry thought. Do we have the courage and wisdom to preach *"the Lord will inherit Judah his portion in the holy land and choose Jerusalem again. Many nations shall be joined to the Lord in that day for behold I come. They shall be my people and I will dwell in the midst of them?"[37]*

How can anyone refute decisive instructions of the divine word that agree in content about the coming of God's kingdom in perpetual obedience to his new covenant in Christ? This plan of inclusive sanctity in his Eucharistic reign is repeatedly manifest as *"You, O Lord, will endure forever and your remembrance to all generations. The nations will fear the name of the Lord and all kings of the earth your splendor when he appears in his glory. He built his sanctuary like high places, like the earth he established forever. Come into his courts, worship the Lord in the majesty of his holiness. All the earth fear before him, he comes to judge the earth."[38]*

In allegory to Christ rising from the dead after his passion, the church will experience a universal rebirth after its harsh times of purification and chastisement because *"The Lord will consume all the gods of the earth and men shall adore him, everyone from his own place even all the isles of the Gentiles. Therefore wait you upon me until the day I rise up to the prey for my judgment is to assemble the nations and gather the kingdoms to pour upon them my anger and fierce wrath for all the earth will be devoured in the fire of my jealousy. Then I will turn to the people a pure lip that they all may call on the Lord and serve him with one consent."[39]*

Much of prophecy pertains to the salvation and land inheritance of the Jews since God will be glorified in them according to his word. They will repent of iniquity to know the Lord as their

204

Savior in his spirit and Eucharistic presence for *"in mercy shall the throne be established and he will sit upon it in truth in the tabernacle of David. They shall say no more, the ark of the covenant of the Lord nor will it come to mind. I will make them one nation in the land upon the mountains of Israel and I will set my sanctuary in the midst of them for evermore. My tabernacle also will be with them and the nations will know I am the Lord who sanctifies Israel."*[40]

The true tabernacle and ordinance of divine service was established by Jesus at the Last Supper after which he as high priest in heaven consecrates through the clergy. This sacrifice in the Liturgy of the Mass is an eternal sacrament for the forgiveness of sins and Jews along with all humanity will partake in this sacred homage when *"The Lord reigns, let the earth be glad. Rejoice in the Lord, all you saints, and give thanks at the remembrance of his holiness. The desire of our soul is to your name and to the remembrance of you. From the end of the earth I will cry to you. I will abide in your tabernacle forever so I may daily perform my vows."*[41]

Reverence to the Ark of the Covenant is a prelusive sign of the Eucharistic tabernacle where Christ's spirit dwells in the living manna. He is the bread of life and path of divine law as we commune with him in obedience to the Sabbath. Of the Messiah, *"Your throne is established of old, you are from everlasting. Holiness becomes your house, O Lord, forever. The law made nothing perfect but a bringing in of a better hope did by which we draw near to God. Christ entered into heaven itself in the presence of God for us, a minister of the sanctuary and true tabernacle. Enter into the holiest consecrated for us through the veil that is his flesh."*[42]

For believers throughout the world, Jerusalem will be a saintly place of veneration in one true faith and Jews seen as a holy chosen people *"for in my wrath I smote you, but in my favor I had mercy on you. The nation and kingdom that will not serve you will perish and I will make the place of my feet glorious. I will make you an eternal excellency, a joy of many generations and they will call you the city of the Lord, The Zion of the Holy One of Israel. Your people will all be righteous: they will inherit the land forever, the branch of my planting, the work of my hands that I may be glorified. You will call your walls Salvation and your gates Praise."*[43]

Distinct parallel between the permanent renewal of Jewish society and restoring of the church reveals Christianity will remain in the hearts of mankind where *"I will raise up the tabernacle of David that is fallen and raise up his ruins. I will plant them upon their land and they will no more be pulled out of the land I have given them. Then I will sprinkle clean water upon you, cleanse you and put my spirit within you. He who blesses himself in the earth will swear by the God of truth. Behold, I create new heavens and a new earth. The former troubles will not be remembered, but rejoice forever for I create Jerusalem a rejoicing and her people a joy."*[44]

Repetition in quotes about divine promise provides solid evidence for the victory of Jesus as a fact of theology we need to study and accept. We should realize that envy has no place in our service to him and his favor to Jews reflects his mercy to all who obey the gospel as *"they will build the old wastes, they shall raise up the former desolations and repair the ruined cities. Men shall call you Ministers of our God and Priests of the Lord. I will direct their work in truth. You will eat the riches of the Gentiles and in their glory you will boast yourselves. Their seed and their offspring shall be known among Gentiles which seed the Lord has blessed."*[45]

Conditions for peace in the Holy Land will come to pass once the Jews believe in Jesus and *"David my servant will be king over them. They shall walk in my law, observe my customs and do them. I will make a covenant of peace with them and showers of benefits. The field will yield its fruit and the earth its increase. Again it shall be heard the voice of joy and of praise into the house of the Lord. Old men and women will dwell in the streets and the city will be full of boys and girls playing therein. As you were a curse among the Gentiles, you will be a blessing. Many peoples and strong nations will come to seek and entreat the Lord in Jerusalem."*[46]

Oppression, wars and falsehood will cease when divine grace is poured out upon all people to follow Jesus and his love in fellowship with the living God. His favor will result in long life, peace and prosperity. Humanity will obtain a new dominion *"for as the days of a tree are the days of my people and my elect will long enjoy the work of their hands. The wolf will dwell with the lamb and the leopard lie down with the goat. The calf, lion and sheep will abide together while a little child leads them. The cow and bear will feed together and the lion will eat straw like an ox. A baby child will play on and put his hand in the hole of the viper."*[47]

These visions of prophecy are not an illusion, nor something we can shun off as the past. We have never experienced the great hope of the bible where even animals rest together without harm, but *"When the Lord has purged the blood of Jerusalem by the spirit of judgment and by the spirit of burning, he who is left in Zion written among the living will be called holy. The branch of the Lord shall be glorious and the earth's fruit be excellent for them who are escaped of Israel. His judgments are in all the earth. He remembered his covenant forever, the word ordered to a thousand generations. I will perform the good thing that I promised."*[48]

Divine mercy on the Jewish nation as a chosen race is not due to moral superiority or any other merit above others, but their amends with God as disciples of Christ will earn them global respect. It is for his glory to finish the work of salvation in his oath when *"The daughter of Zion is left as a city laid waste. Your country is desolate, your cities are burned with fire. Except the Lord had left us a very small remnant, we would be as Sodom and Gomorrah. I do this not for your sakes: be ashamed and confounded for your own ways. Jerusalem will be called a city of truth. The cities will be filled with men as the holy flock who know I am the Lord."*[49]

In order to comprehend the full extent and phase of end wrath, physical plagues of the sixth seal must be separated from the former seven vial woes. These extraordinary events are final signs before Christ comes in glory to judge the wicked and all demonic angels into damnation. This framework exposes a rational sequence of curses in the prior five seals of the Apocalypse that relate to the gospel since all prophecies of the last days end with the great day of Almighty God. The sixth seal is not an aberration misplaced in context, but it shows the inclusive nature of opening each seal and its disasters will astound those who survive other afflictions.

Before the battle of Armageddon when spirits of devils actually bring kings of the earth to a vain revolt against Christ, a mighty earthquake and great hail from a hurricane such as never seen appears in the seventh vial curse. These disruptions will cause terrible global disasters of crumbling buildings, violent seas and flooding. At that time the Antichrist's throne in Rome will come to complete ruin, but in the sixth seal it seems another earthquake will occur along with untold wonders in the heavens and earth that will literally move mountains and islands out of their place.[50] Affairs connected with the Second Advent reveal the omnipotence of God.

Fright, misery and death will overcome most of the human race as it passes through stages of growing apostasy and divine retribution, but beyond all these incredible things Jesus taught *"after the tribulation of those days, the sun will be dark and the moon won't give her light. The stars of heaven will fall and the powers of heaven will be shaken. Then they will see the Son of man coming in the clouds with great power and glory."*[51] In that time, *"The Lord alone will be exalted and he shall utterly abolish the idols. They will go into the holes of the rocks and caves of the earth for fear of his majesty when he arises to shake terribly the earth."*[52]

Scientists have observed many asteroids in our solar system and warned about the extreme impact of even smaller ones hitting the earth, but when many smash *"The day of the Lord comes to lay the land desolate and he will destroy the sinners out of it. I will punish the world for their evil and cause the arrogance of the proud to cease. Thus, I will shake the heavens and the earth will remove out of her place. For the windows from on high are open and the foundations of the earth do shake. The earth is utterly broken down, crushed, dissolved and moved exceedingly. It will reel to and fro like a drunkard. Great iniquity will fall and not rise again."*[53]

Obstinate blasphemy, idolatry and all sorts of evil will persist in the public despite dreadful results of their sins, yet their rebellion will turn into despair *"For the wrath of the Lord is upon all nations and his fury upon their armies. He has utterly destroyed them and the mountains will be melted with their blood. All the host of heaven shall be dissolved and the heavens rolled together as a scroll. All their host will fall down as a leaf off the vine and fig from a tree. In that day men shall cast their idols of silver and gold they made to moles and to the bats."*[54] The host of heaven dissolved refers to evil angels while stars are the heavens' host falling to earth.

Some verses of prophecy must be examined closely because a cursory reading often reflects error in interpretation. We must look below the surface or mere appearance to understand the real meaning. It would seem at first glance both the heavens and earth will completely burn up physically since St. Peter knew *"the heavens shall pass away with great noise and the elements melt with fervent heat. The earth and the works that are therein shall be burned up."*[55] Darkness will cover the heavens and violent explosions from falling stars will cause global fires, but the light of Christ will burn all the wicked people and demons into damnation.

Precisely why physics will be affected to create a sky which seems unreal or how a sudden barrage of asteroids hit the earth are questions of speculation, but a dramatic change in the existence of things does not eliminate reality as St. Peter wrote of the day of God *"Nevertheless we look for new heavens and a new earth wherein dwells justice."*[56] Analysis needs to be made of what he indicated by elements of the heavens and works committed on earth since these terms relate to devils and to iniquity of people. Natural fire is different from the flaming fire of God's spirit in Christ and his army that dissolves evil angels and their children among men.

Supernatural power emanating from Christ, his holy angels and risen saints will destroy wicked powers in the heavens and in earth as *"His going forth is from the end of heaven and his course unto the ends of it. Nothing is hid from the heat thereof. The gods who made not the heavens and earth will perish from earth and under the heavens. The Lord shall punish the host of high ones who are on high and the kings of the earth. They will be gathered together as prisoners in the pit and shut up in the prison. The moon shall blush and the sun ashamed when the Lord reigns in Mt. Zion and Jerusalem, glorified before his ancients."*[57]

Scrutiny of St. Peter's reference to the elements of the heavens melting with fervent heat reveals he taught about devils rather than material composing the universe. The root sense of the word element translated from Greek writings is in the order, principle or rank of things. St. Paul used the same term and explained herein *"we wrestle not against flesh and blood, but against principalities, powers and rulers of darkness of this world in high places. Those who are not gods, how is it you turn again to serve the wretched elements in bondage. Beware no one spoil you by philosophy and vain deceit after human traditions and elements of the world."*[58]

The Antichrist's empire will be sorely stricken by a series of great plagues, but *"The Lord has opened his armory and brought forth the weapons of his indignation. Though Babylon should mount up to heaven and fortify the height of her strength, yet from me shall spoilers come unto her. For the Lord God of recompenses will surely requite. They will sleep a perpetual sleep and not wake. Their day is come, the time of their visitation. He will smite the earth with the rod of his mouth, with the breath of his lips he shall slay the wicked. For the terrible one is brought to nothing, the scorner is consumed and all who hasten iniquity cut off.*"[59]

While the earth is jolted off its axis and the immense force of asteroids devastate already desperate living conditions, people will realize their summons to judgment *"For behold the Lord comes out of his place to punish the inhabitants of the earth for their iniquity. Therefore you have visited them, destroyed them and made their memory to perish. The Lord brings forth the army and the power. They are extinct and quenched as tow. You suddenly hurl them down to ruin, consumed with horrors. So you will arise and despise their image. Let fire devour your enemies, you will ordain peace for us and only in you let us remember your name."*[60]

This world's end as we know it is a real conflict where heavenly forces will condemn all who are joined to the Antichrist's kingdom since *"The Lord will consume with the spirit of his mouth and shall destroy with the brightness of his coming. He touches the land and it will melt. He builds his journey in the heaven and founded his troops in the earth. I have called my mighty ones and ordered my sanctified ones in my wrath. The noise of a multitude of great people, a violent noise of kingdoms of nations gathered together. The Lord leads the host of battle who come from a far country, from the end of heaven to spoil for the Almighty."*[61]

Somewhat like strong radiation which dissolves human tissue in a form of melting, wicked people will perish from the hot light rays of Christ and his army as *"The Lord comes out of his place and will come down to tread on the high places of the earth. The mountains shall be molten and the valleys as wax before the fire. He will come with chariots like a whirlwind to render his fury and rebuke with flames of fire. I will gather all nations and tongues: they will come and see my glory. I will gather you and blow upon you in the fire of my wrath and you shall be melted in the midst. As silver is melted in the furnace, so will you be melted."*[62]

Readers may be surprised at the many verses about how judgment day happens in a battle between heaven and earth, but this is its view: *"the Lord of hosts will come down to fight for Mt. Zion. As birds flying so shall he defend Jerusalem, deliver it and preserve it. His wrath burns and his tongue as a devouring fire to sift the nations with a sieve of vanity. The heathen are in turmoil, kingdoms totter and the earth melted when he uttered his voice. Let death seize upon them and go quick into hell. You, O God, will bring them down to the pit of destruction. He burns the shields with fire and makes wars to cease unto the ends of the earth."*[63]

Mankind will never achieve peace on earth because of its selfish deficiency in vanity shown by pride, greed and hedonism. The destructive falsehood of apostasy will fail for *"The Lord will be hope of his people and strength of the children of Israel. He will roar out of Zion and utter his voice from Jerusalem. The heavens and earth will shake, the sun turned dark and the moon into blood before the great and dreadful day of the Lord come. He uttered his voice to his army, his camp is very great and strong who execute his word. When you came down as melting fire, the nations trembled at your presence, the waters boiled and mountains melted away."*[64]

Metaphors of waters and mountains apply to people who follow the great whore of the Apocalypse in satanic worship.[65] The futile denial of God in a false church has a shocking end when *"All the proud and corrupt will burn up as stubble so that it will leave them neither root nor branch. God is jealous and the Lord reserves wrath for his enemies. He will not acquit the profane for the earth burned at his presence, yea the world and all who dwell therein. This shall be the plaque how the Lord will smite the people: their flesh will consume away as they stand, their eyes consume in their holes, their tongue consume away in their mouth."*[66]

Creation itself was formed out of nothing while humans were later made out of the earth's dust endowed with souls and spirits in the image of God. Heat from the light of Christ which shines in his army is from his indestructible spirit and set apart from quantum phenomenon. Although this spiritual force can penetrate physical things, no material substance can withstand that kind of power. It is the origin of all things by God through Christ and the source of eternal life, but all beings who oppose this heavenly breath will face damnation. Despite death of our flesh, there is an unceasing second death in resurrection to an eternal lake of fire.

Since the Messiah's army will be drawn from the heavens and cover the earth, it seems odd their path is described as *"I have raised one from the north and he will come from the rising of the sun upon princes like mortar and the potter treads the clay. He gave the nations before him and made him rule over kings. Babylon is taken for out of the north comes a nation against her to make her land desolate. They are removed and none dwell therein. The Lord laid Babylon waste and desolate forever for the spoilers come to her from the north. In that time the children of Israel and Judah will come together and join the Lord in an everlasting covenant."*[67]

Armageddon will display supernatural power at Megiddo on the plain of Esdraelon in Israel. Christ's forces against the Antichrist's military are not a fairy tale of Santa Claus and his elves from the North Pole, but St. John saw *"heaven opened and behold a white horse. He who sat upon him was called Faithful and True and in justice he does judge and make war. His eyes were as a flame of fire and on his head were many crowns. His name is The Word of God and the armies of heaven followed him on white horses. Out of his mouth goes a sharp sword to smite the nations and rule them. He treads the winepress of wrath of Almighty God."*[68]

Sorceries will end upon the earth at the Second Advent when all who belong to an evil reign will be damned. Of those who attempt to fight against the Messiah, *"These will make war with the Lamb and the Lamb shall overcome them for he is the Lord of lords and King of kings. They who are with him are called, chosen and faithful. I saw the beast and kings of the earth with their armies gathered together to make war against him who sat on the horse and his army. The beast was taken with the false prophet and both cast alive into a lake of fire burning with brimstone. Their remnant were slain and all the fowls were filled with their flesh."*[69]

Imagery of a hopeless society drawn by demonic spirits in worthless defense is a drama of deception where actual weapons will be formed which logically are designed to diffuse the light of Christ. Human flesh will be melted from the brightness of his coming so it is rational to assume the instrument of warfare stated in Scripture is a type of gun to disperse this light since *"What do you image against the Lord? For they intended evil against you: they invented a mischievous device which they are unable to perform. You will make them as a fiery oven in the time of your anger. The Lord shall swallow them up and the fire will devour them."*[70]

Biblical prophecy is very explicit about judgment day affairs and thereafter for *"I know my redeemer lives and that he shall stand at the latter day upon the earth. His feet will stand in that day upon the mount of Olives over Jerusalem towards the east and the mount of Olives will be divided in the midst thereof to the east and west with a very great valley. The Lord my God shall come and all the saints with him. He will be king over all the earth and there shall be no more utter destruction, but Jerusalem will be safely inhabited. Everyone who is left of all nations will go up from year to year to worship the Lord to keep the feast of tabernacles."*[71]

Prediction of the saints coming with Christ and his holy angels to judge mandates that they be resurrected before the sentence. Those who are taken up into heaven at the third watch will be transformed with all souls who dwell there in spirit as then *"We shall not all die, but we will all be changed. In a moment, in the twinkling of an eye at the last trump, the dead shall be raised incorruptible and we will be changed."*[72] Jesus urged us to be ready when *"he will come in the*

209

second or come in the third watch. Those servants whom the lord finds watching, he shall gird himself and make them to sit down to meat and will come forth and serve them."[73]

Mystery in resurrection still awaits us, but we need to recognize no person can eat without a body. Jesus appeared to his disciples from the dead saying *"Behold my hands and my feet that it is I myself. Handle me and see for a spirit has not flesh and bones as you see I have."[74]* He ate food with them and a colossal banquet will be prepared in heaven for all who put on immortal life and make war with Christ. Thus, *"Let us be glad and rejoice, and give honor to him for the marriage supper of the Lamb is come, and his wife was arrayed in fine white linen of sanctity in the saints. Blessed are they who are called to the marriage supper of the Lamb."[75]*

The marriage supper in heaven where a solid meal will be served precedes the final battle of good and evil in a war that baffles our imagination. An innumerable company will partake in this feast with Jesus and then *"the armies of heaven followed him on white horses clothed in fine linen, white and clean. To you who fear my name shall the Son of righteousness arise with healing in his wings and you will tread down the wicked as ashes under your feet. The Lord will beautify the meek with salvation. Let the faithful exult in glory to execute vengeance on the nations and punish on them the judgment written. All the saints have this honor."[76]*

Either those who preach God will rapture the church before he plagues the world or believe the church must suffer all prophetic tribulation until the Second Advent and then taken bodily into heaven must rethink their perception. The faithful will experience times of redemption into heaven during apocalyptic wars prior to God's wrath poured out in the seven vials. Then the saints will come with Christ in glory to destroy his enemies. What Jesus taught about global wars, watches, the end and his judgment are not understood. The idea of Armageddon marking an end of time also contradicts the fullness of salvation in promises to Abraham.

Catholic scholars' mainstream thought about rapture called the parousia holds this is a single event on judgment day when resurrection will take place. How do they rectify this and explain teaching *"to increase and abound in love toward one another and all men to the end our Lord confirms your hearts in holiness before God at the coming of Christ with all the saints?"[77]* The fact that *"God has not appointed us to wrath"* does not refer to damnation but instead to terrors of the end whereof we need to *"await Jesus from heaven who delivered us from the wrath to come. You brethren are not in darkness so that day overtakes you as a thief."[78]*

We should be reminded of the times and seasons discussed in chapters of this text because they lead to incorruption of all faithful who battle evil angels and apostate people for *"Do you not know that the saints shall judge the world? Know you not that we will judge angels?"[79]* How can spirits condemn these enemies of Christ unless they have immortal bodies? The issue of a triple rapture is crucial in regard to when resurrection will occur as *"The Lord will descend with a shout, with the voice of the archangel, and with the trump of God. The dead in Christ will rise first, then we who survive will meet the Lord in the air and so be ever with the Lord."[80]*

St. Paul stated in this passage *"We say this to you by word of the Lord. Wherefore comfort one another with these words."* He was writing in agreement with other apostles whose tutor was Jesus, but the doctrine is based in Scripture. Belief in rapture is a soothing anchor of hope that builds faith in troubled times since *"Hear the word of the Lord. Your brethren who hated you and cast you out for my name's sake, he will appear to your joy and they will be ashamed: A voice of noise from the city, a voice from the temple, a voice of the Lord that renders wrath to his enemies. Come my people, enter your chambers until the indignation pass away."[81]*

Grasping the sequence of rapture is essential to signs of prophecy Jesus told about the last days. This adjacent return to deliver his loved ones from death before plagues of the end time is for the sake of his mercy and glory shown by his power, but also to prepare his army for war. We must distinguish resurrection of the third watch from the Second Advent. Thus St. Paul taught that *"Christ is risen from the dead and even so in Christ will all be made alive. But every man in his own order: Christ the first fruits, after they who are Christ's at his coming. Then comes the end when he delivers the kingdom to God with all enemies under his feet."*[82]

As we pray to God our Father for his kingdom to come on earth as it is in heaven we must realize great struggles of temptation and evil, yet hope of deliverance. Our desire for universal peace will come to pass where *"The God of heaven shall set up a kingdom that will never be destroyed and it will stand forever. I beheld until the beast was slain and his body destroyed and given to the burning flame. I saw the Son of man come with the clouds to the Ancient of days and he was given dominion so all people, nations and tongues will serve him. The saints of the most High shall take and possess the kingdom forever, even forever and ever."*[83]

God's kingdom on earth was prepared from the foundation of the world and *"all the tribes of the earth will mourn when they see the Son of man coming in the clouds of heaven with power and great glory."*[84] His triumph is with Our Lady who is Queen of Heaven and will not happen until she bears the faithful in rapture *"for as soon as Zion travailed, she brought forth her children. Shall God bring to the birth and shut the womb? He will come to me who will be ruler in Israel whose goings forth are from everlasting. He will give them up until she who travails brings forth. Then the remnant of his brethren will be converted to the children of Israel."*[85]

Hope in eternal life will be revealed at the third watch when Jesus taught those who endure until the end will be saved.[86] All souls who abide in spirit before God with the redeemed from earth will take on new bodies to avenge injustice with Christ as *"He sent from above, he took me, he drew me out of many waters. He brought me into a large place and delivered me for his judgments were before me. By my God I leaped over a wall who girded me with strength and set me on high places. You gave me the shield of salvation and teach my hands to war so my enemies were consumed as dust in the wind and cast out as dirt in the streets."*[87]

Events in Revelation of Our Lady's battle with the red dragon of atheistic Marxism that span the periods she foretold at Fatima of dreadful wars and her conquest with Christ are summed up in the words *"Now is come salvation, and strength, and the kingdom of God and the power of his Christ."*[88] These times include the watches and end wrath so *"in the days of the voice of the seventh angel when he begins to sound, the mystery of God will be finished. As he sounded the last of seven trumpets, God took great power and reigned, he gave reward to the prophets, saints and them who fear his name, and will destroy them who destroy the earth."*[89]

Reward of resurrection is when the last trumpet begins to sound since the saints will delight in the marriage supper and then help destroy evil. There is a continuing timeframe in the days of the voice of the seventh angel wherein *"the nations were angry and your wrath is come, and the time of the dead that they should be judged."*[90] We must confront the complexity that *"the Lord Jesus Christ will judge the living and dead at his appearing and his kingdom."*[91] These are two different times which apply to the start of the last trumpet and to its end when all evil souls in hell and earth will be damned forever, yet rising up from the dead of a just remnant.

The concept of our world ending with all the dead and everyone alive either being risen to immortal life or sent to torment in everlasting fire is mistaken. It is not going to happen all at once and an elect segment of humanity will remain alive to inherit Christ's kingdom. Distinction in phases between fate of the just and unjust shows *"judgment must begin at the house of God and if it first begin at us, what will be the end of them who obey not the gospel of Christ? The*

211

Lord knows how to deliver the godly out of temptations, but the heavens and earth that now exist are reserved unto fire against the day of judgment and perdition of ungodly men."[92]

Questions about syntax have a vital function in determining the grammar used in certain quotes of the bible. One such linguistic problem is evident as St. Paul wrote *"there is laid up for me a crown of justice which the Lord, the just judge, will give me at that day and not only me but unto all who love his appearing."* This coincides with the last trumpet as he taught in other epistles of resurrection at the third watch. Why then did Jesus say *"Everyone who knows the Son and believes on him has everlasting life and I will raise him up at the last day?"*[93] At denotes a fixed position in time to enter the day of end wrath rather than its completion.

Subtle words or phrases can often be confusing, but there is no disparity in revealing the real nature of inspired prophecy. The Antichrist will arise to conquer the world and during his reign God's wrath will unleash amazing terrors on earth. When Christ comes in flaming fire with his angels and saints *"He who rejects me and receives not my words, the word I have spoken will judge him in the last day."*[94] The wicked will be damned in that day, not at that day but Jesus still said *"These will go into everlasting torment, but the just into life eternal."*[95] This puzzle involves beheaded martyrs, others in heaven who die during the end and souls in purgatory.

During the cruel tyranny of the Antichrist many faithful will suffer martyrdom while other believers die from great plagues or medical and natural causes. We must consider their glorious fate in the urging to *"Fear God and give glory to him for the hour of judgment is come. If any man worship the beast and his image and receive his mark, the same will be tormented with fire and brimstone and the smoke of their torment ascends up forever and ever. Here is the patience of the saints who keep the law of God and faith in Jesus. Blessed are the dead in the Lord from henceforth. They will rest from their labors and their works do follow them."*[96]

Most inclusive of any doctrine declared by Jesus dealing with the matter of judgment states *"For as the Father raises up the dead and gives them life, even so the Son gives life to whom he will. The Father committed all judgment to the Son so all men should honor the Son even as they honor the Father. The hour is coming in which all that are in the graves will hear his voice and come forth: they who have done good unto resurrection of life and they who have done evil unto resurrection of damnation."*[97] This extensive scope includes all souls in hell, every soul of the end not yet risen in heaven and also those who remain in what the church calls purgatory.

Similar to denial of an eternal hell, even more people do not believe in purgatory. This place of temporal amends and purification of souls who die in sins not worthy of damnation was a concept originated by Jewish custom. When they fought with the Greek empire, a godly high priest found bodies of his soldiers who took forbidden idols as personal spoil. Prayers were made to the Lord *"that the sin they committed be forgiven concerning the resurrection for if he had not hoped they would rise again it would be vain to pray for the dead. He sent twelve thousand drachmas of silver to Jerusalem to be offered for the sins of the dead."*[98]

Jesus described justice of the kingdom of heaven to include confinement where guilty souls are penalized, but not in endless agony. He said *"if your brother has anything against you, go to be reconciled to your brother unless the judge cast you into prison. You will not come out from it until you pay the last penny."*[99] He also spoke of a king who nullified his servants' debt, but the servant did not have pity on those who owed him money and then *"his lord delivered him to the tormentors until he pay all he was due. So likewise my heavenly Father will do unto you if you from your hearts do not forgive everyone his brother their trespasses."*[100]

Understanding purgatory is more than theory relating to human laws of correction based on the severity of crimes, but penance of the dead for unrepentant sins within bounds of divine grace is a biblical reality for mercy. This intricate difference of heaven, purgatory and hell is manifest in instruction written about judgment day for *"many of them who sleep in the dust of the earth shall awake, some to everlasting life and some to shame and everlasting contempt."[101]* The places of the dust of the earth are unlike flesh of people who *"all are of the dust and turn to dust again. The Lord pities his children for he knows our frame that we are dust."[102]*

Variation in meaning is apparent for our mortal frame of dust and the subterranean worlds of departed spirits whereof *"at the name of Jesus every knee will bend of those in heaven, on earth and under the earth. Every tongue shall confess Jesus Christ is Lord to the glory of God the Father."[103]* With respect to hell, *"Why do the wicked live, become old and are mighty in power? They will lie down in the dust and the worms shall cover them. Their worm will not die, nor their fire be quenched."[104]* But to purgatory, *"The Lord raises up the lowly from the dust and lifts the poor out of the dunghill to seat them with the princes of his own people."[105]*

Survival of an elect remnant of the human race from the end wrath as a chosen holy seed to inherit the kingdom of God will complete his salvation in Christ. Jesus will come to avenge injustice, to resurrect spirits not yet risen and to fulfill the promise of a new heavens and new earth. It is *"at that time your people shall be saved, everyone who is found written in the book. They who are wise will shine as the brightness of the sky and they who instruct many to virtue as stars for all eternity. This is eternal life that they know the true God and Jesus Christ whom he has sent. He who believes will not be condemned, but is passed from death into life."[106]*

Tragedies of the end times result from denial of the bible as men or women seek after their lusts without guilt or fear. This shame of ignominy and falsehood is an act of choice, but God will *"shake not the earth only, but also heaven removing those things that are shaken so those things which cannot be shaken may remain whereof we receive a kingdom that will not be removed. In that day the deaf will hear the words of the book and the eyes of blind will see out of obscurity and darkness. The meek will joy in the Lord and the poor among men rejoice in the Holy One of Israel. They who erred in spirit and murmured will learn doctrine."[107]*

Blessings and curses of divine law which apply to fidelity or vanity were foretold long ago. It is sad to contemplate why people scorn the truth and deep pity to know the consequences. There is no force or reason against God who will reveal the atonement of his Son in shocking power and glory. The gospel has many facets for the creation of mankind whose future is laden with severe troubles and mysteries of hope to an end purpose of lasting peace. Moses said of his people's captivity *"When you are in tribulation, even in the latter days, if you turn and obey the Lord your God, he will not forget the covenant of your fathers he swore unto them."[108]*

Although God will accomplish his oaths to Abraham about his seed through Isaac and by his seed in Christ, how many who study the prophets see these things as reality? This patriarch is known as the father of faith since he doubted not the promise to his son Isaac when asked to offer him in sacrifice *"reasoning that God was able to raise him up even from the dead so he received him as a type."[109]* An angel told him not to kill his son who was a prefigure of Christ whom Abraham is the father of many nations by lineage and his obedience. Yet in Isaac, *"I will bless you and multiply you and in your seed shall all nations of the earth be blessed."[110]*

Migration of a small remnant of Hebrews from the lands of captivity to their homeland will again take place after the Messiah ushers in the kingdom of God as *"The days come that I will raise unto David a just branch and a king will reign, prosper and execute justice in all the earth. He will be called, The Lord Our Righteousness. They shall be my people and I will be their God that they may fear me forever for the good of them and of their children after them. I will make* an everlasting covenant with them and not turn away from them to do them good. I will rejoice over them and plant them in this land with my whole heart and with my whole soul."[111]

Ezekiel wrote in a great vision of the third Jewish temple, ministry of the priests and detailed land descriptions to heirs that "the glory of the Lord came into the house and he said to me, the place of my throne and the place of my feet. I will dwell in the midst of the children of Israel forever and my holy name the house of Israel will no more defile."[112] After all the ages of wars and deceit in history, victory of truth and love will conquer for "Bless God in the congregations, even the Lord from the fountain of Israel. Because of your temple at Jerusalem shall kings bring presents to you. Sing to God you kingdoms of earth: sing praises to the Lord."[113]

Pattern in the temple's structure revealed to the ancient King David reflects God's design of our sense in human existence. The outer and inner courts are symbols of our mortal bodies and interior souls which contain intellect along with emotion, but the middle place in the Holy of Holies is an image of our spiritual hearts whereby we can commune with divine grace. Outward appearance of the temple is not only a sign of our faculties, but it is a means of ministry since the stones of divine law in the Ark of the Covenant will be replaced by the Eucharist in Christ's tabernacle.[114] The new covenant will be established to receive the bread of life.

Scripture does not feign God's purpose in plagues of the last days. Some teachers dismiss prophecy of the restored temple in Jerusalem as a figure of the church in its present day, not a physical building which is the centerpiece of a future rebirth of faith among all nations. Like the church, this temple will rise up from its ruins. The promise of land between the Nile and Euphrates rivers was specified by Moses and by Ezekiel in sum saying "This shall be the border concerning the land of your fathers you shall inherit according to the twelve tribes of Israel. The strangers among the children of Israel will have inheritance in what tribe he sojourns."[115]

Should we not do as Abraham did when he was told an heir would still be born from his loins despite his old age or lack of children "he believed the Lord who credited it to him as justice. He staggered not at the promise of God through unbelief, but was strong in faith being persuaded that what he promised he was able to perform?"[116] We know the just live in faith by hearing the word of God. Jesus foretold "I have many things to say unto you, but you cannot bear them now. The Spirit of truth will guide you into all truth and will show you things to come. Everyone who is of the truth hears my voice."[117] Prophecy is not bound in secrecy.

Institutions of public education serve to train students in skills needed for careers to sustain their livelihood and to increase awareness of the world around them, but these things of our secular society pertain mainly to our bodies, minds or emotions "having a form of piety denying its power, ever learning yet never able to attain knowledge of truth."[118] That quest is spiritual. When St. Peter realized Jesus is the Christ, the Son of the living God he notably replied "Blessed are you for flesh and blood has not revealed this to you, but my Father in heaven. It is the spirit that gives life, the flesh profits nothing. He who is of God hears my words."[119]

Faith is an innate part of our being which enlightens our souls by means of our spirit, but we can exercise our conscious contact with God or block his path for whatever reasons we choose. No doubt seems evident that radical changes need to be made within the echelons of Christian theology and the lax obedience to discipleship of those who don't practice their faith or know not Christ as their Savior. We must see warnings of our times in which apathy prevails so "Blessed is he who reads, and they who hear the words of this prophecy and keep those things written therein. Seal not the words of the prophecy of this book for the time is at hand."[120]

True revelation of a sound mind and spirit is of divine love. This opening of the door of our hearts to Jesus is more than personal salvation for in him we are sent as he was to proclaim the

214

gospel in its entirety. Many people who cross all lines of race and religion may be startled by these writings because my presentation goes well beyond their usual mode of thought, yet *"if this counsel or work be of men, it will come to nothing. But if it be of God, you cannot stop it unless you are found to fight against God."[121]* Some have despised calls to repent in the past, but *"He who is unjust, let him be unjust still and he who is holy, let him be holy still."[122]*

Prudence advises those who are skeptical about stages of prophecy shown in prior chapters to think twice because *"Nobody pours new wine into old wineskins or the new wine will burst the skins. New wine must be put in fresh skins and both are saved. Every scribe learned in the kingdom of God brings out things new and old."[123]* Seasons of our times have not been defined, but my thesis defends ardent doctrines of the church. It is now *"in the latter days you will consider it perfectly. None of the wicked shall understand, but the wise will understand."[124]* Following topics include the seventh seal and other visions in the book of Revelation.

---

[1] Genesis 3,1-15

[2] Genesis 15,1-7&18; 17,1-7&19-21

[3] Psalm 96,10-11; Mathew 13,38-43&47-50

[4] Mathew 5,5&17; 25,31-41

[5] John 18,33-37

[6] Mark 14,60-64

[7] Ephesians 3,9&21

[8] Psalm 37,9-11&29; 76,6-9

[9] Psalm 85,2-3&10-11; Isaiah 61,11

[10] Ephesians 1,10-23

[11] Psalm 104,1-5&30-35; Colossians 1,19-20

[12] Psalm 86,9; 89,1-14; I John 2,2

[13] Psalm 68,1-3; II Thessalonians 1,7-10

[14] Acts 1,3-11

[15] Micah 7,18-20

[16] Psalm 110; Isaiah 45,16-25; Hebrews 2,1-8

[17] Mathew 24,22; Mark 13,20

[18] Isaiah 6,11-13; 11,9

[19] Mark 13,31

[20] Psalm 102,12-13&22-28

[21] Psalm 9,3-8&17-20; Zechariah 9,9-10; 13,2

[22] Genesis 15,18; 17,4-7&15-21

[23] Psalm 47,1-5; 94,14-15; Jeremiah 33,8-9

[24] Psalm 18,47-50; 72,5-19; Isaiah 25,8; Acts 17,26

[25] Jeremiah 31,16-17&28-34; Ezekiel 6,8-10

[26] Isaiah 48,9-11; Jeremiah 14,21; Ezekiel 36,17-27

[27] Isaiah 32,10-17; Ezekiel 16,42&59-63; 20,34-38

[28] Jeremiah 31,2-3; Ezekiel 11,16-21

[29] Jeremiah 29,11-14; 31,4-10; 32,42; 50,19-20

[30] Jeremiah 31,31-34; Hosea 1,10-11; 2,18-23

[31] Isaiah 66, 22-23; Jeremiah 4,1-2; Micah 4,3
[32] Isaiah 11,11-13; 46,13; Jeremiah 3,18; 16,14-15
[33] Ezekiel 36,8-15&33-38
[34] Deuteronomy 12,5-14; I Chronicles 28,2-13
[35] Isaiah 30,22; 33,20; Jeremiah 30,18; 33,16
[36] Isaiah 2,2-4; 33,22; Jeremiah 3,17; Micah 4,1-3
[37] Zechariah 2,10-13
[38] Psalm 78,65-71; 96,8-13; 102,12-16
[39] Zephaniah 2,11; 3,8-9
[40] Isaiah 16,5; Jeremiah 3,16; Ezekiel 37,21-28
[41] Psalm 30,4-6; 61,1-8; 97,1-12; Isaiah 26,8
[42] Psalm 93; Hebrews 7,19; 8,1-2; 9,24; 10,19-22
[43] Isaiah 60,10-22
[44] Isaiah 65,16-18; Ezekiel 36,25-27; Amos 9,11-15
[45] Isaiah 61,4-11
[46] Jeremiah 33,10-11; Ezekiel 37,24; Zechariah 8,3-23
[47] Isaiah 11,6-8; 65,20-25
[48] Psalm 105,6-11; Isaiah 4,1-4; Jeremiah 33,14-15
[49] Isaiah 1,7-9; Ezekiel 36,32&38; Zechariah 8,3
[50] Revelation 6,12-14; 16,14&18-21
[51] Mathew 24,29; Mark 13, 24-26; Luke 21,26-27
[52] Isaiah 2,17-20
[53] Isaiah 13,9-13; 24,18-20
[54] Isaiah 2,20; 34,1-4
[55] II Peter 3,10-12
[56] II Peter 3,13
[57] Psalm 19,6; Isaiah 24,21-23; Jeremiah 10,10-11
[58] Galatians 4,9; Ephesians 6,12; Colossians 2,8
[59] Isaiah 11,4; 29,20; Jeremiah 50,25-28; 51,53-57
[60] Psalm 73,17-20; Isaiah 26,14&21; 43,15-17
[61] Isaiah 13,3-6; Amos 9,5-6; II Thessalonians 2,8-12
[62] Isaiah 66,15-18; Ezekiel 22,20-22; Micah 1,2-4
[63] Psalm 46,6-10; 55,15&23; Isaiah 30,27-28; 31,4-5
[64] Joel 2,11&31; 3,16; Isaiah 64,1-3
[65] Revelation 17,1-6&15
[66] Nahum 1,2-3&5-6; Zechariah 14,12; Malachi 4,1
[67] Isaiah 41,2&25; Jeremiah 50,2-5&9; 51,48&55-56
[68] Revelation 16,13-16; 19,11-18
[69] Revelation 17,14; 19,19-21
[70] Psalm 21,9-11; Nahum 1,9
[71] Job 19,25; Zechariah 14,3-5&9-11&16
[72] I Corinthians 15,51-54; I Thessalonians 4,15-17
[73] Luke 12,35-38
[74] Luke 24,36-43
[75] Revelation 19,6-9
[76] Psalm 149,4-9; Malachi 4,1-3; Revelation 19,14
[77] I Thessalonians 3,12-13
[78] I Thessalonians 1,10; 5,3-9
[79] I Corinthians 6,2-3; Jude 6&14
[80] I Thessalonians 4,13-18
[81] Isaiah 26,18-21; 66,5-6
[82] I Corinthians 15,19-26
[83] Daniel 2,44; 7,9-14&18
[84] Mathew 24,30-31; Revelation 1,7
[85] Isaiah 66,5-9; Micah 5,2-4; Revelation 12,5&17

[86] Mathew 10,21-22; 24,13-14; Mark 13,13
[87] Psalm 18,16-42
[88] Revelation 12,10
[89] Revelation 10,7; 11,15-18
[90] Revelation 11,18
[91] Acts 10,38-43; II Timothy 4,1; I Peter 4,5
[92] I Peter 4,17; II Peter 2,9; 3,7
[93] John 6,39-40; II Timothy 4,8
[94] John 12,47-48
[95] Mathew 25,46
[96] Revelation 14,6-13
[97] John 5,21-23&28-29
[98] Deuteronomy 7,25-26; II Machabees 12,38-46
[99] Mathew 5,19-26;
[100] Mathew 18,21-35
[101] Daniel 12,2
[102] Psalm 22,15; 103,14; Ecclesiastes 3,20
[103] Philippians 2,9-11
[104] Job 21,7&22-26; Isaiah 66,24; Mark 9,43-48
[105] Psalm 113,5-8
[106] Daniel 12,1-3; John 4,23-24; 5,24; 17,3
[107] Isaiah 29,18-24; Hebrews 12,25-29
[108] Deuteronomy 4,30-31
[109] Hebrews 11,17-19
[110] Genesis 17,4-7; 22,1-18
[111] Jeremiah 23,3-6; 32,37-41
[112] Ezekiel 43,4-7
[113] Psalm 68,26&29&32
[114] Jeremiah 3,14-19
[115] Genesis 15,18; Ezekiel 47,13-23
[116] Genesis 15,1-6; Romans 4,13-21
[117] John 14,16-17; 16,12-13; 18,37
[118] II Timothy 3,1-7
[119] Mathew 16,15-17; John 6,63; 8,47
[120] Revelation 1,3; 22,6&10
[121] Acts 5,38-39
[122] Revelation 22,11
[123] Mathew 9,16-17; 13,52; Luke 5,36-39
[124] Jeremiah 23,20; Daniel 11,33; 12,10

Chapter Ten
OPENING OF THE SEVENTH SEAL
NEW WORLD

"And when he opened the seventh seal, there was silence in heaven about the space of a half hour." Revelation 8,1

Prominence of the seven seals of the Apocalypse is central to all prophecy about the last days. The sequence of world wars mixed with earthquakes, famines, pestilence and signs in the sky before many stars fall on earth at the Second Advent is verified in the gospel and the prophets. Opening of seals concerning the four horses are not a concurrent theme of afflictions taking place all at once while we wait for a full-scale nuclear war to destroy civilization as the Messiah comes to save his people. That catchall in a fast track theory neglects critical events of the end. Armageddon is a battle of Christ against corruption, not an internal human conflict.

Scholars must examine their errors of relating Christ's exoteric homily of the last days to the ruin of the second Jewish temple and isolating the prophets to ancient history. Building of the third temple will not happen without world conflict and the Antichrist is not going to take global power by a cakewalk of peace where all countries yield by passive diplomacy. Nations will not turn against each other or oppose the Antichrist once he gains control so logic in itself implies wars among mankind will then cease, yet Jesus will come in judgment. These matters should be reckoned with common sense and courage, not appeased with false promise or ridicule.

As a church we need to know God's purpose in salvation of a segment of the Jews before his wrath and his design to seal the new covenant with them as a whole nation in a new heavens and a new earth. Have we forgotten the continuation of global strife foretold by Our Lady at Fatima in which entire nations will be annihilated by the spread of atheistic Marxism. These things are not obsolete as they contain the gospel to be preached even now and after by Jewish believers in all the earth prior to the end. We cannot ignore Israel's fate in a political sense or spiritual division among faithful Jews and the builders who reject the cornerstone of Christ.

Prospect of world peace and prosperity for humanity in union with divine grace is a hope expressed in many Christian songs. This concept of a type of heaven on earth is a belief held in many of our hearts, but not a doctrine taught or often touched upon from the pulpit. It is easy to separate the paradise above from our mortal trials and limit sermons to our personal path toward the hereafter. Is that all we need to know or is the Liturgy of the Word as it relates to our times more complex than accepting Christ as Savior? Clergy struggle with uncertainty and mainly avoid readings of prophecy, but they have an obligation to seek and find its meaning.

Discipline is vital in our search for wisdom, knowledge and ministry. Fervor is formed if we *"Study to show yourselves approved of God, a workman who needs not to be ashamed, rightly dividing the word of truth."*[1] His living word applies with piercing conviction to many detailed current affairs that directly affect the whole world around us so why would we shudder to warn of perils to both body and soul? There is reason and reality in these issues for instruction and conversion of many so *"Aim at charity, yet desire spiritual gifts, especially to prophesy. What will I profit you unless I speak by revelation, knowledge, prophecy or doctrine?"*[2]

Biblical predictions are not a nice menu of events we can choose from or combine to suit our individual outlook and station in life. It is a very serious mistake to flout these disturbing events summed up in the book of Revelation *"For every man who hears the words of prophecy of this book, if any man adds to these things, God will add to him the plagues that are written. And if any man takes away from the words of this prophecy, God will take away his part out of the book of life and out of the holy city."*[3] As powerful and unfamiliar these visions are *"the Spirit and the bride say, Come. Let him who is thirsty come and take the water of life freely."*[4]

When the Israelites heard the voice of God utter the Ten Commandments in trembling fear at Mt. Sinai, how is it they soon turned from him to make a golden calf to worship as their god? Moses gave the law saying *"You shall not add to the word I command, nor subtract from it for that is your wisdom and knowledge in the sight of other nations."*[5] This principle applies to the future when *"You will become a byword among the nations and the Lord will scatter you from one end of the earth to the other. So the generation to come after you and stranger will see the plagues and ask why. Then answer because they forsook the covenant of the Lord God."*[6]

In retrospect of this prophecy we know there is a generation to come who no doubt looks back from the end of the world since he said *"Neither with you only do I make this covenant and oath, but with him who is not with us this day. Those things which are revealed belong to us and to our children forever. You will return and obey the voice of the Lord."*[7] Results of our moral behavior are not limited to mortal life but also death and *"Every one of us will give an account of himself to God whether it be good or bad."*[8] Many sins that merit damnation and lead to plagues of divine requital are being justified even by clergy as personal acts of virtuous freedom.

Revelation of Christ coming in glory to judge will eliminate evil and deceit by his divinity with God and the Holy Spirit. The key element of a new world is belief in his Eucharistic service and tabernacles throughout the earth with Jerusalem as headquarters like the Vatican is the Holy See of today since *"Prepare to meet your God, O Israel. The Lord will reign over them in Mt. Zion from henceforth and forever.*[9] *His tabernacle is in Salem and his dwelling place is in Zion. A glorious high throne from the beginning is the place of our sanctuary. Kings and princes will enter this city sitting on the throne of David. The city will remain forever."*[10]

Satan the prince of darkness is described in the Apocalypse as a great red dragon who gives power and reign to the Antichrist such that they are worshiped by all nations. An essential point is made of the Devil's hatred after he takes possession of the Antichrist and gives *"him a mouth speaking great things. He opened his mouth in blasphemy against God, his tabernacle and them who dwell in heaven."*[11] This cursing is toward God and members of his kingdom, but it is also firmly against Jesus in his Eucharistic tabernacle for *"This is the bread that comes down from heaven and the bread I will give is my flesh which I will give for the life of the world."*[12]

Promise of Christ's rule over earth is God's oath to be in us by his spirit and dwell among us in holy flesh of his tabernacle. Of this endless gospel dogma, *"We will not fear though the earth is shaken and mountains plunge into the sea. There is a river whereof the streams make glad the city of God, the holy place of tabernacles of the most High. God is in the midst of her and she will not be moved. The secret of the Lord is with them who fear him: he will show them his covenant. In the secret of his tabernacle he will hide me and set me on a rock. He who dwells in the secret place of the most High will abide under the shadow of the Almighty."*[13]

Reflection on the seventh seal of the book of Revelation is a perplexity involving questions that are difficult to explain. There are just not very many quotes from Scripture relating to the silence in heaven St. John wrote about to indicate what he meant by this silence. Whether the heaven stated in this seal denotes heaven itself or the sky are puzzles left mainly to reason. We could infer paradise is vacant and silent if God leaves his home with the army of Jesus to judge, but the enigma could simply mean the war is over. Also the span of time within the space of half an hour suggests a metaphoric period which may not be easy to accurately decipher.[14]

Instead of lack of sound, the inherent meaning of the silence seems to be used in the sense of calm, security and awe. In the wake of the Second Advent when demons and evil people are damned, corpses of the wicked who die from burning heat in the light of Christ will be left for the birds all over the world. Those of faith who survive will be amazed at this global horror and know for sure the power of Jesus as Lord. The fallen angels of darkness will be bound in hellfire when he and his troops triumph so conflict with these powers in the air will stop. This logic in absence of commotions or confrontation reveals the silence of that aspect of heaven.

The sequence of all catastrophic prophecies occurring in the opening of each seal ends with the seventh seal after the battle of Armageddon. It is rational to perceive this stage as a time of healing and relief for the elect who inherit the earth as a holy seed. Divine justice will be done and the promise of a new world will begin as *"Be silent, O all flesh, before the Lord for he is raised up out of his holy habitation. O sword of the Lord, how long will you not be quiet? Go into your scabbard, rest and be still. When God arose to save all the meek of the earth, you caused judgment to be heard from heaven. The earth feared and was still."*[15]

Holy reverence will fill the hearts of them who belong to God's kingdom in heaven and earth as his vengeance is completed. The work of salvation will finally take root and yield its fruits since *"The Lord will not cast off his people, nor abandon his inheritance. Happy is the man you teach by your law so you may give him rest from the days of adversity when the pit be dug for the wicked. The Lord has broken the staff of the wicked and rod of rulers. It will come to pass in that day he will give you rest from your sorrow and from your fear and from your hard bondage wherein you served. The whole earth is at rest and quiet: it is glad and rejoiced."*[16]

Jesus displayed great power as a storm began to sink a ship he was in with his disciples. He rebuked the wind and directed the sea *"Peace, be still. The wind ceased and there was calm."*[17] His apostles wondered how even the wind and sea obeyed him, but in union with the Father he will cause terror in wrath to end so *"Be still and know that I am God. I will be exalted among the nations. I will be exalted in the earth. O you sons of men, how long will you love vanity and seek falsehood. The Lord has set apart him who is godly for himself. Stand in awe and sin not: commune with your heart and be still."*[18] His grace will settle in their souls.

Salvation of the Messiah is in him who will forever rule Israel and the whole world from the throne of David. Although Jesus will be revealed in glory to everyone and can appear to anyone at any time, he is not going to reign on earth in the person of his risen body. Jews as well as other nations will have their own kings and princes in passage of time. The eternal testament of Christ was established by him in the Eucharist and in this truth he is our Savior and King not only in the tabernacle of David, but in his tabernacles around the world. Why do so many reject this basic doctrine of the cross or partake of this living bread in sacrilege?

Iniquity has been the cause of civil disorder and divine justice from creation of the human race, but debauchery will reach its summit in demonic lunacy of the Antichrist's egoism and in worship of the Devil by an apostate church led by the false prophet. This may be a fitting end of pride and deceit, but Christ will overcome and to the Hebrews *"I will make my fury toward you to cease and I will be quiet and be angry no more. In that day it will be said to Jerusalem, Fear not and to Zion, Let not your hands be weak. The Lord God in the midst of you is mighty, he will save, he will rejoice over you, he will rest in his love and his joy of you in praise."*[19]

Homage will cover heaven and earth after Christ sits at the right hand of the Father to judge the living and the dead.[20] His kingdom will come despite the lust for fame and fortune of those who set up their own empire. The gospel will dominate all mankind albeit by force as *"O God of our salvation, the hope of all the earth and distant seas, you purge away our transgressions by terrible things in justice. You still the roaring of the seas and tumult of the people. Unto you all flesh will come. We will be satisfied with the goodness of your house, even your holy temple. Bless God in the congregations, even the Lord, from the fountain of Israel."[21]*

Water is a primary source of life and spiritually it refers to the divine word of which Christ became Incarnate. He is the Word of God by which we have our being and live even risen from the dead like him in eternity. As he took on flesh by power of the Holy Spirit, he is also present through consecration in the Eucharist. From these pure fountains or tabernacles, *"With joy you will draw water out of the wells of salvation. Sing unto the Lord for he has done great things. This will be known in all the earth. The Holy One of Israel is in the midst of you. He who has mercy on them will lead them, even by the springs of water he will guide them."[22]*

Faith without works is dead and obedience to divine law in keeping the Sabbath holy is not an option. Despite hypocrisy of some, many who still attend the Liturgy of the Mass are true in their devotion. It is Jesus in the bread of life we seek as he said *"It is written in the prophets, they shall be taught of God. Everyone who is learned of the Father comes to me. I am the bread of life so anyone who eats of it will not die. He who believes in me out of his belly will flow rivers of living water."[23]* This living water is replenished in the Eucharist for *"The Lord is my shepherd. He leads me beside the still waters. I will dwell in the house of Lord forever."[24]*

Mystery of Christ's reign in his divine role as the Son of David to inherit his throne is in his tabernacle in Jerusalem. According to God's promise *"I will set up your seed after you and he will build a house for my name and I will establish the throne of his kingdom forever. I will be his father and he shall be my son."[25]* The house of God is his kingdom and we who believe are living stones of his spiritual temple where *"We will go into his tabernacles, we will worship at his footstool. Arise into your rest, you and the ark of your strength. The Lord swore unto David: of the fruit of your body I will set on your throne."[26]* That fruit is the Eucharist.

Jerusalem is the place of Christ's throne and footstool of his kingdom in the Ark of the New Covenant, but his tabernacles are over all the earth. King David knew the promise was of God's own eternal house, not of his mortal house as he wrote *"You spoke of your servant's house of a great while to come, the Christ of the God of Israel, the Rock of Israel, the just ruler of men in the fear of God. My house is not so great with God, yet he made with me an eternal covenant ordered in all things and sure. He is my salvation and my desire. There is nothing thereof that springs not up, but the sons of evil will be set on fire and burnt to naught."[27]*

Our rest is in his rest and our testimony is in the blood of atonement ever present in the Last Supper. There Christ created the clergy in his command to *"Do this in remembrance of me."[28]* Let us not be misled about this fact or how it relates to promise for Jews since *"I will clothe her priests with salvation and her saints will abound for joy. I will satisfy her poor with bread. If your children keep my covenant and my testimony that I will teach them, their children will sit upon your throne for evermore. The Lord chose Zion, he desired it for his habitation. This is my rest forever: here I will dwell for I prefer it. I have ordained a lamp for my anointed."[29]*

Houses of worship are not complete without embracing that Eucharistic lamp which is the light of the world. We cannot separate spirituality from the true tabernacle of God or deny the ongoing unity in his spirit, his word and his flesh for *"The cup of blessing that we bless, is it not the communion of the blood of Christ? The bread we break, is it not the communion of the body of Christ? We being many are one bread and one body as we are all partakers of one bread. Let a man examine himself and eat of that bread and drink of that cup. He who eats and drinks unworthily will eat and drink damnation to himself, not discerning the Lord's body."[30]*

Many years will pass as people make their ways to a national homeland, populate the world and rebuild civilization. Hard work will be done to pick up the pieces of a desolate society, but *"Drop down you heavens from above, let the skies pour down justice, let the earth open, bring forth salvation and let holiness spring up together. The ends of the world will remember, turn to the Lord and all tribes of nations shall worship before you. The kingdom is the Lord's and he is governor among the nations. A seed will serve him and declare his justice to a people who shall be born. He will give you rest and you will be as a watered garden whose springs fail not."*[31]

Is it a lack of faith and courage or apathy, sloth and personal gain that doomsday has swept public theology of the end of the world? Why do we pacify ourselves and others about serious issues of the last days with the excuse it is none of our business since only God knows these things? His word is full of specifics about signs of our times and we must *"speak the wisdom of God in a mystery, even hidden wisdom, ordained to us before the world for the Spirit searches all things. We have the mind of Christ."*[32] We should heed stern warnings to those who *"have forsaken me the fountain of living waters and made cisterns that can hold no water."*[33]

There is no end of the world, but our society will be changed with the common bond of truth and charity. When Jesus stands on the Mount of Olives, a great valley will split to the north and south so *"in that day living waters will go out from Jerusalem, half of them to the east sea and half to the utmost sea."*[34] This is an actual physical event occurring at that point in time and should not be dismissed in symbolism of preaching the gospel. It is written of a vision in which Ezekiel was brought into these great real waters coming from under the third Jewish temple, *"it was a river I could not pass over and everything will live where the river comes."*[35]

These prophecies mean what they say and have no room for us to distort in a manner which fits our views. If our theories or hypotheses are based on the wrong premises, interpretation of the seasons of our times becomes a muddled form of imagination. We must align our thoughts and ways with Scripture. God is not calling various kinds of animals Noah brought into his ark to save them from uncharted waters of the flood, but he is calling us to get on board of his word. In our secular society *"we ought to obey God rather than men."*[36] Readings not yet examined which include discussion beyond the seven seals are found in the ensuing chapter.

---

[1] II Timothy 2,15
[2] I Corinthians 14,1&6
[3] Revelation 22,18-20
[4] Revelation 22,17
[5] Exodus 19,10-20; 20,1-19; 32,1-14
[6] Deuteronomy 4,1-6; 28,37&64; 29,22-25
[7] Deuteronomy 29,14-15&29; 30,1-8
[8] Romans 14,10-12; II Corinthians 5,10
[9] Amos 4,12-13; Micah 4,7-8
[10] Psalm 76,2; Jeremiah 17,12&25
[11] Revelation 13,4-7
[12] John 6,48-51

[13] Psalm 25,12-14; 27,5; 46,2-5; 91,1

[14] Daniel 12,11-12

[15] Psalm 76,8-9; Jeremiah 47,6; Zechariah 2,10-13

[16] Psalm 94,12-15; Isaiah 14,1-7

[17] Mark 4,36-41

[18] Psalm 4,2-4; 46,9-11

[19] Ezekiel 16,42; Zephaniah 3,12-17

[20] Mathew 26,64; Mark 14,62

[21] Psalm 65,1-7; 68,26

[22] Isaiah 12,3-6; 49,7-10

[23] John 6,45-50; 7,37-38

[24] Psalm 23,1-2&5-6

[25] II Samuel 7,10-16; Mathew 1,17

[26] Psalm 132,7-11

[27] II Samuel 7,19; 23,1-7

[28] Mathew 26,26-28; Mark 14,22-24; Luke 22,19

[29] Psalm 132,12-18

[30] I Corinthians 10,16-17; 11,23-29

[31] Psalm 22,27-31; 67,4; Isaiah 45,8; 58,6-11

[32] I Corinthians 2,7-10&16

[33] Jeremiah 2,13; 17,13

[34] Zechariah 14,4&8

[35] Ezekiel 47,1-9

[36] Acts 5,27-29

Chapter Eleven
WHITE THRONE JUDGEMENT

"I saw a great white throne and I saw the dead stand before God. Books were opened and the dead were judged according to their works. Whoever was not found written in the book of life was cast into the lake of fire." Rev. 20,11-15

Controversy surrounds many readings of the bible even those concerning the person of Jesus Christ of whom it was foretold he would be a sign of contradiction. Nearly all prophetic truth revolves around him and the gospel he proclaimed with the miracles he performed was given to and recorded by his disciples. Yet for centuries his divinity, atonement and resurrection have been disputed. It is a grave insult to our integrity that we possess great technical skills, but reject the most basic facts of history and are blind to a future fraught with horrible plagues. These events are of our own making and this moral deficiency leads to damnation.

When Jesus was brought to the temple for circumcision, a devout Jew named Simeon *"said to Mary his mother, Behold this child is set for the fall and rising again of many in Israel and for a sign which shall be spoken against."[1]* That fall and rising again applies to the last days when Jews as a nation forsake him since Moses plainly foretold *"You are unmindful of the Rock who begot you and have forgotten the God who formed you."[2]* The angel Gabriel spoke to Mary before her virgin birth saying *"You shall name him Jesus and he will be called the Son of God. He will reign over the house of Jacob forever and his kingdom will have no end."[3]*

Those mysteries were explained in prior chapters by extensive detail of putting together a coherent picture of the seven seals in Revelation. Order of these periods is guided by reason and by a literal belief in the divine word. Realism is the object of this research so we can see the ruling existence of our Creator, his salvation and knowledge of all things. We cannot distort his teaching or substitute our own perspective as a wish list of blessings without regard to principle. The bible is not a myth or some type of poetic fantasy, but a direct communication of divine law and justice about our times. Why would anyone choose to live in a false daydream?

Visions of the prophets and related preaching of Christ may be hard to understand, but we have already entered stages of the end times in global wars of the last century and all isolated commotions of wars since then in various places in the world. Perilous conflicts are yet to come as the faithful look to the hope of redemption and await a new world at the Second Advent. Jesus claimed he would be seen sitting at the right hand of power so if God comes with him to judge, there is still another distinct time and place of general judgment after Armageddon. This is an obvious question of confusion or dispute for many who study the Apocalypse.

Analysis of what comes after peace and prosperity are settled on earth does not exhibit an idealistic society of every person without sin. Human beings can choose to obey or transgress divine law, but have recourse to confess faults and stay on the right path. Despite the majesty of Christ to destroy all evil, *"The nation and kingdom that will not serve you shall perish. Those nations will be utterly wasted. The sinner being a hundred years old will be accursed."[4]* Jesus is a just Savior who remains to *"judge and reprove with equity for the meek of the earth. He will smite the earth with the rod of his mouth and with his breath slay the wicked."[5]*

History will certainly reflect prophetic aspects of the gospel and these hard lessons taught in coming generations. Although the church will rise in new strength over the whole world, some people will follow after their flesh rather than abide in God's spirit to keep his law. He will reign in Jesus by love and also fear so *"His seed will endure forever and his throne as the sun before me. It will be established forever as the moon and as a faithful witness in heaven. If his children forsake my law and walk not in my judgments, then I will visit their iniquity with the rod and with stripes. Yet I will not break my covenant, nor alter the promise gone out of my lips."[6]*

Sequence in a new world begins with victory for Jesus as he conquers servants of a wicked kingdom and angels of darkness, but his domain is in continuing justice since *"out of his mouth goes a sharp sword so with it he should smite the nations and he shall rule them with a rod of iron."[7]* Immortal saints will join in his ruling power for *"to him who overcomes I will grant to sit with me in my throne, even as I overcame and sit down with my Father in his throne."[8]* Their role in his grace is amazing *"for you have redeemed us to God by your blood from every tongue, people and nation. You made us kings and priests and we will reign on earth."[9]*

The idea of Jesus, angels and risen saints visibly walking around earth in a playground with mortal people or sitting on judicial benches giving sentence to unjust people or nations is false. They will reign over or above our planet, but as in the ancient past great wonders were done by unseen angels and saints will possess these gifts as *"in the resurrection of the dead, they neither marry or are given in marriage, but are as angels of God in heaven."[10]* Jesus told his apostles *"in the regeneration when the Son of man sits in the throne of his glory, you will sit upon twelve thrones judging the twelve tribes of Israel."[11]* Their thrones of justice are in heaven.

Distinction in the paradise of heaven above from a new world on earth will always be part of the reality for mortal beings because *"God has chosen things which are not to bring to nothing things that are so no flesh can glory in his presence. But of him you are in Christ Jesus who is our wisdom, justice, sanctity and redemption."[12]* The unseen reality of heaven and presence of Christ in the Eucharist are known by faith. God told Moses *"You cannot see my face for no man sees me and still lives. Before the eyes of all your people I will work marvels not done in all the earth, nor in any nation. This people will see the awesome deeds I the Lord will do."[13]*

Notice of the spiritual renewal in our world was given by Jesus in his prophecy about the time he termed the regeneration when his apostles will judge the twelve tribes of Israel. Even he spoke directly of the change in morality and the privilege to reign with him. Their thrones are with him as he sits at the right hand of God *"For we know if our earthly house is dissolved, we have an eternal house not made with human hands in the heavens. We do groan that mortality might be swallowed up of life."[14]* Exactly how those who defy the church are cursed is not clear, but it appears any rebellion against it will be an exception to global harmony.

No matter how long anyone lives or what good quality of life they enjoy, we must realize *"it is appointed unto men once to die, but after this the judgment."[15]* We have only one life to live which we must account for after death in hope of being rewarded with eternal life or in dread of damnation. No person can be judged in this manner more than once, nor does anyone pass death on and on in some innate form of reincarnation. God is an Almighty being with both reason and emotion who made salvation known in the risen Christ. There is no other means apart from his spirit to obtain his inner peace in this life or way to escape utter sorrow of the abyss.

An intrinsic issue is found in the Apocalypse that stands separate in time and place from the Second Advent. This vision of God the Father sitting on his throne to judge the dead cannot be ignored as if it were not written or distorted by symbolic theories which neglect its premises. When Jesus comes in flaming glory to judge the living and the dead St. John saw a holy angel *"holding the key of the bottomless pit and a great chain in his hand. He bound Satan, cast him into the pit, shut him up for a thousand years and set a seal upon him to deceive the nations no more until the thousand years are finished. Then he must be loosed a little season."[16]*

This timeframe of a millennium may seem like an eternity to some, but *"a thousand years is as one day with the Lord."*[17] People will enjoy extremely long lives in plenty of sustenance and health with security from harm. The world's population from the remnant left will multiply in a dramatic way since more women will be seeking the fewer men who survive coming wars so *"in that day seven woman shall take hold of one man saying, we will eat our own bread and wear our own apparel only let us be called by your name to take away our reproach."*[18] Finding a wife will be easy for men since so many women won't want to end up as an old maid.

Christ's reign with the risen saints is verified in the millennium era while the dragon who is the old serpent that deceived Adam and Eve named the Devil and Satan is bound in hell. In a corresponding vision *"I saw thrones and they who sat upon them and judgment was given to them. I saw the souls of them who were beheaded for their witness of Jesus and for the word of God who had not worshiped the beast or his image, nor received his mark upon their foreheads or in their hands. They lived and reigned with Christ a thousand years. But the rest of the dead lived not until the thousand years were finished. This is the first resurrection."*[19]

What is referred to as the first resurrection includes all souls who receive the gift of immortal life at the last trumpet and at the Second Advent, but in contrast also those who are resurrected from hell and from a burning death into the eternal lake of fire. The mere fact of an event being called first suggests a similar occurrence to follow. It is repeated of saints that *"Blessed and holy is he who has part in the first resurrection. On such the second death has no power, but they shall be priests of God and of Christ and will reign with him a thousand years."*[20] This period of generations is not figurative or fictional, but literally real and actual.

Finality of God's power and vengeance for his glory in the church founded and upheld by his Son is impeccably shown in a test of faith soon after the millennium reign *"when the thousand years are expired, Satan will be loosed out of his prison and go out to deceive the nations in the four quarters of the earth, Gog and Magog, to gather them together to battle whose number is as the sand of the sea. They compassed the camp of the saints about the earth and the beloved city. Fire came down from God out of heaven and devoured them."*[21] This assault is against the church and there seems little doubt the angels and risen saints will execute judgment.

Reference to Gog and Magog relates to Marxist atheism born in Russia which is the basis of ideology of the red dragon in demonic control over nations. The relation is in a spiritual sense much like the Babylon of Revelation or Jerusalem when it is mentioned as *"the great city that spiritually is called Sodom and Egypt where also our Lord was crucified."*[22] Tendency in people to follow their pride is beyond reason after Christ already came in glory but *"the Devil who deceived them was cast into the lake of fire where the beast and false prophet are. He will be tormented day and night forever and ever."*[23] Satan will see his ugly end of evil power.

Clues are given in the passage concerning the millennium to reveal the difference in time and place of judgment by Christ and by God. It is said of the faithful who live and die in that age they lived not or rise in incorruption until after this period. They will dwell in spirit in heaven or purgatory until they stand before God in resurrection. Satan is cast into the lake of fire. This is the place where the Antichrist and false prophet are since they were damned previously at the Second Advent. Jesus will leave heaven to judge, but the souls in heaven, purgatory, hell and those consumed with fire in final rebellion will be judged by God in heaven.

Discrepancy in judging of Christ and of God does not mean Jesus has no part in justice of the Father for he is one with him in the midst of his throne and sits with him on his throne.[24] St. John wrote of the mystery of a final general judgment *"I saw a great white throne and him who sat upon it from whose face the earth and heaven fled away for there was found no place for them. And I saw the dead, small and great, stand before God. The books were opened and another book was opened which is the book of life and the dead were judged out of those things written in the books according to their works."*[25] Our deeds are recorded for a witness.

Reading about the heaven and earth having no place as they fled away gives the impression of a sudden wasting away of our universe in a cosmic explosion. This is not the meaning of that verse since only the dead are judged and St. John saw things set apart from physical reality *"And the sea gave up the dead who were in it, and death and hell delivered up the dead who were in them. Every man was judged according to their works. Death and hell were cast into the lake of fire. This is the second death. And whoever was not found written in the book of life was cast into the lake of fire."*[26] There is no escape from that place of eternal damnation.

Some scholars deny the millennium era and associate the white throne judgment with the Second Advent surmising it is curtains for mankind in the end of time, but this view defies logic and divine promise as *"I John saw the holy city, new Jerusalem, coming down from God out of heaven prepared as a bride adorned for her husband. Behold the tabernacle of God is with men and he will dwell with them. They shall be his people and God himself will be with them and be their God. I saw a new heaven and a new earth for the first heaven and earth passed away, and there was no more sea."*[27] The church will remain with its Eucharistic tabernacle.

Lapse in time from the start of a new creation at the Second Advent to its final formation at the white throne judgment is confirmation of God's supreme power in the affairs of humanity. If flaming fire of Christ and his army at Armageddon is not enough to convince mankind to obey the new covenant, the consuming fire of God similar to Sodom and Gomorrah will devour his enemies for a fearful memory.[28] There will be no more sea from which the dead arose. This image of departed souls is not material waters on earth and is separate from death and hell. It seems the dead will then not wait to be resurrected in heaven or damned to the lake of fire.

Mortal people will not lose their free will and all who yet follow in future generations must give an account of their lives upon death, but *"he who sat upon the throne said: Behold I make all things new for these things are true and faithful. It is done. I will give to him who is thirsty of the fountain of the water of life freely. He who overcomes shall inherit all things, but they who are cowardly and unbelieving will have their part in the lake that burns with fire and brimstone which is the second death."*[29] In that world without end the sacramental life of the church will endure as the path to immortal life, yet they who reject it will burn forever.

It is senseless to read the bible and believe damnation is just a form of oblivion or all people are part of God's kingdom regardless of their moral way of life. Everything we do is written in books kept in heaven, but anyone can repent and be forgiven in Christ. Why lie to ourselves thinking God is too loving to curse anyone or there is no place of eternal torment? Jesus taught that those who die in iniquity will be *"cast into a furnace of fire. There will be weeping and gnashing of teeth in fire that never will be quenched."*[30] They will not enter heaven *"for without are dogs, sorcerers, fornicators, murderers, idolaters and all who do falsehood."*[31]

Paradise in heaven is described by St. John as a city made of pure gold even its streets with pearl gates and foundations of precious stones, but surpassing more than all this extreme beauty and luxury *"the glory of God did lighten it and the Lamb is the light thereof. And I saw no temple therein for the Lord God Almighty and the Lamb are the temple of it. His servants will serve him and see his face and his name written in their foreheads. Nothing will enter into it that defiles, but only they who are written in the Lamb's book of life. Blessed are they who keep his commandments and have the right to the tree of life and to enter the city."*[32]

Little else can be said in this chapter except the word of God is endless. We must deal with our lives in the present tense with our eyes open to the signs of our times. The warnings and hope are not written in vain or unsolvable mystery. In relation to the promise of God to his only begotten Son *"I will give you the nations for an inheritance and the ends of the earth for your possession. And now be wise O kings, take heed you rulers of the earth. Give homage to him lest you perish from the way when his anger blazes suddenly. I will give power to him who overcomes over the nations to rule them with a rod of iron as I received of my Father."*[33]

---

[1] Luke 2,21-35
[2] Genesis 49,24; Deuteronomy 32,17-18&31-33
[3] Luke 1,26-33
[4] Isaiah 60,12; 65,20
[5] Isaiah 11,4
[6] Psalm 89,27-36
[7] Revelation 19,15
[8] Revelation 3,20-21
[9] Revelation 1,4-6; 5,9-10
[10] Mathew 22,28-32; Luke 20,33-38
[11] Mathew 19,28; Luke 22,28-30
[12] I Corinthians 1,27-31
[13] Exodus 33,12-23; 34,10
[14] II Corinthians 5,1-4
[15] Hebrews 9,27
[16] Revelation 20,1-3
[17] II Peter 3,8
[18] Isaiah 4,1
[19] Revelation 20,4-5
[20] Revelation 20,6
[21] Revelation 20,7-9
[22] Revelation 11,8
[23] Revelation 20,10
[24] John 17,21-24; Revelation 3,21; 7,17; 22,1-3
[25] Revelation 20,11-12
[26] Revelation 20,13-15
[27] Revelation 21,1-3
[28] Genesis 19,24-28; II Peter 2,6; Jude 6-7
[29] Revelation 21,5-8
[30] Mathew 13,41-42; Mark 9,43-44
[31] Revelation 22,15
[32] Revelation 21,10-27; 22,1-5&14
[33] Psalm 2,6-12; Revelation 2,26-27

Chapter Twelve
CONCLUSION

"Return you children of men. We spend our time as a story that is told. Teach us to number our days so we may apply our hearts to wisdom. Let your work appear to your servants and your glory to their children." Psalm 90,3-16

The bible is not only a guide to spiritual matters of divine law so we can obtain its blessings in our personal lives and eternal life in heaven. These writings reflect a detailed forecast of the church's journey through its own passion in Calvary before rebirth in a new world. We need to awake from our deep slumber in seeing how specific prophecies develop in rational phases. Common thought of the Apocalypse is in a frivolous concept of doomsday that ignores trials of purification and chastisement. Growing secularism in apostasy and imperial goals of radical cultures threaten global stability in a climate of economic despair and incessant violence.

Politics and religion are subjects some people would rather avoid since they consider them as private opinion closed to opposing argument. These issues are part of everyday life affecting everyone regardless of their beliefs or desire to stay away from controversy. This book opens many questions among diverse religions or nations and answers puzzles to anyone who seeks to know basic facts in times of the last days. Those events are presented in an informative manner much like simple arithmetic and can be thoroughly understood by any literate person. Study and meditation of Scripture is a science of reason and reality, not a mystery of blind faith.

Beside its historical value, records and prophetic teachings of God's word are a living force in the past, present and future. Most Christian scholars concentrate mainly on ancient themes and the atonement of Christ in a view stuck in history. They have poor grades in determining the distinct timeframe of catastrophic seasons before the Second Advent. This standstill is mainly due to the general idea we cannot know actual secrets of those things, but also since they don't want to offend anybody fearing rebuttal of objection to their claims. The desire to remain neutral and isolate doctrine from how Israelites fit into prophecy rejects the gospel itself.

Critical points of our times are in debate of whether or not we live in the generation Christ said would not pass away until all events he described are fulfilled. Jesus was not talking to Jews of his time when he told about the end of the world. We have witnessed the first periods he predicted in global wars of the last century and all regional battles since then. Signs he gave of natural disasters are increasing everywhere in record breaking intensity, but great sorrows remain in what he called the by and by as nation rises against nation and then kingdom rises against kingdom with conventional and nuclear weapons before his final wrath and triumph.

Many people never heard of or have forgot Fatima during WWI when Our Lady announced serious warnings about Christ's gospel against a sinful world by the onslaught of apocalyptic wars beyond WWII in which entire nations would be annihilated. Some think these accounts are fraud or have no bearing on our future, but the divine word provides specific information of coming human conflicts that lead to global reign of the Antichrist. Political aspects of this turmoil as it develops are clearly written in the various ancient names of peoples that align together against each other at separate times with different outcomes in future tense.

Our attention should be focused on who these nations are and why they are drawn into such calamity. Breaking news almost on a daily basis reveals new tensions of bloodshed, abnormal weather conditions and huge financial woes. All the trouble and misery are causing the public to wonder if anyone can offer a solution. We face even greater concerns as the groundwork of

WWIII has already taken place and many potential triggers exist that draw tragically close such as the danger of Iran making nuclear bombs. A widespread counter insurgency within allies of Russia is plainly being formed against oppressive regimes linked to a terrorist agenda.

It seems even the intelligence community is not aware of ties Russia has with an interlocked vortex of peoples and tribes who come against Israel and its allies, particularly the United States of America.[1] The notion of Russians being a timid or defeated post-Soviet era foe is absurd since they have shown their defensive might when provoked in crushing the Georgian army in its bordering provinces. Russia was until now off our radar screen in any scenario of some major explosive events in the Middle East. That dreadful war will turn into chaos as missile guidance systems are targeted and shut down while brother turns their swords against brother.[2]

Threats to world security go further than stigma of a fiscal cliff as we stand on the brink of destruction not seen in prior wars. Moral and political principles are bound together in divine law with more severe curses resulting from worsening iniquity.[3] The final plague is a sword of battle, but while hedonism rises in our society prosperity has failed with much hardship and dire amounts of debt, families are broken by divorce and child abuse, addictions to sex, drugs and alcohol become epidemic, physical and mental medical problems skyrocket, our prisons are overcrowded, weather causes extensive damage and terrorism has stressed our military.

Anyone who thinks God does not lose his patient temper needs to know he is rightly jealous for his names' sake. He has not changed although general philosophy about who he is and the way of life he expects has turned into mockery. His commandments are still in effect, but loss of faith and ethics in our world is a bondage marked with massive bloodshed, not new freedom of pleasure in a perverted conscience of right and wrong. This corruption of our souls is a dead end and that gap of secularism in our laws and education is in ignorance and deceit. Careless trust in the materialism of our own pride and military power will surely be met with justice.

In the U.S. we are a democracy and many states have passed laws and amendments to their constitutions concerning heterosexual marriage and pro-life stances against abortion only to be struck down by slight of a few judges in courts. Matters of right to life and sexual unions are core examples of morality that divide our society and their legal status should be determined by the people. Why have promises repeatedly been made for Congress to start an amendment process to the U.S. Constitution without action to allow states to ratify if they choose? Our citizens should have the final say in social struggles of a broad spectrum of our nation.

Decency has become a forgotten cause for numerous lawmakers because of aberrant court decisions about freedom of speech. We have come to accept the flood of filth in pornography as sexual promiscuity is glorified in our television, movie theaters and internet. Fornication and adultery are sins that prohibit us from the kingdom of God, yet these behaviors go on with no sense of guilt or any need of repentance. We need to examine our lifestyles in light of biblical doctrine and realize the dangers to our own souls and retribution for collective iniquity on our nation. Fire and brimstone are physical realism, not just a place of despair in damnation.

Is the federal government afraid to start an amendment process to stop abortion and prohibit gay marriage? Are some members of Congress worried about staying in office and what would happen if their liberal political spotlight on fetal life or equal rights was overturned by enough states to ratify conservative laws? Pro-life or heterosexual lobbies in multiple localities lost huge amounts of money and labor by not pursuing a prime goal to focus their efforts on amending the U.S. Constitution. They have to form a national agenda of We the People which targets and exposes dignitaries who refuse legislation to let America as a whole decide its values.

Officials who vote to legalize gay unions cost all taxpayers on things like health insurance. Those who claim to be Christian disgrace the very person of Jesus who is the Word of God. Are they incompetent or just dishonest because there is no vagueness about his vow to vomit out any nation for this disgusting sin. Many bishops have expressed scandal against so-called Catholic politicians who deny clear teachings of the church. These taboos have not changed, nor has Pope Francis diverged from his conviction that same-sex marriage is a total rejection of God's law engraved in our hearts and hence the identity of family and its survival are in jeopardy.

Let us be certain about the serious result of sexual sins many believe do not harm anyone as *"The Lord knows how to reserve the unjust to judgment, especially those who follow the flesh in unclean lust and despise authority."*[4] This dominion is divine power where adultery, incest and homosexuality are primary reasons for very severe correction so *"You shall not lie with a man as a woman. It is an abomination. Defile you not in any of these things or the land will vomit you out just as the nations before you. They are without excuse who dishonor their bodies for women changed the natural use and men likewise burned in their lust one toward each other."*[5]

Instead of a code of self-evident principles, the U.S. Constitution has become a twisted theory adapted to deceit about true ethics of justice. That denial of its original intent spurns life itself by legalized abortion and through gay marriage humiliates our creation since God made Eve from Adam's rib as *"he took one of Adam's ribs and made a woman."* The purpose of this design was first because *"It is not good the man should live alone: I will make him a help mate. They will be one flesh."* Their union parallels Christ's bond with his church and provides succession to *"be fruitful and multiply."*[6] These standards are not a subject of metamorphosis.

The historic but narrow decision by the U.S. Supreme Court to legalize same-sex marriage was a clinching blow to home rule powers of all states in our country. This marred claim to sagacity is about a new era of liberty requiring more prudence than the past. Sanctioned misuse of our human bodily form edifies an unholy lust as a sacred act of affection. It is a sad day for our nation and the atrophy of our judicial psyche may be the death bell with respect to a clear indictment against our sinful deeds made by the prophets unless we undo the shame. Sexuality is a teaching of physiology, not licentious rationalism. What will pupils learn in school?

America may not have yet changed into the jungle displayed by a contagious malaise of bad news occurring in other lands where fight or flight are the only options, but this biblical morass of brother against brother will ultimately transpire into an evil scheme of survival upon all our earth. Its self-serving motive shown by thugs who murder, steal and rape defies the rule of love which is built in the family and church. The very foundation of civil society is falling apart and being replaced by debauchery of our own ego in submission to depraved lusts. That hedonism does not consider unborn human beings, natural laws or irrevocable judgments.

Freedom of religion is at odds with a sentiment of secular liberalism which restricts public displays of faith and now regulates procedures for adoption and health insurance requirements contrary to church dogma. These actions have harmed related charitable programs that have long served our welfare. Oaths of office sworn on the bible to so help me God have become a fallacy of so help yourself. If there are so many laws about discrimination, how does it apply to the right to practice our faith? Who are the real bigots? Our founding fathers never intended to separate government and its society from a sober conscience guided by divine law.

Citizens of faith have to unite and speak out to move mountains eroding our precious liberty which bring adverse justice upon us. We may not have yet removed IN GOD WE TRUST from our currency, but how many have taken him out of their hearts and put trust in themselves? The widespread solidarity in his grace is why autocracy of the Soviet Union fell apart and this same

231

grace led the civil rights march to success against racial prejudice. We should accept the motto Moses gave to the ancient Pharaoh to 'Let My People Go' for an allied caption to free us from corruption. The Bill of Rights gives us a two way street for equity in our statutes.

Revival spread by leaps and bounds in the early church since the apostles gained conversion of so many Jews and Gentiles by reason of Scripture they were said to have turned the world upside down.[7] It takes more than idle talk, inner cliques or a facade to go into the world and make new disciples while drawing back those who stray. Where is our zeal? It should not be in our pockets or in lavish building projects, but labor and funding need to be spent in reaching souls for Christ. Our welcome mat must extend beyond our regular members to fill empty pews in renewal and the divisions in creed among us need to be corrected with transparency.

Something has to be done to fulfill a new evangelization so desperately appealed for by the papacy and bishops over many years. Problems have only grown worse due to apathy and we must face the horrible result of judgment. These pervasive changes are no longer just personal choices having little effect on others, but we are looking at unmeasured danger if we don't make amends and intercede for transgression. An urgent call must be made to bring us together in one accord to accept our mutual challenge and speak with one voice. We need to pray and get out in the field with a message of warnings in truth of the gospel to plant seeds for harvest.

Perception of the Catholic Church and its funds suffered greatly during the sex abuse scandal of priests, yet disgrace also involved the Leadership Conference of Women Religious (LCWR) which represents eighty percent of U.S. Catholic nuns. The Vatican found serious theological errors about abortion, homosexuality, ordained women, euthanasia and radical feminism. Steps were taken to ensure that publications or programs of the LCWR are based on sound doctrine. American nuns were applauded for their work in services such as hospitals and for the poor but most have veered from traditional roles with less than a third of prior numbers.

Stains of the consecrated lives of priests and sisters are hard to remove since some have gone farther than taking off their priestly garb or religious habits. They have joined a rebellion within the church which wilily claims to be progressive, but aligns with heresy and seeks sympathy by justifying sin. The honor they seek is in their own circles, not from God. But why do many of those who share the same vocations in obedience to teachings of church hierarchy not speak out against falsehood? Views of all women religious are not reflected by defiance, but fear to stop these waters of deception, complacency and iniquity is induced by a lack of virtue.

Devout Catholics must come out of their closets with fervor of the Holy Spirit inspiring their families, friends and neighbors to reverse the Protestant Reformation which has broken off in divisions and splintered into so many denominations there is no particular character. We need to open our doors to the poor in spirit including many Protestants who oppose schisms in morality and individualistic approaches to Christianity. Pastors and laity need to focus on effective ways of outreach to bring people into the faith and teach them the truth of our times in living out Christ's passion as his mystical body yet redemption in sacraments of the church.

The crux of my thesis is in a threefold theory of rapture occurring over periods of world wars before divine wrath against the Antichrist's reign ending in Armageddon. New profound lesson in the seven seals of Revelation clearly diverges from common theology of the four horses all acting at once to bring havoc on earth. Making the linkage of ancient names of nations to those of today and how these powers fit into the last days has never been done. Much discussion is made about the pretext of coming nuclear wars and who will fight in them. Passages relating to Israel first defend it as a state then remove it until the Messiah restores their kingdom.

Great irony of Scripture is in history repeating itself for the Jewish nation in their freedom, captivity and return. Prophetic proverbs such as *"like mother, like daughter"* refer to idolatry of the latter days.[8] We cannot dismiss the struggle to liberate them from their enemies, nor the warning Jesus gave saying *"the days will come upon you that your enemies will compass you on every side and lay you even with the ground because you knew not the time of your visitation."*[9] The mistake of their enemies who know this prediction of defeat is God will defend them in WWIII and it is the Antichrist who conquers them and all nations on earth in WWIV.[10]

Where many scholars error is in how the Antichrist takes global tyranny and once this evil society is put in place there will be no opposition within its ranks to destroy itself. The Second Advent is set apart from human strife as this judgment is from Christ's heavenly army against an apostate world. Following WWIII and first watch in the second seal, plagues of seven trumpets and seven vials of wrath are a sequence of afflictions which include WWIV and then massive cosmic curses specified on those who had the mark of the beast. It is wrong to link the great army of the sixth trumpet with gathering of kings to Armageddon in the sixth vial.[11]

Overwhelming evidence of my research supports the contention that the forth seal reveals the Antichrist will obtain his reign by force. To accept this puts the fourth seal in a very central place of prophecy. It makes you think about the order and importance of other seals by putting the sixth seal judgment of the Lamb's wrath in perspective and also isolates the great sword of the second seal over earth as a separate war. Theologians would rather side-step the landmark of a third Jewish temple, but plans now exist by orthodox Jews to build it in place of the Al-Aqsa Mosque in East Jerusalem. This project is no classified secret, but it cannot be negotiated.

Prophecy needs to be recognized from the present, not buried in the past or brushed off in the distant future. The most glaring premise we must realize is creation of the State of Israel from the bloodbath of WWII, its early battles for survival and migration of Jews to that land are all based in the prophets.[12] Long standing disputes over control of Jerusalem and failed peace accords with Palestinians are an insolvable deadlock due to the wide range of hatred to destroy Israel. This outright denial of their right to exist will result in a global war which is a ticking time bomb in God's hand, but we must analyze our current reality to see how close it is.

Armed conflict goes on between Israel and militants in the Gaza Strip. Blockades continue to hamper the lives of many people who live there. West Bank Palestinian leaders refuse to alter demands for complete sovereignty over prior 1967 borders with East Jerusalem as their capital while Israeli settlements expand. Incredible vast uprisings dubbed an Arab Spring have engulfed many nations with no promise of peace, but instead more division and discord. Worries abound if chemical weapons have fallen into demented hands. Instability in the Middle East is in a power grab infiltrated by despotic leaders and insurgents who despise Israel and its allies.

Americans must reconsider careless attitudes about safety due to many homebred suspects of death squads in western countries seen as an enemy within. This shocking alert prompted broad surveillance operations in Europe aimed at surprise raids. Terrorist gains persist by assault in places like Iraq to take back areas they once held before the U.S. and its allies pushed them out. That country is mired in violence and paralyzed by feuds in its government to the point of becoming a failed state with Iran seeking political or military control. The same kind of upset and defeat loom over Afghanistan, yet it is centered on the main core of fascist designs.

U.S. and NATO nations decided to stop fighting the war and exit troops, but new and severe problems in sweeping hostile zones crop up that draw them back into offensive modes. Afghan forces and police squads rely heavily on foreign aid since that country cannot pay for its defense. Billions of dollars will still be needed even if any ongoing combat mission is over. Most nations

233

are in financial straits so claim to a viable pro-western Afghan democracy is unlikely given the resilience of rebels and sanctuaries in remote areas of Pakistan for al-Qaida and the Taliban. This ethnic region and Pashtun community is part of the lives of those in Pakistan.

Sharp polarization exists in the Moslem world, but this inner conflict of civil unrest is not confined to areas where tragedy has sprung up in awesome measures. Threat of terror is growing greater as resolve weakens to fight with some false idea that either the war is contained or it won't come back to our homeland. There is no crystal ball to predict how or when some kind of disaster will take place, but threats are real and include defense against sophisticated viruses of cyber sabotage by computer hackers who could knock out industries with electronic grids, water plants, railroads or other vital services. That kind of espionage is hard to detect.

The eminent factor of combined forces in an expansive array of nations and terrorist factions against Israel said to come like a cloud to cover the land is in leadership of Russia.[13] A huge group of people and bands will unite together under the superpower of Russian military and the U.S. will be forced to marshal its allies to confront the mammoth battalion. It does not seem that Russia wants this immense gamble, but an extraneous factor called a bit in their jaws will draw them into WWIII with an evil thought to take spoil and prey. What will happen is unknown, but Iran is its strategic and major commercial partner and also a member of its alliance.

Sanctions against Tehran's assets, trade and oil industry over several years severely cut Iran's exports and effectively disrupted its economy. Further tough measures would have driven it into bankruptcy if they didn't compromise over their nuclear program. These restrictions by the U.N., U.S. and EU were enforced to persuade Iran to halt its upgraded uranium enrichment labs at their very modern facilities that were close to quickly having enough material to arm an atomic warhead. A negotiated solution seems to be the only way to prevent Israel's plans for a pre-emptive strike on Iran's nuclear plants. Only God can tell what would follow.

Iran's hawkish foreign policy stance and stalled talks with the U.N. took a surprising change with the presidential election of new well-respected leader. His common sense appeals for compromise on Tehran's nuclear production activities to resolve questions of enrichment and monitoring its reactor sites in exchange for lifting of sanctions was a victory for moderates on the verge of mass protests. Seeking a pragmatic agenda to improve the livelihood of its citizens and promise to reform domestic repression such as greater freedom of speech and women's rights, he appointed a cabinet of technocrats who were educated in Western university cultures.

The long paradigm of antagonistic rhetoric toward the U.S. shifted with a desire to achieve better relations and a feasible treaty. This bold new face for a state seen as a pariah by many in the international community brought a sense of hope, but easing tensions by diplomacy over fears that Iran wants to build a nuclear arsenal requires an ongoing process of transforming attitudes. Callous hatreds of warmongers are hard to stop and diminish the idea of harmony to mere illusion. These inside and outside unruly factors hinder the whole spectrum of transparent cooperation so any final deal could wane or otherwise quickly turn useless.

As NATO pulls out of major battles, rapprochement has fortunately replaced particularly dangerous military options. Russian intervention to mend Middle Eastern affairs promoted the Kremlin's importance as a geopolitical mediator. The eminent status of persuasion among their allies is a presence critically needed in dialogue concerning security issues. In all simplicity to the vulture-like nature of expansive violence, Russia's seat in promoting peace can only benefit all parties who want to avoid world war. There are no alternatives to welcoming this entrenched broker since some armed force tactics carry thoughtless tragic results.

Civil revolt of March 2011 in Syria turned into an arena of foreign rebel groups including extremists who want to draw the U.S. and Russia into a nuclear weapons confrontation thinking they will be left to pick up the booty. It became a magnet for savage crimes exhibited by rape, torture, relentless bombings, chemical warfare and denial of humanitarian aid. Countless victims were killed or injured while several millions of innocent people fled to camps in other nations and like numbers left homeless in a country that could end up as a primary breeding ground for terrorist cells. The dramatic exodus and displacement of Syrians are horrifying.

Influx of radical opposition forces pushing for harsh Islamic rule obscured a Western backed ideology of the Free Syrian Army to move away from tyranny. Bloody struggles soon sprung up among the insurgents fighting for much money and arms supplies donated primarily by Arab Gulf states and Turkey leaving divided fiefdoms in many areas. Ruthless cruelty shown by the Syrian government and by militants goes against any code of human rights or doctrines of religious purity. Similar to events in other lands, the towns and places of worship in Syria have become a shambles and ended tranquil coexistence of Islamic and Christian neighbors.

There is a great warning to be learned from concessions by Syria to give up its exceedingly bulky stockpile of deadly chemical weapons, armed munitions to deliver them and their ability to manufacture them in compliance with a U.N. mandate. This agreement was mitigated by Russia whose unwavering support in advanced weapon shipments to Damascus thru Iran and sudden buildup of precision force with naval, air and land bases in Syria obviously draws a red line in Russian defense against U.S. hegemony. Danger in the balance of power there is far more than most analysts thought and any solution requires close multilateral cooperation.

Rivalry caused by opportunistic mercenaries and inherent blazing discord in diverse regional ambitions and religious sects leaves uncertainty about who will rule in Syria. Its alliance to Iran and Russia cannot be ignored by America, nor connections to strong anti-Israeli troops such as Hezbollah in Lebanon be seen as a non-existential threat. Political resolution to the conflict involves unfettered partnership by those who are waging a proxy war to establish any kind of order. These big guns need to recognize the interests of each other and use their resources in funding or influence to repair damage, not get caught in a net of awesome doom.

Troubling signs of our times not only reveal emergence of Russia's military alliance detailed in Scripture, but backing of Saudi Arabia, Qatar and Turkey of the rebellion to topple the Syrian regime is clear evidence of a predicted wider conflict. Arab Gulf states are sandwiched by Iran and ancient kingdoms of Ethiopia and Libya while Turkey deals with an expanding Kurdistan. This pro-western league will strangely find itself defending their sovereignty against enemies of Jews. They have strong armed forces and high technology for warfare against vast opposition from African and other armies when nations collide over reign of the Holy Land.

Atrocities continue on massive scales from the Horn of Africa to Sudan and its surrounding countries. Beside a brutal force history of the Sudanese government, many rebel tribes rove over lawless districts to pillage leaving a tragedy for millions, especially orphans. This repulsive situation in South Sudan, Darfur, Central African Republic, Chad, Kenya, Nigeria and other areas reflects a scenario in the prophets that will turn into complete anarchy. Peacekeeping forces and compassionate aid groups have been stymied by their inability to overcome the madness or deliver sufficient supplies for survival of those in desperate need.

Crucial issues revolve around whether or not Israel will either choose or be cornered into full-fledged strife. Apart from small scale bombings, what exit is available if Jews and Jerusalem become the center of fray? How Syria, Lebanon and Iraq fit into the biblical scheme are of great concern because war could spill over their borders and no doubt Israel stands ready to act unilaterally if threatened. Mighty militant factions have consolidated and are based on all sides of this tiny state. While Israel looks at the U.N. nuclear treaty with Iran as a historic mistake, their Supreme Leader openly calls them an illegitimate regime led by rabid dogs.

Despite concession to curb its enrichment of uranium to levels used by most civilian reactors and also dilute near nuclear grade stockpiles to produce atomic bombs, Iran refused to halt the process. Very little was done to change the infrastructure of existing facilities or their ability to manufacture more centrifuges, but complete access was granted for daily U.N. inspection of key factories to insure knowledge of ongoing procedures as a source for energy. The short range plan does not alter pugnacious foreign policies or deter those who want to derail it. Terms are temporary while this nation is dubiously left as a threshold nuclear country.

Optimism concerning the Middle East must be viewed with caution because Shia and Sunni sides of the Islamic sectarian divide created spasms of military stalemate where large swathes of turf in many places could flare up in new battles. Like Iraq, Afghanistan and other states, many militias who looted arsenals of weapons in Libya smuggled them into conflict zones. Egypt remains shaken in efforts to quash the Moslem Brotherhood and is circled by insurgent gangs. Siding with Saudi Arabia, the Egyptian military joined a broad coalition of forces against the adversaries who bitterly oppose the West in onward chaos on earth.

Estimates of frozen assets to be put back in Iranian hands total multiple billions of dollars. Assuming they do obtain that lofty wealth and regain former amounts of income from oil sales or other losses in trade, their diplomatic and combat strength would greatly increase. The nuclear deal for sanction relief may have undermined foreign aggression, but alliances with governments who frown on U.S. policy like Venezuela, Bolivia and Nicaragua will solidify. Tehran does not want any foreign soldiers on the doorsteps of its long borders with either Iraq or Afghanistan. It supports a regional security coalition in which they would have a swaying voice.

No guarantee can be made of success to contain Iran's nuclear program since any final deal is shaky at best due to strong dissent and lack of trust on both sides. Although failure of the pact would open old wounds with no means for cure, Iran remains a decisive factor in the course of unceasing violence. Problems to stabilize the turmoil in Afghanistan, Iraq and Syria by some form of truce with al-Qaida and Taliban through an Iranian grapevine could materialize. This concealed leverage might appeal to some of their leaders including those in Pakistan who have sought to stop terror and complete a pipeline from Iran to import gas to Islamabad.

Competition for economic and political gains may swing in Russia's favor due to its efforts to enlist nations in a consortium that challenges any other trade groups. The Moscow-led Customs Union with Belarus and Kazakhstan is a developing scene with swooping interest from former Soviet republics in Central Asia. The savvy of this mammoth enterprise to become the Eurasian Economic Union is in capital, not force. Yet mutual financial profits and investments work hand in hand with joint military exchanges. Membership in this lineup could extremely boost Russia's banking and industrial complex including the arms build-up of its partners.

Critics argue there is no need to finish a European missile defense shield in a phased approach of land and sea launching systems since Iran put limits on its nuclear plants. Steps to create anti-ballistic missile stations in Romania by 2015 and Poland by 2018 along with more equipped warships are now being neutralized by Russian mobile ballistic batteries. The offensive could include its enclave on the Baltic Sea. Deployment of missiles that may include interceptors in Alaska is a serious source of much contention where Russia expressed regret about a regressive orientation by the West and prepared for a pre-emptive strike with modern weapons.

Who is the real target in an expensive defense movement said to protect Europe? Why have joint councils of these installations with Russia refused to promise that bombs will not be used against them nor agreed to equal footing with a nation who has sought peace? Are we expecting a war or inviting one? Stout words were spoken against the U.S. program to make long range non-nuclear missiles capable of hitting anywhere in the world in as little as an hour. Moscow said it nullifies the strategic nuclear balance and they will take counter measures to insure there is no possibility to achieve military superiority. The war machine is alive and well.

Revelation of prophecy is coming together on a grand scale unveiling unknown aspects before our eyes. Russia's ally in ancient Gomer with all his bands refers to eastern Ukrainians and their neighbors. This large east area of the Ukraine is industrialized with factories designed to make Russian military hardware as in nearly all engines for their helicopters. Both political and public dissent over identities with either Russia's Customs Union or Europe shows a distinct vision of who forms the tribal nation of Gomer. That cultural line is a source of stark internal tension and also discord between East and West trade blocs who seek more member states.

Exactly what will transpire in the Ukraine whose bankruptcy was first averted by Russia and then tied to EU loans is yet to be realized. Protests of the 2004 Orange Revolution were revived and the separatist question remains in any prospect for peace. Ethnic and financial worries combine in a tinderbox that could explode within the country and its borders. Cold War actions have taken a different shape since the new European Union structure fractured fraternity with Russia. These and other reasons relating to the terrorist agenda present circumstances for the once feared Russian bear to come out of hibernation to feed and defend its habitat.

Acts of war are not receding and world security is in serious doubt. New crisis develops as a dire turn of events that ousted elected leaders of Ukraine points to the historical juncture among civilian rivals in a state of flux with an unstable partition of borders. Russia's response to the so-called Maiden rebellion named after protests in Kiev's central square prompted jitters in the U.S. and Europe. It branded the coup as mutiny led by neo-Nazis who are linked to western powers on a one sided agenda. Anger was displayed by suspending loans and energy write offs until the course to both function in government and pattern of a financial lifeline is complete.

Alarming drama in the Ukraine leaves no doubt about Russia's intent to use troops to protect its military or commerce bases and stand with those who favor help from them. Massive combat moves on land, sea and air were taken to patrol adjacent sides. Soldiers in Crimean airports and naval facilities were put on alert to keep them safe. Moscow's view of a greedy extremist ploy to sever it from the Ukraine was said to backfire since its people are not guinea pigs in a science experiment. The decision to suddenly organize an army, navy and air force capable of defeating local aggression and resisting outside armor created a standoff NATO did not expect.

Tensions escalated from a counter-coup of dissent that raised Russian flags in eastern cities with scuffles by opposing parties. This issue of secession of the Crimean peninsula and other parts of the Ukraine to Russia either by elections or blunt force reflects a startling aspect of the prophetic ethnic stock of Gomer and their other ingrained bands which form a block against the allies of Israel. It is from the lens of the past that we can determine prospects of the future. We must look to the cradle of civilization to trace peoples who do not now have the same identity. The origin of Cossacks seems to be in Gomer and they thus have a hand in destiny.

Western leaders and media outlets spun out in a frenzy to condemn the Kremlin's move as an imperialist invasion in violation of sovereign integrity. U.S. officials at the highest levels humiliated Russia's president as a tyrant in a propaganda campaign to depict the new coalition from Kiev as legitimate, yet confirmed reports indicate that ultra-right wing radicals instigated the nationalist plot for self-proclaimed rule with snipers who shot protesters and police. Alleged scam to subvert a valid political assembly by third party insurgents casts doubt about who was behind mobs throwing firebombs. Was this a scandal or triumph for democracy?

Local defense units came out in very large numbers to guard against right sector fanatics in volunteer support of the Crimean army and Russian forces for controlled access to the region. The West portrayed itself as good guys against the bad guys of new Soviet communism, but ignored bigotry by Kiev lawmakers against Russian speaking people. Crimean residents sought protection under the Black Sea fleet agreement where Russia already sustained major troop deployments in their province. These rights to democratic choice and traditional defense matters in place by law were battered by U.S. sanctions and threats of diplomatic boycott.

Misleading and overblown accusations against Russia in a determined effort to break its ties with the Ukraine strain its overall dealings with NATO. Double standards shown in past armed incursions by the U.S. versus inconsistent limits on security measures of other nations displays open hypocrisy. It is reckless to pursue an all or nothing policy and substitute a just us approach for justice. There is a moment of truth in resolving murder claims of a conspiracy to form a bias rebel regime in Kiev. Pundits said the West is blind and dumb to facts on the ground for its own advantage. Given the status of global discord, aims to punish Russia are stupidity.

Tripartite accords were logical from the start of decisions for banking loans to the Ukraine and for projects in business plans to build its economy. Kiev urgently needs large amounts of cash in the short and long term that require strict austerity conditions of lending by Europe. Recession has severely cut funding from U.S. and EU coffers so it is unlikely they can carry the debt alone. Similar bailouts have weakened livelihood in countries like Greece, Italy and Spain where taxes jumped, property values sunk and social programs slashed. Better life in Ukraine won't happen without Russia who holds wealth, family bonds and vital trade leverage.

Crimea's parliament voted unanimously to join the Russian Federation. The formal annex was approved by referendum rather than a choice to declare independence from Ukraine. This bold conduct stirred patriotic fervor in Russia and served as a model for other local areas that resisted the Kiev coup as illegal. Outcome of bloodshed caused defection in the Ukrainian army and broad distrust among the public who fear the real struggle led by foreign powers. Disturbing news reflects this divided state facing issues of default and widening spite or strife. Military debate scrambles in a febrile mood while NATO set up a strike force to deter Russia.

Discredit of the strong popular vote in Crimea to split from its mainland and become part of Russia contradicts past precedents of accepting self-declared states such as Kosovo and South Sudan. Mentality of contempt for the Kremlin's consent to a unified treaty solidified paranoia of a rebuilt Berlin wall. Instead of working in harmony to calm unrest and confront welfare issues, America intimidated and provoked Russia with false impression of forcing the decision. It is a sad breach of trust with anyone who has empathy for joy of celebration by virtually all Crimean inhabitants. This situation raised many eyebrows in distaste of warmongers.

Domination of neo-Nazi factions and rich oligarchs in the Ukraine's ruling class creates an internal dimension of harm and venal ethics that exceeds any cultural spat. Interim authorities displaced many pro-Russian activists while recruiting a new national army to subdue resistance brigades. Demand to restore a nuclear arsenal is an obvious prospect for escalating a total fiasco. Puppet masters of this propped up stage are caught in a confusing media quarrel between war stream hogwash and objective remarks. The idea of Russia as a menace to contain by rules made for other nations is bogus. Freedom cannot be won by empty outrage or might.

Pages of predictions made in Scripture are passing by without due knowledge and sensible discourse. For those who seek truth and want to apply wisdom in their communities, current events must be highlighted in regard to divine purpose of parted end time periods. The Ukraine is vulnerable to a civil or regional war because of its social history and economic pressure. We need to comprehend how this danger fits into the prophetic puzzle by reference to Russia's ally in Gomer which poses a geographical change to restructure its boundary. This query is akin to the Kurds within borders of Turkey, Syria and Iraq. The warpath is being paved.

Measuring the Customs Union impact on global affairs has some observers rankled as a new resurgence of the Soviet Union. Russia is making an assertive advance with perks to sign up nations within its orbit of family and commerce links. This long list includes Moldova, Georgia, Armenia, Ukraine, Tajikistan, Uzbekistan and Kyrgyzstan. These people have rich resources but sorely need foreign investment to develop and profit from them. Any economic pact would also boost defensive contracts fulfilled by Russia essentially regaining much of its former realm yet the danger of internal conflict is from political oppression or radical ideologies.

Decades of mostly low profile battles in northern and southern Caucasus states started with individual nationalist goals, but became a guerrilla war to conquer broader districts in global jihad with bombings inside the Russian heartland. There is no prospect of ending these sudden attacks anytime soon while diffuse jihadist franchises relocate, consent together and strike far outside their origins creating long range security concerns for Russia. The war within a war of rebels against rebels exhibits vicious moves by al-Qaida branches seizing much Iraqi ground tied to bases in Syria with a tactical trajectory threatening Jordan, Saudi Arabia and Israel.

Success stories against terror elapsed and replaced by more awful prospects with a perilous front forging in Yemen. No champions have emerged as an Iranian-Saudi contest drums for political and military power through channels of an adverse arms build-up. Protracted warfare has seen shifting clashes, but the strangle hold around the Middle East reflects swelling of the confederacy found in Psalm 83 whose ardent intent is to destroy Israel and its allies. This ambition to govern Jerusalem attracts other Moslems to restore former Palestine and clever plots could trigger Russia's swing to imperialism that will spell untold desolation.

Facts on the ground indicate a precarious future unless we accept warnings of the divine word and do something to change our way of thinking about the last days. Many people are trapped in unrealistic ideologies that will not prosper and others stuck in their comfort zones unaware of pending dangers or ignore them in a carefree life. It is our solemn duty to understand the ruin and bloodshed of wracked nations since 9/11. We may have rebuilt the World Trade Center, but are we blind to the thought of a nuclear war? Can international peace talks resolve the dilemma of suffering in Syria, Iraq, Afghanistan, Africa, Gaza, Ukraine and other places?

Numbers of displaced people on the earth have jumped at an astounding rate reaching levels of over 50 million individuals forced from their homes by an expanding web of cruel hostility aimed at glory, might and wealth. Should we not stagger at this pressing pattern of dramatic brutality as a sign of somber warning? Humanity has turned away from the saving care of divine blessings and in response its casualties may soon be counted in unthinkable slaughter. God has a controversy with our lack of faith and conceited hedonism. The road to peace is blocked because judgment is being pronounced to proclaim his praise in due process of his holy gospel.

Consent to bargaining answers for difficult issues of foreign policy will hopefully result in a reprieve from disaster, but deadly schisms may worsen and open ways for expanding transition of an extremist federation whose hidden mischief has persisted and risen up beyond anyone's expectations. Containing these forces rests on a choice that must be made in our conscience and cognition to accept inspired truth. Why be deceived about that vision? Can we not determine omens of our times or calculate the useless and destructive path that has brought terrible misery to fellow brothers? When will it end or how does it benefit? The price is our soul.

Whatever occurs on regional levels is far superseded by Russian capacity in conventional and nuclear weapons. Western nations have been led by the U.S. to extend its NATO power base and alienate Russia since the Soviet Union fell. The time of reckoning will surely come, but to our reproach, its spurring motive seems to be in their pride and resentment rather than reason that will rise up to battle. Why else would someone boldly defy God who spoke directly to a Russian leader saying *"Are you he of whom I spoke in old time by my servants the prophets of Israel? In that day when my people of Israel will dwell safely, shall you not know it?"[14]*

Foreign policy is shadowed by financial troubles which have not recovered as some falsely perceive. The U.S. must still cope with an ocean of debt, unfunded entitlement programs, its bulky military budget, trade deficit, unemployment and dismal household net worth. Average citizens have higher living costs and taxes while most can only find part time jobs with pay cuts and no benefits. Housing rentals sprung for many Americans who lost their homes in bankruptcy. Gains in stocks went to the wealthy, but a new frantic crash is likely. Corporate profits largely resulted from cutting costs, making lay-offs and contracts with outsourced labor.

There is no quick fix to all our adversity and we should not ignore its connection to divine law and to prophetic events that have or are now taking place. The future is laden with sorrows having enormous impact on the world's power structure and increasing persecution of the true faith. Jesus gave parables of these stages relating them to the great flood in Noah's era coming heedlessly on the earth and to Lot's time when Sodom and Gomorrah were consumed suddenly by fire. In ancient history some Jews fled to Babylon before others were killed as they believed divine warnings, but for we who heed our surrender must be to Christ in his church.

Armageddon and the Apocalypse are commonly used in a careless or casual sense, but these biblical concepts involve a complex series of plagues we can know and prepare for. Plurality of the last days is divided in the day of redemption and the day of judgment.[15] No one has access to God's calendar and clock to tell the exact time of watches in rapture or day of wrath and hour of the Second Advent. Of the signs Jesus said *"when you see these things come to pass, know it is near even at the doors. Watch unless he finds you sleeping."[16]* He referred to the by and by of WWIII and WWIV and noted the distinct doors in the parted seasons of each watch.

Redemption of the faithful spared from death and taken alive into heaven cannot be proved by science, but it is a hope clearly explained by Jesus, his apostles and the prophets. This event is verified in three separate visions in the book of Revelation and we need to discern the start and end of those seasons as *"Let us now fear the Lord our God who gives rain, both the former and the latter in his season: he has reserved unto us the appointed weeks of harvest. Repent and be converted that when the times of refreshing will come from the presence of the Lord, he will send Jesus Christ whom heaven must receive until the times of restitution of all things."[17]*

We now live in the former rain of grace while the latter rain will come among Jews and to all ends of the earth. These are those times of refreshing in the Eucharist when Jesus will save us until the end wrath and judgment to restore mankind in a new world so *"be patient brethren unto the coming of the Lord. Behold the husbandman waits for the precious fruit of the earth and has long patience for it, until he receives the early and latter rain."[18]* These surges in our spiritual awakening pour in periods of world wars before the end as *"Know that in the last days perilous times shall come. Because iniquity will abound, the love of many will wax cold."[19]*

Admonition to be delivered was made by Jesus to *"Take heed to yourselves not to be filled with surfeiting, cares of this life and drunkenness so that day comes upon you unaware. For it will come as a snare on all who dwell on the face of the earth. Watch then and pray always to be accounted worthy to escape all these things and stand before the Son of man."*[20] The acceptable year of escaping this day of vengeance is in the day of redemption from when global wars start until they will end.[21] News is evident throughout the world that battle lines are even now being drawn for overwhelming bloodshed of WWIII and we need holiness to meet the Lord.

Span of conflicts Jesus called the beginning of sorrows corresponds to the day of redemption because he warned *"when these things begin to come to pass, then look up and lift up your head for your redemption draws near."*[22] On the other hand he taught *"He who endures until the end shall be saved."*[23] That end is in the seven vials of wrath and Second Advent when the heavens and entire earth shake, but trials of nuclear wars and growing assaults on the church cannot be taken lightly. Tribulation theory is relative to the timing and intensity of curses. The only hope in the end is survival, yet many are redeemed before then while others succumb to death.

Most Christians ask how long it will be until the end of the world. This query is answered in the timeframe of prophecy and Jesus gave a clue to *"learn a parable of the fig tree. When the branch is yet tender and leaves break forth, you know summer is near even at the doors. This generation will not pass away until all these things are fulfilled."*[24] The first watch is signaled by WWIII and many will be taught and know the hope of redemption in piety and prayer since *"the pastures of the wilderness do spring: for the tree bears her fruit, the fig tree and the vine do yield their strength."*[25] Analogy of the fig tree is revealed in this encompassing verse.

Our Lady is the mother of Christ and the Queen of Heaven in a spiritual war against the great red dragon of the Apocalypse. She is wisdom of the tree of life whose womb bears the fruit of redemption in rapture.[26] Her seed who keep the commandments of God and the testimony of Jesus are at enmity with the seed of Satan.[27] Pastures of the wilderness are houses of worship in the Eucharistic Liturgy that spring forth her seed. The fig tree reflects this renewal coming in the present while the vine refers to a future revival caused in a new Epiphany among Jewish men who become priests to preach the gospel of hope and divine justice in all the earth.

What we can say about the generation of the end of this world is we now live in that time and signs of when nation will rise against nation are in plain view. The battlefield of this war is being set and those who are keen to Scripture should take heed and follow the path Jesus made in his church. Why are blatant sins of some Catholics who go to the Liturgy of the Mass used as a scapegoat by others of their own hypocrisy? If we don't like the way things are, Jesus does not change in his presence of the Eucharist. We have an obligation to him and to his body of those who serve him, but also to help those in error. Where is our charity or our faith?

My motive in writing is not in malice toward other religions or races, but it was born out of a sense of reason and pure compassion. People need to comprehend the outcome of world power struggles and hope of redemption before the Second Advent. My sincere desire is to prompt dialogue about prophecy and cause many to rethink their positions on a practical and spiritual level. The intent is to save lives and souls for it would be amiss to ignore either. Hopefully this labor of love will postpone the inevitable and lessen the impact of curses by its instruction. Our public forums and global leaders should stand back and look into the mirror of truth.

Frank discourse is made to excite readers to do their part in exposing lack of foresight by all means of communication which have access to nearly everyone in our world. Networks of web pages are primary ways to interact about realities of contemporary and future affairs. We need to light our candles and take initiatives to break down the walls that divide us. Study groups can be formed in many places or by our skills in technology to draw response from diverse cultures. Prophets of the bible reveal serious issues confronting our society so don't take the easy way out and leave it to someone else. If our teachers cannot teach us, then we should teach them.

This book is not dull except to those who are hard of hearing. My effort to deal with matters which depart from common theology in realism of our times is academic for hungry minds and hearts. These things need to be said or there would be no urgency to fill a vacuum of deceit and closed opinion by a new perception of fate. Clergy and students of Scripture most likely have not heard my views, but we should see orthodoxy as it relates to knowledge of the apostles and patriarchs like Jacob, Moses and King David who knew what they talked about. Prophets taught regarding their predictions, *"in the latter days you will consider it perfectly."*[28]

Who can argue with the divine word of God who spoke by his Son to give fearful signs of the end? The prophet Isaiah at first backed away from a heavenly vision, but *"heard the voice of the Lord saying whom shall I send? Then I said, Here I am send me."*[29] When Moses was called he said *"Who am I that should go to the Pharaoh and deliver the children of Israel out of Egypt? I am not eloquent, but of slow speech and a slow tongue."*[30] Jeremiah also resisted his ministry by saying *"Ah, Lord God! Behold I cannot speak for I am a child."*[31] Jonah fled and cried from the belly of whale before he warned Nineveh.[32] Why balk at being the mouth of God?

Braggarts who vaunt themselves in vanity often act like they are the voice of a higher power, but selfish pursuits lead to oppression, envy and graft. There is a different code in Christianity where the least of all believers is the greatest and it has been extremely humbling for me to accept the work to rightly divide the word of truth with efficacy. This learning experience was done with much study and prayer in wary care of avoiding defects. Many verses are outwardly clear, but certain metaphors were very difficult to explain their proper context and distinguishing quotes that apply to different wars, watches and a new world was a tedious task.

A main issue of mine in doing research and composing this literary addition to interpret bible prophecy was not in the labor itself because of my faith and yearning need to share my thoughts. What bothered me is not in my ability to finish this mission since the Lord has been my guide, but I wondered if it was worth-while enough to thwart resistance expected from those who are set in their own ways and would slight or scoff at these ideas. Hindrance of unbelief, apathy and opposing theories or morals is far outweighed by countless people who are tired of the same old sermons having no bearing on how critical themes relate to the world we live in.

Several years were spent sorting out the maze of verses in coherent chapters and during this time there was strong interest from nearly everyone I talked to who wanted to read my text. Some priests asked me where did you go to school? A former bishop of mine said God does not call qualified people, but he qualifies those he calls. David was a shepherd when brought to be anointed king of Israel and many apostles of Jesus were fishermen. I've used much effort in comparing my concepts with footnote theories of my bibles. My mother once told me nobody studies like you and a priest would decline that drudgery to avoid contention.

In the first attempt to write, print and publish my thesis of the Apocalypse copyrighted in 1996 titled The Book of Seven Seals, my pastor allowed me to lead bible studies and a seminar which drew people from other churches. He told someone I was rewriting the bible and my response was laughter since no person can change it, but he was not joking and this thorough review is much more comprehensive and accurate in its profile. There simply is not much left out of Scripture in the extraordinary number of citations. I do not consider myself a prophet, but rather a messenger gifted with wisdom and knowledge of the truth written long ago.

Elijah worked great miracles and the wicked king Ahab asked him *"Are you he who troubles Israel? And he said, I have not troubled Israel but you and your father's house who forsake the Lord and follow Baal."*[33] When Jezebel wanted to kill Elijah he fled and thought *"Only I am left, and they seek my life to take it away."* The Lord said to him *"I have left me seven thousand in Israel who have not bowed to Baal."*[34] Even now many still persist in fidelity to the church and of its apostolic ministry *"I have set watchmen upon your walls, O Jerusalem, who will not hold their peace day or night. Keep not silence you who make mention of the Lord."*[35]

Although I desired help from clergy in writing, it seemed nobody could assist or counsel me except by their encouragement. It was a strange and lonely feeling to do what now is done, but I have no doubt these teachings will produce the fruit of my dreams come true. My expectation is very high as many have gone before me to move the heart of God to bless their obedience, yet some readers will say *"You are beside yourself, much learning has made you mad."*[36] It is truth I've sought for his praise rather than mine. Rejection of the prophets' admonition was habitual as *"Then I said, Ah Lord God! They say of me, does he not speak in parables?"*[37]

If Jesus said the end would come when his gospel was preached in the whole world, why has it not occurred?[38] Christianity has been spread over the earth for over two thousand years, but prophecy he gave of wars, wrath and his glory are not taught in the meaning of context. The end phase will not come until these wars are declared and finished. It is wrong to bury the prophets in ancient history and look backward at the warnings Christ gave to Jews. We must grapple with hatred against Jews and their allies, how the Antichrist takes his reign and purpose in judgment for a new world. Our theology is clouded with erroneous symbolism and conjecture.

The paramount question of pending disaster is can we do anything about it? Vital challenge confronts the church to *"Blow the trumpet in Zion, sanctify a fast and call a solemn assembly."*[39] This command seems to apply for an urgent Vatican III since *"If my people who are called by my name will humble themselves and pray, seek my face and turn from their wicked ways, then I will hear from heaven and heal their land."*[40] Likewise to any society on earth *"At what instant I speak of a nation and a kingdom to pluck up, pull down and destroy it, if that nation against whom I entreat turn from their evil, I will repent of the evil I thought to do against them."*[41]

Faith the size of a mustard seed can move mountains, but this requires work in the wisdom and power of God. If the Catholic Church is to carry out a new evangelization, it must embrace the fulgent charisma of the Holy Spirit. St. Paul wrote *"this I pray that your charity may abound yet more and more in knowledge and all discernment. So in everything you are enriched in him and come behind in no gift."*[42] There are a variety of wondrous gifts we should strive after and cultivate in an orderly practice, but our love must overcome fear of exposing harsh truths and stubborn ways *"giving all diligence, add to your faith virtue, and to virtue knowledge."*[43]

Preachers have not come forth with clear answers about threats to global security since 9/11 or many other maladies resulting from rising iniquity and *"where there is no vision, the people perish."*[44] This publication provides sight to political and religious leaders or to individuals in hope of amends. It is a <u>Book of Remembrance: A Story That Is Told</u> since it recalls and reveals hidden prognostic prospects of the gospel, epistles and prophets. Also, the remembrance to all generations in the Eucharist is a prophecy Jesus ordained in his holy priesthood as an everlasting covenant with his living presence as the center of our faith and communion with God.

Timing for these things to be revealed is today in this earth, not to aliens in another realm on some other planet. Jesus is the Alpha and Omega, the beginning and the end. It is time for us to learn the alphabet he taught about the last days as *"your words have been stout against me. You say it is vain to serve God and we call the proud happy and they who tempt God are delivered for the wicked are built up. Then they who feared the Lord spoke often one to another. He gave ear and a book of remembrance was written for them before the Lord. They shall be mine when I make up my jewels and spare them as man spares his son who serves him."*[45]

Should there be a place for me in the bible, it is in the parable Jesus gave about the fig tree and generation of the end times *"For the Son of man is as a man taking a far journey who left his house, gave authority to his servants, to every man his work and commanded the porter to watch."*[46] Before his passion he prayed to his Holy Father *"As you sent me into the world, even so I also sent them into the world for those who also shall believe on me through their word."*[47] We all have duties to do for him who is our shepherd and only door to eternal life so *"To him the porter opens and the sheep hear his voice."*[48] That voice is in his word and his spirit.

A colloquialism often used to measure good taste or gauge effectiveness asserts the proof is in the pudding. Only time will tell and stand the test of presumption or truth in what is written, but my analysis is an effort to show the divine word as we have received it with no more or less. My theology strongly supports the moral and sacramental doctrines of the church, but offers a new approach to modern events concerning prophecy. We must be mindful of the Father who tends the vine of Christ for *"every branch in me that bears no fruit he takes away. When I say to the wicked you will surely die and you give him no warning, his blood will be on your hands."*[49]

Christ's message of atonement is a way of life found in the Eucharist, but traumatic signs of his gospel will continue to be told until the end. His word will not return to him void of harvest yet *"The vision of all is become to you as the words of a book that is sealed which men deliver to one who is learned saying, Read this I pray you and he answers I cannot for it is sealed. And the book will be given to him who is not learned saying, Read this I pray you and he shall answer I am not learned. The Lord has closed your eyes as this people honor me with their lips, but their soul is far removed from me and their fear of me is taught by the precept of men."*[50]

Does the attitude of what will be will be excuse us from pleading for mercy? Will man blame God and say he made them that way in denial of sin and deceit? Are they afraid of their peers more than him or create falsehood to hide from reality? Do people cling to doctrines of men to save their reputation or lying wares they sell? Divine law does discriminate and the heart of Christ beats in the secret of his tabernacle. If we do not obey the Sabbath and follow this path of his living remembrance where is our treasure? Our vigil must be kept in his body and blood so who will be left behind in times of the watches? Who will be left to inherit the earth?

Separating the overlap of citations relating to the three watches is an arduous endeavor, but many passages confirm reality of these distinct events happening in trials of intense wars. The unique transformation in the church of conversion for a segment of Jews following WWIII and the role of these priests in proclaiming final signs of the gospel is a crucial element of prophecy. This renewal of faith in the latter rain will be matched with great apostasy when the Antichrist rises in power and takes his reign, but Jesus said *"What I say to you I say to all, Watch."*[51] He made a difference between those taken in rapture and they who await a new world.

After deliverance in the watches beyond the end wrath *"Those who wait upon the Lord shall inherit the earth. Wait upon me until the day I rise up to the prey for then I will turn to the people a pure tongue to serve me with one consent. The upright will have dominion over them in the morning."*[52] This morning or birth of peace and love on earth follows the other watches as *"My soul waits for the Lord more than they who wait for the morning. I say more than they who watch for the morning. He will redeem Israel from all his iniquities. Your people will be willing in the day of your power, in the beauties of holiness from the womb of the morning."*[53]

Summary of the watches in rapture and rebirth of the church is to our generation so *"Watch therefore, You know not when the master of the house comes: at evening, or midnight, or at the cockcrowing, or in the morning."*[54] Nobody can predict exact times or number the years of this generation, but we can know the warnings and *"Seek him who makes the seven stars and Orion and turns the shadow of death into morning. Give thanks at the remembrance of his holiness. Weeping may endure for a moment, but joy comes in the morning and in my prosperity I will never be moved. I will come into your house and worship toward your holy temple."*[55]

Clouds of mystery surely cover my work since it involves a union of witnesses in heaven and on earth who will respond together in the calling to Christ. Moses said evil would befall Jews in the latter days, but before then a potent prophecy will be revealed to *"Give ear, O you heavens and I will speak, and hear O earth the words of my mouth. My doctrine will drop as the rain, my speech shall distil as the dew, as the small rain upon the tender herb and showers on the grass. Because I will publish the name of the Lord: ascribe greatness unto our God."*[56] This buss about the end times will be shouted from the housetops of our communication.[57]

Pages of my bibles are very worn and their bindings are loose from use in meditation. Piles of notes to sort out my vision have turned into a non-fiction product not meant to scare our wits, but to give refuge for souls that can provide more solace than an underground bunker. Its purpose is to promote truth with firm footing and remove the veil of uncertainty. In this grace, *"O God, you did send a plentiful rain whereby you confirmed your inheritance when it was weary. The Lord gave the word: great was the company who published it."*[58] This company is a campaign of an army of servants or mass of persons organized for a spiritual war.

Stock in that firm may never reach trade markets, but everybody has a stake in sharing the word and enlisting new recruits. Our primary battle is against ignorance since *"wisdom and knowledge will be the stability of your times, and strength of your salvation."*[59] This problem is both practical and moral as we need to know the facts about our times and also the right path to our redemption. The great multitude from all corners of the earth in the first watch could not be numbered because they heard the news and were ready. That moment is approaching us so it seems many will quickly intervene together in the heavenly drawing of preparation.[60]

Compliments were received quite a while ago from a variety of sources in response to the limited printing of my first book about the seven seals of Revelation. Many senior editors of major publishing companies were impressed with the read as fascinating, interesting or worthy but said the timing was not right for it. Religious media networks, political leaders, prominent people and inter-faith groups spoke of my creative talents, fervency and well done research on an important message. In that early time several high ranking priests applauded my work including an official stamp by the U.S. Apostolic Pro-Nuncio of Pope John Paul II.

Legitimate reasons existed why my initial writing did not make the best sellers list. It was not God's timing and lack of having scan numbers on copies stopped me from contracts with book store chains and distributing companies. Also, marketing of electronic books was not popular at that time and I decided to stop selling and then wait until a better and updated version would be completed in the future. My text is vastly improved in every way being easier to read, very comprehensive, more professional and acutely accurate. It stands alone, complete and apart from the prior effort with footnotes of biblical quotes or passages which before were absent.

My exegesis of the divine word has a striking nature in ongoing controversy we cannot hide from because everyone on earth is affected by its physical, mental and spiritual dimensions. Current events continue to support basic tenets as time passes and with each stroke to note these things, the stunning echo in this subject does not fail to astound me. The bible is a sounding board to the music of existence as a living testimony from Christ who is author and perfection of faith. We have to practice the way of life in him as a remedy for ourselves and others. His redemption and kingdom draws near so we need to earnestly prepare and be ready.

Much weeping and appalling sorrow has already come upon us, but the Lord said no one is greater than his master. It is very sad to watch these affairs take place and expect even more terrible hardships, but pondering why mankind causes them brings pity limited by regret. Our capacity to save souls or educate knowledge has no effect on those who refuse divine grace and defy their ability to reason with good sense. Evil powers are at work on a deceptive course of global curses that will prove the vanity of pride and lust. We cannot stop that vile spirit from showing its ugly head, but God can conquer and will do what he said written long ago.

Multitudes of people seem oblivious to the deep troubles going on in our world while our stadiums and convention halls are packed with sports and entertainment fans seeking excitement of fun with their comrades. Who is taking time to keep the Sabbath holy and cheer in song for fellowship in the church? Do we have to be brought to our knees by tragedy or can we perceive foretold signs of contemporary scourges which urgently call us to make amends and pray? Let us intercede for the winds of revival to blow across our lands before the floods of battle rise over their shores and cities. The Lord's Eucharistic ark is our safe haven and salvation.

All research, writing, editing and proofing of this work was done by myself. There were moments when I shook my head at the daunting task before me and could only look to Jesus for answers to puzzles hidden in mystery. My understanding and belief grew in certainty because it is happening in a time for reflection. Readers may observe lengthy paragraphs, but thought patterns and biblical passages require that mode of spacing which became as a melody ringing out in uniform rhythm. Business of being my own publisher included cover design with book and print size. I trust the format meets approval apart from a minor margin glitch.

Concern of mine now is not whether the job will succeed, but when the church hierarchy will confirm the substance in interpretation. Scripture tells me formal support will be offered for *"the preacher was wise, he still taught the people knowledge. Yea he gave good heed, searched out and set in order many proverbs. The preacher sought to find acceptable words, and that which was written was upright, even words of truth. The words are as goads and as nails, fastened by the masters of assemblies which are given from one shepherd."*[61] Christ is the true shepherd who will secure this complex theme of logic, hope and stimulus among his bishops.

God willing, my plan is to schedule seminars and panel discussions, respond to inquiries and interview requests, develop outreach through the media and internet links, structure a funded discipleship program in Catholic dioceses and find ways to translate copies in other languages. What kind of publishing contract that might be worked out in due time is not clear to me, but my own publishing company named Eccles Living with its trademark is legally established for commercial sales. The business title stems from our ecclesiastical path to Christ. I wrote a draft manuscript of a sequel to this book about Fatima confirming its concepts in detail.

I've often thought of pursuing arrangements for a movie production in the form of a trilogy that reflects three primary phases of our times in global wars and in the Second Advent. The art of literature has prompted many performances in theater and my thesis gives a new face of our world unlike anything seen in the past. Drama for this script is already written, but the star studded cast, the stage and the lines of speech in acting out a powerful motion-picture have not been set. Opportunity is open for Hollywood directors to use their talents and resources in making a blockbuster show of Holy Writ having much spiritual and profitable significance.

Crossing the threshold of publication is in the hands of Jesus with hope of ministry, exchange of dialogue among sundry religions and calming hatred of violence which threatens our society. These objectives require toil of charity, use of reason and fidelity to him in pleading for mercy. My bold pioneering journey in the bible reflects a prophetic story that is told as it precedes us in a fate not yet lived out. God keeps the books, but we make the choices. As for myself, *"Lord I have loved your house where your honor dwells. I will compass your altar with thanksgiving and tell of all your wondrous works. In the congregations I will bless the Lord."[62]*

Narration of reality in relation to the word of God is frozen in the present tense which stops anyone from filling in the blanks of his omnipotence to follow on the morrow. His spirit is the power of victory that can reach every plane of knowledge if his servants do his bidding. We all should take on the role of curator about our evolving state of being because there is much left unsaid to be revealed in the divine plan. This snapshot of civilization reflects a status quo of when it went to print, but the range of topic matter spans eternity. Salvation messages unfold in a process of remarkable judgments that release us from a prison of ignorance.

In closing, my former example in leading an evangelization committee in a suburb of Chicago gives incentive and direction for the kind of grassroots system other parishes need to follow. We created new ways to invite people to our church, urged our laity to do their part and went to thousands in our area going door to door with pamphlets about our activities. Newspapers came with cameras and wrote articles on the leg work of Catholics seeking souls. The result was a healthy ethnic mix in our members. Although the harvest is plenty and the laborers few we can do more with less as Gideon routed a great army in chaos without the sword.[63]

Truth became a forgotten memory in ancient Hebrew society throughout periods of plagues when a cycle of repentance and order was restored. In one such instance the Book of the Law given by Moses was found in the temple and delivered to King Josiah who *"took away all the abominations out of the land of Israel and they departed not from following the Lord all his days."* God told him *"your eyes will not see all the evil I will bring upon this place."[64]* Public reply to his warning is pivotal and what has been lost in our foresight must be faced with disaster unless we humble ourselves to turn from pagan ways. The cup of divine justice is full.

---

[1] Ezekiel 38,1-16&21; 39,6
[2] Zechariah 12,2-9
[3] Leviticus 26,15-33; Deuteronomy 28,15-47
[4] II Peter 2,9-10
[5] Leviticus 18,6-28; 20,10-16; Romans 1,21-32
[6] Genesis 1,26-28; 2,7&18-24
[7] Acts 2,40-47; 4,4; 6,1; 17,6; 20,20-21
[8] Ezekiel 16,43-44
[9] Luke 19,42-44
[10] Ezekiel 38,8&14; Zechariah 12,3&8-9
[11] Revelation 9,13-19; 16,1-2&12-16
[12] Ezekiel 16,3-6; 38,8

13 Ezekiel 38,3-12
14 Ezekiel 38,8&14&17
15 Mathew 10,15; Ephesians 4,30; II Peter 2,9
16 Mark 13,29-36; Luke 12,35-40; 21,9-10
17 Jeremiah 5,24; Acts 1,7-8; 3,19-21
18 John 15,1-5; James 5,1-8
19 Mathew 24,12; Mark 13,8; II Timothy 3,1
20 Luke 21,34-36
21 Isaiah 61,1-3
22 Mark 13,8; Luke 21,28
23 Mathew 24,13; Mark 13,13
24 Mathew 24,32-34; Luke 21,29-32
25 Joel 2,21-23
26 Proverbs 3,13-18; 8,34-36; 9,1-5; Isaiah 66,5-9
27 Genesis 3,14-15; Revelation 12,1-5&17
28 Jeremiah 23,20; 30,23-24
29 Isaiah 6,1-8
30 Exodus 3,2-12, 4,10-12
31 Jeremiah 1,5-9
32 Jonah 1,1-3&17; 2,1; 3,1-3
33 I Kings 16,29-30; 18,17-18
34 I Kings 19,1-10&14&18
35 Isaiah 52,6-8; 62,6-7; Jeremiah 6,17; Micah 7,4
36 Acts 26,24-29
37 Ezekiel 20,49
38 Mathew 24,14
39 Joel 2,12-17
40 II Chronicles 7,14
41 Jeremiah 18,7-8
42 I Corinthians 1,4-8; Philippians 1,9-10
43 I Corinthians 12,4-11; James 3,13; II Peter 1,5-8
44 Proverbs 29,18
45 Malachi 3,13-18
46 Mark 13,34
47 John 17,13-20
48 John 10,1-11
49 Deuteronomy 18,22; Ezekiel 3,17-21; John 15,1-7
50 Isaiah 29,9-14
51 Mark 13,37
52 Psalm 37,9-11&34; 49,14-15; Zephaniah 3,8-9
53 Psalm 110,3; 130,6-8
54 Mark 13,35
55 Psalm 5,3-7; 30,4-5; Amos 5,8
56 Deuteronomy 31,29-30; 32,1-4
57 Mathew 10,27; Luke 12,2-3
58 Psalm 68,9-11
59 Isaiah 33,6
60 Revelation 7,9-14
61 Ecclesiastes 12,9-11; Isaiah 41,1-7
62 Psalm 26,6-8&12
63 Judges 6,11-17; 7,7-22
64 II Chronicles 34,14-33; Nehemiah 8,1-8; 9,2

BREAD OF LIFE

Salvation is in the tabernacles of the righteous. Bind the sacrifice
with cords, even unto the horns of the altar. This is the bread
from heaven for life of the world. O taste and see that the
Lord is good. Psalm 34,8; 118,15&27; John 6,47-58